English Drama: Shakespeare to the Restoration 1590–1660

Alexander Leggatt

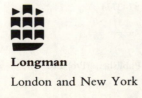

Longman

London and New York

Longman Group UK Limited,
Longman House, Burnt Mill, Harlow,
Essex CM20 2JE, England
and Associated Companies throughout the world.

Published in the United States of America
by Longman Inc., New York

© Longman Group UK Limited 1988

First published 1988

BRITISH LIBRARY CATALOGUING IN PUBLICATION DATA
Leggatt, Alexander
  English drama: Shakespeare to Restoration
  1590–1660. — (Longman literature in English
  series).
  1. English drama — Early modern and
  Elizabethan, 1500–1600 — History and
  criticism 2. English drama — 17th century —
  History and criticism
  I. Title
  822'.3'09   PR651
ISBN 0-582-49310-2 CSD
ISBN 0-582-49311-0 PPR

LIBRARY OF CONGRESS CATALOGING IN PUBLICATION DATA
Leggatt, Alexander.
  English drama: Shakespeare to the Restoration,
  1590–1660.

  (Longman literature in English series)
  Includes bibliographies and index.
  1. English drama — Early modern and Elizabethan,
  1500–1600 — History and criticism. 2. English drama —
  17th century — History and criticism. I. Title.
  II. Series.
  PR651.L44 1988   822.3'09   87–3774
  ISBN 0-582-49310-2
  ISBN 0-582-49311-0 (pbk.)

Set in Linotron 202 9½/11pt Bembo
Produced by Longman Singapore Publishers (Pte) Ltd.
Printed in Singapore

Contents

Editors' Preface

The multi-volume Longman Literature in English Series provides students of literature with a critical introduction to the major genres in their historical and cultural context. Each volume gives a coherent account of a clearly defined area, and the series, when complete, will offer a practical and comprehensive guide to literature written in English from Anglo-Saxon times to the present. The aim of the series as a whole is to show that the most valuable and stimulating approach to literature is that based upon an awareness of the relations between literary forms and their historical context. Thus the areas covered by most of the separate volumes are defined by period and genre. Each volume offers new and informed ways of reading literary works, and provides guidance to further reading in an extensive reference section.

As well as studies on all periods of English and American literature, the series includes books on criticism and literary theory, and on the intellectual and cultural context. A comprehensive series of this kind must of course include other literatures written in English, and therefore a group of volumes deals with Irish and Scottish literature, and the literatures of India, Africa, the Caribbean, Australia and Canada. The forty-seven volumes of the series cover the following areas: Pre-Renaissance English Literature, English Poetry, English Drama, English Fiction, English Prose, Criticism and Literary Theory, Intellectual and Cultural Context, American Literature, Other Literatures in English.

David Carroll
Michael Wheeler

Longman Literature in English Series

General Editors: David Carroll and Michael Wheeler
University of Lancaster

Pre-Renaissance English Literature

* ★ English Literature before Chaucer   *Michael Swanton*
* English Literature in the Age of Chaucer
* ★ English Medieval Romance   *W. R. J. Barron*

English Poetry

* ★ English Poetry of the Sixteenth Century   *Gary Waller*
* ★ English Poetry of the Seventeenth Century   *George Parfitt*
* English Poetry of the Eighteenth Century, 1700–1789
* ★ English Poetry of the Romantic Period, 1789–1830   *J. R. Watson*
* ★ English Poetry of the Victorian Period, 1830–1890   *Bernard Richards*
* English Poetry of the Early Modern Period, 1890–1940
* English Poetry since 1940

English Drama

* English Drama before Shakespeare
* ★ English Drama: Shakespeare to the Restoration, 1590–1660
  Alexander Leggatt
* ★ English Drama: Restoration and Eighteenth Century, 1660–1789
  Richard W. Bevis
* English Drama: Romantic and Victorian, 1789–1890
* English Drama of the Early Modern Period, 1890–1940
* English Drama since 1940

English Fiction

* ★ English Fiction of the Eighteenth Century, 1700–1789
  Clive T. Probyn
* English Fiction of the Romantic Period, 1789–1830
* ★ English Fiction of the Victorian Period, 1830–1890   *Michael Wheeler*
* English Fiction of the Early Modern Period, 1890–1940
* English Fiction since 1940

English Prose

* English Prose of the Seventeenth Century, 1590–1700
* English Prose of the Eighteenth Century
* English Prose of the Nineteenth Century

Criticism and Literary Theory

Criticism and Literary Theory from Sidney to Johnson
Criticism and Literary Theory from Wordsworth to Arnold
Criticism and Literary Theory from 1890 to the Present

The Intellectual and Cultural Context

The Sixteenth Century
The Seventeenth Century
★ The Eighteenth Century, 1700–1789 *James Sambrook*
The Romantic Period, 1789–1830
The Victorian Period, 1830–1890
The Twentieth Century: 1890 to the Present

American Literature

American Literature before 1880
American Poetry of the Twentieth Century
American Drama of the Twentieth Century
★ American Fiction, 1865–1940 *Brian Lee*
American Fiction since 1940
Twentieth-Century America

Other Literatures

Irish Literature since 1800
Scottish Literature since 1700

Australian Literature
Indian Literature in English
African Literature in English: East and West
South African Literature in English
Caribbean Literature in English
★ Canadian Literature in English *W. J. Keith*

★ *Already published*

Acknowledgements

Since I have tried to keep footnotes to a minimum, my debts to others who have written on this period are on the whole acknowledged only in the most general way, in the bibliographies. For any particular debts that should have been recorded and are not, my apologies. Since this is a book written with students in mind, I am particularly aware of how much I owe to my own students, both graduate and undergraduate, who over the years have helped me to think about Shakespeare and his contemporaries. This is a debt so great as to amount to collaboration. Finally, I wish to thank Doreen Morton for her help in preparing the final typescript, and David Carroll for his generous encouragement and his wise advice.

Alexander Leggatt
Toronto, 1987

For
Judith, Helen, Jillian and Rosalind

Chapter 1
Introduction

To anyone living through them, the last years of Queen Elizabeth's reign would not have seemed like a golden age. They were marked by crop failures, economic unrest, and the general malaise of living under an ageing queen who would not name a successor and whose imminent death threatened chaos. The rebellion by the Earl of Essex in 1601 was easily put down, but it was the first serious challenge to the regime for years and it broke the long internal peace of England. Under these circumstances the orderly accession of King James was greeted with relief. But disillusionment soon followed, and it was not long before Elizabeth was missed. As the new king journeyed south from Scotland, there was an incident at Newark-upon-Trent that was to prove ominous. A cutpurse was taken red-handed and when King James heard of it he ordered the man executed at once. This reflected his belief in absolute royal authority and his corresponding failure to grasp the English belief in the due process of law, with the king as simply part of that process. In the conflicts between Crown and Parliament that occurred under James and his son Charles, the key issue was to be just that: was the king under the law or above it?

Elizabeth had managed to avoid confrontation on such points. By force of personality combined with political cunning, she maintained through the inevitable strains and conflicts of political life a feeling of national consensus. She created the perception – so strong that it became, as perceptions do, a political reality – that she and her people were bound by ties of mutual affection. Her reign was accordingly marked by relative stability. Under the earlier Tudors the religious policy of the government had swung sharply and dangerously. Elizabeth's reign saw the settlement of the Anglican *via media*, with its compromise between Protestant theology and Catholic liturgy. Under the Stuarts the cracks were to reappear, as the Puritan wing of the church became increasingly disaffected, not only challenging the establishment but splitting away from it by mid-century into a bewildering variety of sects. In the reign of Charles, Archbishop Laud exacerbated the problem with his High Church policies; and his attempt to impose the Prayer Book on Scotland led to the astonishing chain reaction that culminated in the Civil War, the execution of the king and the temporary abolition of the monarchy itself.

Of course the appearance of consensus was possible only because certain problems were temporarily shelved. It was when people began to debate, to define their positions (as at the Hampton Court Conference of 1604, when James tried and failed to reconcile the Puritans) that the cracks became impossible to hide. At the beginning of the Tudor period there had been some vigorous and thoughtful political writing, of which More's *Utopia* is only the most conspicuous example. The seventeenth century was to see a return of this spirit of inquiry, ranging from Hobbes's *Leviathan* to the pamphlet wars of the Civil War period. But under Elizabeth this spirit was temporarily dormant. Philip Styles has observed, 'There is probably no period of English history during the past five hundred years when political speculation was less active or more discouraged'.[1] There is probably, by the same token, no period at which the celebration of the reigning monarch was so deeply ingrained in the national life.[2] The anniversary of Elizabeth's accession was observed as though it were one of the festivals of the church. There was some compensation for the loss of the cult of the Virgin Mary in the new cult of the Virgin Queen. Elizabeth's public appearances were marked by a carefully orchestrated pageantry that seems to borrow from the language of liturgy. A foreign visitor watching one of her appearances at Greenwich describes the preparation of the Queen's dinner table: 'A gentleman entered the room bearing a rod, and along with him another who had a table-cloth, which after they had knelt three times, with the utmost veneration, he spread upon the table, and after kneeling again they both retired'. It reads like the beginning of a High Mass, and it goes on from there. The Queen at this point is not even present. The same visitor notes that when she did appear 'wherever she turned her face as she was going along, everybody fell down on their knees'.[3]

This pageantry was part of the air Elizabeth breathed. The formal allegorical shows that were regularly presented to her sometimes required her active participation. Sidney's *The Lady of May*, in which the Queen is asked to settle a debate between a forester and a shepherd on the value of their different ways of life, is a case in point. As Jonathan Goldberg has argued, she was *in* the pageantry, part of it, as James never was.[4] For one thing, she could dance, and this was not just a social accomplishment. Sir John Davies' poem *Orchestra* expresses the important commonplace that the dance symbolizes the harmony of all things. Ben Jonson used it this way in his court masques for King James. But James, whose legs were so weak he could barely walk without support, was largely confined to watching other people dance in his honour. (His notorious love of hunting may be accounted for by the fact that he was not a cripple on horseback.) Elizabeth's entertainments tended to be outdoors. The Stuart court masque is very much an indoor affair, and in place of the free-wheeling staging of the earlier pageants, it involves the first important use in England of perspective scenery, which imposes a rigid pattern of sightlines and means there is only one really good seat in the house, the king's.

Elizabeth was celebrated, then, in communal and quasi-religious occasions in which she was a participant. James watched elaborate and expensive allegorical shows created in his honour. In theory the celebration of order centred on the monarch was the same in both cases; in practice it was, and had to be, more worked-up and artificial under James, and there was a more embarrassing split between the tributes to his wisdom and goodness and the rather seedy reality. Sir John Harington recounts an entertainment for the visiting King of Denmark that was reduced to chaos by the drunkenness both of the participants and of the royal audience:

> His majesty then got up and would dance with the Queen
> of Sheba; but he fell down and humbled himself before
> her, and was carried to an inner chamber and laid on a
> bed of state; which was not a little defiled with the
> presents of the Queen which had been bestowed upon his
> garments; such as wine, cream, jelly, beverage, cakes,
> spices and other good matters.

Faith and Hope, speechless and staggering, were unable to play their parts; Charity did a little better before retiring 'to Hope and Faith, who were both sick and spewing in the lower hall'.[5] When he came to the throne in 1625 Charles restored the court's dignity, but the political tensions that had begun in his father's quarrels with Parliament got worse. Shy, withdrawn and devious, Charles reduced the court to a closed fantasy world that had lost contact with the nation. From 1629 to 1640 he ruled without Parliament, calling it only at the end of the period when he needed money for the war with Scotland. Within two years the war with Scotland had bred civil war in England.

The broad picture, then, is of a fragmenting society. Small wonder that people looked back to Elizabeth's reign as a golden age of stability. But society was also changing, or was felt to be changing, in more pervasive ways. Under Elizabeth the population of London had doubled in size from roughly 100,000 to 200,000. By the Jacobean age the growth of London was becoming alarming, and it was seen as indicative of a general collapse of old social values. The city was well on the way to becoming Cobbett's 'great wen'. King James himself addressed the problem in a speech in the Star Chamber in 1616, complaining that the new population, clustered in the suburbs, was a charge on the city and contributed nothing to it. He blamed the pride of the women and the idleness of the men, who treated London as a place to follow new fashions and as a marriage market. He recalled his Christmas proclamation of the previous year 'that all gentlemen of quality should depart to their own countries and houses, to maintain hospitality amongst their neighbours'.[6] He was drawing on a view, eloquently expressed in Jonson's 'To Penshurst', of the country as a place of natural order, where tradition and neighbourly hospitality bound society together. The city was a symbol of the new age, in which human relations turned into cash transactions and old identities dissolved. In Middleton's comedy *Michaelmas Term* the country folk who come to London quite literally lose their names in the process. London, besides being the centre of political and social life, was a place where men and women became dehumanized, the victims of a change from old agrarian values to commercial and industrial ones. There is a reference to 'mills for iron, /Oil, corn, or men to grind 'em into powder' that might be Blake or Wordsworth complaining of the Industrial Revolution but is in fact Ben Jonson speaking through the mouth of Volpone (I. 1). King James himself turned royal honours into counters in a cash transaction, selling knighthoods for thirty pounds a time.

The seventeenth century had no monopoly on this problem. Elsewhere in this series Michael Wheeler has pointed to the change in Victorian England 'from direct emotional bonds of rural life to acts of exchange in urban life as the basis of human relationship'.[7] Shakespeare's contemporaries were worrying about the disappearance of woodland, and Michael Drayton lamented the shrinking of the Forest of Arden in particular.[8] Yet in the early twentieth century there was enough greenwood left for E. M. Forster to imagine (if only just) the hero of *Maurice* disappearing into it to find the freedom denied him in society. The nostalgia for a rural past that has only just been lost, and the complaint that city life has of late become inhuman and things were much better in our grandfather's days, are met in age after age. With due allowance for the exaggerations of the imagination, they reflect a reality that can be traced through such objective evidence as population figures; but rural England was, it seems, a long time dying, and we need to be wary of the claim each age makes that it is specially afflicted.

The order the Jacobeans saw vanishing was not just a social one. While there was nothing like the *Origin of Species* to produce a crisis of faith on a national scale, the sectarian disputes of the time put many details of faith to the test, and the still current belief that the ordering of human society and of the larger universe were bound up with each other meant that both were shaken together. In *Troilus and Cressida*, Ulysses's much-quoted speech about order and degree is in fact a speech expressing the fear of universal chaos:

> Take but degree away, untune that string,
> And, hark, what discord follows. Each thing meets
> In mere oppugnancy. The bounded waters
> Should lift their bosoms higher than the shores
> And make a sop of all this solid globe;
> Strength should be lord of imbecility,
> And the rude son should strike his father dead;
> Force should be right, or rather, right and wrong,
> Between whose endless jar justice resides,
> Should lose their names, and so should justice too.
> Then everything includes itself in power,
> Power into will, will into appetite;
> And appetite, an universal wolf,
> So doubly seconded with will and power,
> Must make perforce an universal prey,
> And last eat up himself.
>
> (I. 3)

Donne relates the loss of social order to the spirit of inquiry, and sees the end not as self-consuming chaos, but as the emergence of the solipsistic individual:

> And new philosophy calls all in doubt,
> The element of fire is quite put out;
> The sun is lost, and th' earth, and no man's wit
> Can well direct him where to look for it.
> And freely men confess that this world's spent
> When in the planets and the firmament
> They seek so many new; they see that this
> Is crumbled out again to his atomies.
> 'Tis all in pieces, all coherence gone;
> All just supply, and all relation:
> Prince, subject, father, son, are things forgot,
> For every man alone thinks he hath got
> To be a Phoenix, and that then can be
> None of that kind of which he is, but he.
>
> ('The First Anniversary', 205)

The solitary hero, poised between excitement and absurdity, who insists on defining the universe in his own terms, will be met again in Jacobean drama.

As part of the breakdown of consensus, a new individuality can be seen in literature as the age advances. For example, we may compare the faceless narrator of *The Faerie Queene* with the very personal and particular figure of the old blind poet in *Paradise Lost*. The spiritual struggles of Donne and Herbert, however much they draw on the larger experience of Christianity, are distinctly their own. The lovers of Sidney's *Astrophil and Stella* are seen against the backdrop of a courtly world, whose values and demands matter to them. Donne's lovers stay in the bedroom, insisting it is all the universe they need; or rather the male speaker of the poems insists on this, imposing his own vision on the world, and on the lady. All this is bound up with what we might call the Protestantism of the age. The individual Christian reading scripture for himself and working out his own salvation becomes the Baconian scientist studying the evidence with his own eyes and not taking the authority of Aristotle for granted. In prose, this is the age of the great solitary eccentrics: Burton, Browne, Aubrey. At the end of Webster's *The White Devil* Flamineo can say 'at myself I will begin and end', and so speak for an age in which all other certainties seem to have vanished.

Yet not altogether so, for he is not the speaker of a lyric poem but a character in a play. There are still the other characters, and there is the unchanging facade of the stage. Drama is a social art, and deals in relationships. Prince, subject, father, son, can never quite be things forgotten where a playwright is concerned, whatever he may have his characters say. Throughout this study, we will be looking at the way drama reflects a world in which old, shared values are collapsing and yet the individual, however compelling he may be, cannot quite emerge as the final reality. We will also see, as the period develops, an attempt ·to restore a sense of shared values, either in new, untraditional terms or in deliberately limited ones. We will see more than that, of course, for these plays were never written to conform to a thesis, however broad. But this will be our recurring theme.

For Shakespeare's more serious-minded contemporaries, drama was not the respectable literary form it has since become. When Sir Thomas Bodley was establishing his great library he took care to exclude such 'idle books, and riff-raffs' as 'almanacs, plays, and proclamations'. It was not until the eighteenth century that this omission in the Bodleian Library began to be repaired.[9] Playwrights conventionally referred to themselves as 'poets' but they were not universally regarded as literary artists. Early in the period the title page of a play book would be more likely to name the acting company than the author. The first seven texts of Shakespeare's plays to be printed in Quarto form (including *Romeo and Juliet*, *Richard II* and *Richard III*) make no mention of his name. He is first identified on the title page of *Love's Labour's Lost* (1598) and disappears again in *1 Henry IV* (also 1598). By the 1608 edition of *King Lear* his name appears in large print at the top of the page, and we may conclude that the publisher had decided he was important. Later Jacobean and Caroline playtexts are not usually anonymous. But the view that drama was an ephemeral entertainment, and the resistance to seeing playwrights as serious literary artists, died hard. Ben Jonson was ridiculed for publishing in 1616 a Folio edition of his plays, poems and masques as his 'Works'. He set the precedent, however, for two of Shakespeare's fellows, who used the folio format again in 1623 to preserve the works of their colleague. Had they not done so a large part of the canon, not published in Quarto form, might well have disappeared for good, including such essential plays as *As You Like It*, *Twelfth Night*, *Macbeth*, *Antony and Cleopatra*, *The Winter's Tale* and *The Tempest*. Shakespeare himself, so far as we can tell, took an interest in the publication of only two of his works, the narrative poems *Venus and Adonis* and *The Rape of Lucrece*. If we are curious about Shakespeare's view of his own achievement, this may give us a clue.

But, if drama was not always taken seriously by the literati it was taken seriously by the state authorities, and with reason. At a time when information and ideas were strictly controlled by the state, any public assembly was potentially dangerous. Queen Elizabeth was known to object, on the spot, to sermons that took a line she disapproved of. Plays had to be licensed by the Master of the Revels, who could demand cuts or even block a performance altogether. The play of *Sir Thomas More*, by several hands possibly including Shakespeare's, drew this order: 'Leave out the insurrection wholly and the cause thereof and begin with Sir Thomas More at the Mayor's sessions, with a report afterwards of his good service done being sheriff of London upon a mutiny against the Lombards only by a short report and not otherwise at your own perils'.[10] The play as it survives shows the difficulty of touching on sensitive political and religious questions; it is clear that More is executed for displeasing King Henry VIII but the issue is never identified. Nor was the office of Master of the Revels the only means of control. Ben Jonson, having examined political corruption at the court of Tiberius Caesar in *Sejanus*, found himself before the Privy Council on a charge of treason. Charles I intervened personally to suppress an 'insolent' speech on the subject of taxation in Massinger's *The King and the Subject*. Censorship, as always, could be capricious. Middleton's *A Game at Chess*, an allegory of the relations between England and Spain including an obvious caricature of the

Spanish ambassador, ran for an incredible nine performances, the longest run on record up to that point, before the Privy Council closed it. Censorship can also be seen in some surviving play texts. *Richard II* was first printed with the entire deposition scene cut. The oaths in Shakespeare's First Folio have been watered down as the result of a 1606 Act of Parliament to curb the profanity of the stage. We cannot always repair the damage with reference to a Quarto text; thus, we will never know whether Shakespeare meant Malvolio in *Twelfth Night* to attribute his good fortune to Jove, as in the Folio text, or to God.

Dramatists, then, were kept on a fairly short lead. While they regularly took an interest in the issues of the day they could deal with them only in the most circumspect and general terms. Their main business was public entertainment. Like the scriptwriters of modern film and television, they were professionals turning out a product, often to order, often in collaboration; the serious literary aspirations of writers like Jonson and Chapman were the exception, not the rule. The loss of a large proportion of the plays of the period has distorted the picture for us. The literary canon that has emerged, including the plays to be discussed in the following chapters, should be imagined as the product of the best talents in a generally unpretentious entertainment industry. Their initial audience was London. Though there was plenty of theatrical activity in the provinces, including frequent tours by London companies, the capital was the main centre for original work. Despite contemporary complaints that it was too big, it was still by our standards a small city and the number of regular playgoers was even smaller.[11] Though popular plays would go on being performed for years, the demand for new work was relentless. As old plays stayed in repertory they would sometimes be revised to keep them fresh: hence the suspect 'Hecate' scenes in *Macbeth*, and, it has recently been argued, the differences between the Quarto and Folio texts of *King Lear*.[12]

Much that we take for granted in the circumstances of performance would have seemed strange to Shakespeare and his contemporaries. The long run, with a company engaged to act one play over and over as long as there was an audience for it, was unknown. So was the figure of the director. The repertory was much larger than that of a modern organization such as the Royal Shakespeare Company; it has been calculated that an Elizabethan actor would have to keep thirty or forty parts in his head, while learning a new one every other week.[13] We may imagine shorter rehearsal periods, and more frequent and audible prompting, than we are used to; in *Romeo and Juliet* Benvolio refers sourly to a 'without-book prologue, faintly spoke /After the prompter' (II. 4). There were several factors that made this system possible. One was the absence of what we would think of as scenery.

While the visual taste of the period was anything but austere, and the actors' costumes seem to have been lavish,[14] plays were acted against an unchanging stage facade, varied only by the occasional use of portable scenic elements. (Shakespeare, for example, seems to have required trees in *As You Like It* and a cave-mouth in *Cymbeline*. Other writers made even more elaborate demands, as we will see in considering Heywood's *Four Ages* in Chapter 10.) There was no designer to create total stage pictures unique to each production. Also, companies were by our standards unusually stable. The same actors would work together, year after year, often for most of their adult lives.

This was particularly true of Shakespeare's company. Before 1603 they were the Lord Chamberlain's Men: this and other company titles reflect the legal requirement that players had to be attached to an important official; the other main company of the 1590s, for example, was the Admiral's Men. Shakespeare's company became the King's Men when at the accession of James the players were taken under direct royal patronage. They were, in effect, Britain's first National Theatre. They had the most eclectic repertoire of any company of the period, they owned their own theatre, the Globe, and they were the company most often asked to perform at Court. The theatre has never been a steady way to make a living, and the hazards in Shakespeare's day included not only poor houses but closure by plague and the destruction of buildings and playscripts by fire. The King's Men were the only company to survive through this period to the closing of the theatres in 1642. At the centre (and this is also true of the other major companies) was a group of 'sharers' or shareholders who played the leading roles and conducted the company's business. They were used to working as a team, on stage and off, and while there is some evidence that authors were expected to conduct rehearsals,[15] performances would really depend on the experience and teamwork of the central group of actors.

Shakespeare's reference to the 'wooden O' (*Henry V*, Prologue) makes us think of his theatre as circular; but it is more revealing to imagine it as a hollowed cylinder. When at the 1982 International Shakespeare Conference at Stratford-upon-Avon C. Walter Hodges traced out the likely dimensions of the Globe theatre in the grounds of the Shakespeare Institute, the general comment was that they looked surprisingly small. The answer is that the audience was packed in layers, vertically. The general effect can still be seen in older theatres and opera houses in London and elsewhere. When an Elizabethan actor walked on stage, he would be confronted with a wall of faces. The actor-audience relationship was an intimate one and the spectators themselves – who, unlike the modern audience, were in the same light

as the actors – were voluble and sometimes ruthless in their reactions.
York's description of the entry of Richard II and Bolingbroke into
London (*Richard II*, v. 2) suggests how quickly an audience's mood
could swing when a 'well-grac'd actor' was succeeded on the stage by
a less favoured one. Ben Jonson complained that the first audience of
The New Inn hissed 'Because the Chambermaid was named Cis'
('Another Epilogue . . .', 8). It sounds like a childish joke on the part
of the self-styled wits of the audience, but it made Jonson change the
character's name in the printed text to Prue.

Open to the elements, with the audience surrounding the stage on
three sides, the public theatres resembled from the outside the bear-
baiting and bull-baiting establishments that also catered to the London
public, and on a rough day the mentality of the audience may have
been similar. Indeed, the Hope Theatre was used alternately for playing
and bear-baiting; Jonson refers to this in the Induction to *Bartholomew
Fair*. But the public stage was only one of two principal forms of
theatre. For the first dozen or so years of the seventeenth century the
tradition of all-boy companies was revived in so-called 'private' theatres: small indoor halls with artificial lighting, higher admission prices,
and, they flattered themselves, a more exclusive clientele. The boys'
companies faded, however, and in 1608 the King's Men took over one
of their principal theatres, the Blackfriars. From that point on
England's leading company worked in two theatres: the old-fashioned
Globe and the modern Blackfriars, where subtler acting and more elaborate visual effects were possible. The Globe is to us the most famous
theatre of its time, but the future lay with the Blackfriars.

The notion of all-boy companies seems to us strange, and though
the satiric bent of their repertoire had a significant influence on Jacobean theatre as a whole, they did not last. But even in the adult
companies female roles were played by boys. We should not think of
this as an eccentric concession to prudery about women showing themselves in public, an odd arrangement that Shakespeare and his fellows
simply had to put up with. A survey of world theatre throughout
history would show all-male companies as the rule, not the exception.
The boys were highly trained artists and, especially in the Jacobean
period, some of the most demanding roles in the English repertoire
were written for them. In 1611 Thomas Coryat, travelling on the
Continent, saw a theatrical innovation in Venice: 'I saw women act,
a thing that I never saw before . . . and they performed it with as good
a grace, action, gesture, and whatsoever convenient for a Player, as
ever I saw any masculine Actor'.[16] The note of surprise is unmistak-
able, and implies a compliment to the boys. Charles's Queen Henrietta
Maria raised Puritan eyebrows by appearing in private theatricals at
Court; but it was not until the Restoration that actresses came to the

public, professional stages of London, and even then they did not instantly replace the boys. Old customs linger in the theatre, and it was not universally obvious that this one needed changing.

'The past', wrote L. P. Hartley in *The Go-Between*, 'is a foreign country; they do things differently there'. Shakespeare and his fellows wrote for a theatre whose conventions are strange to us, and they wrote from within a culture we would find rich in some ways, intolerably repressive in others. We may, for example, think with envy of the Elizabethan barber-shops that kept musical instruments for customers to play while they were waiting; we may be less envious of the Elizabethan who had to answer to the authorities if he did not appear regularly in church on Sundays. If we could travel by time-machine to the Globe theatre, we would likely find the acting style bizarre, the behaviour of the audience barbarous, and the smell intolerable. But if we were lucky enough to catch a performance of *King Lear*, or *Volpone*, or *The Duchess of Malfi*, we would find that through all the cultural barriers there was something that spoke to us. These texts were created amid social and cultural tensions peculiar to their time and amid theatrical conditions we cannot now reproduce. However, the social problems, as I suggested earlier, can be paralleled in other periods and are still broadly recognizable. And for all the changes in the language of the theatre the difficult, dynamic relationship of text, performer and audience is a constant. Reading the plays we lose that relationship, substituting the rather different relationship of text and reader. As with history, so with the medium itself, we are taking the plays out of context, and it requires an effort of imagination to repair the damage. In the pages that follow I will not confront questions of this sort very directly, and I will not be able to linger long over any one play. But I hope to suggest why so many of these plays, and not just Shakespeare's, still live in the theatre, why more deserve revival, and why the effort of the solitary reader to understand them, including his effort to imagine them in their original time and circumstances, is still worth making.

Notes

1. 'The Commonwealth', *Shakespeare Survey*, 17 (1964), 103–19 (p. 110).

2. See Roy Strong, *The Cult of Elizabeth* (London, 1977).

3. Paul Hentzner, *Travels in England*, 1598, quoted from John Dover Wilson,

Life in Shakespeare's England (Cambridge, 1911, reprint Harmondsworth, 1944), pp. 245–6.

4. *James I and the Politics of Literature* (Baltimore, 1983), p. 31. For representative Elizabethan pageants, see Jean Wilson, *Entertainments for Elizabeth I* (Woodbridge, 1980). Stuart masques can be sampled in *A Book of Masques: In Honour of Allardyce Nicoll*, edited by T. J. B. Spencer and S. W. Wells (London, 1967).

5. Quoted in G. P. V. Akrigg, *Jacobean Pageant* (Cambridge, Mass., 1962, reprint New York, 1967), p. 80.

6. *The Political Works of James I*, edited by Charles Howard McIlwan (Cambridge, Mass., 1918), p. 343.

7. *English Fiction of the Victorian Period, 1830–1890* (London, 1985), p. 112.

8. See A. L. Rowse, *The England of Elizabeth: The Structure of Society* (London, 1950, reprint 1973), p. 84.

9. Gerald Eades Bentley, *The Profession of Dramatist in Shakespeare's Time 1590–1642* (Princeton, 1971), pp. 52–3.

10. On this and other cases of censorship, see Bentley, *Profession of Dramatist*, pp. 145–96.

11. The composition of the theatre audience is still a matter of debate. Ann Jennalie Cook, in *The Privileged Playgoers of Shakespeare's London 1576–1642* (Princeton, 1981), has argued for a relatively élite public. Her conclusions have been disputed by Martin Butler, *Theatre and Crisis 1632–1642* (Cambridge, 1984), pp. 293–306.

12. See Steven Urkowitz, *Shakespeare's Revision of King Lear* (Princeton, 1980).

13. See Bernard Beckerman, *Shakespeare at the Globe 1599–1609* (New York, 1962), p. 130.

14. See Gerald Eades Bentley, *The Profession of Player in Shakespeare's Time 1590–1642* (Princeton, 1984), p. 88.

15. See David Klein, 'Did Shakespeare Produce his own Plays?', *Modern Language Review*, 57 (1962), 556–60.

16. Quoted in Bentley, *Profession of Player*, p. 114.

Part One:
Shakespeare

Chapter 2
Early Plays

The theatre William Shakespeare (1564–1616) found when he first came to London was a recent creation, little more than ten years old. Both in the public, professional theatres, and in the private children's companies that flourished in the 1580s the keynote was experimentation. Language, whether the glamour of Marlowe's verse or the studied artifice of Lyly's prose, was boldly stylized. By later standards, characterization was simple and dramatic construction haphazard. For example, in the anonymous *Edmund Ironside; or, War Hath Made All Friends* (c. 1595) only the title signals the ending, in which two claimants to the British throne are suddenly and unexpectedly reconciled just as they seem about to fight to the death. The conclusion comes, not from some impulse earlier in the play, but from the author's desire for a striking effect. Sometimes the haphazardness produces fascinating results. In Robert Greene's *The Scottish History of James IV* (c. 1590) the Induction purports to introduce a story that happened in the past: then two characters from the Induction, the clowns Nano and Slipper, are sent out into the main play, which for them is not a finished, past action but a developing future. The freedom Greene exercises here goes back to mediaeval drama, where Noah and his wife swear by Christ and his saints, and shepherds from contemporary Yorkshire find themselves, with no sense of incongruity, at the cradle of the infant Jesus. Maddening to the literal-minded, such devices toy provocatively with the very nature of theatrical story-telling, and make serious points of their own about the continuities of life, and about time other than clock time.

Shakespeare must have been attracted by such experimental boldness as Greene's, and in some of his plays we can almost match it. But he is never quite so brazen. It is more characteristic of him, when we compare him with his older contemporaries, to impose control. We can see this if we compare his *Henry IV* and *Henry V* with the anonymous *Famous Victories of Henry V* (c. 1586), a comparison from which the earlier play does not suffer so much as we might expect. The early Hal is a roughly drawn but vivid character: an impulsive, emotional youth who begins as a rioter and criminal, repents noisily and sincerely when rebuked by his father, and in his later career as king sweeps through France with the same breezy energy he brought to petty crime. He really is, in other words, what Shakespeare's Hal pretends to be. Shakespeare's story of a careful politician who manipulates his own legend involves unquestionable gains in psychological and political sophistication, but there are losses as well: the earlier playwright assaults our emotions and imaginations more directly. For all its acknowledgement of the horror of war there is nothing in *Henry V* that catches the stench of a battlefield so acutely as the scene in *The Famous Victories* in which one of the clowns steals shoes from dead French soldiers.

It is tempting to say that Shakespeare found Elizabethan drama a rough beast and, for good or ill, tamed it. Tempting, and not altogether untrue. For all his range, he is never quite so eclectic as his predecessors could be. He uses clowns in tragedy, of course; but they never take on an independent life of their own quite as thoroughly as do the clowns of Marlowe's *Doctor Faustus* (*c.* 1592). (That some of those clown scenes may not be Marlowe's does not affect the comparison: their bumptious independence is a fair reflection of standard Elizabethan practice.) This does not mean, however, that the experimental quality is lost; it leaves the surface and goes inward. Kyd in *The Spanish Tragedy* (*c.* 1587) and Marlowe in *Doctor Faustus* display their supernatural machinery before our eyes: their heroes are playthings of supernatural beings we can actually see. Shakespeare's Romeo defies unseen stars, and his Titus questions unseen gods. When the supernatural returns to the stage in *Hamlet*'s ghost and *Macbeth*'s witches, it has a new enigmatic quality. Shakespeare's surface is less artificial, more apparently normal, than that of earlier drama, but his probing of human actions and beliefs strikes deeper, and takes less for granted. When Greene's James IV debates whether or not to kill his wife he weighs alternatives simply and clearly, then makes his decision like a man flipping a coin. Hamlet never debates whether or not he should kill Claudius; instead, he questions why he cannot do so when he so clearly wants to, or thinks he wants to, and never finds the answer.

We do not know if the *Henry VI* trilogy (*c.* 1590–2) was Shakespeare's first work in the theatre, for the beginning of his career is shadowy. But it makes a convenient starting point, for its public action, high rhetoric and overweening heroes show him working in the territory of his greatest predecessor, Marlowe, yet taking a very independent line.[1] Marlowe aims for obvious excitement; Shakespeare is more exploratory. Marlowe's first major work, *Tamburlaine the Great* (1587–8), tells over two parts the story of a spectacular hero who marches from victory to victory with only death to stop him. *Henry*

VI has no such hero, and takes three plays to recount a protracted tale
of national failure. Early in Marlowe's play the title character, having
begun as an obscure brigand, casts off his shepherd's weeds and
announces his intention to conquer the world. Marlowe opens with
the birth of a legend. Shakespeare opens with the death of one, and
goes on from there. His concern is not with a single great figure but
with the whole body politic.

1 Henry VI begins with the state funeral of Henry V, the hero of
Agincourt, including formal laments in which the cosmos decorously
mourns with England: 'Hung be the heavens with black, yield day to
night!' (I. 1). Within a few lines the mourners are quarrelling with each
other and news of disaster in France begins to pour in. The decorum
of the occasion is broken not only by the news itself but by the tough
realism of the messenger who explains the English failure:

> No treachery, but want of men and money.
> Amongst the soldiers this is muttered,
> That here you maintain several factions,
> And whilst a field should be dispatch'd and fought,
> You are disputing of your generals.
>
> (I. 1)

The realism continues throughout Part One. With Henry V dead the
hopes of England are set on Lord Talbot, who is no superman but
makes a good showing in the field as long as he has enough support.
He is betrayed in the end by York and Somerset, who are too busy
quarrelling with each other to send him the soldiers he needs. Talbot
and his son John have a long, stylized death sequence that celebrates
their heroism, chivalry and piety and gives them a final triumph:

> Thou antic Death, that laughs us here to scorn,
> Anon, from thy insulting tyranny,
> Coupled in bonds of perpetuity,
> Two Talbots, winged through the lither sky,
> In thy despite shall scape mortality.
>
> (IV. 7)

This vision is countered by the cynicism of Joan La Pucelle, whose
view of Talbot gives death the last laugh: 'Him that thou magnifi'st
with all these titles /Stinking and fly-blown lies here at our feet' (IV. 7).

The destruction of Talbot in a world that is barren ground for his
chivalric deeds is the key event of Part One; its equivalent in Part Two
is the fall and murder of the Protector, Humphrey, Duke of
Gloucester, who stands for civil order in England. Though

Shakespeare does not sentimentalize him, Gloucester is virtually the only one of the important peers surrounding King Henry who is not out for his own power. He has even some belief in the rule of law: 'I must offend before I be attainted' (II. 4). But he soon realizes he is surrounded by animals, and predicts what his fall will mean for the King: 'Thus is the shepherd beaten from thy side /And wolves are gnarling who shall gnaw thee first' (III. 1). The principal wolf is the Duke of York, who has an opposing claim to the crown. York asserts that claim towards the end of Part Two with a speech of Marlovian aspiration – 'Ah, sancta majestas! Who would not buy thee dear?' (v. 1) – only to fritter away his advantage in a series of compromises. He too is hunted down and killed, in a gruelling scene in which he is placed on a molehill, crowned with paper, and given to wipe away his tears a napkin steeped in the blood of his son (Part Three, I. 4). Here Shakespeare seems to be reaching back to the miracle plays for a parody Crucifixion.[2] As England breaks down into barbarism the play becomes increasingly formal and stylized, given to set-pieces of violence and long formal speeches of defiance and lament. In the most powerful of these formal scenes, Henry's reverie of escaping from the world of history into the simple life of a shepherd is juxtaposed, damningly, with the laments of two of history's victims, identified only as a Son who has killed his Father and a Father who has killed his Son (Part Three, II. 5). The civil war breaks down into a series of private revenge actions: 'Thy father slew my father; therefore, die' (Part Three, I. 3). The next step seems to be complete anarchy.

We get one glimpse of what anarchy might look like in Part Two, in the brilliant depiction of the peasants' revolt led by Jack Cade. Cade touches on some real grievances, and the rallying-cry, 'The first thing we do, let's kill all the lawyers' (IV. 2) may seem irresistible. But the brutal violence of the rebellion aims not at liberty but at a new tyranny under Cade himself: 'Away, burn all the records of the realm. My mouth shall be the parliament of England' (IV. 7). The past is obliterated and the body politic becomes a single man. Cade is defeated, but something like his anarchic spirit revives and takes a more formidable shape in the last major character to emerge from the mayhem, Richard of Gloucester. After killing the saintly but ineffectual King Henry, Richard makes a formal announcement about himself that shows him as the final embodiment of the self-seeking power drives of his whole world:

> I have no brother, I am like no brother;
> And this word 'love' which greybeards call divine,
> Be resident in men like one another
> And not in me. I am myself alone.
>
> (Part Three, v. 6)

This claim will resonate through Jacobean tragedy. The hero of Chapman's *Bussy d'Ambois*, and Giovanni in Ford's *'Tis Pity She's a Whore*, are two of many characters who try to reshape the world according to their own imaginations, as though their wills were the only reality that mattered. The claim is touched on in Donne's words, 'every man alone thinks he hath got / To be a Phoenix' ('The First Anniversary', 216) and in Tamburlaine's boast, 'I hold the fates bound fast in iron chains, / And with my hand turn fortune's wheel about' (Part One, I. 2). Marlowe lets us feel the excitement of the boast, while Donne complains of it as a sign of social breakdown. Shakespeare is somewhere between the two. Richard's language has none of the sweep of Tamburlaine's, for his focus is more narrowly political, and he is less inclined to look out into the universe. But it has a compelling rhythm, and the boldness of its commitment catches our admiration. Richard meets with resistance, as Bussy and Giovanni will do. But while they meet it directly, in the conflicting claims other characters exert, the effective opposition to Richard grows slowly through the final play in the group. Though it carries on in theme, character and action from the *Henry VI* plays, *Richard III* (*c.* 1593) is fundamentally different in spirit. At first the difference seems to be that it is dominated by a single individual. It opens with a soliloquy, the only play of Shakespeare's to do so. While the issues of *Henry VI* are thrashed out in the council chamber and on the battlefield, the scale of *Richard III* is at once more domestic and more universal. Though Richard operates privately, working on one person at a time, he seems to be not just serving his own political ambition by contriving a death here and there but calling the fundamental bond of humanity into question, and it is this bond – one of the master-themes in Shakespeare – that will finally provide the opposition to the villain-hero.

His brutal, levelling wit makes human life a cheap commodity:

> But yet I run before my horse to market.
> Clarence still breathes, Edward still lives and reigns;
> When they are gone, then must I count my gains.
>
> (I. 1)

Yet the wit is seductive, and he has an ingratiating manner with the audience. He also seems to be the only source of energy in an exhausted world. In the laments of the bereaved women the past becomes a blur of names:

> I had an Edward, till a Richard kill'd him;
> I had a Harry, till a Richard kill'd him;
> Thou hadst an Edward, till a Richard kill'd him;
> Thou had'st a Richard, till a Richard kill'd him.
>
> (IV. 4)

The play is full of reminiscence; we are at the end of a long age of suffering, and we are surrounded by the dead. It seems appropriate that Buckingham, the last of Richard's victims, dies on All Souls' Day. The living, notably Edward and Clarence, also bear a weight of guilt from the past and Richard can be seen as the unwitting agent of retribution. But if there is a larger process at work Richard is its victim as well as its agent. Margaret has an apocalyptic vision of what is happening in England:

> Earth gapes, hell burns, fiends roar, saints pray,
> To have him suddenly convey'd from hence.
> Cancel his bond of life, dear God, I pray,
> That I may live and say, the dog is dead!
>
> (IV. 4)

Shakespeare prepares for Richard's end in other, less showy ways. He becomes exhausted and confused; he loses his power to charm; his support melts away. Finally the past comes on stage to haunt him in the procession of ghosts the night before Bosworth Field. More damagingly, Richard judges and condemns himself by the standards of conventional humanity he mocked so wittily in the early scenes: 'I shall despair. There is no creature loves me, /And if I die, no soul will pity me' (v. 3). He is imprisoned in the solitude he once saw as a liberation. Against him Richmond asserts not the devious claim of the historical Tudors – Shakespeare tactfully keeps that out of the picture – but a deeper, more mysterious power. If we think back to *3 Henry VI*, we remember the old King addressing the boy Richmond as 'England's hope' (IV. 6). More immediately, he brings a restoration of the social and family ties Richard has violated, invoking a range of values in which Marlowe was hardly ever interested:

> If you do fight in safeguard of your wives,
> Your wives shall welcome home the conquerors;
> If you do free your children from the sword,
> Your children's children quits it in your age.
>
> (v. 3)

Landing at Milford Haven, he associates himself, as the historical Henry VII did, with the mysterious West of Britain, centre of the Arthurian legend.[3] *Henry VI* begins with the death of a legendary king whose achievement is swept away by history. *Richard III* ends not so much with the rescue of England as with the lifting of England from history into myth. Richard in a way begins the process, representing as he does a fundamental evil. Richmond seems to be hardly a character from history, indeed hardly a character at all, but an embodied principle of order. The vision is, up to a point, reassuring. But it would be more reassuring still if it were more firmly grounded, as some of Shakespeare's later visions of order are, in recognizable human reality. If Shakespeare's early history plays speak to their time, what they appeal to is a sense of national disillusionment and frustration in which the forces of disorder are palpable enough but the powers that might rescue England are, like Arthur's tombstone and Drake's drum, the stuff of dreams.

The procession of ghosts who haunt Richard on the eve of his death stretch back not only to the early scenes of the play but to *Henry VI*. While a play like *Edmund Ironside* seems to pick its ending out of the air, Shakespeare's ending is part of a sustained effort of consolidation. This consolidation is the formal expression of Shakespeare's concern with the human bond. No action is finally isolated, because no one, not even Richard, is entirely alone. This concern shapes what may have been Shakespeare's first comedy, *The Comedy of Errors* (*c.* 1590). At first glance we have Elizabethan eclecticism, as Shakespeare grafts on to the Plautine farce of *Menaechmi* a romantic story of shipwreck, loss and miraculous restoration. But the two stories work together, both being addressed to the same anxieties. The two sets of identical twins (Shakespeare doubles Plautus's number) confront not just mechanical confusion about lost property but a fundamental challenge to their identities. As other characters address them with total confidence about their names and total inaccuracy about their actions, they are made to question not only what is happening but who they are. The instability of identity will become, as we will see later, a tragic theme for Shakespeare. Here our laughter is seldom nervous, for we have seen at the beginning of the play the father who holds the key to the identity problem, just as we see in the following scenes the sons who will give a happy ending to his own tale of loss. The reuniting of the broken family, a motif to which Shakespeare will return in the final romances, restores identity by restoring the family ties that first created it. The Abbess of Ephesus, appealed to as an authority figure to settle the problems even the Duke cannot manage, turns out to be the lost mother, and greets the recovery of her children as a new birth:

> Thirty-three years have I but gone in travail
> Of you, my sons, and till this present hour
> My heavy burden ne'er delivered.
>   (v. 1)

The twin Dromios, source of much knockabout comedy throughout the play, are left alone on stage at the end, and settle the question of precedence, so fundamental to Elizabethan society, by deciding to ignore it: 'We came into the world like brother and brother, /And now let's go hand in hand, not one before another' (v. 1).

If *The Comedy of Errors* enriches the farce of mistaken identity beyond anything Shakespeare's audience could have expected, *The Two Gentlemen of Verona* (*c.* 1593) takes a story of romantic love and seems deliberately to shrink it. The lovers Valentine and Proteus and their ladies Julia and Silvia are contained within a series of neat plot ironies, and subject to comic counterpointing by the servants Speed and Launce – not to mention Launce's dog Crab,[4] who in performance generally steals the show by his obvious indifference to the whole proceeding. Far from enriching the lovers, love seems to diminish them, Valentine to an innocent and Proteus to a schemer. The opposing value of male friendship, celebrated at length in Lyly's *Endimion* (1588), is reduced to Valentine's brisk gesture of surrendering his lady to his friend, who has just tried to rape her. No sooner has Valentine uttered his notorious 'All that was mine in Silvia I give thee' (v. 4) than Julia, who is disguised as a boy and who has her own claims on Proteus, conveniently faints, thereby calling attention to herself and starting the next plot twist. The sheer speed of the dénouement seems to reduce the characters and give a diminished view of the satisfactions they achieve,[5] and the passage that sticks most easily in the mind is Proteus's lament, early in the play:

> O, how this spring of love resembleth
> The uncertain glory of an April day,
> Which now shows all the beauty of the sun,
> And by and by a cloud takes all away!
>
> (I. 3)

In this case Shakespeare's control has a somewhat levelling and sardonic effect. Taken together, *The Comedy of Errors* and *The Two Gentlemen of Verona* establish the poles of celebration and irony between which Shakespearean comedy will continue to turn.

Both comedies reverse expectations: put simply, *The Comedy of Errors* is warmer than we might have expected from its farcical premises, *The Two Gentlemen* colder than its romantic material might have allowed. *The Taming of the Shrew* (*c.* 1594) contains a double reversal. The shrew is a familiar laughing-stock, who in earlier comedies if she is cured at all is (sometimes literally) beaten into submission. Katharina is a much subtler portrayal: a difficult girl with an ostentatiously sweet sister, she has, it seems, deliberately made herself hard to get along with.[6] Petruchio subjects her to a brutal physical ordeal that involves depriving her of food and sleep; she is tamed as a hawk would be tamed. But she is also made to see the value of ordinary decent comfort by being denied it.[7] Later Petruchio tests her obedience by making her play a game in which the sun is the moon if he says it is and an old man is a 'young budding virgin, fair and fresh and sweet' (IV. 5). She obliges with a fine passage of rhetoric that shows her pleasure in being a full partner in the game. This is not really a romantic affair, though it is sometimes played as though it were; and Petruchio's view of marriage is not much to modern taste. But we should grant that in goading Katharina's mind into action he is paying her the compliment of assuming she has one. The taming plot has the outline of a conventional and rather brutal shrew comedy; but there is surprising psychological richness in its development. The corresponding surprise in the subplot is that Bianca, who is the desirable prize at the centre of a conventional rival-wooer intrigue, and who is won by the young romantic Lucentio, turns out to be the real shrew, as anyone who listened carefully to her earlier dialogue could have predicted. Once again farce and romance are turned inside out.

In *Love's Labour's Lost* (c. 1594) the very form of comedy seems to be turning against itself. A damaging spirit of mockery and scepticism is in the air. Granted the different tone appropriate to the genre, we are in a world like that of *1 Henry VI*, where heroism, legend and chivalry confront the brute facts of reality. The King of Navarre and his three friends are 'brave conquerors' (I. 1), seeking to triumph over time and death by the fame of their enterprise: a three-year period of study, fasting and celibacy. The first scene, like that of *1 Henry VI*, is a violated ceremony. One of the King's companions, Berowne, stands out against the formal oath-taking, insisting the scheme is unrealistic. He subscribes under pressure from his fellows, but before the scene is over we learn that the King's rules of celibacy have already been broken by the clown Costard and will have to be broken again by the King himself to accommodate a diplomatic mission led by the Princess of France. With comic predictability, the King and his fellows fall in love with the Princess and her ladies. The way is led by the fantastical Spaniard Don Armado, who is already in love with the country wench Jaquenetta, and tries to preserve his dignity with the thought that he is following the precedent of such heroes as Samson and Hercules (I. 2). Similarly, the King and his fellows beg Berowne to find some 'authority' for their oath-breaking. He replies with a speech that begins with a romantic celebration of the power of love as a way of recovering the heroism they have lost – 'For valour, is not Love a Hercules, /Still climbing trees in the Hesperides?' – but ends with flat sophistry:

It is religion to be thus forsworn,
For charity itself fulfils the law,
And who can sever love from charity?
(IV. 3)

This new dedication to love combines the men's desire to be
conquerors with the practical bawdry that is never far from their
minds:

KING
  Saint Cupid, then! and soldiers, to the field!
BEROWNE
  Advance your standards, and upon them lords;
  Pell-mell, down with them!
(IV. 3)

The play's evocation of a lost world of heroism is an important part
of its comic irony. This comes to a head in the show of the Nine
Worthies, where figures like Alexander, Hercules and Pompey are
incongruously impersonated by the local amateurs. The show is brutally mocked by its aristocratic audience, and breaks up in disorder.
One of the victims seems to be theatrical illusion itself, which is given
the lie direct when Costard declares, 'I Pompey am' and the French
lord Boyet retorts, 'You lie, you are not he' (v. 2).[8] The pretensions
of language are similarly challenged. Sometimes the challenge is direct,
as when Berowne begs, 'White-handed mistress, one sweet word with
thee' and the Princess retorts, 'Honey, and milk, and sugar; there is
three' (v. 2). Armado's language is self-deflating: 'the posteriors of this
day, which the rude multitude call the afternoon' (v. 1). Finally,
Berowne is brought to renounce 'taffeta phrases, silken terms precise'
and promises to woo 'in russet yeas and honest kersey noes' (v. 2). So
far all this sounds like the normal business of comedy: pretensions are
deflated, the power of love is asserted. But it is not that simple. The
three-years' vow, ridiculous though it was, involved a commitment,
and the breaking of that commitment leads the Princess to insist, 'Nor
God, nor I, delights in perjur'd men' (v. 2). The ladies' mockery of
the lords' wooing is not the sort of teasing that leaves room for serious
affection. It is merciless and destructive, and leaves the men simply
helpless. As they embark on their courtship, Berowne ruefully predicts
the outcome and declares it is no more than they deserve: 'Light
wenches may prove plagues to men forsworn; /If so, our copper buys
no better treasure' (IV. 3). The mockery itself leaves us a little uncomfortable; there is something unsporting in attacking such easy
victims. This is certainly the effect when the lords attack the Nine

Worthies. The joking becomes tasteless and irritating and Armado, who has been a laughing-stock for much of the play, replies to it with touching dignity, thinking not of himself but of Hector: 'The sweet war-man is dead and rotten, sweet chucks, beat not the bones of the buried. When he breathed he was a man' (v. 2).

Armado's plea for a decent hearing suggests that our common mortality ought to make us gentle with one another. And while comedy normally constructs happy endings in defiance of time and death, *Love's Labour's Lost* breaks this fundamental rule by letting mortality have its way. The sport of the final scene is interrupted by the news of the death of the Princess's father. The shock has been fairly prepared, not just by our knowledge of his illness but more subtly by earlier moments when we feel a chill in the air: when Katharine talks of the sister who died of love, or when the page Moth promises lightly that he will prove 'a man, if I live' (III. 1) and we remember how commonly Elizabethan children died. As the Princess prepares to return to France the King demands an instant happy ending, and she refuses:

KING
    Now, at the latest minute of the hour,
    Grant us your loves.
PRINCESS
                          A time, methinks, too short
    To make a world-without-end bargain in.
                                  (v. 2)

The men will be tested by being made to wait for a year. Not only is this, as Berowne remarks, 'too long for a play' (v. 2) but in the test on Berowne in particular the play's own spirit of mockery is challenged. Katharine, herself the most sharp-tongued of the ladies, orders him to 'jest a twelvemonth in an hospital' as 'the way to choke a gibing spirit' (v. 2). But the play does not just turn on itself and leave us with nothing. The men are given a new and shorter period of trial, a chance to prove that they can fulfil something like the vows they undertook so foolishly before; in that sense the play circles back to its beginning. And in the final songs of winter and spring time ceases to be a forward movement to death and becomes cyclical. The action of this courtly, enclosed and learned comedy is finally absorbed into the workings of nature, and in a characteristic Shakespearean act of consolidation a structure is broken only to be re-made.

In *Love's Labour's Lost* the great figures of legend were shadows in the past, suggesting the littleness of the characters we saw; *A Midsummer Night's Dream* (c. 1595) opens with two legendary figures,

Theseus and Hippolyta, present before our eyes. The inset play of Pyramus and Thisbe is, like the show of the Nine Worthies, threatened by the incompetence of its performers and the mockery of its audience; but unlike the earlier show it is played out to the end. Bottom, Quince and company aim to delight their audience without giving offence, and while they may not succeed in quite the way they intended, they do succeed. They also manage to exorcise the tragic side of love, telling in comic form a story of fatal passion and confusion that seems at times a parody of *Romeo and Juliet*. In the play as a whole we see comedy's answer to mortality, as it celebrates the special occasion of marriage, fixing closely on one moment of happiness. The play begins with Theseus impatient for his wedding night, and ends with his going off stage to enjoy it while the fairies prepare to bless the bride-beds. Other possibilities are set against the ideal of marriage, but are made to keep their distance. Hermia, under pressure from her father to marry Demetrius, is threatened with the equally undesirable alternatives of a contemplative life of chastity like Navarre's, and death. She chooses neither but escapes from the city with her lover. Chastity is both ideal-ized and distanced in Oberon's description of the 'Imperial vot'ress' (II. 1) whom Cupid's arrow misses. It hits a common flower, infecting it with the power to cause love, and the play concerns itself with that. In the same scene Titania tells the story of another votaress, one of her own order, whose pregnancy made her look like a ship 'rich with merchandise' but whose fate reminds us that human fertility has its dangers too. 'But she, being mortal, of that boy did die'. The reminder is brief; the play is not her story either. In moments like this we seem to see the play selecting its own material.

The boy himself, though we never see him, survives to cause disorder in the fairy world as Oberon and Titania quarrel over him. Oberon's trick on Titania is potentially grotesque; she could, he threatens, fall in love with a beast. Instead we find her courting Bottom, whose natural clownishness is enhanced by an ass's head. The haunting power of this image is suggested by the number of times illustrators have used it to represent the play. Unlike earlier stage pictures in Shakespeare – York crowned with paper, for instance – it cannot be reduced to a simple meaning. In part, however, it mocks the claim of love to endow its victims with special perception. Though Berowne declared, 'A lover's eyes will gaze an eagle blind' (IV. 3), in the fate of Titania and in the simpler fates of Lysander and Demetrius we see love as a comic distortion of the senses. Theseus ranks lovers with lunatics and poets: 'The lover, all as frantic, /Sees Helen's beauty in a brow of Egypt' (V. 1). But the sceptical voice, destructive in *Love's Labour's Lost*, touches *A Midsummer Night's Dream* very lightly. Theseus mocks lovers, but he is a lover himself. He disbelieves the story of the wood, but we have seen it with our own eyes, and he himself has had an affair with Titania. He mocks artificial fables and the dreams of poets; but he is an antique fable himself, and as a character in a play he owes his very existence to a poet.[9] Not only is scepticism turned against itself; it becomes the occasion for belief. The gentle reception Theseus recommends for *Pyramus and Thisbe*, saying, 'The best in this kind are but shadows; and the worst are no worse, if imagination amend them' (v. 1), is precisely the reception Puck's epilogue asks for the whole play. Hippolyta adds that, *Pyramus and Thisbe* being such silly stuff, 'It must be your imagination then, and not theirs' (v. 1). In the fairy scenes we watch life-sized actors pretending to be characters who can hide in acorn-cups; by agreeing to accept this illusion, we become collaborators in the artistic process. Our first reaction of disbelief simply throws the responsibility on us: it must be our imaginations, not theirs.

When they first wake after their night in the forest the lovers are poised in confusion between dream and reality; but as they talk together the mystery dissipates, their forest experience is placed as a dream (though it was, theatrically, as real as the experience of Athens) and they go off to talk about it. Bottom wakes alone, and for him the dream retains its sense of mystery. He may be a fool, but he has an artist's respect for the experience itself, a mistrust of interpretation:

> Man is but an ass, if he go about to expound this dream,
> Methought I was – there is no man can tell what.
> Methought I was – and methought I had – but man is but
> a patch'd fool, if he will offer to say what methought I
> had. The eye of man hath not heard, the ear of man hath
> not seen, man's hand is not able to taste, his tongue to
> conceive, nor his heart to report, what my dream was. I
> will get Peter Quince to write a ballad of this dream. It
> shall be call'd 'Bottom's Dream', because it hath no
> bottom.
>   (IV. 1)

The dream cannot be expounded; but it can be turned into art. It is the egocentric art of the actor who in the casting of *Pyramus and Thisbe* wanted to play all the parts himself, and now wants to claim the dream as *his* dream. Literal dreams are, of course, private in just this way. But we can supplement Bottom's respect for his vision with the lovers' awareness, equally mysterious in its own way, of the dream as a communal experience like the play itself. For Shakespeare the play is a breakthrough; after the radical and at times near-destructive experiments of the earlier comedies he has turned scepticism against itself and produced the most perfectly finished of his early works.

Few have thought of *Titus Andronicus* (*c.* 1592) as perfectly finished, and there is a consensus that Shakespeare's least promising beginning was in tragedy. But the play cannot be dismissed as a random collection of atrocities. Like *Henry VI* it shows the death of an old order but it is more focused, as tragedy usually is, on the responsibility of an individual, and its imaginative reach in its best scenes is much greater. Titus is a pious old Roman general, a servant of the state with a strong sense of family. When at the start of the play he has the Gothic prince Alarbus killed to appease the ghosts of his sons, dead in the Gothic wars, it is emphasized that this is a ritual sacrifice. But it also involves ignoring pleas for natural pity from Alarbus's mother Tamora. Though Titus makes his decision easily it is a tragic decision that starts an avalanche of horror. Beneath the funeral and election ceremonies of the early scenes, which suggest a formalized society, there are brutal passions waiting to be released. Titus makes another fatal decision when he is asked to pick the next emperor and, with characteristic piety, chooses the arrogant Saturninus over the apparently more decent Bassianus simply because Saturninus is the late Emperor's eldest son. Within minutes Saturninus has turned against him and betrothed himself to Tamora. Titus is left to brood, like Lear and Timon after him, on ingratitude; but he soon has worse to cope with. As though we were looking at the dark underside of *A Midsummer Night's Dream*, the action moves to a wood outside Rome, where, in ironic juxtaposition with the Emperor's hunt, Titus's daughter Lavinia is raped and mutilated by Tamora's sons. At the centre of the same wood is a 'detested, dark, blood-drinking pit' (II. 3) in which two of Titus's sons are trapped with the murdered body of Bassianus, in a trick that leads to their being falsely accused of his death. As the atrocities mount, Titus finds himself pleading for the pity he has denied Tamora; and since the tribunes of Rome will not listen he pleads with bitter irony to the stones. His sons are killed, another son is exiled, he is tricked into chopping off his own hand. The forest seems to have come to the city: 'Rome is but a wilderness of tigers' (III. 1). Titus's suffering combines the elemental anguish of 'I am the sea' (III. 1) with the dream-like bewilderment of 'When will this fearful slumber have an end?' (III. 1). Then, with an unsteady combination of madness and bitterly sane irony, he has his kinsmen look for justice by fishing in the sea, digging in the earth, and firing off arrows with messages for the gods. At last he turns to revenge, and the play retreats to the conventional as Shakespeare's later tragedies do not. Significantly, the arrows fired at the gods are redirected into the emperor's court. The business ceases to be questioning the universe and becomes simply getting back at one's enemies. Titus kills Tamora's sons in a characteristically ritualized scene, and serves them to their mother in a pie, forcing her to imitate the man-eating pit in the wood and 'like to the earth, swallow her own increase' (v. 2). It is all brutally appropriate, but we lose our concentration on Titus as a tragic figure; in the last scene he is one of three people killed in four lines, just another corpse. Later some dignity is restored as his kinsmen kiss him, formally honouring the body that was earlier mutilated; but the general effect of the last act is that a potentially tragic vision has been contracted into a revenge melodrama.

There is also something bookish about *Titus Andronicus*. The dialogue is heavy with learned allusion. Lavinia, tongueless, describes her fate by ransacking her father's library for appropriate references; verses of Horace are wrapped around weapons; Titus kills Lavinia on the precedent set by Virginius. The violence is contained within a somewhat academic artifice. *Romeo and Juliet* (*c.* 1595), though in some respects it is not so seminal for the later tragedies, is a more profoundly original work. Here too the lovers are contained within an artificial framework. At each major manifestation of the feud – the opening brawl, the aftermath of Tybalt's death, the final scene in the tomb – the stage fills symmetrically with Capulets and Montagues, and the Prince takes the centre to speak for the whole community. The Prologue packages the story in the neat formulae of a Shakespearean sonnet. But the forms are there to be broken. Juliet is first seen trapped by social convention; as her family talks over her head, arranging her marriage, she says little and is clearly not expected to say anything. But when she caps the Nurse's 'It stinted and said "Ay"' with 'And stint thou too, I pray thee, nurse, say I' (I. 3) the quiet pun makes us sit up and take notice. Romeo is trapped by literary convention, mooning over Rosaline in coldly patterned verse; but we notice that he can stand back from his own posturing and ask, a bit sheepishly, 'Dost thou not laugh?' (I. 1). When he sees Juliet the painting-by-numbers paradoxes of his early verse – 'Feather of lead, bright smoke, cold fire, sick health' (I. 1) – are replaced by more daring and richly textured language:

> O, she doth teach the torches to burn bright!
> It seems she hangs upon the cheek of night
> As a rich jewel in an Ethiope's ear –
> Beauty too rich for use, for earth too dear!
>
> (I. 5)

Their first meeting is a kissing game enclosed in a sonnet, but followed by an extra quatrain and a second kiss. As in Shakespeare's comedies, love is expressing itself formally and at the same time straining against the formality. Fourteen lines are not enough. In the next scene there is the physical barrier of the balcony between them; but they work across that barrier, with Juliet (like the ladies of *Love's Labour's Lost*) purging Romeo of his conventional language and finally tearing up both literary and social convention by proposing marriage herself.

Their resemblance at this point to the lovers of the comedies has suggested to some critics that the play 'becomes, rather than is, tragic'[10] as the characters are forced into a tragic plot in which they do not really belong. It is true that some of the most confident writing in the early scenes includes the flashing wit of Mercutio and the comic garrulity of the Nurse, and that after the death of Tybalt Juliet's language becomes as painfully artificial as Romeo's when he was pining for Rosaline. But as the imaginations of Romeo and Juliet expand, even explode, in the excitement of love we see that this is, as the Prologue called it, a death-marked love. There is more to their fate than the opposition of the stars. Juliet's passionate, witty speech anticipating her wedding night goes straight from sex to death:

> Come, gentle night, come, loving, black-brow'd night,
> Give me my Romeo; and, when I shall die,
> Take him and cut him out in little stars,
> And he will make the face of heaven so fine
> That all the world will be in love with night
> And pay no worship to the garish sun.
>
> (III. 2)

In the ensuing action the lovers are not just caught in the machinery of coincidence; they drive the action forward by their own passionate impulses. One arrangement of scenes is particularly significant: we hear of the misfortune that delays Friar Laurence's letter only *after* we have heard Romeo's reaction to the misleading news of Juliet's death: 'Is it e'en so? Then I defy you, stars!' (v. 1). Literally, the plot incident happens first and Romeo reacts to it; but theatrically Romeo's decision takes priority. The responsibility is his.

The grim simplicity of Romeo's line marks a significant advance over the noisy passions of the preceding scenes. It also embodies a central paradox: Romeo is at once defying his fate and fulfilling it, doing what the stars have determined but doing it as an act of his own will. For most of the play he seems an untypical tragic hero, a decent, likeable young man who has no great guilt on his soul and who kills Tybalt only under intolerable pressure. But in the last act he acquires something like the terrible isolation from normal humanity we see more fully in later tragedies. Paris arrives at Juliet's tomb with sweet water and flowers, Romeo with a mattock and a crowbar. They have become Edgar Linton and Heathcliff. 'The boy gives warning something doth approach' (v. 3) – Romeo must seem hardly human. His language is, briefly, the language of *Titus*:

> The time and my intents are savage-wild,
> More fierce and more inexorable far
> Than empty tigers or the roaring sea.
>
> (v. 3)

He goes on to speak as a man for whom death has become familiar, even domestic: 'here will I remain /With worms that are thy chambermaids' (v. 3). The lovers die together, yet separately. Shakespeare contrives it so that each addresses a final speech to the other's unconscious body. In the end they are hidden from view as Friar Laurence delivers a long plot summary that leaves out everything we have found exciting and the bereaved fathers promise each other to replace their dead children with opulent statues. *Romeo and Juliet* is, like Shakespeare's other early plays, an experiment, and some of the risks will not be repeated: the machinery of coincidence, the closeness of the tone to romantic comedy, the use of likeable and essentially innocent young people as tragic figures. But in the increasing isolation of the lovers from their community, as they break through to a new level of experience even the audience cannot always grasp, *Romeo and Juliet* takes its place with the great tragedies that are to come.

In Shakespeare's early plays the language is frequently stilted and the characterization thin, though in both areas there are hints, and often more than hints, of achievements to come. But the construction is already masterly. The atrocities of *Titus Andronicus* make the play look wild: but in the organization of imagery, verbal and theatrical, we notice a careful design: Romans go to the wilderness, and the wilderness comes to Rome. At the end of *Henry VI* disaster abroad and disaster at home are neatly related as Talbot dies betrayed by his feuding countrymen. And few even of Shakespeare's plays are as closely woven as *A Midsummer Night's Dream*. This sense of control, of an imaginative purpose working through the deepest levels of the play, is perhaps the most striking feature that separates Shakespeare from his brilliant, erratic predecessors. Yet this ordering strains against a fascination with the anarchic: Cade's desire to undo civilization, Richard's determination to be himself alone; Kate's resistance to taming; and the mockery of the Princess and her ladies, that seems to leave nothing standing. In general, Shakespeare's way with anarchy is neither to let it have its way nor to suppress it altogether, but to focus it and redirect it. Titus's revenge is as violent as the atrocities it responds to, but more neatly emblematic. Kate's address on marriage shows her not only obedient to her husband but superior to her fellow wives; her energy, and her interest in scoring points, are not suppressed but redirected. And yet Kate is also a rebel who finally capitulates; so is Richard III, who turns his sceptical gaze at last against himself and admits the judgement of conventional society. Romeo, coming to die with Juliet, takes care to have his servant deliver a final message to his father. There is in all these plays an underlying conservatism, a desire to hold to the ordering patterns of family and society. The family in particular matters. The reunion in *The Comedy of Errors*, and the way the Andronici work together in adversity, show the importance of this theme in two otherwise very different plays. Richard's crimes are against the family no less than against the state. Shakespeare was of course no unquestioning proponent of order. The early comedies seen as a group are finely balanced between celebration and scepticism. The edge of fantasy in the ending of *Richard III* anticipates the endings of many later tragedies, where the final consolidation of the state leaves us not so much sceptical as uncaring, and the ending of *2 Henry IV*, where the rejection of Falstaff leaves us disturbed by the price of order. But that lies in the future. Shakespeare's desire to pull together the disparate material of Elizabethan drama, and the full range of possibilites it exemplifies, is best summed up in the ending of *A Midsummer Night's Dream*, where the clowns pay their backhanded tribute to the wedding of Theseus and the other lovers, and spirits of the forest, their own disorder resolved, come to the city to bless the bride-beds.

Notes

1. On the relation between the two writers see F. P. Wilson, *Marlowe and the Early Shakespeare* (Oxford, 1953), and Nicholas Brooke, 'Marlowe as Provocative Agent in Shakespeare's Early Plays', *Shakespeare Survey*, 14 (1961), 34–44.

2. See Emrys Jones, *The Origins of Shakespeare* (Oxford, 1977), pp. 54–56.

3. See Emrys Jones, 'Stuart *Cymbeline*', *Essays in Criticism*, 11 (1961), 84–99.

4. See Harold F. Brooks, 'Two Clowns in a Comedy (To Say Nothing of the Dog): Speed, Launce (and Crab) in *The Two Gentlemen of Verona*', *Essays and Studies*, 16 (1963), 91–100.

5. See Clifford Leech, Introduction to the Arden edition (London, 1969), p. lxix.

6. See Ruth Nevo, *Comic Transformations in Shakespeare* (London, 1980), p. 41.

7. See G. R. Hibbard, Introduction to the New Penguin edition (Harmondsworth, 1968), p. 21.

8. See Anne Righter [Barton], *Shakespeare and the Idea of the Play* (London, 1962, reprint Harmondsworth, 1967), p. 99.

9. See G. K. Hunter, *John Lyly: The Humanist as Courtier* (London, 1962), p. 328.

10. Susan Snyder, *The Comic Matrix of Shakespeare's Tragedies* (Princeton, 1979), p. 57.

Chapter 3
History and Comedy

In the celebration of order there is inevitably a public, ceremonial quality. The public ceremonies of politics – a coronation, a procession – have a certain kinship to the private ceremonies that mark a marriage – a feast, a dance, a church service. All proceed by set forms, making a virtue of predictability. When a king is crowned or lovers are married they speak what is set down for them, losing their individuality in a design that belongs to the community. What this meant for the public life of Elizabethan England is suggested in the elaborate artifice of the occasions surrounding Elizabeth, touched on briefly in Chapter 1. But of course the lack of individuality the royal occasion imposes, its refusal to admit that the monarch is anything less than splendid, the subjects anything less than enthusiastically loyal, is a fiction. The life of the occasion comes from symbols, not realities. And sometimes individuality intrudes: the execution of Mary Queen of Scots is a case in point. Mary used recognizable colour-coding to control the occasion. She appeared on the scaffold dressed from head to foot in black. Then, removing the black robe, she appeared from head to foot in blood red, the colour of the martyrs of the Church. A Catholic queen was dying in a Protestant country. Then, as she knelt to receive the blow, her wig fell off revealing the close-cropped grey hair beneath. The symbol became the woman. So in the love poetry of the period, experience is highly conventionalized: the worshipping lover, the disdainful lady who preserves her honour against the wittiest or most desperate entreaties. But in certain of Shakespeare's sonnets we hear the bitter reflections of a lover who is not only sleeping quite regularly with his lady but knows he is not the only one. We know nothing about her beyond the poems, not even her name. But here too there was a woman, and in this case the art itself preserves her, no less than it preserves the beauty of the young man who is the rival centre of attention.

C. L. Barber has described the Renaissance as a period when an ordered, ceremonial view of life was being replaced by an historical one, acknowledging individual realities in a way that challenged communal forms.[1] In. the ceremonial view, symbols have fixed and predictable meanings. The surrender of individual reality to the demands of the occasion is suggested by a picture of the coronation procession of Henry VIII, which shows Henry with the face of his father. To the painter the individual does not matter: a king is a king.[2] And yet the fact that we can detect the error, and know it *is* an error, implies that in the visual art of this period even at its crudest we expect to see individuals, not icons. The same is true of Shakespeare. The ordering vision of his earlier plays sometimes lets his characters slip into anonymity. In *A Midsummer Night's Dream* we can distinguish Hermia and Helena readily enough when they are troubled and confused: but as soon as harmony is achieved their voices chime together interchangeably, and in the last act they are completely silent. What Richmond stands for is plain enough, but as a character he is somewhat faceless. In the mid to late 1590s, however, Shakespeare's work enters a second phase in which the conditions that create order, and the cost, are examined more closely and the intractable reality of individuals emerges more sharply. The forms he worked in, history and comedy, both have a public dimension; both are concerned with the fate and interests of a community, and in both there is a natural tendency to convention. Lovers and loyal subjects alike behave according to the book. But Shakespeare is now starting to explore more deeply. In the later histories the political analysis is more searching and uncomfortable than it was in *Henry VI* and *Richard III*; and in the later comedies stylized fantasy is set against a deeper exploration of psychological reality than Shakespeare previously allowed himself in that form.

King John (c. 1596), like *Henry VI*, deals with the question of disputed succession, an anxiety that must have deepened in England as the old Queen got closer to death with no heir in sight. But this time there is no Richmond to settle the problem. Nor does Shakespeare take the route of John Bale, whose morality-cum-history propaganda piece *Kyng Johan*, written during the sectarian conflicts of mid-century, had made the King an early Protestant martyr.

Shakespeare largely ignores the chance to exploit that issue. His John is an insecure ruler, who holds the crown, as his mother frankly tells him, by 'your strong possession much more than your right' (I. 1). He is blustering, devious and liable to panic. He indulges in anti-papal rhetoric when he feels secure enough to do so but submits to Rome when he needs Cardinal Pandulph's help. The other claimant is Arthur, a child who is essentially the tool of the adults around him and whose own view of the question is 'I am not worth this coil that's made for me' (II. 1). Shakespeare presents on the whole an ironically detached view of a world driven by expediency and self-interest, by what the Bastard Philip Faulconbridge calls 'Commodity'. The Bastard himself, like Berowne in *Love's Labour's Lost*, tries to stand aside from the action and comment sardonically on it but finds himself drawn in, losing his detachment and becoming part of what he had mocked. He himself embodies a variation on the theme of legitimacy. He first appears in a debate over his family's land, an ironic reflection of the debate over England. He cheerfully surrenders his claim in order to try his fortunes in a larger, more open world where the rewards may be greater: 'Brother, take you my land, I'll take my chance' (I. 1). At the same time he is the spiritual heir of his natural father Richard Coeur de Lion, avenging his death by killing the Duke of Austria. As the breezy cynicism of his earlier manner disappears, he takes a deeper and more serious view of England than anyone else on stage. After Arthur's death he recognizes that something irreplaceable has gone from England: 'The life, the right, and truth of all this realm /Is fled to heaven' (IV. 3). As the action becomes darker and more confused he clings to the virtues of loyalty and courage; but there is no satisfactory subject for his loyalty to fix on. In the last scene he promises, Kent-like, to follow John into death, and a few lines later is dedicating the rest of his life to the new king Henry. This final confusion is symptomatic of the fragmented world of the play, in which the moral and political centre the crown should provide is missing,

> and England now is left
> To tug and scamble and to part by th' teeth
> The unowned interest of proud-swelling state.
>
> (IV. 3)

King John is a noisy, frantic, somewhat disorganized play. Against it, *Richard II* (1595) is measured and stately. But it shows a breakdown that is finally more terrible. This time the crown is not so much fought over by competing claimants as violated by the man who wears it. Richard sees his kingly function as that of a tax-gatherer who has to raise revenue, by any means that will work, to support a court he himself admits has been too lavish (I. 4). The dying John of Gaunt tells him, 'Landlord of England art thou now, not king' (II. 1). Far from taking the accusation to heart, he shows its truth by seizing Gaunt's estate before the old man's body is cold. The Duke of York points out that in denying the inheritance to Gaunt's son Bolingbroke Richard is denying the principle by which he himself holds office: 'for how art thou a king /But by fair sequence and succession?' (II. 1). When Bolingbroke returns to England, ostensibly to claim his inheritance, he is guilty of treason in ignoring the sentence of banishment Richard passed on him; but the deeper treason is Richard's. His support melts away and he surrenders his kingship to Bolingbroke; it all happens so fast that Richard seems to be yielding not just to the pressure of events but to his own desire for self-destruction. It is fitting that he gives the crown away with his own hands:

> I give this heavy weight from off my head
> And this unwieldy spectre from my hand,
> The pride of kingly sway from out my heart;
> With mine own tears I wash away my balm,
> With mine own hands I give away my crown,
> With mine own tongue deny my sacred state,
> With mine own breath release all duteous oaths.
>
> (IV. 1)

In Richard's imagination the symbols become desanctified as he removes them: the crown is just a heavy weight, the sceptre is merely unwieldy. But as he speaks he evokes the whole structure of social and political order that centres on kingship. What is happening is not just a transfer of power but the untuning of all the instruments of society.

Seen in pragmatic terms the political action ought to be satisfying: a neurotic and destructive ruler is replaced by a demonstrably more competent one. And that indeed is part of the play's political vision. But Richard, as he himself insists, has also a sacred right to his office, no matter how badly he behaves:

> Not all the water in the rough rude sea
> Can wash the balm off from an anointed king;
> The breath of worldly men cannot depose
> The deputy elected by the Lord.
>
> (III. 2)

Yet it happens, and Richard expects it to happen. Having declared,

> For every man that Bolingbroke hath press'd
> To lift shrewd steel against our golden crown,
> God for his Richard hath in heavenly pay
> A glorious angel. . .

Richard then asks Salisbury. 'How far off lies your power?' (III. 2) and when told that Salisbury has no soldiers for him sinks into despair. No angels come to the king's defence; God seems to have lost interest in His deputy. The sacredness of the office is affirmed not by the prevention of Bolingbroke's usurpation but by the dire consequences that follow. As Bolingbroke prepares to ascend the throne, the Bishop of

Carlisle prophesies, 'The blood of English shall manure the ground /And future ages groan for this foul act'. England will become 'the field of Golgotha and dead men's skulls' (IV. 1). Carlisle's prophecy encompasses not only the troubled reign of Henry IV but the later consequences of the unresolved dynastic question in the long chaos of the Wars of the Roses, which Shakespeare had already dramatized. As in *King John*, there is a sense that something in England is broken forever; but the culprit this time, though Carlisle does not see it that way, is the King himself.

Richard is regularly identified with the sun:

> See, see, King Richard doth himself appear,
> As doth the blushing discontented sun
> From out the fiery portal of the east.
> (III. 3)

But as Richard himself puts it, the sun falls out of the sky: 'Down down I come, like glist'ring Phaethon, /Wanting the manage of unruly jades' (III. 3). His words combine spectacular, symbolic ruin with a pragmatic awareness of how that ruin came about. And since he is so identified with his office the removal of his kingship means his destruction as a man. If he is not king he is nothing, and when we last see him in prison the role-playing and self-dramatization that have distinguished his earlier behaviour have turned into a nightmare. Though his body is imprisoned his mind is free, yet he finds no satisfying way to use that freedom:

> Thus play I in one person many people,
> And none contented. Sometimes I am a king;
> Then treasons make me wish myself a beggar,
> And so I am. Then crushing penury
> Persuades me I was better when a king,
> Then am I king'd again, and by and by
> Think that I am unking'd by Bolingbroke,
> And straight am nothing.
> (v. 5)

Role-playing in a void will be enough for some Jacobean heroes. It is not enough for Richard, who yearns for the order he himself has violated. As he meditates, music plays from the next room; but the musicians fail to keep time, the music goes sour, and Richard sees in it an image of his own fate. Marston's *The Malcontent* will open with vile out-of-tune music as a sign of the discord the title character thrives on. Richard still believes the music ought to be better.

Henry IV becomes the effective king of England, and in the process kingship ceases to be a sanctified office and becomes a job, to be earned and held by practical effort.[3] In *1 Henry IV* (1597) Henry tells his son that the rebel Hotspur

> hath more worthy interest to the state
> Than thou the shadow of succession.
> For of no right, nor colour like to right,
> He doth fill fields with harness in the realm.
>
> (III. 2)

Henry's own way of earning power, he tells Hal, has been through a careful management of his public appearances. At the Battle of Shrewsbury Douglas, who has killed several underlings disguised as the king, confronts Henry himself with the words, 'I fear thou art another counterfeit; /And yet, in faith, thou bearest thee like a king' (V. 4). Both points are valid: Henry will never be the true king Richard was, but he is a good imitation. He is constantly threatened by rebellion, however, and in Part Two (c. 1598) by his own growing melancholy and sickness. He promised at the end of *Richard II* to lead England on a crusade, and the dream of going to the Holy Land becomes a futile obsession, like the dream of Moscow in *The Three Sisters*. He saw it first as a way of expiating the guilt of Richard's murder, and his failure suggests the guilt is irremovable. On his deathbed, he tells Hal it was a plot 'to busy giddy minds /With foreign quarrels' (IV. 5) and advises him to use the same strategy; but by now he is so identified as a role-player that we cannot be sure even this view of the crusade is the true one.

Hal sets out to construct a career for himself along his father's lines. In the soliloquy that ends the first Eastcheap scene he announces he is only playing the role of prodigal prince in order to make his later reform more impressive:

> Yet herein will I imitate the sun,
> Who doth permit the base contagious clouds
> To smother up his beauty from the world,
> That, when he please again to be himself,
> Being wanted, he may be more wonder'd at
> By breaking through the foul and ugly mists
> Of vapours that did seem to strangle him.
>
> (I. 2)

This is one of Richard II's key images, but we note that all Hal can do is promise to *imitate* the sun. A natural right to succeed, as his father warned him, is not enough any more, and so Hal cultivates a talent to impress. He demonstrates this talent twice, to his father's satisfaction: once by his promise to take on Hotspur and beat him at his own game of honour; and once by excusing his apparently inexcusable act of taking the crown from his father's deathbed:

> O my son,
> God put it in thy mind to take it hence,
> That thou mightst win the more thy father's love
> Pleading so wisely in excuse of it!
>
> (IV. 5)

Hal, like Richard II, lays his hands on the crown. Richard's gesture was a surrender that was also a violation; Hal's asserts a right, but in terms that suggest his right depends on his own efforts.

Throughout Part One Hal is compared with Hotspur. On the surface they are wastrel and hero; in reality they are pragmatist and dreamer. Hotspur's life is governed by the ideal of honour, but there is something obsessive and fantastic in the way he talks about it:

> By heaven, methinks it were an easy leap
> To pluck bright honour from the pale-fac'd moon,
> Or dive into the bottom of the deep
> Where fathom-line could never touch the ground,
> And pull up drowned honour by the locks.
>
> (I. 3)

As his uncle Worcester complains, 'He apprehends a world of figures here, /But not the form of what he should attend' (I. 3). Both Hal and Hotspur are lively and witty, but while Hal can control his moods Hotspur is in the grip of a manic energy that never lets him go. In death, he breaks like a machine that has been driven too hard. Losing honour in his defeat by Hal, he considers he has lost everything; honour is to him what kingship was to Richard. But while Richard was preoccupied with his own nothingness, Hotspur's final nihilism, like Macbeth's, encompasses all life:

> thoughts, the slaves of life, and life, time's fool,
> And time, that takes survey of all the world,
> Must have a stop.
>
> (V. 4)

The dying King Henry is preoccupied with his son's future, and England's; for Hotspur the future is a blank.

Hal is also set against Falstaff, whose views on honour are conspicuously different from Hotspur's but whose penchant for fantasy gives them an unexpected kinship. Like Hotspur he uses a moon-image; Hal is associated with the sun. Falstaff does not like to be thought of as a thief:

> when thou art king let not us that are squires of the
> night's body be call'd thieves of the day's beauty. Let us
> be Diana's foresters, gentlemen of the shade, minions of
> the moon; and let men say we be men of good
> government, being govern'd, as the sea is, by our noble
> and chaste mistress the moon, under whose countenance
> we steal.
> (I. 2)

The last word brings us down to reality. Falstaff, on this sort of question at least, never fools himself. But he maintains a splendid indifference to mere facts. His account of the Gad's Hill robbery, in which eleven rogues in buckram grow out of two as though it were the most natural thing in the world, is offered directly to Hal and Poins, who were the original two and who are perfectly placed, the audience knows, to give Falstaff the lie direct. They do. But against all odds Falstaff escapes their trap: 'By the Lord, I knew ye as well as he that made ye. Why, hear you, my masters, was it for me to kill the heir-apparent?' (II. 4). Flushed with this triumph he goes on to construct, in the extempore play that follows, a fantasy world of which he is the centre. He and Hal alternate the parts of Hal and his father. The King as played by Falstaff has a high opinion of the fat knight. The King as played by Hal takes the opposite view, to which Falstaff (as Hal) retorts, 'banish not him thy Harry's company – banish plump Jack, and banish all the world'. Hal's reply, 'I do, I will' (II. 4), takes us in an instant out of the play and into the future. Rich and triumphant though it seems, Falstaff's world can vanish like a bubble.

But he does not break suddenly, like Hotspur. Throughout Part Two we see him subject to the slow erosion of time. He puts up considerable resistance, turning his diseases into jokes: 'A pox of this gout! Or, a gout of this pox! For the one or the other plays the rogue with my great toe' (I. 2). But his guard slips, as it never does in Part One, and we hear the naked confession, 'I am old, I am old' (II. 4). We also have a closer view of the petty conniving that keeps him going from day to day. Eastcheap is no longer the holiday world it seemed in Part One. The centre of innocence has shifted to Gloucestershire, where the scenes with Shallow evoke a settled, pleasant, amiably mindless country life and Falstaff becomes an urban con-man, an intruder.

It is a low but human world, and the recruits Falstaff takes from it, despite bearing names like Mouldy and Feeble, are individuals with voices of their own, not the mere caricatures Falstaff takes them for. With the news of the old king's death we glimpse briefly what Falstaff's dream of the new reign would come to if he could turn it to reality: 'Let us take any man's horses; the laws of England are at my commandment' (v. 3). But there is no real threat of a Cade-like anarchy here. Falstaff is pathetically out of his depth, and the new king's public rejection of him, followed by the extra kick of sending him and his followers to prison, leaves Falstaff with nothing to say but a flat, helpless 'my lord, my lord'. The Chief Justice's response, 'I cannot now speak. I will hear you soon' (v. 5). seems to be not cutting Falstaff off in mid-flight but forestalling the revelation that he has nothing to say. The rejection, coupled with his reconciliation with the Lord Chief Justice, consolidates King Henry's public role as a strong and principled ruler. But when he says of his stay in Eastcheap, 'being awak'd, I do despise my dream' (v. 5), we see the cost to his full humanity. Bottom and the lovers of *A Midsummer Night's Dream* also came back to daylight after a period of disorder. While Eastcheap is hardly the Athenian wood, it offers the same chance to expand beyond the rational and respectable; the contrast between King Henry's view of his dream and the view of Bottom and the lovers is a revealing one.

Henry V (*c.* 1599) shows not a sanctified king but a successful leader. Henry's success takes the form of a series of brilliant performances; as the Archbishop of Canterbury claims, he has the right manner for every occasion (I. 1). He plays the careful statesman, stern conqueror, gallant underdog, practical joker, and finally, in his courtship of the French Princess Katharine, the blunt good-hearted fellow with no command of language. We may wonder what lies behind these performances, particularly when he greets the execution of Bardolph, an old Eastcheap crony, with no hint of personal recognition, merely the statement of a principle: 'We would have all such offenders so cut off' (III. 6). Is there an authentic human being here at all? When we catch a glimpse of the inner Henry, the night before his great victory at Agincourt, it is a glimpse of darkness. The King chafes against the responsibility imposed by his role, and claims that he gets nothing in return but ceremony. The crown and sceptre, powerful symbols for Richard II, are for Henry external shows that cannot heal the ordinary ills of the flesh: 'O, be sick, great greatness, /And bid thy ceremony give thee cure'. Besides his general discontent, the guilt of Richard's deposition still haunts him, and he fears the prayers he is having offered for the late King's soul are 'nothing worth'. Yet for all this he carries on and shoulders his duty: 'The day, my friends, and all things stay for me' (IV. 1). Henry is a pragmatist. Lacking a sanctified office he seeks fulfilment in action; if he cannot be a king as Richard was he must do the feats of a hero. We see his pragmatism in the scene with Katharine. He mocks the protestations of conventional lovers, and insists, like Rosalind in *As You Like It*, on keeping in touch with reality: 'If thou canst love me for this, take me. If not, to say that I shall die, is true; but for thy love, by the Lord, no. Yet I love thee too' (v. 2). He insists also on the political reality that lies behind his courtship:

> KING HENRY
> Wilt thou have me?
> KATHARINE
> Dat is as it sall please de roi mon pere.
> KING HENRY
> Nay, it will please him well, Kate. I shall please him, Kate.
> (v. 2)

The final reality for Henry, as for Falstaff and Hotspur, is time. Though he fulfils himself in action the achievement passes; the final Chorus reminds us that Henry's successors not only lost everything he had gained but ruined England into the bargain. The first historical tetralogy ended with a mythical England, a purified vision of order. The second ends more realistically, with the revelation that even the achievement of Agincourt was swept away by time.

The chorus of praise that surrounds Henry, in which even his enemies join, suggests a need to believe in something, and in the sheer insistence of that chorus there is something a little desperate. For what Henry achieves is so limited, so temporary: a single victory, a pragmatic achievement whose erosion Shakespeare has already shown in detail, as he reminds us in the Epilogue. He orders his state, but on a temporary basis, for a limited purpose. There is no sense that, like Richmond, he is restoring an order that is fundamental and immutable, to which any damage was bound to be temporary. But Shakespeare does what he can to celebrate and admire what Henry does achieve. By the same token, the assertion of loyalty at the end of *King John* is a little desperate, and Richard II's assertion of the sanctity of his kingship is even more so. The belief in order that characterized the early Shakepeare is replaced by something subtly different: what registers now is the *need* to believe in order. In the darkness of *King John*, and the débâcle that follows Richard's violation of his kingship, the conditions that would make such a belief secure – a monarch with an unquestioned right coupled with the ability to enforce that right – do not exist. In the second tetralogy the two most striking scenes involving the crown show that fundamental symbol violated: passed from hand to hand in *Richard II*, prematurely snatched in *2 Henry IV*. The symbol ceases to function. What matters now is the individuality of the man who wears the crown: the neurotic self-destructiveness of Richard II, the practical competence and panache of Henry V. The latter can rescue kingship for a while, but only by turning it into leadership; and that means that kingship itself is a diminished thing.

Seen from a distance the figures of the history plays have the glamour and power of myth: the ruined sun-king Richard II, the gallant Hotspur, the prodigal Prince Hal who becomes the hero of Agincourt. But Shakespeare's analysis of them, without denying the attraction of these myths, explores the human reality behind them. There is a similar exploration throughout the comedies, whose stories, fantastic in bare outline, Shakespeare uses as a means to probe human relations. *The Merchant of Venice* (*c.* 1596), described by Harley Granville-Barker as 'a fairy tale',[4] is a case in point. As in many old tales, the action centres on solving riddles. The suitors who come to win Portia must decide which one of three caskets contains her picture. Portia, in turn, must find the trick in the wording of Shylock's bond that allows Antonio to be released. Finally Bassanio, who has won the casket game with confidence and ease, is presented with a problem he cannot solve. The young doctor who has saved his friend Antonio demands Portia's ring in return, and Bassanio has to make a hard choice between the claims of love and the claims of friendship. In the last scene, after some comic embarrassment, Portia solves the riddle: Bassanio's painful choice was no choice at all. She was the doctor, he has given her own ring back to her, and now she returns it through Antonio. The arithmetic of love is more mysterious than that of Shylock's law. But the play does not show a simple opposition between love and commerce, for both involve risks. Bassanio wins Portia by declaring himself ready to 'give and hazard all he hath' (II. 7). Bassanio only has to make a gesture; Antonio actually hazards his life to save his friend. His willingness to risk all is of a piece with his commercial behaviour; Shylock, while acknowledging he is 'sufficient', remarks sourly on the ventures he has 'squander'd abroad' (I. 3). Portia gives up Bassanio as soon as she has gained him so that he may go to his friend, and she seems to chafe against her position as a wealthy heiress, impatient to start giving her money away. What we seem to have, then, is a morally significant fairy tale, based on the Christian paradox of gain through loss.

But there are problems. It is not clear that Antonio has really gained anything by hazarding his body for Bassanio; he greets the restoration of his wealth with a rather flat 'I am dumb' (v. 1), and his subdued manner throughout the last scene suggests that his mysterious melancholy, which opens the play, has not really lifted. There is certainly the material for a Christian allegory in the opposition of Shylock and the other characters: he stands for the Law, they stand for grace, mercy and sacrifice. But in practice the characters, and our responses to them, are not so simple. Portia's famous speech on mercy serves only to show the powerlessness of such an appeal, and eventually she has to defeat Shylock with his own weapons, not overriding the law with grace or even equity, but turning the law, with grim precision, against itself:

> If thou tak'st more
> Or less than a just pound, be it but so much
> As makes it light or heavy in the substance
> Or the division of the twentieth part
> Of one poor scruple, nay, if the scale do turn
> But in the estimation of a hair,
> Thou diest, and all thy goods are confiscate.
>
> (IV. 1)

We wanted to see Shylock defeated; but when, like Shylock, we are given what we want, it is unexpectedly alarming. Shakespeare does not sentimentalize the Jew, though some actors have done so; but he allows misgivings about the opposition to him. Antonio's violent anti-Semitism – spitting, spurning, name-calling – is a dark side to an otherwise amiable character, and one does not have to be a modern liberal to be disturbed by it. When Jessica escapes from her father, we might think our sympathies were meant to be simple; her Christian lover is rescuing her from a dark, joyless house and freeing her from the bondage of the Law. But the dramatic emphasis falls on the money she steals as she leaves, and this ironic variation on spoiling the Egyptians keeps our reactions a little uncertain. Lancelot Gobbo's claim that the fiend is tempting him to run away from Shylock while his conscience is urging him to stay may not be quite so simple a comic inversion as it looks. Lancelot also points to the commercial disadvantages of Jessica's conversion: 'This making of Christians will raise the price of hogs' (III. 5).

Shylock himself is not quite the alien he seems. He is built into Venetian society, and Antonio points out that the Duke cannot deny him justice, 'since that the trade and profit of the city / Consisteth of all nations' (III. 3). Shylock puts it more dramatically, threatening the Duke directly: 'If you deny it, let the danger light /Upon your charter and your city's freedom' (IV. 1). Of all the ways Antonio could have raised money, he goes to Shylock; what looks at first like a piece of arbitrary plotting may also be symbolic of Shylock's essential place in society. The law and the profit-making materialism he stands for are unlovely but fundamental parts of the social fabric. Shylock's conspicuous absence in the last act suggests that the harmony of the close, in which the conflicting claims of love and friendship can be easily resolved in riddles and laughter, is achieved only by narrowing the play's vision. As the name of Portia's estate, Belmont, suggests, we have retreated to a mountaintop somewhat removed from the traffic of the world. Venice, we may remember, is at sea level. The ending is limited in other ways. Early in the last act Lorenzo's contemplation of the music of the spheres places this harmony as something man can know about but not experience directly:

> Such harmony is in immortal souls,
> But whilst this muddy vesture of decay
> Doth grossly close it in, we cannot hear it.
>
> (v. 1)

As the act develops there is a sharp descent in tone to the bawdy joking of the ring sequence and the play ends not with a graceful gesture by a major character but with a low joke by a minor one: 'Well, while I live I'll fear no other thing /So sore as keeping safe Nerissa's ring' (v. 1). The eclectic manner of the last scene does not produce a full harmony: between the music of the spheres and Nerissa's ring there ought to be some middle term, a vision of love that harmonizes the spiritual and the sensual. The play suggests this need, but does not satisfy it.

Much Ado About Nothing (c. 1599) is more down-to-earth. Leaving aside the special case of Lyly, this is arguably the first great prose comedy in English. A substantial part of the first three acts is in prose, and when verse takes over, as in Claudio's attack on Hero at their wedding, it is generally the vehicle for strained, even unhealthy passions. Leonato's household is filled in with almost novelistic detail. Music has to be arranged, dances have to be organized. Beatrice, on Hero's wedding morning, has a cold. Beatrice and Benedick are not just a stock pair of witty lovers but fully realized characters whose wit is a function of personality and whose need to score points off each other reflects an underlying anxiety to which wit itself is sometimes sacrificed:

BENEDICK
    Well, you are a rare parrot-teacher.
BEATRICE
    A bird of my tongue is better than a beast of yours.

BENEDICK

> I would my horse had the speed of your tongue, and
> so good a continuer. But keep your way, a God's
> name; I have done.

BEATRICE

> You always end with a jade's trick. I know you of
> old.
>
> (I. 1)

Neither character can let the other have the last word, and the jokes
deteriorate into simple rudeness. Beneath their obsession with each
other, and their obsessive jokes against marriage, it is not hard to
detect the romantic interest that is drawn out by trickery in the two
eavesdropping scenes. Though these scenes are quite different in style,
Benedick's being long, relaxed and casual, Beatrice's short and for this
play suprisingly lyrical, they show a common method. In each case
the character's self-esteem is broken down; their friends, speaking
behind their backs, are deeply critical of them. At the same time each
is told of the other's love. They are cut out of their old relationships
and driven towards each other.

We should notice, however, that this relatively realistic depiction
of a love affair is not just accompanied but buttressed by the more
conventional Claudio–Hero plot. Their story is stylized and arbitrary.
It is resolved not by any intelligent action on the part of the high-life
characters, but by Dogberry and Verges, who muddle through to a
solution without realizing what they are doing. The song of mourning
at Hero's tomb, the only song in the play that is not in some way
mocked, adds a touch of ceremony, which is also a touch of the
impersonal: after it, day comes and the story is resolved, as though the
action is simply part of the cycle of nature. Beatrice and Benedick's
realization of love follows the engagement of the other couple, with
Don Pedro playing match-maker in each case, and in both engage-
ments there is an element of comic trickery. The disaster of Hero's
broken wedding precipitates a deeper test on Beatrice and Benedick's
devotion to each other, and in both cases we are driven beyond the
comedy of the early scenes into something more sombre. When
Beatrice demands, 'Kill Claudio' (IV. 1), the potential for laughter is
there, but audiences and performers often feel uneasy if the laugh
comes. Finally, after the restoration of Claudio and Hero the love of
Beatrice and Benedick is cemented, and they are caught in the conventional gesture of writing sonnets to each other. The characters of
Beatrice and Benedick bring a new psychological depth to Shakespearean comedy, but the action in which they are involved is finally
a conventional one. The surface of the play is social and realistic, and

as in *The Merchant of Venice* the normal emotional range of comedy is extended; but beneath it we hear the rhythm of the old dance.

Social observation also figures prominently in *The Merry Wives of Windsor* (*c.* 1600). The country town, with its comfortable routines – 'we'll have a posset for't soon at night, in faith, at the latter end of a sea-coal fire' (I. 4) – is invaded by outsiders associated with the court. Sir John Falstaff offers the Windsor wives promises of high life and quotations from Sidney's aristocratic sonnet sequence, *Astrophil and Stella* (III. 3). Fenton is a gentleman who wooed Anne Page for her money at first, and now woos her for herself, but must overcome her parents' suspicion that 'he is of too high a region; he knows too much' (III. 2). Fenton gets the girl, in the upshot of a conventional but entertaining rival-wooer plot. Falstaff, whose motive for paying court to Mistress Ford and Mistress Page is simply financial, gets dunked in the Thames, disguised as an old witch, beaten, pinched and burned. The traditional objection that this Falstaff is a diminished version of the great character of the history plays is partly based on the sheer number of his humiliations. But the Falstaff of the histories was finally destroyed, and this character is not. He has the protection of the comic form itself. Always resilient, he keeps coming back for another beating; in the end he is forgiven and allowed to join in the final merriment:

> let us every one go home,
> And laugh this sport o'er by a country fire –
> Sir John and all.
>   (v. 5)

But the reference to the *country* fire may remind Sir John that he is still an outsider. Windsor is a tolerant community, which can find places for a comic Welshman and even a comic Frenchman; but Mistress Page's 'Now, good Sir John, how like you Windsor wives?' (v. 5) suggests that the townspeople make a point of not letting anyone get the better of them. The play is mostly in prose, and its comedy borders on farce. But we are constantly reminded that we are in the shadow of Windsor Castle, and references to the Order of the Garter and its ceremonies[5] suggest a social structure that finally goes deeper than the pleasant routines of hunting, dining and gossiping the Windsor citizens engage in. Falstaff's disguise as Herne the Hunter, with horns on his head, and his ordeal of being pinched and burned by fairies, are more farcical than mysterious: 'Heavens defend me from that Welsh fairy, lest he transform me to a piece of cheese!' (v. 5). But they also hint at a ritual action beneath the comedy and give (as in *Much Ado*) a touch of ceremony to this most prosaic of Shakespeare's plays.

As You Like It (*c.* 1600) returns to the opposition of court and country, and develops it much more elaborately. We are never told the name of the principality Frederick has usurped. This may reflect a causalness about geography appropriate to romance; or it may relate to the concern with novelty that makes this fantasy court a reflection of some basic Elizabethan worries. This community is nameless because it is rootless, with no respect for tradition. The question is, 'what's the new news at the new court?' (I. 1). The will of Sir Rowland de Boys is set aside by his heir Oliver, who abuses his position as elder brother by treating Orlando as menial. Oliver refers to the servant Old Adam as 'you old dog', drawing the retort, 'God be with my old master! He would not have spoke such a word' (I. 1). Respect for age is one of the tests of a society, as *King Lear* shows; and Adam, who for Orlando represents 'the constant service of the antique world' (II. 3), knows this new world well enough to have saved some money against the time 'when service should in my old limbs lie lame, /And unregarded age in corners thrown' (II. 3). The settled principles of loyalty and obligation will not protect him when he can no longer work for his wages. The Forest of Arden, which, we note, has a name, though one that leaves us uncertain whether to place it in France or Warwickshire, is associated with a lost past. There men live 'like the old Robin Hood of England . . . and fleet the time carelessly as they did in the golden world' (I. 1). The old Duke rules over a free and informal court where courtesy and hospitality are still alive. When Orlando comes to this better world, his reflexes are at first wrong; he assumes he has to enforce charity with his sword. He soon learns his mistake, and when he and Adam, now 'your venerable burden' (II. 7), sit down to share the Duke's banquet and to talk of his late father Sir Rowland, we see a picture of old bonds and old values restored.

With the security of a decent society thus established, Orlando can devote his leisure to his love for Rosalind, not knowing that the shepherd boy who is teasing him for it and pretending to cure him is Rosalind herself. Their love had its origin in the tense world of Frederick's court, where Rosalind is melancholy and out of sorts, and where she and Orlando, both 'out of suits with fortune,' (I. 2), are at first shy and tenative with each other. In a moment of slightly forced gaiety she thinks of falling in love as a sport to pass the time, and Celia warns her not to take it further than that: 'But love no man in good earnest, nor no further in sport neither than with safety of a pure blush thou mayst in honour come off again' (I. 2). This is before she meets Orlando; but beneath the witty, outspoken banter of the forest scenes there may be a touch of the shy, tentative woman we see in the court. She turns Orlando's courtship of her into a game, for her amusement and ours; but she is also acting out her desires without making any overt commitment. As in *Love's Labour's Lost*, the conventional language of courtship takes a drubbing: 'Men have died from time to time, and worms have eaten them, but not for love' (IV. 1). As in *Much Ado About Nothing*, the major love scenes are in prose, and there is a recognizable psychological reality beneath the gamesmanship. But Rosalind's prose can encompass a range of effects, from the promise, or threat, to Orlando 'to wash your liver as clean as a sound sheep's heart, that there should not be one spot of love in't' (III. 2), to the startling 'his kissing is as full of sanctity as the touch of holy bread' (III. 4) – this, of a man who has never kissed her. At times her wit creates a fine balance of commitment and detachment in a single passage: 'O coz, coz, coz, my pretty little coz, that thou didst know how many fathom deep I am in love! But it cannot be sounded; my affection hath an unknown bottom, like the bay of Portugal' (IV. 1). There is never any question about what she wants; when Silvius has led the other lovers in a stylized contemplation of the pangs of unrequited love, Rosalind, having joined it for a while, suddenly orders, 'Pray you, no more of this; 'tis like the howling of Irish wolves against the moon' (V. 2), and starts arranging weddings.

What Arden has given her is a period of liberty in which, using her disguise as the boy Ganymede, she can express all her commonsense misgivings about the follies of love, and enjoy the experience of being wooed by Orlando, without committing herself either way. Finally she makes her commitment, turning quite pragmatically towards marriage: 'I will weary you then no longer with idle talking' (V. 2). For all the bluntness of her manner, there is a sense of miracle in her entrance as a bride. She is accompanied not by a forester dressed as Hymen, but by Hymen himself.[6] The song that accompanies the entrance suggests that harmony of high and earthly visions that finally eluded us in *The Merchant of Venice*:

> Then is there mirth in heaven,
> When earthly things made even
> Atone together.
>   (V. 4)

The rest of the finale reflects the full range of the play's vision, from the celebration of wedlock as 'great Juno's crown' to Jaques' send-off for Touchstone and Audrey: 'and you to wrangling, for thy loving voyage /Is but for two months victuall'd (V. 4).

The range of the last scene reflects the great human variety found in Arden itself. While in Frederick's court Touchstone had to be warned, 'you'll be whipp'd for taxation one of these days' (I. 2), the forest is a free place where Duke Senior not only enjoys the insults of Jaques but seeks him out when he hears he is in a railing mood. There is a place in the forest for the very urban figure of the melancholy satirist, just as there is for the courtly clown. The native population is mixed, to say the least. It ranges from Silvius and Phoebe, who are from a stylized pastoral, to Corin and Audrey, who have the smell of actual farming about them. Even within a single character, Corin, we discern different kinds of pastoral experience. When we first encounter him he seems, like old Adam, the victim of a society whose integrity is breaking down, in which work becomes a job for hire rather than an essential part of one's life: 'I am shepherd to another man /And do not shear the fleeces that I graze' (ii. 4). Elsewhere he exemplifies a stable, self-sufficient life set against the rootless frivolity of the court as reported by Touchstone: 'Sir, I am a true labourer: I earn that I eat, get that I wear, owe no man hate, envy no man's happiness, glad of another's good, content with my harm, and the greatest of my pride is to see my ewes graze and my lambs suck' (iii. 2). It is his opposition to Touchstone that brings out this quality in him, and throughout the relaxed, seemingly plotless middle scenes Shakespeare keeps our attention with piquant juxtapositions of characters.[7] The play is, one might say, like the forest itself: it admits the trials of 'winter and rough weather' (ii. 5) but it is a free, civilized place where a variety of characters can be welcomed and a full range of experience explored.

The need to imagine such places is suggested by the early scenes, which evoke a less civilized kind of society. The same concerns touch *Twelfth Night* (c. 1600). Olivia runs a relaxed household, or thinks she does. Her routine of mourning for her brother does not prevent her from enjoying the jokes of Feste, including a very impudent joke about her brother's soul being in Hell. As licensed fool he has an accepted place: 'There is no slander in an allowed fool, though he do nothing but rail' (i. 5). It is Maria, not Olivia, who threatens he will be turned away. Olivia is also prepared to tolerate her uncle Sir Toby, a living example of the uselessness of a younger son without an occupation. Even when she finds him brawling with Sebastian, she orders him out of her sight but not out of her house, and she offers to tell Sebastian

> how many fruitless pranks
> This ruffian hath botch'd up, that thou thereby
> Mayst smile at this.
> (iv. 1)

Sir Toby is a nuisance, but paradoxically this gives him an accepted place in the household, as resident drunk and troublemaker. It is

Malvolio who threatens Sir Toby with dismissal, attributing the threat to Olivia (II. 3); but elsewhere we see him put words into her mouth,[8] and there is every reason to believe that the threat is his, not hers. Malvolio cannot conceive why Sir Toby should be allowed to stay in the house, any more than he can conceive why a wise man should laugh at a fool (I. 5).

As well as having no feeling for the kind of social order in which such things are possible, Malvolio is a social climber who imagines he can marry Olivia, and her title, on his own self-evident merits. He is in his own way a 'new man'. Maria gives an important insight into his character when she declares, 'The devil a puritan that he is, or anything constantly, but a time-pleaser' (II. 3). If he seems a puritan, it is because puritanism is the coming movement. When he is locked in his dark room and Feste, disguised as Sir Topas, asks his view on 'the opinion of Pythagoras concerning wild fowl', his reply, 'I think nobly of the soul, and in no way approve his opinion' (IV. 2) is at first sight touching; but Malvolio may just be saying what he thinks a priest will want to hear. Sir Andrew Aguecheek can also be placed socially. He is a gentleman with more money than sense, who squanders his inheritance and tries to recoup his losses with a good marriage. He sees Olivia as Bassanio first saw Portia, as a hazardous but necessary commercial venture: 'If I cannot recover your niece, I am a foul way out' (II. 3). (Is it just coincidence that the annual income he is squandering, three thousand ducats, is precisely the sum Antonio borrows from Shylock on Bassanio's behalf?) The realities of class and position also touch the romantic plot. Olivia first signals her interest in Cesario by asking 'What is your parentage?' (I. 5). When she finds herself married to Sebastian, Orsino assures her she has not made a mistake: 'Be not amaz'd; right noble is his blood' (V. 1). And class, as well as character and style, put her other suitors, Sir Andrew and Malvolio, out of court.

Twelfth Night is as romantic and fantastic as any of Shakespeare's comedies, but it is rooted in social reality. It takes its title from a religious observance which is also an important social occasion, the only play of Shakespeare's to do so. But of course that is far from being the full range of its interest. In the background of the romantic plot is a story of shipwreck and apparent loss that looks back to *The Comedy of Errors* and forward to *The Tempest*. In the foreground is a tale of unrequited affections, at once comic and painful: Viola in love with Orsino, but restrained by her male disguise; Olivia in love with Viola *because* of her male disguise; Orsino thinking he is in love with Olivia, but showing an increasing interest in the boy he does not realize is a woman. Viola touches the sympathies of both Orsino and Olivia with her eloquent depictions of unrequited love:

Make me a willow cabin at your gate,
And call upon my soul within the house;
Write loyal cantons of contemned love
And sing them loud even in the dead of night;
Halloo your name to the reverberate hills,
And make the babbling gossip of the air
Cry out 'Olivia!'

(I. 5)

Describing Orsino's feelings for Olivia, she is also, we may assume, drawing on her feelings for him, and without meaning to she triggers in Olivia the same feelings for her. Her male disguise, which is part of the problem, is also part of the solution. She represents the female half of the mysterious double being who is Cesario; the male half is her brother Sebastian, who in the end settles the problems of the love-plot not by being clever, but simply by being there.

When Viola and Cesario come together in the last scene, their reunion has a still, poised quality that fixes in our minds a mysterious image of love: a single being in a double body, 'a natural perspective that is, and is not' (v. 1). This image having been achieved, the pairing of the lovers follows naturally. The ending of the love-plot is boldly stylized and finally convincing at its own level; but it also seems, as the ending of *As You Like It* did not, a bit remote from ordinary experience. There is a sharp contrast between the satisfaction of the lovers and the battered condition of Sir Toby and Sir Andrew, for whom Sebastian's masculinity has been not the answer to a dream but merely a rude awakening. And there is the irreconcilable bitterness of Malvolio's 'I'll be reveng'd on the whole pack of you!' (v. 1). The ending reflects a radical split in the whole fabric of the play. The Malvolio plot, in which the pompous steward is gulled as he deserves to be, is at first so funny that the cruelty does not bother us. But when we find him locked in a dark room, begging for light, ink and paper, the laughter turns a bit sour. His story, unlike that of the lovers, is not really resolved. It suggests an uncertain future. This picks up suggestions of the passage of time that touch the play at various points, usually in the comic plot, and come to a head in Feste's final song in which, to the recurring chorus of the wind and the rain, human life is seen as deterioration through time. That time erodes human achievements was also the burden of the ending of *Henry V*; and the wind and the rain will be heard again in *King Lear*. What resists these darker suggestions, and keeps *Twelfth Night* comic, is the final assertion of the artifice of the play itself, which moves to an ending through time but is always available to entertain us tomorrow, balancing the changeableness of a time-bound art with the permanence of a recurring experience: 'But that's all one, our play is done, /And we'll strive to please you every day' (v. 1).

The comedies, no less than the histories, suggest a need to believe: in this case, in an ordered, reciprocal society of which marriage is the central but not the only symbol. We think also of the Duke's banquet in the Forest of Arden, where Orlando and Old Adam are welcomed, and of the country fire to which the Windsor wives invite Sir John. It can be argued, in fact, that the comedies examine social relations in greater depth than the histories, which are more concerned with rulers. Here we see not just rulers or even lovers but kinsmen, heirs, parties to a contract, masters and servants – a whole network of relations. The disrespect for tradition we see in Malvolio and Oliver, and for ordinary decency we see in Shylock, makes them more than just blocking characters in a love-plot. In *As You Like It* the satisfaction of the lovers is accompanied by the recovery of good order in the forest and its anticipated restoration in the court; in *Twelfth Night*, by the defeat of the socially insensitive Malvolio. I have said that the comedies, like the histories, register a *need* to believe, rather than the achievement of belief. The final harmony of *The Merchant of Venice* is limited, that of *Twelfth Night* stylized and somewhat fantastic. Yet we seem closer to belief here, not just because of the expectations of the genre itself but because marriage as a symbol of order seems less damaged, more viable, than kingship. That it does so is partly because of the honesty with which Shakespeare makes his characters face up to the problems of the world they live in, and of their own natures, before they come to this final reward. This is the equivalent of the histories' examination of the merits and weaknesses of the individuals who wear the crown. Portia, before her marriage with Bassanio can be secure, must face up not only to Shylock but to the more insidious challenge posed by Antonio's claim on her husband. Bassanio must face conflicting loyalties; so must Benedick, when Beatrice tells him to kill Claudio. Some of these plays end with a sense of unfinished business, notably *Twelfth Night*: the sea captain who is keeping Viola's women's clothes, which are needed before her identity and therefore her marriage to Orsino can be locked into place, is 'in durance, at Malvolio's suit' (v. 1), and Malvolio is still unreconciled. It is in the nature of comedy that here Shakespeare's depiction of harmony and order should be more confident than it is in the history plays; to that extent his comedies are more conservative. But it is a mature conservatism that has weighed the cost and the likelihood of the achievements it depicts.

Notes

1. *Shakespeare's Festive Comedy* (Princeton, 1959, reprint Cleveland, 1963), p. 193.

2. Reproduced, uncredited, in Lacey Baldwin Smith, *The Horizon Book of the Elizabethan World* (New York, 1967), pp. 61–62.

3. See Alvin B. Kernan, 'The Henriad: Shakespeare's Major History Plays', *Yale Review*, 59 (1969), 3–32.

4. *Prefaces to Shakespeare*, I (Princeton, 1946, reprint 1952), 335.

5. On this aspect of the play see William Green, *Shakespeare's Merry Wives of Windsor* (Princeton, 1962).

6. See Sylvan Barnet, 'Strange Events: Improbability in *As You Like It*', Shakespeare Studies, 4 (1968), 119–31 (p. 122).

7. On this aspect of the play see the classic article by Harold Jenkins, '*As You Like It*', *Shakespeare Survey*, 8 (1955), 40–51.

8. In II. 2 he clearly exceeds his instructions by the rudeness with which he delivers Olivia's ring to Viola, while claiming he is simply following orders.

Chapter 4
Tragedy

The central figures of the histories seek power; of the comedies, love cemented in marriage. The tragic heroes seek something more basic and intangible: an assertion of their own identities, in which their values, their destinies, and their relations with other people are all bound up. Hamlet speaks for them all, in his urgent words when his friends try to keep him away from the ghost: 'my fate cries out' (I. 4). They all go, as he does, to confront some destiny that is peculiarly their own, though they are not always so conscious that this is what they are doing. The need to believe in something, which we saw as a feature of the comedies and histories, is in tragedy a characteristic of the heroes themselves. Here its range of application is both wider and more personal. They need to believe in the gods, in other people, in themselves. And at every level they encounter betrayal. Self-betrayal, or betrayal by a loved one that makes them question themselves, are the fundamental threats. Like the central characters in *The Comedy of Errors*, the tragic heroes are regularly forced to doubt their own identities, and to feel split off from their communities. They respond to this challenge by consciously reconstructing their natures for their own reassurance, over-dramatizing them, combining truth with fiction in a frighteningly unstable mix. These constructed performances, like the kingship of Richard II, embody values whose currency no longer seems certain even to them. And in certain of the tragedies the social order itself breaks down. What remains unquestioned is the sheer stubborn courage with which the heroes resist a final descent to absurdity.

The great tragic sequence begins with *Julius Caesar* (1599), a history play in its own right, and one that shares the political scepticism of the English histories. While the latter show a king-centred society in which the symbols of kingship have gone dead, *Julius Caesar* shows a republic that has lost faith in itself and its traditions, and has not yet found new ones. It opens with the Feast of Lupercal. But we have little sense of what this festival means, or ought to mean, for Roman society. Instead we see politicians using it for their own ends.[1] Caesar's supporters take the occasion to decorate his statues; the tribunes Flavius and Marullus go around removing the decorations and are, ominously, 'put to silence' (I. 2). During the games Antony offers Caesar a crown, which he thrice refuses, (reluctantly, according to Casca) while the crowd cheers. This particular episode seems theatrical rather than ceremonial. The only reference to the traditional significance of Lupercal comes when Caesar commands Antony to touch Calphurnia during the race:

> for our elders say,
> The barren, touched in this holy chase,
> Shake off their sterile curse.
> (I. 2)

This belief is placed as a tradition from the past. But there is a deeper significance to this moment. Caesar is a man who would be king; for Shakespeare's audience the barrenness of his wife would be a bad omen. There is none of the mystery of true kingship about him; he is a politician who will get the office, if he gets it at all, by his own efforts. Rome is not a traditionally ordered society or even an incipient monarchy but a free political arena where there are no rules and the deciding factors are the skill, judgement, personality and reputations of individual politicians.

The storm that precedes the death of Caesar may suggest divine judgement of some kind; but the actual meaning of the storm is less firm than in the corresponding scenes of *King Lear* and *Macbeth*. The focus is on the different reactions people have to it. Casca is terrified; Cassius is excited and allegorizes the storm as the spirit of Caesar, which he takes pride in defying; for Cicero it is simply a nasty bit of weather. Unusually for the drama of this period, omens do not always work. The Soothsayer correctly predicts trouble on the Ides of March, but the symbolic moment when the sick Ligarius throws away his crutch is a sign of the healing of Rome that turns out to be false. Brutus tries to give ritual dignity to the killing of Caesar by having his fellow conspirators wash their hands in Caesar's blood, in line with his earlier advice to Cassius, 'Let's be sacrificers, but not butchers' (II. 1). But they look like butchers. And the significance of the washing continues to develop beyond Brutus's control. When Antony shakes the hands of the conspirators, he will be stained with blood himself. This looks like implicating him in their guilt; in fact it predicts his own career of butchery. When the gardeners of *Richard II* compare their work to the ordering of the state the allegory is clear and familiar. In *Julius Caesar*, moments that look allegorical develop unpredictably, and characters are often wrong about the significance of their own actions.[2]

This is in keeping with a general openness in the play's structure. Characters who have interested us in the first half are abruptly dropped in the second. For modern taste, the carefully contrived suspense before the killing of Caesar makes the ensuing civil war seem a long anticlimax. In the critical reception and stage history of the play, the climax has actually shifted, being variously placed at the assassination of Caesar, Antony's funeral oration, and the quarrel in Brutus's tent.[3] The ending leaves much unresolved. The tension between Antony and Octavius suggests that the mischief Antony set afoot is far from over. We are left uncertain as to our final judgement of important characters. When, having failed to persuade his friends to assist his suicide, Brutus declares, 'My heart doth joy that yet in all my life /I found no man but he was true to me' (v. 5), are we meant to detect any irony? And when Antony delivers his eulogy to Brutus as 'the noblest Roman of them all' (v. 5) is this a sincere tribute or another piece of showmanship?

We come down to questions of character. Criticism of this sort goes in and out of fashion, but *Julius Caesar* has always responded readily to the study of its central personalities. They have the same open, unpredictable quality we detect in the play as a whole. Cassius at first appears shrewd but petty and spiteful in his opposition to Caesar; in his later scenes he develops touching dignity and humanity. No one takes Marc Antony seriously in the early scenes. His funeral oration reveals him as a brilliant and dangerous man; then the powerful impression he has made is frittered away as Octavius, quietly but steadily, takes the initiative. How people *appear* is another vital matter. Caesar himself seems to be a small man casting a giant shadow; the reputation for greatness that surrounds him is incongruous with the vain, nervous braggart we see. Yet, not in spite of his weaknesses but in a curious way because of them, he emerges as a compelling personality, a study of the deep flaws that accompany, even stimulate, genius. If Caesar postures for the world Brutus, fatally, postures for himself. In the temptation sequence in I. 2 Cassius, ostensibly appealing to Brutus's honour, actually appeals to his vanity. He uses the word 'honour' because it is the word Brutus wants to hear. He urges Brutus to look in a mirror that

> will turn
> Your hidden worthiness into your eye,
> That you might see your shadow.
>
> (I. 2)

Part of Brutus's difficulty is that he is always on his dignity, always trying to keep up his role as 'the noble Brutus'. Each of his many blunders is accompanied by a stately speech defending it. He persuades himself to kill Caesar, not because he has shown evidence of tyranny (though the audience has seen such evidence) but through a somewhat academic argument about what Caesar *might* do if he had power. He provokes the fatal battle of Philippi with the often-quoted 'There is a tide in the affairs of men' (IV. 3). The problem is not just impracticality; he is a pose-striker, and his poses keep separating him from reality. He is not, perhaps, a hypocrite, though he comes dangerously close when he attacks Cassius for raising money by vile means and not giving him any (IV. 3). But his sense of himself leads him to create and play an idealized role, to his own destruction and that of his associates. It is a problem we will meet in other tragedies by Shakespeare and his Jacobean contemporaries.

A fragmented world in which values are uncertain and the individual has to construct artificially a sense of his own identity – these are some of the basic conditions of Shakespearean tragedy.[4] The familiar imperatives of love and revenge shape *Romeo and Juliet* and *Titus Andronicus*, giving clear tasks for the heroes. *Hamlet* (c. 1601) starts with the apparent generic certainties of revenge tragedy – the ghost, the mad scenes, the *contemptus mundi* and of course the revenge action itself – and proceeds to disturb our conventional responses to them. Interestingly, the rightness of revenge is never overtly questioned, as it will be in Tourneur's *The Atheist's Tragedy* and Chapman's *The Revenge of Bussy d'Ambois*. But the whole basis of the action, the command of the Ghost, remains problematic. Revenge ghosts are traditionally voluble; this one unsettles us by his initial silence.[5] Though he is clear and vivid on the battlements, the impression he makes fades in daylight. Horatio and the sentries disagree about how long he stayed (I. 2). Hamlet himself later refers to death as 'the undiscover'd country, from whose bourn /No traveller returns' (III. 1), briefly forgetting the Ghost's very existence. His own difficulty about the Ghost's identity is supported from the play as a whole. Horatio's 'I knew your father; /These hands are not more like' (I. 2) is more guarded than it seems: one's hands are reverse images of each other, and are not quite identical. In claiming to come from Purgatory the Ghost claims to come from a place that according to the official religion of Shakespeare's England does not exist. More immediately relevant to the play is the fact that Hamlet ignores the Ghost's claim. For him the alternatives continue to be Heaven and Hell; this reflects not so much a Protestant upbringing as a tendency to think in moral absolutes. When the final revenge is accomplished the Ghost does not reappear to gloat, like Don Andrea in *The Spanish Tragedy*. Hamlet himself makes no reference to it as he kills Claudius; his last words to the King are 'Follow my mother' (V. 2).

The way the Ghost is left behind is a sign of how far the play's issues go beyond the immediate question of revenge. The longest play in the Shakespeare canon, it owes its length partly to the detailed filling-out of the life of the Danish court, especially in scenes like II. 2, where we are treated to the gossip of court and theatre (the London theatre, in the Folio text) and the café philosophizing of Hamlet and his fellow students. Like his hero, Shakespeare seems in no hurry. A central difficulty in Hamlet's role as revenger is that he is continually subject to distractions. Waiting for the Ghost to appear, he indulges in a digression on the Danish reputation for drunkenness, which broadens into a lecture on how men can be destroyed by a single flaw: the lecture gets so interesting that the Ghost's appearance comes as a surprise. The Ghost wants Hamlet to focus his mind on the task of revenge, and warns him, 'Taint not thy mind, nor let thy soul contrive /Against thy mother aught. Leave her to heaven' (I. 5). Yet no sooner has Hamlet vowed to clear his mind of everything but the single command than he cries 'O most pernicious woman!' (I. 5); and the obsession with Gertrude we see in the first soliloquy never really leaves him. Waiting for the Mousetrap play to prove Claudius's guilt, he subjects Ophelia to gratuitous and offensive jokes about female lechery. Watching the play itself, he seems at least as interested in the references to second marriage as in the poisoning. There are always more issues before Hamlet than he can satisfactorily cope with. In the interview with his mother, for example, he at last confronts her directly with her guilt and wins her repentance. It is a major achievement; but the focus is pulled away from it in a number of ways. Even after Gertrude is clearly repentant Hamlet keeps returning obsessively to the attack, suggesting that there is more in his relations with her than a straightforward desire for moral correction; the Ghost appears, again as an interruption, to remind Hamlet that his business is revenge; and through most of the scene the corpse of Polonius is lying on the floor, ignored by everyone but the audience, who may sense that in killing him Hamlet has started an action larger and more complicated than the initial revenge story.

In Hamlet's own mind there is an improvising, experimental quality. He tries out different reactions to the death of Polonius, from the sardonic 'Thou find'st to be too busy is some danger' to the more dignified

> For this same lord,
> I do repent; but heaven hath pleas'd it so
> To punish me with this, and this with me,
> That I must be their scourge and minister.

(III. 4)

In the 'To be or not to be' soliloquy his fear of death is a fear of the unknown, an uncanny state of consciousness which he thinks of as a sleep troubled by unimaginable dreams. This is strikingly different from the conventional fear of judgement we find in the mangled version of the soliloquy in the First Quarto; and it is different from the orthodox and rather technical view of salvation and damnation on which Hamlet bases his refusal to kill Claudius at prayer. In that scene he thinks as conventionally as Claudius himself. Hamlet's uncertainty about his own reactions is indicated most sharply in a speech that may look at first like a definite statement about himself and the world:

> I have of late – but wherefore I know not – lost all my
> mirth, forgone all custom of exercises; and indeed it goes
> so heavily with my disposition that this goodly frame, the
> earth, seems to me a sterile promontory; this most
> excellent canopy, the air, look you, this brave o'erhanging
> firmament, this majestical roof fretted with golden fire,
> why it appeareth nothing to me but a foul and pestilent
> congregation of vapours. What a piece of work is a man!
> How noble in reason, how infinite in faculties, in form
> and moving how express and admirable; in action how
> like an angel, in apprehension how like a god! The beauty
> of the world, the paragon of animals! And yet, to me,
> what is this quintessence of dust?
>
> (II. 2)

This looks like a definitive statement of late Renaissance disillusionment, as idealism and excitement turn to their opposites. But it is more complicated than that. Hamlet does not say that he used to think man and the universe were splendid but now he knows they are rotten; he says they *are* splendid – and even points to the heavens ('look you') as evidence – but that they have gone rotten *for him*. He recognizes a subjective and an objective reality, each valid on its own terms, yet sharply contradicting one another. This means, finally, a deep split in his own mind. His claim that he does not know how this has come about could be part of the cat-and-mouse game he is playing with Rosencrantz and Guildenstern; but it could also indicate a deeper bewilderment about himself of which we see evidence elsewhere. Later, after surveying possible reasons why he has not taken revenge, he concludes simply, 'I do not know' (IV. 4).

This uncertainty about himself drives Hamlet into role-playing far more elaborate than Brutus's. The antic disposition, the pose of madness, is his most obvious role, and we notice the care with which he dresses the part of the melancholy madman. But while we may speculate as to why he adopts this role he himself never makes the reason articulate: 'I perchance hereafter shall think meet /To put an antic disposition on' (I. 5). The experimental quality has this time a touch of casualness. On two important occasions he measures himself enviously against those who can play their roles with greater confidence and commitment: the Player, who can work up a great storm of passion for Hecuba; and Fortinbras, who can start a war for a patch of ground not big enough to bury the casualties. He recognizes the absurdity of each man's commitment. His overt line of thought is 'if this man can do so much for a trivial cause, why can I do so little for a great one?' But beneath this is a fascination with the irrational that amounts to saying, 'what this man is doing is ridiculous; I wish I could do it'. In the case of the Player, Hamlet tries at first to compete with him in noisy passion: 'Bloody, bawdy villain! /Remorseless, treacherous, lecherous, kindless villain!' He then withdraws, almost sheepishly – 'Why, what an ass am I!' – and decides to use drama in a more purposeful way with *The Murder of Gonzago* (II. 2). But when he sets himself against Fortinbras there is no such withdrawal. The soliloquy ends with a player-like flourish, 'from this time forth, /My thoughts be bloody, or be nothing worth' (IV. 4) and at this point Hamlet is withdrawn from us.[6]

When he returns in Act Five he seems contracted, purposeful, deliberate. We have seen him kill Polonius wildly, in hot blood; he has now killed Rosencrantz and Guildenstern in cold blood, by remote control, with an attention to detail, 'not shriving-time allow'd' (V. 2), that is a little alarming. He seems to think it a great joke. In the grim comedy of his scene with the gravedigger there is also a new steadiness. Death, the great unknown, is also the great certainty, the final answer to all riddles. The sign of this is a solid prop that Hamlet can hold in his hand, the skull of Yorick. But the effect is still not simple: after all the glib joking about the way death levels courtiers, lawyers and landowners there is the mild shock of discovery that the skull Hamlet is holding is that of a man he knew. His memory of Yorick setting 'the table on a roar' (V. 1) opposes the noisiness and vitality of life to Yorick's present silence – a silence, like the Ghost's, which stubbornly resists questions. And Hamlet's discovery that the grave he is joking over is Ophelia's leads to a flash of the old, wild passion. Despite these crosscurrents the awareness of mortality seems to steady Hamlet; that, and the recognition of 'a divinity that shapes our ends' (V. 2). When Hamlet stabs Claudius he himself is dying, and knows he is dying. But the dignity and calm of Hamlet just before the court's last entrance – 'the readiness is all' (V. 2) – are only part of the effect. The killings themselves are as flashy and theatrical as any in Shakespeare. They anticipate the grotesque ingenuities of Jacobean tragedy and are very different from the much simpler deaths of Othello, Macbeth and Lear. There is a moral neatness about them: Claudius's poison works through them all, Laertes is killed with his own treachery, Gertrude does not seem to realize what she is doing. At the same time they share some of the wild, accidental quality of the moment when Hamlet runs his rapier through the arras and then wonders who he has killed.

Hamlet is at one level an exciting narrative with a decisive resolution. Yet our involvement with the narrative is not as straightforward as we might have expected: the moment when Hamlet finally kills Claudius does not seem to have the weight of the whole play behind it as do the deaths of Desdemona and Cordelia. It is simply one incident in a very busy scene. There is formal dignity in Fortinbras's tribute to Hamlet as one 'likely, had he been put on /To have prov'd most royal' (v. 2) and in the military funeral he orders. But both seem meant for someone else: we have not thought of Hamlet as either king or soldier. He himself in his final moments worries about being misinterpreted, and his last words, 'the rest is silence' (v. 2). preserve a sense of enigma. But *Hamlet* is not an absurdist drama either; balanced against the awareness of mystery are the drive and clarity of the narrative, the assurance that death at least is certain, and a conviction that good and evil are not meaningless words. *Hamlet* shows a puzzling world, but not a world falling apart.

We can be less certain about *Troilus and Cressida* (*c.* 1602). It is hard even to say what genre the play belongs to: it has been variously placed as a tragedy, a dark comedy, and even an example of the peculiar Jonsonian form, comical satire.[7] The problem of objective and subjective reality touched on in *Hamlet* returns in a more acute form here. The debate in the Trojan council over whether or not to let Helen go develops into a debate over value itself: whether a thing's value 'dwells . . . in particular will' or 'wherein 'tis precious of itself' (ii. 2). At the end, after Hector's death, the Greeks assume the war is over and Troilus assumes it is still going on. The ending of the love plot is equally indecisive; Cressida fades out of the play and Troilus's resolve to chastize Diomedes leads to a combat whose end we never see. The love-plot, too, carries with it the idea of split reality. Seeing with his own eyes the evidence of Cressida's betrayal, Troilus declares 'This is, and is not, Cressid'. The Cressida on stage is now in a sense unreal: 'This she? No, this is Diomed's Cressida' (v. 2). As in the council debate, when he argued that value dwelt in particular will, Troilus insists on a Cressida of his own, in defiance of objective reality.

Cressida exemplifies the instability of will, even of identity. When Troilus warns her 'something may be done that we will not' (iv. 4) the passive voice suggests how (apparently) unthinkingly she will drift into betrayal. In the kissing game she is caught up in as soon as she arrives among the Greeks – a nasty version of the courtship games of *Love's Labour's Lost* and *As You Like It* – we see virtually a new Cressida created before our eyes. Guarded at first, she submits to the social pressure of the game and enters into it.[8] In the end she summarizes her own split loyalties a bit glibly: 'Troilus, farewell! One eye yet looks on thee; /But with my heart the other eye doth see'. But Thersites's gloss, 'A proof of strength she could not publish more, /Unless she said, "My mind is now turn'd whore"' (v. 2), is equally glib. Behind both formulae is the elusiveness of Cressida herself.

The instability she represents is pervasive. The play's first reference to Hector is to Hector acting out of character:

>   Hector, whose patience
> Is as a virtue fix'd, today was mov'd.
> He chid Andromache, and struck his armourer.
>   (I. 2)

In the Council scene he makes a compelling case for returning Helen, then suddenly abandons his position, yields to his brothers, and announces that he has already sent a challenge among the Greeks. The play begins with an armed Prologue identifying the argument as 'the chance of war'; the next line is Troilus's 'Call hither my varlet; I'll unarm again'. For him the argument is love. But at the end of the same scene he yields quickly to pressure from Aeneas –

> AENEAS
>   How now, Prince Troilus, wherefore not afield?
> TROILUS
>   Because not there. This womanish answer sorts,
>   For womanish it is to be from hence.
>   (I. 1)

– and goes to war after all. Not all the surprises are discreditable: Ajax for most of the play is simply a dolt, but alone among the Greeks he gives a humane and courteous reaction to the death of Hector: 'If it be so, yet bragless let it be; /Great Hector was as good a man as he' (v. 9).

If death is a final reality in *Hamlet*, time – the force we sensed in the background of *Henry V* and *Twelfth Night* – is the final reality in *Troilus and Cressida*. References to time and its work of destruction are pervasive. Ulysses warns Achilles that if he sits idle he will inevitably lose his reputation, 'for Time is like a fashionable host /That slightly shakes his parting guest by th' hand' (III. 3). Cressida, on the other

hand, fears that *not* to hold off will be equally destructive; to consummate is to finish: 'Things won are done, joy's soul lies in the doing'
(I. 2). And when Achilles finally acts, the sense of a tremendous latent
power that has been created by his fellow Greeks' concern to bring him
into the war is immediately dissipated. He is too out of condition to
fight Hector single-handed and so catches him in ambush, unarmed
and outnumbered, and orders his Myrmidons to kill him. We have
seen him in action at last, and we are not impressed.

Time offers two alternatives: rust or consume. There seems to be
no chance of preservation, except one. The lovers speak of projecting
their legend through time. Cressida's speech in particular has an almost
hypnotic sense of the destructive power of time, against which this
legend will be asserted:

> If I be false, or swerve a hair from truth,
> When time is old and hath forgot itself,
> When water-drops have worn the stones of Troy,
> And blind oblivion swallow'd cities up,
> And mighty states characterless are grated
> To dusty nothing, yet let memory
> From false to false, among false maids in love,
> Upbraid my falsehood!
>
> (III. 2)

Troilus imagines a legend of fidelity; her prediction is closer to the
truth. Pandarus clinches the matter: 'If ever you prove false to one
another . . . let all pitiful goers-between be call'd to the world's end
after my name; call them all Pandars' (III. 2). What survives of this
affair is its notoriety. At the end, time itself breaks down as Pandarus
speaks directly to the London audience, addressing them as 'Good
traders in the flesh . . . As many as be here of Pandar's hall' (v. 10)
and offering to bequeath them his diseases. This is what love comes
to. What war comes to is suggested in an eerie sequence in which
Hector kills a man for his 'goodly armour' and finds a 'putrefied core'
inside, as though the dead warrior has already rotted (v. 8). The elaborate speeches of Ulysses come down to Machiavellian playing on
Achilles's envy of Ajax. Even that fails, as Thersites tells us: 'now is
the cur Ajax prouder than the cur Achilles, and will not arm today,
wherefore the Greeks begin to proclaim barbarism, and policy grows
into an ill opinion' (v. 4). We want to admire Hector but he lets us
down. Cressida's best moments are her wry, sad insights into her own
frailty. There is, finally, so little to believe in that the play edges from
tragedy into satire. The breakup of certainty that begins in *Julius Caesar*
and *Hamlet* is here as radical as it will ever be in Shakespeare. The

satiric viewpoint, allowed free rein here, is in the following tragedies absorbed into a larger vision.

The levelling cynicism of Thersites finds a counterpart in *Othello* (*c.* 1603) in the reductive generalizations that are Iago's stock in trade. He presents himself as the man who knows it all: 'These Moors are changeable in their wills' (I. 3). He is in particular an authority on Venetian women:

> I know our country disposition well,
> In Venice they do let God see the pranks
> They dare not show their husbands.
>
> (III. 3)

The knowing manner accompanies a determination not to be fooled. He reduces the courtship of Othello and Desdemona to this: 'Mark me with what violence she first lov'd the Moor, but for bragging and telling her fantastical lies' (II. 1). Love itself comes down to 'making the beast with two backs' (I. 1). He seems almost physically irritated when Roderigo uses the word 'blessed' of Desdemona (II. 1). He likes to present himself as a man of the world, and speaks almost primly of reason and common sense; but as we listen to him we realize he is in the grip of an obsession. He is a compulsive talker, whose motive-hunting[9] suggests that he cannot shut his mind off until he has imagined all the possible ways he could be injured. He is ironically trapped by his own cynicism about women into the strange notion that Othello has cuckolded him, though a less likely pair of lovers than Othello and Emilia would be hard to imagine. Emilia's brisk dismissal of the idea allows us to hear another and healthier voice of common sense:

> Some such squire he was
> That turn'd your wit the seamy side without,
> And made you to suspect me with the Moor.
>
> (IV. 2)

Iago likes to present himself as a diabolical tempter: 'Divinity of hell!' (II. 3); but we may reflect that, as Ben Jonson was to put it, the devil is an ass.

And yet Iago manages to destroy Othello, and through him Desdemona. His strategy is weak – his plot gets out of control and the handkerchief finally destroys him as it destroys the others – but his tactics are alarmingly skilful. In the great temptation scene he works not by direct accusation but by evasive hints, fixing on disturbing words like 'think' and 'if'.[10] When he has Othello so unsettled that he craves any kind of certainty, he warns him *against* jealousy and thus makes the idea of jealousy clear in his mind. Like all effective tempters he leaves the main work up to the victim. And there are reasons why Othello is vulnerable. He is not just, as Emilia calls him, a dolt. His manner in the early scenes shows considerable wit and sophistication; he may be an exotic but he is not a barbarian. At the same time there is something self-conscious about him; he is aware of being watched, he is even aware of playing a role: 'Were it my cue to fight, I should have known it /Without a prompter' (i. 2). Before the Senate he defends his courtship of Desdemona with one of the most eloquent set-pieces in Shakespeare, introducing it with the apology, 'Rude am I in my speech /And little bless'd with the soft phrase of peace' (i. 3). There is more to this than a variation on Antony's ironic claim that he lacks eloquence, which is simply part of his manipulation of the Roman mob. Othello is most comfortable in the role of soldier, and plain speech is expected of a soldier. The role of lover is strange to him, and he is unduly apologetic about his ability to play it. The attraction of Othello and Desdemona is an attraction of extreme opposites: his life has been active, glamorous, ranging over the world; hers has been sheltered and domestic. And of course it is precisely the difference of age, race and background that the fatal common sense of Iago will play on.

Othello has been variously seen as a genuinely heroic figure and an egotistical braggart,[11] and this debate is rooted in Othello's own uncertainty about himself. His grandiloquent manner conveys an uneasy mixture of well-grounded self-esteem and posturing. On the field of battle he knows who he is; in the chambers of love he is not so sure. At the same time, there is something about him Iago cannot taint. What G. Wilson Knight has called the 'Othello music'[12] occasionally yields to a coarse, broken language under the influence of Iago, but the corruption is never final. The vow of revenge at the climax of the temptation scene has an imaginative sweep and a sense of commitment Iago is incapable of. Othello can see 'the pity of it' (iv. 1), and this alarms Iago, who has to bring him back into line. While Iago's mind skims over the surface of experience, capable only of the most cynical observations, Othello can make the deep commitments of the idealist. He has made his marriage the centre of his life: 'there where I have garner'd up my heart, /Where either I must live or bear no life' (iv. 2). When it goes, his whole life goes with it: 'Othello's occupation's gone' (iii. 3). He tries to give the killing of Desdemona sacrificial dignity: 'It is the cause, it is the cause, my soul' (v. 2). This includes a due appreciation of the irreplaceable beauty he is destroying. But the dignity vanishes as he and Desdemona end up shouting and struggling on the bed; like Brutus, he has tried to conduct a sacrifice but simply commits a murder.

For him as for Troilus, identity, even reality itself, are dislocated by his lover's infidelity:[13]

>   I cry you mercy, then,
> I took you for that cunning whore of Venice
> That married with Othello.
>   (IV. 2)

The crucial difference is that Desdemona has not betrayed him. Early in the temptation sequence, one look at her tells him the truth: 'If she be false, O then heaven mocks itself! /I'll not believe't' (III. 3). But he cannot hold on to that truth. His failure to realize the virtue of Desdemona is in the last analysis more serious than his failure to realize the wickedness of Iago. That virtue develops under pressure; she passes from simple fidelity to the refusal to blame Othello even for her death. Once the truth is made clear to him in the last scene, Othello attacks Iago as we might expect, but his relations with his tempter are perfunctory; Iago is no longer that interesting, to him or to us. What matters is what Othello has done to Desdemona, and the only judgement he will accept on that is his own. In a final act of role-playing he splits himself in two, becoming at once 'a malignant and a turban'd Turk' who 'beat a Venetian and traduc'd the state' and the old Othello, who does justice on the offender. His reference to himself as 'he that was Othello' (V. 2) has suggested a loss of his old identity; now that identity reasserts itself as everything he was is invoked in a final condemnation of what he has become.

In *King Lear* (c. 1605) the central character's failure to grasp both the evil and the good around him is the starting point for a fuller and more searching tragic action. This is accompanied by what looks like a favourite Shakespearean device, the interrupted ceremony, recalling the oath-taking in *Love's Labour's Lost* and the trial by combat in *Richard II*. This time Cordelia refuses to co-operate in Lear's love-test. But here there is something deeply wrong about the ceremony itself. It expresses not the values of a group or community, but the egotism and anxiety of one old man. It depends not on set forms but on competitive, improvised eloquence. It represents in itself, in other words, a fundamental violation of the nature and purpose of ceremony. Richard II gave his kingship away. Lear does worse: he actually splits the office in two, giving the responsibility to his sons-in-law while retaining the ceremonial trappings for himself. The awkward gesture of making Albany and Cornwall part a coronet between them suggests the breaking of a circle, a fundamental violation of integrity. Later, when Goneril turns on him, Lear ironically questions his own identity: 'Who is it that can tell me who I am?' (I. 4). He has made his identity depend on other people's recognition of him; but he has himself violated the social and family bonds on which such recognition depends, and his misuse of ceremony is a clue to this.

He finds himself in a bewildering world, from which the signposts have been removed. Behind *Othello*, and suggested by the opposition of Iago and Desdemona, we could detect a framework like that of a morality play: heaven and hell, angels and devils. If such expectations are encouraged by the opposition of good and evil characters in *King Lear*, they are also frustrated. Though the play's interest in sacrifice and forgiveness is recognizably Christian, and though Christian associations surround Cordelia,[14] Shakespeare has taken unusual care to strip the play's language of overt Christian references. Instead, characters imagine the gods that correspond to their own needs, desires and fears. Nature is variously the Darwinian Nature of Edmund, whose law is survival of the fittest, and the nourishing and sustaining Nature of Cordelia: 'All you unpublish'd virtues of the earth, /Spring with my tears!' (IV. 4). Denied long-range certainty, both characters and audience are thrown back on immediate experience. One of the play's most important devices is to set against a character's attempt to come to terms with experience an event, or simply a sight, that breaks his confidence and forces him, and us, to begin again. Edgar has just reached a stoic acceptance of his fate, on the grounds that he is at the worst and his lot can only improve, when he is confronted with his father, blind and led by an old man: 'O gods! Who is't can say "I am at the worst"? /I am worse than e'er I was' (IV. 1). Through the last scene there is much talk of the justice of the gods; then Lear enters with the dead Cordelia.

The play is constantly confounding expectations. In the middle of the storm Lear achieves a significant breakthrough, in his prayer to (not about, but to) the 'poor naked wretches' (III. 4) whose sufferings he has neglected in his concern for himself. It looks like a point of rest, a moment of gentleness; but the effect is broken by the explosive entrance of an actual 'naked wretch', Poor Tom, who is not just pitiable but grotesque and terrifying. Poor Tom is not a final reality either; he is, as several asides remind us, a character invented and impersonated by Edgar, who has paradoxically disguised himself by taking his clothes off. Edgar is the play's chief spokesman for reason and hope; yet as Poor Tom he contributes some of its blackest insights. In this play we cannot settle on one idea as the key to it all, or on one reading of a character. The most acute instance of this is Cordelia. She sounds a little cold at first, as in reaction to her sisters' bogus protestations of love she presents her love for her father as simply a proper return for his nurture of her and reminds him that she must divide her love with her husband. She has at least an awareness that one's human ties cannot be restricted to one person. But it may be she does not yet realize what her own love for that one person is capable of. Like Desdemona she develops under pressure, as she not only commits herself totally to her father but will not even acknowledge he has injured her. 'No cause, no cause' (IV. 7) is forgiveness in its purest form; it may be literally absurd, but it is a saving absurdity. Cordelia embodies as powerfully as any character in literature the redeeming power of love. But the one thing she cannot do for Lear is come back from the dead. If there are Christ-associations around her they serve only to emphasize this final, terrible difference; all through the last scene Lear looks desperately for signs of a life that will never return. Nor can we separate the insights Cordelia gives us: the full pain of her death is dependent on the beauty of her reunion with Lear. And we might reflect that if man were just the poor, bare, forked animal Lear sees in the storm it would not be the outrage it is that a dog, a horse or a rat should have life and Cordelia should die.

It is conventional to observe that Lear learns from his experience; but what is really striking is the titanic resistance he puts up. Even when his elder daughters turn against him he persists in his old folly, measuring their love by the number of knights they will allow him: 'Thy fifty yet doth double five-and-twenty, /And thou art twice her love' (II. 4). But there is more than folly here. His final threats, so blustering and futile that they teeter on the edge of comedy, nonetheless seem to touch some hidden spring in the universe:

>   No, you unnatural hags,
> I will have such revenges on you both,
> That all the world shall – I will do such things –
> What they are, yet I know not, but they shall be
> The terrors of the earth. You think I'll weep;
> No, I'll not weep.   *Storm and tempest.*
> I have full cause of weeping; but this heart
> Shall break into a hundred thousand flaws
> Or ere I'll weep. O fool, I shall go mad!
>
>   (II. 4)

Lear's own voice releases the storm. Though not literally a supernatural event, it described in terms that make it sound supernatural; and there is an obvious correspondence between the storm on the heath and the storm in Lear's mind. Yet he also sees it as something external, something he can both direct and defy. He calls on it to destroy 'ingrateful man' while insisting 'I am a man /More sinn'd against than sinning' (III. 2). The scale of Lear's thought is widening. The movement can be traced in one typical line: 'let them anatomize Regan; see what breeds about her heart. Is there any cause in nature that make these hard hearts?' (III. 6). From his own bitter experience Lear goes to a searing vision of the folly and wickedness of man. But he is still resisting insights into himself.

The storm sequence and the later scene with Gloucester near Dover cliff are full of broken images of the social order: trial and punishment, a king reviewing his troops and ordering his servants about. Beneath the trappings of society Lear smells universal corruption: the beadle lusts after the whore he is whipping, 'the usurer hangs the cozener', 'change places, and, handy-dandy, which is the justice, which is the thief?' This leads to a curious charity, a bitter equivalent of Cordelia's 'no cause, no cause': 'None does offend, none, I say, none I'll able 'em' (IV. 6). There are no offences where all are equally guilty. Lear has also seen beneath the flattery that surrounds his own office: 'When the rain came to wet me once, and the wind to make me chatter, when the thunder would not peace at my bidding, there I found 'em, there I smelt 'em out. Go to, they are not men o' their words. They told me I was everything. 'Tis a lie, I am not ague-proof' (IV. 6). But Lear's insights are still partial. Throughout the middle scenes he is surrounded by examples of love and loyalty in the Fool, Kent, Gloucester and Edgar, whose mere presence is a reminder that there is more to man than corruption. For the most part he does not seem to notice them. This gives special power to the moments of recognition when they do come: 'How dost, my boy? Art cold? /I am cold myself' (III. 2); 'If thou wilt weep my fortunes, take my eyes. /I know thee well enough, thy name is Gloucester'. But within seconds of preaching patience to Gloucester, he is shouting, 'Kill, kill, kill, kill, kill, kill!' (IV. 6).

His stubborness takes a new turn when he wakes in Cordelia's tent; here, it is restoration that is hard to accept. His imagination tries at first to place a great distance between himself and Cordelia: the soul in bliss, the soul in torment. Addressed with titles of respect, he shrinks away: 'Do not abuse me'. Only his ability to feel pain assures him he is alive: 'I feel this pin prick'. As he comes to realize his true condition he is, for the first time, shy, tentative and apologetic:

> Pray, do not mock me.
> I am a very foolish fond old man,
> Fourscore and upward, not an hour more nor less;
> And, to deal plainly,
> I fear I am not in my perfect mind. . . .
>   Do not laugh at me;
> For, as I am a man, I think this lady
> To be my child Cordelia.
>   (IV. 7)

From this point Lear's mind contracts as sharply as it had expanded. Only one thing matters now: Cordelia. Not love, or justice; he has gone beyond abstractions. Simply Cordelia. Everything else is 'packs and sects of great ones, /That ebb and flow by th' moon', and questions like 'who loses and who wins, who's in, who's out' (v. 3), once so vital to him, are subjects of mild amusement. Then Cordelia is taken from him. Again he resists: 'I kill'd the slave that was a-hanging thee' (v. 3). As in the first scene, he asks her to speak, and she is silent.[15] The focus reaches a final narrow intensity – 'Look on her, look, her lips, /Look there, look there!' (v. 3) – and he dies.[16] The survivors seem cowed and exhausted by what they have seen. It may have been possible to moralize about Lear's earlier experience, as it was about the parallel but simpler experience of Gloucester, who trusts the wrong son, is blinded and gains new insight. But there is nothing to do with this final shattering experience but what Lear himself finds so difficult: submit to it.

The violation of the social bond that begins *King Lear* finds an equivalent in *Macbeth* (*c*. 1606) in the murder of Duncan. Duncan does not make a strong impression as a character, but he is associated with images of courtesy and loyalty that give him a significance beyond the personal. The mutual courtesies that accompany the victory of his generals and his arrival at Macbeth's castle, the banquet Macbeth leaves to struggle with his conscience – these evoke the dignity not just of kingship but of the whole social order that depends on it. More important, Macbeth himself knows what it means to kill the King:

> He's here in double trust:
> First, as I am his kinsman and his subject,
> Strong both against the deed; then, as his host,
> Who should against his murderer shut the door,
> Not bear the knife myself. Besides, this Duncan
> Hath borne his faculties so meek, hath been
> So clear in his great office, that his virtues
> Will plead like angels, trumpet-tongu'd, against
> The deep damnation of his taking-off;
> And pity, like a naked new-born babe,
> Striding the blast, or heaven's cherubin, hors'd
> Upon the sightless couriers of the air,
> Shall blow the horrid deed in every eye,
> That tears shall drown the wind.
>   (I. 7)

This is characteristic of the way Macbeth's mind works. He goes rapidly from the plain statement of obligation to an extraordinary poetic image of horror that leaves moral formulae and even logical meaning behind. His apprehension of his own evil goes beyond the straightforward dehumanizing of herself that Lady Macbeth attempts, and far beyond the moral inversions and grotesqueries of the witches. He is temporarily manoeuvred by his wife into a false sense of what his manhood requires. In that way he is made, like other tragic heroes, to play a role. But the role never locks finally into place; his honest awareness of his own evil is always breaking through.

At one level he is the plaything of the witches, and of whatever power they represent. But they never come into focus as clearly as he does: Shakespeare has abandoned the straightforward devils and concrete hellmouth of earlier drama to create a spiritual evil more horrible for being murky. And Macbeth, like Romeo when he defies the stars, makes the fatal actions his own. He himself seems able to unleash evil on the world. On the night of the murder, the images of horror spread outward from Macbeth's own hallucinations to signs of disorder in the external world: strange noises, great winds, horses eating each other. Later, before the murder of Banquo, Macbeth calls on night to come at his bidding; and it does (III. 2). We saw Richard III deteriorate when he became king; Macbeth's deterioration is more painful and protracted, as he becomes coarse, bullying, obsessed with his own fears even as he tries to deny them. And yet we continue, to an alarming extent, to see the action from his point of view. We see the ghost of Banquo, as he does; we share a grim privilege denied everyone on stage, even Lady Macbeth. The vision of the line of Banquo that concludes the cauldron scene ought to be a vision of order, showing the stability of the kingly principle. To Macbeth the relentless march of kings is horrible, and that horror communicates to us.

Here, as in *Othello*, the poles of the moral universe are finally secure:

> Angels are bright still, though the brightest fell.
> Though all things foul would wear the brows of grace,
> Yet grace must still look so.
>
> (IV. 3)

Macbeth is finally destroyed by an army that comes to cleanse Scotland of the sickness with which he has infected it. Behind it lies the good king Edward the Confessor; its ranks include Old Siward and his son, who revive something like the piety and chivalry of the Talbots in *1 Henry VI*. But the main dramatization of the opposition to Macbeth is in the so-called 'England' scene between Malcolm and Macduff – an odd, awkward, disjointed scene full of suspicion and unease. Virtue will not quite come into focus in this play. Banquo looks like a decent, sensible man, but has to pray,

> Merciful Powers,
> Restrain in me the cursed thoughts that nature
> Gives way to in repose!
> (II. 1)

Macduff kills Macbeth in revenge for his family. But we are uncomfortably aware, and so is he, that he himself is guilty of deserting them. Moreover, the final dismissal of Macbeth as 'this dead butcher' (v. 8) does not win our full assent. It is not so much that we admire his last stand, fighting even against the prophecies. It is rather that we have seen too deeply into his mind, and participated in his torment. All along he has been aware of what he has lost: 'honour, love, obedience, troops of friends' (v. 3). Even the terrible nihilism of 'Tomorrow, and tomorrow, and tomorrow' (v. 5) implies an awareness that there ought to be more than this to life. Macbeth acts like a butcher and occasionally speaks like one; but here he speaks as a man, and we can enter into his mind. Tragedy in general focuses on the fate of the individual rather than the community, though it is aware of both; in Macbeth the focus is so radically on the individual that our strongest sense of good comes not from the community but from the one man who has given himself up to evil.

Antony and Cleopatra (c. 1607) ends, like Macbeth, with a society consolidating itself after a period of disorder. We are witnessing the birth of the pax Romana; or, as Caesar puts it, 'The time of universal peace is near' (IV. 6). This achievement leaves us largely indifferent. In his next speech Caesar gives orders for the disposal of Antony's followers who have gone over to him:

> Go charge Agrippa
> Plant those that have revolted in the vant;
> That Antony may seem to spend his fury
> Upon himself.
> (IV. 6)

We think back to another Caesar who was noted for generosity to former enemies, just as earlier the Pompey we saw before us reminded us of a more formidable one: 'Thy father, Pompey, would ne'er have made this treaty' (II. 6). The Roman political world is second-generation and second-rate. Rome itself, which in Julius Caesar and Coriolanus is a palpable city with a full range of social classes and a recognizable geography, is here as neutral and unatmospheric as a committee-room. Ghostly armies march back and forth across the map, and there is much talk of ruling the world; but there is little sense of what this world is like and of what exactly it means to rule it. The most vivid images of empire are the ones that diminish it. In the party on Pompey's galley the ineffectual Lepidus is carried off drunk, and Enobarbus remarks that the servant who is bearing him is 'a strong fellow' for "A bears /The third part of the world' (II. 7). In ironic counterpoint to the treaty between Pompey and the triumvirate is the greeting of Enobarbus and Menas. 'two thieves kissing' (II. 6). Pompey has a chance to be 'lord of all the world' if he will let Menas kill his guests. His refusal,

> Ah, this thou shouldst have done,
> And not have spoke on't! In me 'tis villainy,
> In thee 't had been good service.
>
> (II. 7)

not only reveals scrambled values but makes us wonder what kind of world can be passed so casually from hand to hand. The scene ends with a drunken round dance in which the great men, circling hand in hand, and singing 'Cup us, till the world go round' (II. 7), create a comically diminished image of the world they rule.

There are two complementary images of dissolving empires: Antony's 'Let Rome in Tiber melt, and the wide arch /Of the rang'd empire fall!' (I. 1) and Cleopatra's 'Melt Egypt into Nile! And kindly creatures /Turn all to serpents!' (II. 5). In the first, Rome and its empire simply disappear; the river, neutral in itself, is merely the thing into which they vanish. The second is an image not of annihilation but of transformation. The Nile has its traditional function of breeding mons-ters; the life it generates is low and coarse, but it is life all the same. Throughout the play Shakespeare gives his audience all the local colour they would expect in a play about Egypt: the wealth and feasting, the mysterious river, the serpents, even the insects. Egypt is as palpable as Rome is unreal. This places an ironic perspective on the Roman fear, shared by Antony himself, that he will lose his own reality if he stays in Egypt: 'These strong Egyptian fetters I must break, /Or lose myself in dotage' (I. 2). The loss of self is an understandable fear, especially when we see how much role-playing is involved in his affair with Cleopatra, from the games of mutual challenge in their opening dialogue to the transvestite exchange of clothing (II. 5). After losing his final battle Antony compares himself to a dissolving cloud: 'Here I am Antony, /Yet cannot hold this visible shape, my knave' (IV. 14). Antony's fate, however, is not to be annihilated but to be transformed.

He has one of the most movingly lyrical death scenes in English drama and then fails to kill himself. Flopping on the stage like a landed fish, he begs his followers to finish him off, the only result being that Decretas steals his sword to present it to Caesar. He cannot die as a noble Roman; he has to die as Cleopatra's lover, in her arms. His actual death scene is taken over by Cleopatra herself. In the Folio text there is no stage direction to mark the moment of his passing; he simply fades out during one of her speeches, to be replaced by the legendary Antony of her later dialogue with Dolabella.

As in *Julius Caesar*, we see life-sized characters projecting gigantic images. What the characters say of each other is at least as important as what we see of them directly. The split reality of 'this is, and is not Cressida' is worked into the whole fabric of the play. Part of the reality of Cleopatra is the wayward, devious gypsy trickster we see; but another part is the great queen created for us by Enobarbus's famous description of her barge, a speech that brings Egypt palpably on stage in the middle of a Roman scene. The Antony the actor is given to play is charming, generous, impulsive and fatally inept. But there is another Antony behind him, externalized in the Soothsayer's description of his attendant spirit:

> Thy daemon, that thy spirit which keeps thee, is
> Noble, courageous, high, unmatchable,
> Where Caesar's is not; but near him thy angel
> Becomes a fear, as being o'erpower'd.
>
> (II. 3)

Like the later desertion of Hercules (IV. 3) this establishes Antony as a failure at a high level: noble, heroic and supernaturally doomed. The Soothsayer goes on to insist that Caesar's spirit, though meaner, has 'that natural luck' that makes him bound to win. In the literal action luck has nothing to do with it. Caesar's skill and Antony's incompetence are fully shown, and are all the explanation we need for the outcome of the war. But the literal action does not exhaust our sense of what is happening; behind the historical events is a shadow- play of demigods.

The issue comes to a head in Cleopatra's dialogue with Dolabella. She creates an Antony we have never seen:

> His legs bestrid the ocean, his rear'd arm
> Crested the world, his voice was propertied
> As all the tuned spheres, and that to friends;
> But when he meant to quail and shake the orb,
> He was as rattling thunder.
>
> (V. 2)

She not only expects this vision to be challenged, but actually provokes the challenge so that she can defy it:

CLEOPATRA
Think you there was, or might be, such a man
As this I dreamt of?
DOLABELLA
                                        Gentle madam, no.
CLEOPATRA
You lie, up to the hearing of the gods.
But, if there be nor never were one such,
It's past the size of dreaming. Nature wants stuff
To vie strange shapes with fancy; yet t'imagine
An Antony were nature's piece 'gainst fancy,
Condemning shadows quite.
                              (v. 2)

Asserting the truth of her vision, Cleopatra is putting a strain on the conventional meanings of words, and ends by reversing them. What her imagination creates is nature; the world of history is a world of shadows.

In her death she seems to be rising beyond the world of history, beyond even her own frailty, to a regal immortality:

My resolution's plac'd, and I have nothing
Of woman in me. Now from head to foot
I am marble-constant; now the fleeting moon
No planet is of mine.
                        (v. 2)

But what happens is rather more interesting than this. The Cleopatra who triumphs over history and mortality is not a new, purified Cleopatra but the Cleopatra we have always known. Taking care to dress the part of Queen of Egypt for the first time in the play, she is scoring a political point, putting the republican upstarts in their place. She does not just rise above Caesar's world; she takes a keen delight in beating him at his own game. The life beyond death that she imagines is very different from Antony's somewhat prettified version of the next world, 'Where souls do couch on flowers, we'll hand in hand' (IV. 14). She imagines not a new kind of life with Antony but the old one beginning again: 'I am again for Cydnus, /To meet Mark Antony' (v. 2). Jealous as ever, she resents the thought that Iras, who has died first, will get Antony's first kiss in the next world. The clown who brings the asp gossips about death in a familiar way, and takes the sting out of it. The death scene itself is full of touching, handling and sexual joking. As in *Macbeth*, though to totally different effect, the world and its judgements are blurred as we focus on the imaginative vision of one character. This time, however, we have moved not into a nightmare but into a dream which, like the dream of the Athenian wood, has its own palpable reality.

There is nothing dream-like about *Coriolanus* (*c.* 1609); but it too shows an individual vision at odds with the movement of history. Menenius's fable of the belly and the members is ostensibly an image of an organic, properly ordered state where all work and all benefit. The reality of Rome is that each class is out for its own interests. Menenius shows his true colours when he warns the plebeians,

> you may as well
> Strike against the heaven with your staves as lift them
> Against the Roman state, whose course will on
> The way it takes, cracking ten thousand curbs
> Of more strong link asunder than can ever
> Appear in your impediment.
>
> (I. 1)

Rome as he conceives it is the aristocracy. The popular cry of 'The people are the city' (III. 1) is simply a cruder way of phrasing the same claim from the other side. Again, reality is fragmented: each class has its own Rome, namely itself. Against this background Coriolanus is not so mad as he sounds when he cries to the people, 'I banish you!' (III. 3); he has simply taken the identification of state with self to its logical extreme.

It is also a logical extension of his own single-minded vision. His stubborn, unyielding nature makes him a great fighter, though not necessarily a great general. He is the sword of Rome, a killing machine, 'a thing of blood, whose every motion /Was tim'd with dying cries' (II. 2). The qualities that make him a military hero make him a political disaster: he cannot adjust, he cannot compromise. But it would be wrong to see him as a magnificent brute who can only kill, not think. In the political scenes we see the tribunes, Menenius, and even Volumnia temporize and deceive, manoeuvring for short-term gains, never thinking beyond their own immediate interests and those of their class. Coriolanus is the only character in the play with a general political theory:

> my soul aches
> To know, when two authorities are up,
> Neither supreme, how soon confusion
> May enter 'twixt the gap of both and take

The one by th' other. . . .
                This double worship,
Where one part does disdain with cause, the other
Insult without all reason, where gentry, title, wisdom,
Cannot conclude but by the yea and no
Of general ignorance – it must omit
Real necessities, and give way the while
To unstable slightness. Purpose so barr'd, it follows
Nothing is done to purpose.
(III. 1)

The state does not run itself, like the body of Menenius's fable; it needs to be ordered, and by a ruling class. This may not be an amiable view of society but at least it has been thought out; and while Coriolanus speaks for his party his concern is not just with the possession of power but with its most effective use.

    Coriolanus's own relations with the state are complex. He tries to stand alone. He hates to be praised, he will not show his scars, he reduces the people to 'voices'. But for most of the play he bears a name given to him by his general Cominius, and when in the last scene this name is stripped from him he is furious. In large measure he was made what he is by his mother. There is perhaps no other character in Shakespeare whose nature is so dependent on the training he has received at another's hands. This explains the ultimate futility of his attempt, when banished from Rome, to reject his old nature and form a new identity for himself:

                          Coriolanus
He would not answer to; forbade all names.
He was a kind of nothing, titleless,
Till he had forg'd himself a name o' th' fire
Of burning Rome.
(v. 1)

His new identity, like his old one, will depend on Rome. His attempt to

                                        stand
As if a man were author of himself
And knew no other kin
(v. 3)

is doomed, as was Richard of Gloucester's. But in place of Richard's final acceptance of conventional morality we have something more in tune with the character as we have seen him all along. Coriolanus has always refused to lie about himself, to play a part; but his attempt to turn himself into a nameless thing is a profound lie about his own nature, a role he cannot sustain:

> Like a dull actor now,
> I have forgot my part, and I am out,
> Even to a full disgrace.
>
> (v. 3)

Yet his surrender to his mother is too surrounded by the play's bleak irony to move us as Lear's recognition of common humanity does. It gives Coriolanus's old enemy Aufidius the chance he needs to destroy him; it serves the interests of a Rome whose worthlessness we have seen; and it means Volumnia's final effect on her son is to kill him. Coriolanus is, again, fully articulate about what is really happening:

> O mother, mother!
> What have you done? Beyond, the heavens do ope,
> The gods look down, and this unnatural scene
> They laugh at.
>
> (v. 3)

In the last scene he appears to go sleepwalking to disaster, playing blindly into Aufidius's hands. But for a moment he has a full vision of what is happening to him. He is a figure of heroic size for whom the ordinary world has finally no use; but the final judgement on that world is that Rome simply fades out of the play.

The Rome of *Coriolanus* is at least a recognizable image of party politics; the Athens of *Timon of Athens* (c. 1608) is a satiric caricature. Social and personal relations are on a cash basis; the word 'usury' recurs obsessively. Coriolanus has at least a wife and mother; the world of *Timon of Athens* is a men's club. The only women who appear are amazons and whores, and the principal function of the latter is to spread disease. In the opening scene the Poet's allegory imagines the world not as an organic society but as a casino ruled by Fortune. In the play proper we see Timon as the centre of a vision of social relations more palpably absurd even than Lear's. As Coriolanus cannot stand praise, Timon cannot stand sharing; he must be the only giver: 'There's none /Can truly say he gives, if he receives' (I. 2). His view of ceremony is 'where there is true friendship. there needs none' (I. 2) but his view of friendship is grotesquely material: 'What need we have any friends, if we should ne'er have need of 'em? They were the most needless creatures living, should we ne'er have use for 'em, and would most resemble sweet instruments hung up in cases, that keep their sounds to themselves' (I. 2). The evocation of music, that fundamental image of order, merely emphasizes the absurdity of Timon's thought. In his prodigality we encounter one of the recurring themes of Jacobean drama, the destruction of the countryside as land is sold for city pleasures. Timon's steward Flavius explains where the money has come from: 'his land's put to their books' (I. 2) and the scale of the disaster is shown by Timon's great cry, 'To Lacedaemon did my land extend' (II. 2).

Timon's second career is an ironic mirror of his first; once again he hands out gold to all comers, but this time his intention to destroy society with it is overt. His retreat to the woods recalls the wilderness journey of Lear and the exile of Coriolanus. He strips off his clothes, and tries at one point to shed even his name. He will not identify himself to Alcibiades, declaring only 'I am Misanthropos, and hate mankind' (IV. 3). But his attempt to fix a new role for himself is placed by a number of ironies. Its self-consciousness is indicated by the accusation of the cynical philosopher Apemantus. who is himself something of a *poseur*, that Timon is simply imitating him: 'men report /Thou dost affect my manners, and dost use them' (IV. 3). His misanthropy goes beyond Apemantus's, but there is enough truth in the charge for the barb to stick. Timon's steward Flavius gives the lie to his master's general condemnation of mankind; the scene in which Flavius shares his remaining wealth with his fellow servants after the break-up of the house shows a benevolent use of money. But Timon, while recognizing one honest man, is comically anxious to keep the rest of his vision intact:

> Forgive my general and exceptious rashness,
> You perpetual-sober gods! I do proclaim
> One honest man – mistake me not, but one;
> No more, I pray – and he's a steward.
> How fain would I have hated all mankind!
>
> (IV. 3)

He then tries to bring Flavius under control by instructing him to imitate his own misanthropy. The only role Timon can imagine for the exceptional honest man is to become his understudy.

In the last scene Alcibiades's compromise with the Athenians, whereby he will destroy only offenders, not the entire city, may look like reasonable justice; but the effect is qualified by the Athenians' bizarre claim that his enemies are *all* dead, and the equally bizarre reason for this: 'Shame, that they wanted cunning, in excess /Hath broke their hearts' (V. 4). Ostensibly healed at the end of the play, this society remains a caricature. The larger order in which Timon's misanthropy is finally placed is not social but natural. His first invocation to the sun recognizes that his curses are in fact a perversion of nature:

> O blessed breeding sun, draw from the earth
> Rotten humidity; below thy sister's orb
> Infect the air!
>
> (IV. 3)

He recognizes a split between nature as it is, blessed and breeding, and nature as he would like it to be; this recalls the split Hamlet acknowledges between the world as he perceives it and the world as it is. Later, Timon tries to project onto the cosmos his own view of the corruption of society:

> The sun's a thief, and with his great attraction
> Robs the vast sea; the moon's an arrant thief,
> And her pale fire she snatches from the sun.
>
> (IV. 3)

Behind Timon's satiric fantasy we sense the ordered rhythms by which nature actually operates. In his later scenes the fury of his early curses is replaced by cool, sardonic wit, suggesting a growing detachment and withdrawal. In his mysterious death he is absorbed into the rhythms of nature:

> Come not to me again. But say to Athens,
> Timon hath made his everlasting mansion
> Upon the beached verge of the salt flood,
> Who once a day with his embossed froth
> The turbulent sea shall cover.
>
> (V. 1)

In its focus on an obsessed individual *Timon of Athens* seems like a shrunken version of the greater tragedies. But it also has links with the romances.[17] It is boldly stylized. It deals in the incredible: Timon not only dies at will but buries himself and puts up his own epitaph; not even in *The Winter's Tale* are we asked to swallow anything like this. Above all, it conveys a strong sense of nature as a force larger than man – Apemantus finds Timon among 'moss'd trees /That have outliv'd the eagle' (IV. 3) – and yet working through human life with a mysterious healing power. Timon's epitaph is a snarl; but the location of his grave, Alcibiades suggests, conveys a different message:

> rich conceit
> Taught thee to make vast Neptune weep for aye
> On thy low grave, on faults forgiven.
>
> (v. 3)

The 'rich conceit' that taught Timon, presumably at some level deeper than consciousness, to establish his grave as a symbol of healing and forgiveness is quite at odds with the overt workings of his mind. The split is characteristic: Coriolanus's great act of mercy is at odds with everything he has consciously stood for; Hamlet thinks of himself as a determined revenger, yet cannot take revenge except under the shadow of his own death. The split reality of 'This is, and is not Cressid' affects the heroes' view of themselves: 'That's he that was Othello; here I am'; 'Does any here know me? This is not Lear'. One reason for the split is that for all their integrity the characters are in some measure the creatures of other people. Lear depends on others' recognition of him; Coriolanus is given his name by Cominius and a good deal of his character by Volumnia; Timon is a creature of the society in which he tries to be exceptional; Antony is most securely a hero in the imagination of Cleopatra and the admiration of his fellow Romans. Yet the heroes' relations with their fellows are destructive as well as creative, and not just because they themselves die. More important, they ignore, reject, even destroy the characters who embody the values they themselves most want to believe in. Othello kills Desdemona, Macbeth kills Duncan, Lear banishes Cordelia, and Timon, finding in Flavius the embodiment of the true charity of which his was only a perversion, tries to turn him into another misanthrope. Cleopatra loves one of the world's great heroes, and her love leeches away everything that makes him actually heroic so that she can celebrate him in her imagination alone. Society as a whole is seen as a shrunken, dog-eat-dog world, a vision that comes to a head in *Timon of Athens* but can be seen in varying degrees from *Troilus and Cressida* to *Coriolanus*. It is a world much in need of heroes and much inclined, as in *Coriolanus*, to destroy them when they appear. But the real tragedy is that the heroes need to believe in such values as love, honour, integrity – that need for belief we see elsewhere in Shakespeare – and persistently betray those values when they appear, in others and in themselves.

Notes

1. See Naomi Conn Liebler, 'Thou Bleeding Piece of Earth: The Ritual Ground of *Julius Caesar*', *Shakespeare Studies*, 14 (1981), 175–96.

2. See Harriet Hawkins, *Likenesses of Truth in Elizabethan and Restoration Drama* (Oxford, 1972), p. 146.

3. On the stage history and the shifts in interest it displays see John Ripley, *'Julius Caesar' on Stage in England and America 1599–1973* (Cambridge, 1980).

4. On the construction of artificial personalities in Shakespearean tragedy, and in the Renaissance generally, see respectively J. Leeds Barroll, *Artificial Persons: The Formation of Character in the Tragedies of Shakespeare* (Columbia, South Carolina, 1974) and Stephen Greenblatt, *Renaissance Self-Fashioning: From More to Shakespeare* (Chicago, 1980).

5. See G. R. Hibbard, *The Making of Shakespeare's Dramatic Poetry* (Toronto, 1981), pp. 12–13.

6. The Fortinbras soliloquy is not in the Folio. If this cut was Shakespeare's it may have been that the association of Hamlet's revenge with Fortinbras's attack on Poland made the absurdity of the revenge too strong and wrecked the delicate balance of doubt and acceptance Shakespeare wanted to create. But we can only speculate.

7. See Oscar James Campbell, *Comicall Satyre and Shakespeare's 'Troilus and Cressida'* (San Marino, 1938).

8. See Gayle Greene, 'Shakespeare's Cressida: "A Kind of Self"', in *The Woman's Part: Feminist Criticism of Shakespeare*, edited by Carolyn Ruth Swift Lenz, Cayle Green and Carol Thomas Neely (Urbana, 1980), pp. 133–49 (pp. 135–36).

9. The phrase is Coleridge's: 'the motive-hunting of motiveless malignity'. See *Coleridge on Shakespeare*, edited by Terence Hawkes (Harmondsworth, 1969), p. 190.

10. On the use of 'if' in the play, see Maledeine Doran, *Shakespeare's Dramatic Language* (Madison, 1976), pp. 63–91.

11. For a survey of the debate, see Jane Adamson, *Othello as Tragedy: Some Problems of Judgment and Feeling* (Cambridge, 1980), pp. 11–27.

12. See *The Wheel of Fire* (Oxford, 1930, reprint London, 1960), pp. 97–119.

13. On the experience of split reality in the plays, see Norman Rabkin, *Shakespeare and the Common Understanding* (New York, 1967), pp. 57–58.

14. For example, 'O dear father, /It is thy business that I go about' (IV. 4). Even here, while there is a striking echo of Luke 2.49, any attempt to see a direct analogy in the situation quickly breaks down.

15. On the play's use of silence, see Jill Levenson, 'What the Silence Said: Still Points in *King Lear*', in *Shakespeare 1971*, edited by Clifford Leech and J. M. R. Margeson (Toronto, 1972), pp. 215–29.

16. Michael Goldman relates Lear's experience to the actor's device of keeping

emotion alive by fixing on particular objects. *See Acting and Action in Shakespearean Tragedy* (Princeton, 1985), pp. 72–73.

17. For a reading of *Timon of Athens* as Shakespeare's last play, see F. W. Brownlow, *Two Shakespearean Sequences: Henry VI to Richard II and Pericles to Timon of Athens* (London, 1977), pp. 216–34.

Chapter 5
Later Comedies

If Shakespeare asks his most radical questions about man and society in the tragedies, he makes his clearest statements of faith in the comedies. The structure of comedy in itself means that it deals in problems with solutions: the riddle is answered, the parted lovers are united, the broken family is rejoined, the apparently dead return to life. We see these motifs in the sequence from *The Comedy of Errors* to *Twelfth Night*. We see also, particularly in the mature comedies, an edge of healthy scepticism. The problems the characters have to solve often involve difficult internal conflicts, and the solutions do not always carry full credibility. In *The Comedy of Errors* the element of fantasy did not disturb us, for it was fundamental to the play's stylized idiom. The element of fantasy in the ending of *Twelfth Night*, after the fuller psychological and social examination we find in that play, leaves us wondering how seriously we can take it. In the so-called 'dark comedies' that follow *Twelfth Night* the difficulty of the problem and the fantasy of the solution both become more extreme, and the extra strain is what gives these plays their peculiar tone.

The heroine of *All's Well That Ends Well* (*c.* 1603) is a determined young lady who campaigns to win the man of her choice, first by curing the King of France of an apparently hopeless illness in return for his promise to let her choose her own husband; and second, by tricking her husband, who has refused to consummate the marriage, into bed with her by making him believe he is sleeping with another woman. The story of Helena and Bertram is, like that of *The Merchant of Venice*, the stuff of fairy tale; but the willingness to allow awkward questions about the material is even more pervasive. The curing of the King is impressively romantic, encouraging our belief in miracles; indeed, the King himself is virtually saved not so much by anything Helena does as by his own faith that the cure is possible:

> Methinks in thee some blessed spirit doth speak
> His powerful sound within an organ weak;
> And what impossibility would slay
> In common sense, sense saves another way.
>
> (II. 1)

But when Helena claims Bertram as her prize the tone abruptly changes. Bertram, lightly characterized up to this point, is revealed as a callow young snob whose reaction to his place in the story is 'A poor physician's daughter my wife? Disdain /Rather corrupt me ever!' (II. 3). He is bullied into marriage by the King; and we may reasonably wonder whether the bed-trick is enough to work the required adjustment in his will, especially as it takes place in the most realistic section of the play, where we see an army fighting an indecisive war and a shabby-genteel landlady trying to preserve her daughter's honour.

Shakespeare does not allow himself the easy solution of reforming Bertram's character; if anything, he gets less attractive as the play progresses. Early in the play the King's eulogy for Bertram's late father evokes a lost world of honour – the King emphasizes the old count's courtesy to inferiors – and comments sourly on the levity of modern youth (I. 2). Bertram exemplifies the latter quality in his willingness to give up his ancestral ring, 'an honour longing to our house' (IV. 2) as the price of seducing the Florentine girl Diana. In the last scene he gets his ring back from Helena, as part of a nominally comic ending of restoration and order. Helena has always had a sympathetic rapport with the older generation, and seems to be restoring Bertram's dignity as well as claiming her husband. But the ending is deliberately tentative, and is arguably more convincing and moving because of this. Bertram's acceptance of Helena, 'If she, my liege, can make me know this clearly, /I'll love her dearly ever, ever dearly' and the King's summary, 'All yet seems well, and if it end so meet /The bitter past, more welcome is the sweet' (V. 3) suggest that the final happiness of traditional comedy is something we can glimpse but not hold securely. We may also wonder why Helena should want Bertram; her love might seem an irrational obsession if it were not so sensitively dramatized. Her toughness and dedication make her look like a Shavian heroine, but in her acceptance of Bertram there is both romantic devotion and a measure of charity. There may be a parallel between their relationship and that of the crusty old Lord Lafeu and the comic braggart Parolles. Lafeu sees right through Parolles, but after the latter's exposure and humiliation Lafeu takes him into his household with the words, 'though you are a fool and a knave, you shall eat' (V. 2). He fulfils Parolles's own prediction, 'there's place and means for every man alive' (IV. 3). Bertram, throughout the finale, is humiliated and disgraced; but in the end Helena's love makes a place for him. The plot machinery of *All's Well That Ends Well* suggests miraculous transformations, but the actual writing of the play in the later scenes conveys a wry acceptance of humanity as it is.

Measure for Measure (1604) moves farther still from traditional comedy, taking its characters to the brink of tragedy. But it does so by the way it develops premises that were originally comic. As in *A*

Midsummer Night's Dream, there is an absurd law against lovers, but the threat that Claudio will be executed for fornication is more serious and insistent than the threat to Hermia. As in *Love's Labour's Lost*, characters who want to retreat to an enclosure are forced into the traffic of the world, but this time the results are disastrous. Angelo, like Bertram and the young men of *Love's Labour's Lost*, scorns love and then succumbs to it; but what he succumbs to is not a romantic attachment but a consuming sexual passion that brings out the cruelty of his nature. Isabella when we first see her is about to retreat into a convent, complaining only that the rules are not strict enough. When Lucio asks her to go to Angelo to plead for her brother Claudio's life, she is clearly reluctant. Her reluctance may be unattractive, but in a way it is justified by the event. Like Angelo, she combines a strongly repressed nature with a belief in moral and legal absolutes. Pleading for her brother's life, she is forced to argue against a strict application of the law – ''Tis set down so in heaven, but not in earth' – and this gives Angelo precisely the opening he needs: 'Say you so? Then I shall pose you quickly' (II. 4). His proposition, her chastity in exchange for her brother's life, produces a fierce revulsion: 'Then Isabel, live chaste, and brother, die; /More than our brother is our chastity' (II. 4). In other comedies of the period the heroine's determination to preserve her chastity is seen as natural and right.[1] But the brutality with which Isabella expresses her choice shows that Shakespeare wants us to see it as problematic. Angelo, in the grip of a passion that perverts his better nature, exemplifies the self-betrayal of the Shakespearean tragic hero; like Macbeth he sees what he is doing and is horrified by it. Isabella's dilemma is likewise potentially tragic, though here the situation, as in some later love-and-honour tragedies, is more contrived in that her dilemma is imposed from without. Angelo's belief in justice and Isabella's belief in her chastity are both questioned; and the sense of the world in which there are no values to rely on is extended in the set-speeches on life and death delivered by the Duke and Claudio. The Duke, though disguised as a friar, talks not of a better world to come but of the emptiness of this one. Claudio, pleading with Isabella to accept Angelo's offer, expresses not a love of life but a terrible fear of death. Neither the spirit nor the flesh is seen positively; the characters are hopelessly boxed in.

Shakespeare's solution is to change the nature of the play, turning it into a comedy of intrigue. At the half-way point the disguised Duke suddenly produces Mariana, the ideal substitute for Isabella in Angelo's bed. Her presence, unlike that of Sebastian, a character with an equivalent function in *Twelfth Night*, is not anticipated; the effect is that a new piece is put on the board half-way through the game. The bed-trick, unlike that of *All's Well That Ends Well*, fails of its immediate purpose. Angelo takes his price and orders Claudio's execution anyway. The Duke is temporarily at a loss; then Providence, for its next trick, produces the pirate Ragozine, 'a man of Claudio's years; his beard and head /Just of his colour', who has conveniently died and whose head can be substituted for Claudio's. The Duke declares, 'O, 'tis an accident that heaven provides!' (IV. 3) and we may feel that Heaven is being so very obliging the irony must be intentional. The Duke and his contrivances are problematic in their own way. He seems to make up not just plans but motives as he goes along. His decision to tell Isabella her brother is dead could be seen as a tough way of teaching her the value of the life she was willing to sacrifice, but the Duke announces only a playwright's reason, 'to make her heavenly comforts of despair, /When it is least expected' (IV. 3). Writers may treat their characters this way, but between one character and another it looks heartless. The Duke's motives appear more positive in the last scene, when he makes Isabella plead for Angelo's life, wringing from her an expression of charity that is the more convincing for being obviously difficult. But when at the end he proposes marriage to her he seems again to be imposing a comic plot device; neither Isabella nor the audience has been properly prepared, and her silence in the face of the Duke's offer leaves the actress's options open.[2] We can hardly be more confident about the wedding of Mariana and Angelo. It is clear that she wants him, and there is something of Helena's charity in her insistence, 'I crave no other, nor no better man' (v. 1). But it is equally clear that all Angelo wants is death. It is up to the actor to suggest otherwise, making what he can of the 'quick'ning in his eye' the Duke claims to see (v. 1). In the last moments the other characters fall silent and the only voices heard are those of the Duke, trying to enforce order, and the impudent Lucio, who has heckled the Duke throughout and who goes down protesting to the end. These two voices exemplify the play's main tension, the attempt to impose order on intractable human reality.

After *Measure for Measure* Shakespeare evidently abandoned the comic form for around four years, a significant gap in such a busy career, and when he returned to it in *Pericles* it was in the form of romance. The kind of fantastic story that constitutes one strand of *The Comedy of Errors* and *Twelfth Night* now takes up an entire play. The quality of *Pericles* (c. 1609) is so uneven that both textual corruption and multiple authorship seem required as explanations, though the play can be surprisingly unified in performance. Part of its roughness may be attributed to its deliberate archaism; it not only revives an old dramatic form, but does so quite self-consciously through the use of the poet Gower as narrator. Gower's language is sprinkled with archaism, and the story he tells is a train of episodes, unlike the complex intrigues of earlier plays. But the play is not as disjointed as it may appear: the incest of Antiochus and his daughter is a perversion of the love between Pericles and Marina that gives us, in their reunion, the play's most moving scene. It also suggests the dark view of sexuality that surfaces again in the brothel in Mytilene. There, however, Marina's invincible chastity reduces the menace of her employers to comic futility. They are more broadly conceived than the equivalent characters in *Measure for Measure*, and lack the gritty stubbornness of Pompey in particular. Gower's commentary alternates between simple moralizing of the order of 'to killen bad, keep good alive' (Chorus II) and a sense of Fortune's arbitrary whims: 'Till Fortune, tired with doing bad, /Threw him ashore, to give him glad' (Chorus II). But in the great storm scene that opens Act Three there is a more mysterious sense of man's relations with his world. The death of his wife Thaisa drives Pericles to an almost tragic questioning of the gods and to a sense of nature as a powerful force closely involved with man yet finally, dreadfully separate:

> A terrible childbed hast thou had, my dear;
> No light, no fire. Th'unfriendly elements
> Forgot thee utterly, nor have I time
> To give thee hallow'd to thy grave, but straight
> Must cast thee, scarcely coffin'd, in the ooze;
> Where, for a monument upon thy bones,
> And e'er remaining lamps, the belching whale
> And humming water must o'erwhelm thy corpse,
> Lying with simple shells.
>
> (III. 1)

At its best the play evokes an image of man adrift in a beautiful, frightening, mysterious universe.

An air of strangeness also pervades *Cymbeline* (*c.* 1610). The theophanies of the two plays (Diana in the first, Jupiter in the second) do not really convey the sense of a fully ordered world. Jupiter's explanation of the sufferings of Posthumus, 'Whom best I love I cross, to make my gift, /The more delay'd, delighted' (v. 4), though more acceptable coming from him than from the Duke in *Measure for Measure*, still suggests that man is at the mercy of the whims of the gods. In the dark counterpart of this scene, Imogen wakes from a drugged sleep to find the headless body of Cloten beside her, and to mistake it for that of her husband Posthumus. Her pained cry –

> if there be
> Yet left in heaven as small a drop of pity
> As a wren's eye, fear'd gods, a part of it!
>
> (IV. 2)

– conveys a sense of heaven's desertion to which the vision of Jupiter is not a full answer. However, the elaborate plot contrivance that has brought Imogen to this pass, and our knowledge that she has mistaken the corpse, control the horror and make it more grotesque than tragic. The jealousy of Posthumus, for which both Iachimo's lies and his own priggishness are responsible, reintroduces the problem of evil in a central character that had been largely excluded from *Pericles*. But if these characters seem like versions of Othello and Iago, they are sharply reduced in scale. There is a persistent, witty detachment in the writing, exemplified in the dirge for the dead Imogen, 'Golden lads and girls all must /As chimney-sweepers, come to dust' (IV. 2), and the Jailer's cheerful recommendation of death: 'he that sleeps fears not the toothache' (V. 4). Gower's function as narrator is split among minor characters who take turns explaining or summarizing the story. More important characters, like Iachimo, Belarius and Pisanio, take a hand at contriving the action from time to time; but no one controls it for long, and Pisanio, feeling his well-meaning plots slipping away from him, is reduced to the hope that 'Fortune brings in some boats that are not steer'd' (IV. 3). The simple structure of *Pericles* is replaced by a complex plot that issues in what is probably the most elaborate finale in Shakespeare. As a feat of sheer logistics it is breathtaking; but it leaves us still somewhat detached, marvelling at its technical brilliance. There is, however, one detail in the finale that may take us to a different level. Cymbeline has for much of the play been a rather uninteresting heavy father, swayed by his wicked queen. At the end, his forces having defeated the Romans, he makes the extraordinary gesture, 'Although the victor, we submit to Caesar' (V. 5). We recall that he was trained by Caesar, and was pushed into the war somewhat against his will. Even so this act of reconciliation surprises us, and makes us think again about why the play was named after this character. The only previous association Shakespeare's audience would have had with his name was that during his reign Christ was born.[3] If this point is relevant then the initial strangeness of *Cymbeline* deepens into mystery.

The initial strangeness of *The Winter's Tale* (*c.* 1611) has more to do with the darkness of the human heart. Leontes's sudden, irrational jealousy is deliberately unsettling. It lacks the farcical quality that makes Ford in *The Merry Wives of Windsor* easy to laugh at and it lacks the tragic dignity of Othello. Yet it is more closely observed than the somewhat conventional jealousy of Posthumus. Leontes's view of the world is poisoned, and his mind fills with images of disgust: 'I have drunk, and seen the spider' (II. 1). This is a darker force than anything Shakespeare has tried to contain within a comedy since *Measure for Measure*. It is countered initially not by a god or a powerful intriguer but by the breezy common sense of Paulina, whose manner is that of

a sensible nanny opening the windows of a sickroom: 'Here's such ado
to make no stain a stain /As passes colouring' (II. 2). As in *All's Well
That Ends Well*, a surprising vein of realistic observation accompanies
the fantastic story. Hermione is not a stock Patient Griselda; her resistance to Leontes is sharp as well as dignified:

> Adieu, my lord.
> I never wish'd to see you sorry; now
> I trust I shall.
>
> (II. 1)

In a situation he might have played for easy emotion, Shakespeare
makes us listen to the sound of a human voice.

In the later Bohemia scenes in which we see the young lovers, Flor-
izel and Leontes's lost daughter Perdita, at a sheep-shearing festival,
there is the same quality of fantasy shot through with realistic observation. In the voice of Perdita we hear occasionally the brisk common
sense we heard from the women earlier in the play. But though she
later comes to Sicilia and revitalizes it by fulfilling the oracle, she is
not the character through which the play's final solution comes about.
While his lost daughter has been growing up, Leontes has been fixed
in a cold routine of mourning by Paulina, who will not let him forget
his dead wife and will not let him marry again. The courtiers who urge
him to take a new wife appear now to be speaking for common sense;
against them Paulina looks bitter and fanatical. But it is Paulina who
guards the final secret: the statue of Hermione that comes to life, or
the actual Hermione who pretends for a while to be a statue – the finale
leaves us poised between possibilities, our disbelief in either of them
suspended. The reunion of father and daughter is kept off stage, stylized by the elaborate prose in which the courtiers describe it; the
reunion of husband and wife is what matters. It is more than a
recovery of the past: it is a fusion of art and nature, of the normal and
the miraculous. Hermione is a magical work of art, and a woman who
in sixteen years has become wrinkled. Under Paulina's guidance our
scepticism is both allowed and denied. She prepares the miracle by
declaring, 'It is required /You do awake your faith', and greets its
fulfilment with a smile:

> That she is living,
> Were it but told you, should be hooted at,
> Like an old tale; but it appears she lives.
>
> (V. 3)

Earlier plays, from *All's Well That Ends Well* to *Cymbeline*, have toyed with impossibilities and allowed a tentative attitude towards them. Here, as in Cleopatra's dialogue with Dolabella, the extraordinary is boldly asserted; and yet what is presented as miracle is also presented as ordinary life:

> O, she's warm!
> If this be magic, let it be an art
> Lawful as eating.
>   (v. 3)

A sense of wonder is pervasive in *The Tempest* (1611), and again what seems extraordinary is also recognized by the audience as belonging to common humanity. Miranda sees Ferdinand as 'a thing divine' while Ferdinand sees Miranda as 'the goddess /On whom these airs attend' (I. 2). We might expect this kind of perception as part of love, yet Miranda also greets the court party, a very mixed bag of humanity indeed, with

> O, wonder!
> How many goodly creatures are there here!
> How beauteous mankind is! O brave new world,
> That has such people in't!
>   (v. 1)

Prospero's wry comment, ''Tis new to thee', suggests the voice of sad experience. But in a way he has already given us an image of these people as extraordinary. Normally when a magician draws a circle he is going to call spirits or devils into it. Prospero calls into his circle human beings like himself. To Caliban, Prospero himself is a figure of wonder; this reaction is inspired not by Prospero the earth-shaking magician, whom Caliban despises, but by Prospero when he is dressed as an ordinary man, and by the equally ordinary men who surround him: 'O Setebos, these be brave spirits indeed! /How fine my master is!' (v. 1). Earlier in the play we have seen that capacity for wonder painfully wasted on Stephano and Trinculo; here, there is a more delicate balance between our acceptance of Caliban's insight and our sense that his wonder is sadly undeserved.

Prospero is a later development from the Duke in *Measure for Measure*. Imperfect in himself, he stage-manages an intrigue that makes others feel they are in the hands of Providence. But we have a much clearer view of him and his problems. His various roles of father, magician and exiled ruler with a grievance to avenge are hard to combine. In his long account of his past troubles he keeps insisting that Miranda is not listening hard enough; she is presumably doing her best. but she can never listen hard enough for him, for the story will never matter so much to her; and her reaction of wonder when she sees the courtiers suggests that she has indeed forgotten what Prospero told her of them.[4] The split between the father and the magician is indicated when Prospero puts Miranda into a charmed sleep before calling up Ariel, and we realize that these two characters, both so vital to him, have virtually no relationship with each other. For all we can tell, Miranda does not even know Ariel exists. To work his magic Prospero has to venture beyond his humanity, and the strain tells both on him and on the spirits he commands. His opening quarrel with Ariel, though it blows over quickly, shows that even this most tractable spirit can be hard work; and Caliban's account of what a spirit looks like under Prospero's power,

> Thou dost me yet but little hurt;
> Thou wilt anon, I know it by thy trembling.
> Now Prosper works upon thee.
>
> (II. 3)

suggests a kind of demonic possession in reverse. The freeing of Ariel means not just a holiday for the spirit but a return to his natural form. When he celebrates his freedom with the song, 'Where the bee sucks, there suck I; /In a cowslip's bell I lie' (V. 1) we realize that we have never seen Ariel as he truly is. The life-sized actor who plays him has shown only the shape he assumes for Prospero, a shape he looks forward to casting off at the end of the play.

Prospero's magic, as his speech surrendering it makes clear, is drawn from nature. The play is remarkably free of the jargon that so often accompanies Renaissance depictions of magic, and this helps keep us in touch with Prospero's essential humanity. His treatment of the lovers looks odd: he puts Ferdinand through an ordeal that seems, like the trials imposed by the Duke and Jupiter, a bit of arbitrary plotting:

> this swift business
> I must uneasy make, lest too light winning
> Make the prize light.
>
> (I. 2)

Ferdinand seems to be a decent young man who hardly needs this trial, much less the insistent lectures on chastity to which Prospero subjects him. But we have to remember that Miranda was once nearly raped by Caliban; if Prospero seems touchy about her, he has reason. We notice that Ferdinand's trial is to perform Caliban's task of carrying wood, and it is the thought of Caliban that causes Prospero, in a flash of anger, to break up the vision of ordered fertility he presents to celebrate the lovers' betrothal. Prospero seems more haunted by the attempted rape than Miranda is. If Prospero overshoots the mark with Ferdinand, he falls short in dealing with the court party. He stages for them the spectacular and morally significant show of the vanishing banquet, culminating in Ariel's magnificent denunciation of the 'three men of sin'. It affects Alonso, who loves his son and can be hurt by the news that he is dead. But Antonio and Sebastian, having no capacity for love, cannot be hurt; and as they cannot be hurt they cannot be reformed. Alonso's repentance is clear to the audience and satisfying to Prospero, who spends much of the last scene talking with him, like a teacher with a pupil who has done particularly well. Antonio and Sebastian remain, so far as we can tell, unreachable;[5] Prospero's forgiveness of his brother is coldly worded, and he keeps the pair in order by threatening them with his knowledge of their plot against Alonso.

But if Prospero's art is limited it is more humane for being so. He does not transform or brainwash, but treats his human material with respect, lecturing, reforming and punishing, but in the end accepting and forgiving what cannot be changed. We were not sure how to take the imperfect authority of the Duke in *Measure for Measure*; Prospero's is clearly a reflection of his humanity, and he himself accepts that humanity by surrendering his magic and dealing with his fellow creatures man to man. Our involvement in his story is peculiarly close not only because of this, but because at the end he transfers his magic to us. He appeals to our imaginations to take him off the island, and to our sympathies to see in his faults an image of our own:

> Gentle breath of yours my sails
> Must fill, or else my project fails,
> Which was to please. Now I want
> Spirits to enforce, art to enchant,
> And my ending is despair,
> Unless I be relieved by prayer,
> Which pierces so that it assaults
> Mercy itself and frees all faults.
> As you from crimes would pardon'd be,
> Let your indulgence set me free.
>   (Epilogue)

In *The Winter's Tale* the statue of Hermione was an ordinary woman and a miracle of art. In *The Tempest* the spectators become both god-like powers who receive prayers, and erring fellow mortals who need to pray themselves. Shakespeare's vision of the miracles of ordinary life, a hard-won achievement born of the risks and tensions of the dark comedies and earlier romances, is here applied to the audience.

The central characters of the early comedies seek the normal satisfactions of marriage, as both part and symbol of a decent social order. This order is also embodied in such images as the Duke's banquet in the Forest of Arden, where old ties are restored and the hungry are fed for the asking. The doomed idealism of the tragic heroes demands much more of the world, as we see in Othello's view of his marriage, Macbeth's view of Duncan's kingship, Cleopatra's emperor Antony, and Hamlet's idealized vision of the father whose revenge he so inexplicably delays. The central figures of the later comedies may not always go this far, but they too make extraordinary demands of the world: while Rosalind wants to marry a man who loves her, Helena wants to marry a man who does not. The Duke, disguised as a friar, tries to solve problems he could never solve as a duke. Prospero tries to draw his very mixed fellow creatures into a single charmed circle. There are echoes, too, of the betrayals from within that haunt the tragedies. Angelo sins against his own ideals, Posthumus and Leontes (like Othello) against the women who embody their belief in human perfection. The spiritual universe, inscrutable in *Hamlet* and *King Lear* and full of murky horror in *Macbeth*, seems to have been replaced by a benevolent nature, whose ordered cycles and generative power guarantee that stability we saw Shakespeare valuing in his earliest plays. But Shakespeare, having passed through the tragic vision, has not quite shed it. Close as it comes to man in these plays, nature is finally separate and goes its own way. Prospero draws his magic from it, but knows he must give that magic back in the end; it does not finally belong to him, any more than Ariel does. The beauty of the elemental world can be, as in *Pericles*, remote and terrifying. While the shepherds rescue Perdita Antigonus is eaten by a bear. If some benevolent power is at work to rejoin the sundered families of *Pericles* and *The Winter's Tale*, it takes its own time. And not all the dead return. For a controlling deity Jupiter seems oddly remote from the action of *Cymbeline*, and his salient quality is not benevolence but a testy impatience with the complaints of suffering humanity. From first to last Shakespeare has either believed or tried to believe in order; in the end he locates our best hope for it not in the gods or nature, not in the structures of society, but in the ties people create with those around them. The final embraces of Leontes and Hermione, or of Posthumus and Imogen, are perhaps expected. But we should notice too the clasped hands of Lafeu and Parolles, Cymbeline and the defeated Roman general Caius Lucius, Prospero and Alonso.

The final bond, as we have seen, is between Prospero and the audience. If it is not too artificial to see Shakespeare's career as framed by the opening of *1 Henry VI* and the ending of *The Tempest*,[6] then we might note that he begins with an interrupted ceremony, the funeral of Henry V, that indicates a collapsing society; and ends with a restoration of bonds on deeper than social terms as Prospero appeals to the combination of imaginative power and sinful frailty we all share with him. As he wrote *The Tempest*, Shakespeare's Jacobean contemporaries were already pushing their investigation of human breakdown to the point where murder, adultery, the collapse of value and the dehumanizing of mankind were becoming so much the stock in trade of drama that the initial horror was edged with sardonic amusement. What else, they seem to say, can you expect of such a low creature as man? Shakespeare always expects more. Even in the darkest moments of *Troilus, Lear* and *Timon*, where man's life really does seem as cheap as a beast's, there are glimmers of love, idealism, pity and ordinary decency. About the structures man builds and the forces that surround him, Shakespeare was never complacent. Kingship goes dead, marriage is betrayed from within, the city becomes a jungle. The gods hurl their thunder and withdraw, leaving mortal suppliants shaken and cowed. Nature kills, creates and kills again. But Shakespeare's people, like the people of no other dramatist, care for each other. From the Dromios' decision that it is better to go hand in hand than quarrel over precedence to Prospero's decision to throw away his power and appeal to the humanity of his audience, Shakespeare shows that beneath and beyond the structures that express order there is a tie of humanity that only death can break. And when death breaks that tie, as it does in *King Lear*, it cannot destroy its value. If the ending of that play seems to represent the furthest reach of Shakspeare's vision it is because the death of Cordelia is a final reality against which all hope, all faith, all idealism breaks. But not all love. Lear's refusal to be reconciled to that death is of a piece with the folly and blindness that have made him resist reality all through the play, but we react to it very differently. The sheer value of this one life is affirmed in the pain its ending causes, to Lear and to us. Love and loss only sharpen each other. It is Shakespeare's greatest image of what we stand to lose, and of what we have in common.

Notes

1. See Alexander Leggatt, *Citizen Comedy in the Age of Shakespeare* (Toronto, 1973), pp. 100–1.

2. For a discussion of different stagings of the ending, see Ralph Berry, *Changing Styles in Shakespeare* (London, 1981), pp. 37–48.

3. See Robin Moffet, '*Cymbeline* and the Nativity', *Shakespeare Quarterly*, 13 (1962), 207–18.

4. See Ann Righter [Barton], Introduction to the New Penguin Shakespeare edition (Harmondsworth, 1968), pp. 10–11.

5. The unreachable quality of Antonio in particular is expressed in the words assigned to him in W. H. Auden's *The Sea and the Mirror*.

6. One problem is of course the existence of *Henry VIII* and *The Noble Kinsmen*, which will be considered in Chapter 11.

Part Two:

Early
Jacobean
Drama

Chapter 6
The Early Jacobeans

The terms 'Elizabethan' and 'Jacobean' are seductive, inviting a neat contrast between a golden age under a loved and splendid queen and a time of disillusionment and breakdown under an unpopular, neurotic king. But of course the culture of England did not change overnight in 1603. There was a strong vein of satire in the literature of the 1590s, and complaint and disillusion were already in the air. In drama, some of the qualities labelled 'Jacobean' were already in place. The sophisticated violence of Jacobean tragedy would not have been novel to audiences who remembered *Titus Andronicus* and *The Spanish Tragedy*. The tendency for tragedy and satire to converge in dark comedy leading to death was already present in *The Jew of Malta* (*c*. 1589).[1] So, it can be argued, was the uncertainty about the universe in which man finds himself. In *The Spanish Tragedy* and *Doctor Faustus* we see gods, or God, at work and the spectacle is not reassuring. In *Tamburlaine* and *Titus Andronicus* it is hard to be sure what, if anything, is in the heavens.

Nonetheless, there are developments that make Jacobean drama distinctive. The most palpable difference is in verse style: a new freedom of movement, a more sustained conversational tone. We can hear the difference if we put a passage from *The Spanish Tragedy*(*c*. 1587) against one from *The Revenger's Tragedy* (*c*. 1606) Here, from Kyd's play, is Hieronimo lamenting the murder of his son and questioning the universe in which such things happen:

> O eyes, no eyes, but fountains fraught with tears;
> O life, no life, but lively form of death;
> O world, no world, but mass of public wrongs,
> Confus'd and fill'd with murder and misdeeds;
> O sacred heavens! if this unhallow'd deed,
> If this inhuman and barbarous attempt,
> If this incomparable murder thus
> Of mine, but now no more my son,
> Shall unreveal'd and unrevenged pass,

> How should we term your dealings to be just,
> If you unjustly deal with those that in your justice
>   trust?
>   (III. 2)

And here, from the Jacobean play, is the bastard Spurio, on the point of cuckolding his father, speculating about his nativity:

> Faith, if the truth were known, I was begot
> After some gluttonous dinner, some stirring dish
> Was my first father, when deep healths went round,
> And ladies' cheeks were painted red with wine,
> Their tongues as short and nimble as their heels,
> Uttering words sweet and thick; and when they rose,
> Were merrily dispos'd to fall again, –
> In such a whisp'ring and withdrawing hour,
> When base male-bawds kept sentinel at stair-head,
> Was I stol'n softly; O, damnation met
> The sin of feasts, drunken adultery.
> I feel it swell me; my revenge is just;
> I was begot in impudent wine and lust.
>   (I. 2)

Leaving aside the differences in tone and content that can be attributed simply to character and situation, we are left with other differences that are fundamental. Hieronimo's lines are end-stopped, his rhetorical devices consciously displayed. We can *hear* the machinery of the writing. For all his questioning, he thinks in familiar abstractions, and the moral attitudes behind his language are conventional and secure. His emotions are clear and ordered, he thinks of the world as a system, and as we listen to him speak we are aware not of an individual personality but of a voice expressing traditional values. Spurio also deals in abstractions, but the way in which he does so is consciously original, just as his verse imitates the flow of conversational speech in a way that Hieronimo's never attempts. He is interested not in the universe but in himself. He develops, half-seriously and half-mischievously, a private fantasy about his own engendering, one that justifies the evil he is about to commit. He is not questioning the universe from the basis of an established morality but making up a morality as he goes along, using words like 'damnation' and 'adultery' without automatic disapproval – indeed, with a certain relish. His manner is impudent and self-confident, but his attitude is finally less secure than Hieronimo's, for we detect resentment just beneath the surface, an extra aggressiveness in the self-assertion. While each character is stylized, Hieronimo as a posed, formal figure of lament and Spurio as a savage cartoon, the depiction of the bastard is more open and complicated, and gives us more to worry about.

The speed and excitement of his manner create an intense concentration on the present moment, a quality we find throughout Jacobean drama. We hear it in a characteristic speech from Dekker and Webster's *Westward Ho* (*c*. 1604):

> Why, there's no minute, no thought of time passes, but
> some villainy or other is a-brewing: why, even now, now,
> at holding up of this finger, and before the turning down
> of this, some are murdering, some lying with their maids,
> some picking of pockets, some cutting purses, some
> cheating, some weighing out bribes. In this city some
> wives are cuckolding some husbands. In yonder village
> some farmers are now – now – grinding the jawbones of
> the poor: therefore sweet scholar, sugared Mistress
> Honeysuckle, take summer before you, and lay hold of it!
> Why, even now must you and I hatch an egg of
> iniquity.
> (II. 1)

We sense the excitement of living in a sharply felt present, one in which the driving forces are material and sexual appetite.

Money, property and class matter in these plays; there is a brisk trade in all three, as there is in sex. Usurers and prostitutes are regularly associated: as business partners, in Chapman, Jonson and Marston's *Eastward Ho* (1605); or as inadvertent marriage partners, brought together symbolically by the mechanism of the plot, in Middleton's *A Trick to Catch the Old One* (1605) and Lording Barry's *Ram Alley* (*c*. 1608). The point of the association is to suggest that trade has cheapened human relations, in money and in sex. James's sale of knighthoods involved another kind of cheapening. For more conservative minds, the interclass mobility naturally created by the rise and fall of families meant that the class structure was breaking down. In Edward Sharpham's *The Fleer* (1606) the title character complains that he has just been at court, 'where I saw a farmer's son sit newly made a courtier, that sat in the presence at cards, as familiar as if the chair of state had been made of a piece of his father's barn door. O, 'tis a shame. I would have state be state in earnest and in game'.[2] The picture of the farmer's son playing cards in the presence chamber is a fair indication of what some people thought was going wrong with

England. The protest at the end of the speech is a striking departure from the normal tone of the play, which is flippant to the point of triviality. This is one thing about which the playwright is serious.

The degree to which Jacobean drama is in fact serious about the issues it deals with is sometimes a real problem. There is a good deal of overt moralizing, but it runs alongside a gleeful fascination with the vice and folly under attack, a quality we hardly ever see in Shakespeare. This is true not only in comedy, where we might expect it,[3] but in tragedy as well. Tourneur's *The Atheist's Tragedy* (c. 1611) and the anonymous *Second Maiden's Tragedy* (c. 1611) are both plays that advertise traditional moral visions. In the first, we see a clear and systematic exposure of the folly of a freethinker who is trying to find his satisfaction in this world. At the end, vice is punished and virtue rewarded. But there is something distinctly grotesque in the way it happens: the atheist villain d'Amville, raising an axe to behead the passive, virtuous hero, accidentally knocks out his own brains. This seems intended as an image of the mysterious ways of Providence, but the absurdity of the moment, underscored by a bystander's helpful comment, 'In lifting up the axe, I think h'has knocked /His brains out' (v. 2), leaves us wondering if the irony is pointing against the villain or against the moralizing plot that destroys him.

Tourneur, we may conclude, has simply lost control. The author of *The Second Maiden's Tragedy* seems more intelligent, but presents us with similar problems. His concern is with sexual morality but his *pièce de résistance* is a long sequence in which the Tyrant steals from its tomb the body of the Lady, who would not yield to his lust. Evidently we are not meant to approve of this; but as the sequence develops morality shades into sensationalism and the necrophilia threatens to become fascinating in the wrong way. Earlier, when the Lady kills herself to preserve her honour, her lover Govanius, generally a sympathetic and serious character, is allowed a cynical joke about the difference between the Lady's action and normal female behaviour:

> Few of your ladies
> In ord'nary will believe it. They abhor it.
> They'll sooner kill themselves with lust than for it.
>
> (III. 1)

In the subplot Anselmus's desire to test his wife's chastity is indicative of what happens to virtue in much Jacobean drama. It is not allowed simply to exist, or to express itself naturally: it must be displayed, goaded and if possible corrupted. Anselmus does not express the last motive overtly, but it is clearly there:

> Give not me
> The thing that is thought good, but what's approved so.
> So wise men choose. O, what a lazy virtue
> Is chastity in a woman if no sin
> Should lay temptation to't!
>
> (I. 2)

In the ensuing action he is not satisfied with the test until his wife fails it.

To risk a few generalizations: in Jacobean drama virtue is withdrawn and under attack, and much of the energy belongs to vice. Even morally appropriate rewards and punishments do not help us get our bearings, for they are too grotesque to suggest a natural process. Playwrights work for the effect of the moment, even if it means being flippant or sensational. The result is a fragmented vision: at its best, the legitimate reflection of a fragmented world; at its worst, mere writing for effect. The art that Shakespeare consolidated is starting to break apart. In the early years of James's reign a theatregoer who had been unlucky in his choice of plays might have wondered if the dramatic form itself was becoming exhausted. The danger was real; that it was averted can be credited to a number of remarkable playwrights who took the liabilities of Jacobean drama – fragmentation, sensationalism, moral incoherence – and turned them into assets.

Learned and ambitious, author of the first notable English translation of Homer, George Chapman (c. 1560–1634) might have been expected to bring a certain gravity to English drama. But his first extant play, *The Blind Beggar of Alexandria* (1596), is a startling extravaganza. The central character, Irus, is a quick-change artist who appears in several different roles. In part, this is a chance for the actor to show off: in one scene Irus appears in three parts in rapid succession, with only a few lines between. But it is also a chance for the playwright to show off, as Chapman exploits the possibilities for complicated plotting. Irus intrigues against himself, reveals his own secrets, and cuckolds himself twice, with different wives. Later, the disguised character working against himself will suggest self-destructiveness: Vindice in *The Revenger's Tragedy*, Bosola in *The Duchess of Malfi*. But Irus is always in control of his own intrigue, and works against himself essentially for the sake of amusement, his and ours. He succeeds in every sphere in which he operates, gaining sex, money and power. Women who profess chastity succumb to his persuasion; the cynical sexual comedy anticipates *The Widow's Tears*. In his capacity as the banished lord Cleantes, he avenges his injuries by making himself King of Egypt. His essential identity seems to be that of the Blind Beggar of the title,

though he is not really blind. He was born a shepherd's son; we may
think back to Tamburlaine, who also began as a shepherd. His victory
is a victory for aspiring. chameleon man, for the dispossessed figure
who has to live by his wits. The play's cheerful acceptance of its own
eclecticism, unlike the harsh clashing of styles in, say, Marston's
Antonio plays, makes it Elizabethan; its date is 1596. But its hero,
carving out his own way in the world, will appear in various guises
throughout Jacobean drama.

He returns, considerably toned down, in Chapman's later comedies.
In *An Humorous Day's Mirth* (1597) Le Mot plays a series of sometimes
hair-raising practical jokes on the other characters, exploiting their
follies and weaknesses. He himself has some of Irus's free-wheeling
quality. Offering to kiss a lady's hand, he bites it instead, and then
makes a speech summing himself up:

> my father and my mother died both in a day, and I rung
> me a peal for them, and they were no sooner brought to
> the church and laid in their graves, but I fetched me two
> or three fine capers aloft, and took my leave of them, as
> men do of their mistresses at the end of a galliard; *Beso las
> manos.*
>   (scene 11)

The central intriguer of *All Fools* (*c.* 1604), Rinaldo, is a younger
brother who sees himself making his way in a world ruled by Fortune:
'my fortune is to win renown by gulling' (v. 2). This time, however,
the trickster is gulled himself at the end of the play, by one of his own
victims. This is in keeping with the view of humanity given in the
play's title, a view that finally extends to the audience: 'We can but
bring you meat, and set you stools, /And to our best cheer say, you
are all (   ) welcome' (Epilogue). Tharsalio in *The Widow's Tears*
(*c.* 1605) is also a younger son, who complains to his older brother,
'You were too forward when you stepped into the world before me
and gulled me of the land that my spirits and parts were indeed born
to' (I. 1). He begins the play by formally renouncing Fortune and
declaring his dependence on 'a more notable deity, sole friend to worth
/And patroness of all good spirits, Confidence' (I. 1). His cynicism
helps set the tone of the comedy, and is largely justified by events. But
like Rinaldo he does not have everything his own way. Impatient with
Tharsalio's mockery, the servant Lycas issues what may be taken as
a significant minority report: 'I marvel what man, what woman, what
name, what action, doth his tongue glide over, but it leaves a slime
upon't?' (IV. 1).

However, Chapman's comedies as a whole participate in this cynicism. In the more light-hearted ones trickery is accepted as mere sport, 'unhurtful motives of delight' (*An Humorous Day's Mirth*, scene 14); 'good tricks of youth, i'faith, no indecorum' (*All Fools*, v. 2). But there is something ultimately cold-blooded in the way Chapman's characters make pastime with one another. The women are generally characterless, prizes in the game. *May-Day* (*c.* 1609) is ostensibly a comedy of courtship, but its real tone is set by *double-entendres* about backsides and sweeping women's coal-houses. In *Monsieur d'Olive* (*c.* 1604) and *The Widow's Tears* characters who have withdrawn from the world into enclosed routines of mourning are brought back to participate in life, but there is nothing particularly warm or romantic in the effect; the world they return to is a grubby one. The light-hearted parading of 'humour' types in *An Humorous Day's Mirth* becomes in some later comedies a darker vision of human weakness. Authority figures, cheerfully gulled along with everyone else in the early plays, are more deeply questioned in the later ones. The Governor who presides over the finale of *The Widow's Tears* wrings this complaint from one of his subjects: 'O desert, where wert thou when this wooden dagger was gilded over with the title of Governor?' (v. 3). *The Gentleman Usher* (*c.* 1602) combines sardonic courtly comedy with grotesque and threatening actions that take it closer to tragicomedy. At one point the apparent injustice of Duke Alphonso leads Strozza to make a speech that might have come from one of Chapman's tragedies:

> And what's a prince? Had all been virtuous men,
> There never had been princes upon earth,
> And so no subject; all men had been princes.
> A virtuous man is subject to no prince,
> But to his soul and honour; which are laws
> That carry fire and sword within themselves,
> Never corrupted, never out of rule.
>
> (v. 4)

The buccaneering licence of Irus has become something more serious: an assertion of individual freedom in a world in which authority has no value except as an expedient for controlling human wickedness.

This idea is central to Chapman's best known tragedy, *Bussy d'Ambois* (*c.* 1604). Bussy is in some respects a development from the dispossessed trickster heroes of Chapman's comedies. But the treatment of the character is more far-reaching, complex and ironic. Bussy begins the play 'poor', complaining of a world in which 'Fortune, not reason, rules the state of things, /Reward goes backwards, Honour on his head'. He attacks the emptiness of human greatness:

> As cedars beaten with incessant storms,
> So great men flourish; and do imitate
> Unskilful statuaries, who suppose
> (In forging a Colossus) if they make him
> Straddle enough, strut, and look big, and gape,
> Their work is goodly; so our tympanous statists
> (In their affected gravity of voice,
> Sourness of countenance, manners' cruelty,
> Authority, wealth, and all the spawn of Fortune)
> Think they bear all the kingdom's worth before them;
> Yet differ not from those colossic statues,
> Which with heroic forms without o'erspread,
> Within are nought but mortar, flint and lead.
> Man is a torch borne in the wind, a dream
> But of a shadow, summ'd with all his substance.
>
> (I. 1)

The startling shift in images from the statue full of rubble to the torch borne in the wind prepares us for one aspect of the play's double vision, its combination of sardonic social observation with a spiritual vision of human greatness and frailty, seen in images drawn from the elements. This is to be, in fact, a characteristic of Chapman's tragedies in general: the follies of court life are as closely observed as in any comedy of the period, but the language is constantly striving for spiritual grandeur.

Another and related aspect of the play's double vision lies in our dilemma about the hero. His answer to the storm of life is, 'We must to Virtue for our guide resort, /Or we shall shipwreck in our safest port' (I. 1). Later he declares, 'I am for honest actions, not for great' (I. 1). By the end of the play his actions have consisted of three killings and an adultery. He never seems aware of the incongruity. He claims the freedom to be a law unto himself, a king in his own right:

> since I am free
> (Offending no just law) let no law make
> By any wrong it does, my life her slave:
> When I am wrong'd and that law fails to right me,
> Let me be King myself (as man was made)
> And do a justice that exceeds the law:
> If my wrong pass the power of single valour
> To right and expiate; then be you my King,
> And do a Right, exceeding Law and Nature:
> Who to himself is law, no law doth need,
> Offends no King, and is a King indeed.
>
> (II. 1)

The trouble is that Bussy is making this speech on his knees before
the King, requesting permission to enjoy the freedom he talks of so
grandly. Later he sees himself as a satirist, exposing the corruption of
the court, the church and the law; but his way of putting it is to
describe himself as the King's hawk, flying at his command (III. 2). If
Bussy could stick to monologues, he might convince us of his independence; but he is a character in a play, brought constantly into
relation with other characters, and frequently dependent on them in
a way that works against his claim of self-sufficiency.

The perspective can also shift the other way, as actions that might
look foolish or degraded are dressed up in heroic language. A trivial
quarrel of courtiers leads to a duel described as a clash of titanic heroes
(II. 1). Bussy's adulterous affair with Tamyra is subject to a similar
double perspective. Tamyra herself describes it as 'licentious fancy'
(II. 2) yet asks the powers of the night to

> make the violent wheels
> Of Time and Fortune stand; and great Existence
> (The Maker's treasury) now not seem to be,
> To all but my approaching friends and me.
>
> (II. 2)

Friar Comolet, the lovers' go-between, describes the affair in images
that suggest both ordinary deception and the creation of a microcosm:

> And (with another colour, which my Art
> Shall teach you to lay on) you yourself must seem
> The only agent, and the first Orb move
> In this our set and cunning world of Love.
>
> (II. 2)

One reason this double vision is possible is that traditional land-
marks have been removed; otherwise it might be tempting to settle for
a conservative reading of Bussy as a pretentious braggart. But the King
is a weak figure of authority; he thinks wistfully of the ordered court
of Elizabeth's England, but seems unable or unwilling to control his
own squabbling courtiers. The supernatural machinery is treated ironically: the devil Behemoth, summoned twice to give information, is
surrounded by grand poetry and striking stage effects, but speaks like
a minor bureaucrat, disobliging and pernickity, insisting on the limits
of his authority. The Friar not only acts as pandar for an adulterous
love but is regularly seen rising from the stage trap as though he were
a devil. On the last such occasion he ascends to find Tamyra being
tortured by her husband Montsurry, cries 'what rape of honour and
religion?' (v. 1), and drops dead. His protest is justified, but not in

quite the terms he uses. His final moments seem at every point to parody the action of a *deus ex machina*. The effect is grotesque and confusing and is, I think, meant to be. Frustrated by our contradictory reactions to the hero and his career, we may be looking for some point of reference that will make the play's vision fall into a single shape; Chapman ensures we do not find one.

Our difficulty persists to the end. Bussy, now far removed from his early choice of honesty over greatness, has come to see himself as a master of secrecy and deception:

> A politician must like lightning melt
> The very marrow, and not print the skin:
> His ways must not be seen.
> (IV. 2)

Yet he is tricked into his death, ignoring or misinterpreting all warnings with a stubbornness that verges on stupidity. His enemies, however, pay tribute to him even as they work towards his destruction. In a development from the image of the storm-beaten cedar in Bussy's first speech, Monsieur sees him as a man who will fall *because* of his greatness, while lesser spirits survive:

> Yet, as the winds sing through a hollow tree,
> And (since it lets them pass through) let it stand;
> But a tree solid, since it gives no way
> To their wild rages, they rend up by th'root:
> So this full creature now shall reel and fall,
> Before the frantic puffs of purblind Chance
> That pipes through empty men, and makes them
>   dance.
>   (v. 3)

This scene reflects a view of Nature not as ordered and reasonable but as an idiot power that 'lays /A mass of stuff together' and gives merit to a man only to effect his ruin. Bussy's own death speeches combine cosmic self-assertion, as he dies standing, propped by his sword,[4] and broken passion triggered by the sight of Tamyra's wounds. He sees himself in his final lines as a falling star, a warning fire that signals the 'frail condition of strength, valour, virtue' (v. 3); but in the play's last speech the ghost of the Friar gives Bussy's images a very different turn:

> Farewell brave relics of a complete man:
> Look up and see thy spirit made a star,
> Join flames with Hercules: and when thou set'st

Thy radiant forehead in the firmament,
Make the vast continent, crack't with thy receipt,
Spread to a world of fire; and th'aged sky,
Cheer with new sparks of old humanity.

(v. 3)

It looks like a final choric utterance, a point of rest. But, even if we ignore the incongruity of such a pagan image in the mouth of a Friar, we may note a certain remoteness in the vision. Bussy in life was never a pure fire, but constantly compromised by his own nature and his dealings with others; and the nature of the world he leaves behind him is indicated by the final parting of Montsurry and Tamyra, who, far from achieving the 'Christian reconcilement' (v. 3) the Friar has urged on them, have reached out to each other but realized they can never join. We are left in a world of division, compromise and impurity, a world from which Bussy, for all his claims of integrity, could be freed only by death.[5]

Of Chapman's later tragedies the most notable are *The Revenge of Bussy d'Ambois* (c. 1610) and the two-part *Conspiracy and Tragedy of Charles Duke of Byron* (c. 1607); in both Chapman returns to some of the issues of *Bussy*. *The Revenge*, the later of the two, presents a new character, Bussy's brother Clermont, an exemplar of Stoic virtue and self-sufficiency who is caught like Bussy in the ironies that the social vision of drama naturally creates. Proclaiming his self-sufficiency, he becomes one of the court's star turns, holding forth in front of admiring audiences. Finally he commits suicide because of the death of his friend and greatest admirer, the Guise. We are torn between admiration of his virtue and an ironic recognition of the compromises this virtue suffers in the world. Byron, like Bussy and Clermont, is a character seen from a double perspective: but his grandeur and folly are even more extreme and the gap between them is wider. This time there is an effective figure of authority, King Henry IV, whose wise, firm and good-natured rule acts as a counter to Byron's *folie de grandeur*. The most powerful passage is Byron's death scene, which is terrible in its unsparing depiction of a man unable to accept his fate, veering between heroic self-assertion and the panic of a cornered animal. In his last lines we hear in succession a lament for his mortality, bitterly contrasted with the regeneration of lower nature; an attempt to draw a self-critical moral; and a final ambiguity:

And so farewell for ever. Never more
Shall any hope of my revival see me;
Such is the endless exile of dead men.
Summer succeeds the Spring. Autumn the Summer,

The frosts of Winter the Fall'n leaves of Autumn;
All these, and all fruits in them yearly fade,
And every year return: but cursed man
Shall never more renew his vanish'd face.
Fall on your knees, then, satists, ere ye fall,
That you may rise again; knees bent too late,
Stick you in earth like statues: see in me
How you are pour'd down from your clearest heavens;
Fall lower yet, mix'd with th' unmoved centre,
That your own shadows may no longer mock ye.
Strike, strike, O strike; fly, fly, commanding soul,
And on thy wings for this thy body's breath,
Bear the eternal victory of death.

                                                    (v. 4)

Does the last line mean Byron's victory over death or death's victory
over Byron? We cannot be sure.[6] We are not helped by the rest of the
speech, which veers between acceptance and defiance, a calm elegiac
tone and one of desperation. The play ends at this point: we do not
see the death, nor is there a concluding speech from another character.
Though the text has been mangled by censorship, it may be that this
technically unusual ending reflects Chapman's intention. His concentration on the extraordinary central figure is such that the play actually
ends in the hero's mind; and we are still not sure what to make of him.

   The role-playing of Shakespeare's tragic heroes is taken further in
Chapman's. Their heroism tends to be a matter of assertion only, never
shown in action. This brings it close to pure performance, divorced
from reality. It depends on their language, and on other people's
language about them, insisting on spiritual grandeur in images drawn
from the elements, images that are at once impressive and somewhat
disembodied. This grandeur is compromised by a world conceived not
as corrupt, like the world of Lear or Timon, but as trivial and petty-
minded, like that of Chapman's own comedies. In that world the
heroes participate, and they remain to some degree creatures of it, their
social actions and attitudes observed with a satiric eye. Yet the world
needs their heroism, even if it can find no satisfactory place for it. The
only attractive figure of order is Henry IV in the Byron plays, and even
he must resort to shabby means to bring down the hero, losing some
dignity in the process. His existence shows that Chapman, at least in
some phase of his thought, wanted to believe in a reasonable order
based on good temper and common sense. But the real excitement of
the plays lies with the heroes, and the centre of that excitement is their
demand for independence, for the primitive freedom of the first created
men before the structures of society closed in. Chapman's heroes

compromise that ideal themselves, but they never altogether destroy its attractiveness.

John Marston (1576–1634) began his career as a writer of scurrilous satires, and ended it as a priest. For the most part his plays are obviously closer to the first pole of his career than to the second; but through them we detect a certain yearning for order, a wish that there were something to believe in, that may not be unconnected with the last phase of his life. For the most part this is expressed ironically. The dedication to his comedy *Antonio and Mellida* (*c*. 1600) evokes serious values by addressing the dedicatee as 'honour's redeemer, virtue's advancer, religion's shelter and piety's fosterer'. But the dedicatee is Nobody. This comedy, and its tragic sequel *Antonio's Revenge* (*c*. 1600) are at first glance as chaotic as anything in Jacobean drama. They are full of striking stage effects: processions and spectacles, bloodstained corpses, offstage cries. The language is highly self-conscious:

> Fly, call, run, row, ride, cry, shout, hurry, haste,
> Haste, hurry, shout, cry, ride, row, run, call, fly;
> Backward and forward, every way about.
>
> (*Antonio and Mellida*, III. 2)

The vocabulary is full of ear-grating novelties:

> Straight chops a wave, and in his slifter'd paunch
> Down falls our ship, and there he breaks his neck,
> Which in an instant up was belk'd again.
>
> (*Antonio and Mellida*, I. 1)

The second play in particular deals with heavy matters – treachery and fidelity, murder and revenge, philosophy and despair – but leaves us persistently uncertain how seriously to take it. The villain Piero, for example, is an unstable mixture of cosmic evil and schoolboy mischief:

> Excellent, excellent! I'll conquer Rome,
> Pop out the light of bright religion;
> And then, helter skelter, all cocksure!
>
> (*Antonio's Revenge*, IV. 3)

In the final revenge action the hero includes among his allies the idiotic Sir Geoffrey Balurdo, whose buffoonery clashes persistently with the heated passions of the other characters.

One persistent factor seems to be a self-conscious preoccupation with style for its own sake:

> and thou and I will live –
> Let's think like what – and thou and I will live
> Like unmatch'd mirrors of calamity.
>   (*Antonio and Mellida*, II. 1)

The switch from the comedy of the first play to the tragedy of the second reflects not a darker vision but a conscious playing with genre. The conclusion of the first play, 'Here ends the comic crosses of true love' (v. 2), suggests a formula for comedy, as does Antonio's return from the dead, popping out of his own coffin. The Prologue to the second play is equally self-conscious: 'O now, methinks, a sullen tragic scene /Would suit the time with pleasing congruence'. We are constantly reminded that we are in a theatre watching a play:

> Now looks down providence
> T'attend the last act of my son's revenge.
> Be gracious, Observation, to our scene;
> For now the Plot unites his scattered limbs
> Close in contracted bands.
>   (*Antonio's Revenge*, v. 1)

This theatrical self-consciousness can be used to sabotage any attempt to take the characters or the action seriously. This is certainly the effect when Antonio sums up the second play, 'Never more woe in lesser plot was found' (v. 6). But the theatricality can also be used to make a point that is in its own way quite serious, if a bit hackneyed. In the Induction to the first play, the actor playing Antonio, having complained about his double role as hero and Amazon, receives this rebuke: 'Not play two parts in one? away, away; 'tis common fashion. Nay, if you cannot bear two subtle fronts under one hood, idiot, go by, go by, off this world's stage. O time's impurity!'

If this seems a little too easy, *Antonio's Revenge* gives the idea more interesting development through the character of Pandulpho Feliche, whose first reaction to his son's murder is to rise above it:

> Wouldst thou have me turn rank mad,
> Or wry my face with mimic action,
> Stamp, curse, weep, rage, and then my bosom strike?
> Away, 'tis apish action, player-like.
>   (I. 5)

If the world is a stage, even our natural emotions are the worked-up rant of a player, or so Pandulpho's Stoic philosophy claims. But later that philosophy breaks down, and appears itself to be a performance:

Man will break out, despite philosophy.
Why, all this while I ha' but played a part,
Like to some boy that acts a tragedy . . .
                              I spake more than a god,
Yet am less than a man.
(IV. 5)

Pandulpho's recognition of his childishness is given extra point by the
fact that this is a play for boy actors.[7] But if we think we have cut
through all the posturing and arrived at human reality in this
expression of grief, Antonio's reaction is disillusioning. At Pandulpho's
claim 'I am the miserablest soul that breathes' he demands indignantly,
'Who dare assume that but Antonio?' This competition of grief, in
which Antonio behaves like a prima donna who cannot bear to be
upstaged, suggests that the conflict between philosophy and passion
is simply a choice of performances. The role-playing we see in the
heroes of Shakespeare and Chapman acquires in Marston a satiric edge,
becoming a series of self-referential jokes about theatricality itself.

Finally Antonio, aided by Pandulpho, seeks relief in action. But his
revenge against Piero is so lurid, so gloatingly sadistic, that its main
purpose seems to be not justice or even revenge but merely a series
of striking effects appealing to the audience's own baser feelings. It
begins with Antonio's murder of Piero's son Julio, who is introduced
simply in order to be killed. Antonio admits the boy's innocence, and
killer and victim express mutual affection, but this only adds to the
sadism of the scene an unpleasantly contrived pathos: 'And you kill
me, 'deed, /I'll tell my father' (III. 3). Antonio tries to give the killing
ritual dignity by offering the boy's blood to Andrugio (Antonio's
father, whom he is avenging):

> I sprinkle round his gore
> And dew thy hearse with these fresh-reeking drops.
> Lo, thus I heave my blood-dyed hands to heaven,
> Even like insatiate hell, still crying 'More!
> My heart hath thirsting dropsies after gore.
> (III. 3)

The result, however, is not ritual dignity but coarse sensationalism.
This is carried over into the killing of Piero himself, a scene whose
manner is sufficiently indicated by the stage direction '*pluck out his
tongue and triumph over him*' (V. 5). We might like to think that Marston
is showing Antonio falling into evil in response to the evil of Piero.
But the play offers no encouragement to do so; Antonio is simply
reacting to his own demand for 'More!'. In the end, he and his fellow

killers compete for the glory of presenting 'this gory spectacle' (v. 6), receive praise for their virtue, and retire to a life of contemplation.

In the last analysis Marston seems content to leave the *Antonio* plays as a collection of striking effects, sometimes entertaining, sometimes lurid. But there is enough intelligence in them to prompt reflections on the absurdity of life and the littleness of man. In his best known play, *The Malcontent* (*c.* 1603), Marston returns to the idea of role-playing and gives it a more thoughtful, deliberate presentation. Antonio adopts a number of roles – Amazon, sailor, fool – but none of them is given sustained or consistent development. In *The Malcontent* the banished Duke Altofront appears throughout the play as the title character, Malevole, and while this role seems for much of the play to be his primary identity the fact that it *is* a role is never quite lost sight of. It allows a provisional quality, a final detachment, in every gesture he makes. As Malevole he is a satirist fascinated by the vices he attacks; as Altofront he is a good man who has lost power through lacking 'those old instruments of state, /Dissemblance and Suspect' (I. 4), but who can use the role of malcontent to meet a wicked world on its own terms. His sense of how that world operates, embodied in lines like 'Make me some rich knave, and I'll make myself /Some great man' (III. 3), occasionally expands into a cosmic disillusionment that recalls Hamlet's, though the tone is coarser:

> Think this – this earth is the only grave and Golgotha
> wherein all things that live must rot; 'tis but the draught
> wherein the heavenly bodies discharge their corruption; the
> very muck-hill on which sublunary orbs cast their
> excrements. Man is the slime of this dung-pit, and princes
> are the governors of these men.
>
> (IV. 5)

But the opening words, 'Think this', give this speech the quality of a consciously contrived set-piece.

Occasionally we glimpse the conservatism that is the basis of so much Jacobean satire, an outrage at the way the old decencies of life have been violated: 'I ha' seen a sumptuous temple turn'd to a stinking privy; more beastly, the sacredest place made a dog's kennel; nay, most inhuman, the stored coffins of long-dead Christians burst up, and made hog's troughs. *Hic finis Priami*'. (II. 5). Occasionally we catch glimpses of an older world, cleaner and more decorous than the 'Italian lascivious palace' (III. 2) that forms the setting of this and so many Jacobean plays. It is embodied in the chastity of the old duchess Maria, the loyalty of the captain of the citadel, the citadel itself, the sea-cliffs, and the hermit's cell to which the usurping Duke Pietro claims he has retired, where 'usherless the air comes in and out' (IV. 5). But Pietro, though truly repentant, is only disguised as a hermit; and the ending seems to be not so much the return of a good old order as simply the ending of a play. Malevole disposes briskly of fools, villains and allies, leaving us with a sense that none of it really matters:

You o'er joy'd spirits, wipe your long-wet eyes.
(*Kicks out Mendoza*) Hence with this man: an eagle takes
                                                    not flies.
(*To Pietro and Aurelia*) You to your vows; (*To Maquerelle*)
                                    and thou unto the suburbs.
(*To Bilioso*) You to my worst friend I would hardly give;
Thou art a perfect old knave. All-pleased live
(*To Celso and the Captain*) You unto my breast,
(*To Maria*)   thou to my heart.

The rest of idle actors idly part.
And as for me, I here assume my right,
To which I hope all's pleased. To all, good night .
                                                    (v. 6)

The same final detachment can be seen in *The Dutch Courtesan* (*c.* 1605). It deals with serious issues: the place of sex in love, the necessity of knowing sin, the impurity that taints even actions done for the best of motives. Malheureux has a theoretical view of sexual virtue and vice that has never been tested against experience; when he falls in love with a prostitute he is made, like Shakespeare's Angelo, to confront the corruption of his own nature. Like Angelo he is finally rescued, but only at the foot of the gallows. The tone, however, is lighter than that of *Measure for Measure*. Malheureux and the temptress Franceschina are broadly drawn, the intrigue is brisk and clever, and the play's lectures on sexuality have the quality of set-pieces, including a couple of paradoxical defences of prostitution that fit neatly into the tradition of mock-encomium, a stock rhetorical exercise in which the orator praises a trivial subject (I. 1, I. 2). In the subplot the trickster Cocledemoy plays a series of practical jokes on the vintner Mulligrub. He brings Mulligrub, like Malheureux, to the foot of the gallows, and makes an assignation with his wife while the victim awaits execution; but the tone even of this scene is farcical enough to justify Cocledemoy's final claim that he has done it all 'only *euphoniae gratia* – for wit's sake' (v. 3). It is Cocledemoy who speaks the Epilogue, describing the play as 'hurtless mirth' whose only claim to respect is skill of execution. That is not the whole truth, but it is a fair indication of the final lightness with which the play's serious themes are disposed of. *The Fawn* (*c*. 1604) is lighter still. The central character, Hercules-Faunus, is a double role in the manner of Altofront-Malevole, but he is playing a game in which the stakes are lower. The play ends with a comic trial in which characters who have exemplified folly and vice are sentenced to the Ship of Fools. Much of the misconduct is sexual, and the play's vision is steadied by the ease with which Marston dramatizes a positive sexual ideal in the princess Dulcimel. She is not the wax figure of a good woman Jacobean drama too often uses, but clever, warm and frank about her erotic feelings; and she inspires similar qualities in her intially cold lover, Hercules's son Tiberio.

Marston returns to sexual themes in his last complete tragedy, *Sophonisba* (*c*. 1606). Here we are at the opposite extreme from the instability of the *Antonio* plays; the control is if anything rather frigid. The saintly heroine is set up to win our admiration, but little else. Exalted and severe, the play is an important precursor of heroic tragedy; but in one respect it draws on Marston's work in satire and develops it with a new and powerful seriousness. The scenes involving the villain Syphax and his attempt on the heroine's chastity are as grotesque as anything in Marston, but this time the grotesquerie is controlled and pointed. In a characteristic sequence Syphax calls up the gruesome enchantress Erichtho to get Sophonisba to his bed, and finds himself in bed with Erichtho herself. The effect, half grim and half farcical, shows the irony of Syphax's position throughout the play: obsessed with his own power, he is in fact the victim of his own passions. In the Erichtho sequence Marston gives a more serious and protracted treatment to the image of the desecrated temple he used in *The Malcontent*. Erichtho herself describes it:

> Where statues and *Jove's* acts are vively limn'd
> Boys with black coals draw the veil'd parts of nature,
> And lecherous actions of imagined lust;
> Where tombs and beauteous urns of well dead men
> Stood in assured rest, the shepherd now
> Unloads his belly, corruption most abhorr'd
> Mingling itself with their renowned ashes,
> Our self quakes at it.
>   (IV. 1)

In his work as a whole Marston's manner veers between feverish excitement and flippant irony; he seems able to control his vision only when he can detach himself from it. But in this passage the indignation is sombre and measured, and suggests the conservatism, the sense of a good world violated, that lies behind so much Jacobean writing.

This conservatism is more deeply rooted in Marston than it is in

Chapman. Marston's aspiring rebel-heroes tend to be more ridiculous than heroic. Piero in the *Antonio* plays postures and struts like the child actor he literally is; the brusque dismissal of Mendoza in *The Malcontent* suggests that he is hardly worth bothering about. At the same time, while Chapman's satire on court life concerns itself with trivial squabbles and petty pride, Marston deals in lust and murder. He has what Chapman seems to lack: a sense of sin. But in his early work this expresses itself so luridly, and with such conscious theatricality, that the moral vision seems to mock itself and the world dissolves into a meaningless charade. In *The Malcontent* and *The Dutch Courtesan* the stylistic touch is light, and keeps the moral questions, urgent though they are, at some distance. There is probably no writer of the period who reminds us so persistently that we are in a theatre watching a play, or who is so given to trivialize matters his characters regard as important. Yet he could be serious, as *Sophonisba* shows; and to describe any play of his as simply a burlesque is to ignore moments when his posturing child actors put us in touch with a real yearning for order, and a real shock at its violation.

The 'Italian lascivious palace' of *The Malcontent* achieves its most vivid embodiment in *The Revenger's Tragedy* (*c.* 1606). The traditional attribution of this play to Cyril Tourneur rests on late and unreliable evidence; there has been a vigorous campaign to assign it to Middleton; but it seems best, in the present state of our knowledge, to treat it as anonymous. Whoever wrote it, it is not only one of the most brilliant plays of the period but in its themes and devices one of the most characteristic. The speech of the bastard Spurio, quoted earlier, exemplifies the cynical vitality of a court where the driving forces are lust and ambition. Spurio's reaction to his father's death is typical of both the play's vision and its manner:

> old dad dead?
> I, one of his cast sins, will send the fates
> Most hearty commendation by his own son;
> I'll tug in the new stream, till strength be done.
>
> (v. 1)

Spurio begins to plot against the Duke's son and successor, Lussurioso; at the end of the action he sets in motion, three claimants to the dukedom are despatched in as many lines. The main resistance to this corrupt world comes from the hero Vindice and his family, but even they are to some degree creatures of it. Vindice's father died 'of discontent, the nobleman's consumption' (i. 1); his brother Hippolyto takes pride in his ability to hold a place at court, by whatever means:

'Faith, I have been shov'd at, but 'tis still my hap /To hold by th'
duchess' skirt' (I. 1); and his mother Gratiana, tempted to work against
her daughter's chastity, admits that her 'poor estate' (II. 1) is her most
vulnerable point. There are glimpses of virtue as an old-fashioned value
associated with the country and scorned by the court. Chastity is 'that
foolish country girl' (II. 1). Vindice, introduced to Lussurioso as a
useful malcontent, amuses him with his old-fashioned rustic greeting,
'How don you? God you godden'. Lussurioso remarks, 'should we
[at court] name God / In a salutation, 'twould ne'er be stood on't'
(v. 2). In *As You Like It* the good, secure order that the court had lost
could be recovered in the Forest of Arden; in *The Malcontent*, in the
windswept cliffs above the palace. In each case we move outside to
recover old values. The old values – chastity, piety – are still there in
the countryside of *The Revenger's Tragedy*; but now they look passé,
and a little ridiculous.

Like Malevole-Altofront, Vindice deals with a corrupt world through
a disguise that allows him to meet it on its own terms, even participate
in it. Hippolito introduces him at court as the pandar Piato:

> This our age swims in him, and if time
> Had so much hair, I should take him for time,
> He's so near kin to this present minute.
>
> (I. 3)

In this capacity he is hired by Lussurioso to seduce Castiza, Vindice's
own sister. Though expressing his horror at the idea, he takes on the
assignment to see what will happen. He has the itch to tinker with
virtue till it breaks that we see in Anselmus in *The Second Maiden's
Tragedy*. Failing with his sister, he turns to their mother, urging her
to

>   think upon the pleasure of the palace;
> Secured ease and state; the stirring meats,
> Ready to move out of the dishes, that
> E'en now quicken when they're eaten;
> Banquets abroad by torchlight, music, sports,
> Bare-headed vassals, that had ne'er the fortune
> To keep on their own hats, but let horns wear 'em;
> Nine coaches waiting, – hurry, hurry, hurry.

To the urgency and excitement of the court he opposes the enclosed
sterility of virtue:

Who'd sit at home in a neglected room,
Dealing her short-liv'd beauty to the pictures,
That are as useless as old men, when those
Poorer in face and fortune than herself
Walk with a hundred acres on their backs,
Fair meadows cut into green foreparts – O,
It was the greatest blessing ever happen'd to women,
When farmers' sons agreed, and met again,
To wash their hands and come up gentlemen;
The commonwealth has flourish'd ever since.
Lands that were mete by the rod, that labour's spar'd,
Tailors ride down, and measure 'em by the yard;
Fair trees, those comely foretops of the field,
Are cut to maintain head-tires – much untold,
All thrives but chastity, she lies a-cold.

(II .1)

The satire, like that of Marston, is based on a conservative vision. The old stable values of land and property have been sacrificed to luxury and novelty; the court has eaten up the city. But there is also the suspicion, in both speeches just quoted, that Vindice, like Malevole, is a satirist fascinated by what he attacks, and his temptation of his mother and sister may be more in earnest than he cares to admit.

Certainly he is fascinated by his own cleverness. When in his own person he rebukes Gratiana for yielding to him, her sophistical excuse, 'No tongue but yours could have bewitch'd me so', is enough to silence him: 'I am confuted in a word' (IV. 4). When she adds, 'I'll give you this, that one I never knew /Plead better for, and 'gainst, the devil than you', he replies, simply, 'You make me proud on't' (IV. 4). The same pleasure at his own performance affects his handling of the revenge action. The old Duke has poisoned Vindice's beloved, Gloriana, whose skull, 'once the bright face of my betrothed lady' (I. 1), we find him contemplating at the beginning of the play. As Piato, he is hired by the Duke to supply a woman. He dresses the skull up, smears it with poison, and forces the Duke to kiss it. The skull in court attire is a powerful *memento mori*, an image of what lies behind the sensual luxury of the palace. The killing, during which the Duke is forced to watch his bastard son courting the Duchess, has a gloating sadism that recalls *Antonio's Revenge*, but the contrivance shows greater wit, and the manner of the Duke's death is morally appropriate in a way that the killings of Julio and Piero were not. At the same time, Vindice takes an amoral aesthetic pleasure in what he does, and in his use of the late Gloriana there is something obscene: he is once again acting as pandar to a woman he claims to love, and his flippant reference to her as 'the bony lady' (III. 5) shows how little this bothers him.

Vindice's disguise extends his opportunities for both intrigue and satiric commentary. But it may accidentally reveal his affinity with the people he attacks, and it certainly stimulates an amoral fascination with his own cleverness, which is finally his undoing. Role-playing has its dangers as well as its excitements. It can lead to loss of identity – one of the symptoms of the court's evil, as Castiza suggests in her witty pretence that she does not recognize the woman who is laying siege to her chastity: 'The world's so chang'd, one shape into another, /It is a wise child now that knows her mother' (II. 1). We recall Othello's pretence this he does not recognize Desdemona, but the tone here is more flippant. Vindice's role-playing traps him into working against himself: Lussurioso hires him to corrupt his own sister, and later (as Vindice) to kill himself (as Piato). Finally, unable to hide his own cleverness, Vindice reveals all to the new Duke Antonio: ''twas somewhat wittily carried, though we say it'. Antonio is not amused, and orders Vindice and Hippolito executed: 'Away with 'em! Such an old man as he; /You that would murder him would murder me' (v. 3).

Antonio's concern with his own skin makes him a less than dignified figure of authority at the end. He does not seem to justify Vindice's hope, 'Your hair will make the silver age again, /Where there was fewer but more honest men' (v. 3). Robbed of a final image of true order, we may think that the play is simply a closed circle of irony, a process whose only end is self-destruction. Certainly there is no serious confidence in divine authority. Heaven's thunder is a stage effect that is heard twice, on cue (IV. 2, v. 3). The most powerful image of divine judgement is, like the bony lady, a reminder of mortality: 'that eternal eye, /That sees through flesh and all' (I. 3). Such a vision does not discriminate. There seems to be, despite Gratiana's temporary lapse, an irreducible virtue exemplified in the two women of the play, summed up in their last scene. But it is an enclosed and static virtue, whose function is to protect itself: 'A virgin honour is a crystal tower, /Which, being weak, is guarded with good spirits' (IV. 4). Even Gratiana's final words. 'Be thou a glass for maids, and I for mothers' (IV. 4), are limited in their effect by the fact that the two women at this point are alone on stage. Their virtue is a private matter; if it is exemplary, it is not within the world of the play, but for the audience; no one else is watching. That takes it close to the merely theatrical.

It may be, however, that the merely theatrical is what finally matters to this author. The main distinction between Vindice and his enemies is not that he is morally superior but that he has greater panache. His pride in his own cleverness, though it trips him up, also allows him to rise above his death with a last flourish. When Hippolito seems annoyed at being caught, Vindice rebukes him: 'Thou hast no conscience; are we not reveng'd? /Is there one enemy left alive amongst those?' (v. 3). His last words, 'We're well, our mother turn'd, our sister true; /We die after a nest of dukes. Adieu' (v. 3), combine the throwaway style that is one of the play's characteristic effects with a tribute to the women's virtue and a satisfaction that the pattern of the action is complete. The social order is rotten, God is a series of stage tricks, and the final reality, as the play has insisted from the beginning when Vindice appeared cradling the skull, is death. But the ability to confront that death with style and courage is, for this dramatist, a virtue more interesting than the enclosed chastity of Castiza. When the old Duke is threatened, early in the play, he cravenly begs for 'days, /Nay, months' (II. 3) to confess his sins. Other characters die with curses, broken sentences or inarticulate groans; some have no chance to say anything. Vindice shows how it ought to be done. His self-command in the face of death may not be a final answer to the social and moral chaos of the world, and of his own nature; but it is an answer that works powerfully in the theatre. Webster was to show what more could be done with it.

Irus, Bussy, Antonio, Altofront, Vindice – the plays of this period tend to take as their starting-point a dispossessed hero. The dispossession that Lear, Coriolanus and Timon suffer in the course of the play is the point where these other characters begin. But instead of going outside society to confront or assert themselves, as Shakespeare's heroes do, these figures try to break back into it. It is a world they hate, envy and want to succeed in. They attack it with cleverness and panache, and with a gift for role-playing that allows them to meet the world's duplicity on its own terms. At times, however, it seems that style is all they really have. In that they are like the dispossessed intellectuals of Jacobean England: bright, educated men dependent for their security on a galling patronage system that involved constant begging. Like Hamlet they ate the air, promise-crammed, and it could be said of them, as of the heroes of Jacobean drama, that style was all they had. In the plays, however, the questions and aspirations of the dispossessed heroes are not just social but spiritual. Chapman draws images from the elements, Marston sees the world as a cosmic privy, and the author of *The Revenger's Tragedy* sardonically imagines comets and thunderclaps coming right on cue. The world in which their heroes are dispossessed and reduced to role-playing is not just the social world of the court. The sceptical gaze of Jacobean drama is also trained on the heavens.

Notes

1. Nicholas Brooke has argued that the norm of Elizabethan tragedy was 'violent moral farce' and that Shakespeare's tragedies are not central to the English tradition but exceptional. See *Horrid Laughter in Jacobean Tragedy* (Totawa, N.J., 1979), p. 7.

2. (London, 1607), sig. C$_3$r

3. One of the best comedies of the period is *Eastward Ho*, where an exemplary tale of the relative fates of an industrious and an idle apprentice is told in a straight-faced way that keeps the morality apparently intact, but with enough sly self-parody to give the devil his due and keep the play entertaining.

4. As Jonathan Goldberg points out, this turns him into a heroic statue. See *James I and the Politics of Literature* (Baltimore, 1983), pp. 160–61.

5. The Friar's speech concludes the play in the 1607–8 Quarto. The 1641 Quarto places the speech much earlier, and concludes the play with Tamyra's parting from Montsurry. The relative value of the two texts is still in dispute, but if the revision is Chapman's it suggests he found the early version too simple an assertion to be an adequate ending for the play.

6. See Elias Schwartz, 'Chapman's Renaissance Man: Byron Reconsidered', *Journal of English and Germanic Philology*, 58 (1959), 613–26 (p. 623).

7. In a seminal article R. A. Foakes argues that the boy actors would produce a burlesque effect throughout: see 'John Marston's Fantastical Plays: *Antonio and Mellida* and *Antonio's Revenge*', *Philological Quarterly*, 41 (1962), 29–32. Foakes's conclusions have been qualified by others, but his essential point needs to be kept in mind in any account of plays written for children's companies.

Chapter 7
Jonson

The figure of the dispossessed hero imagined by Chapman and Marston appears in the persona of the writer himself in the work of Ben Jonson (1572–1637). The stepson of a bricklayer, Jonson constructed a literary career for himself with a self-conscious effort for which there is no parallel in any other playwright of the period. That career took him into the highest circles. He wrote masques for the court of James I, and the addressees of his non-dramatic verse include important members of the aristocracy and the intelligentsia. Yet he remained always an outsider, guarding his independence, standing on his dignity, trying as much as possible to depend on his own abilities and not the precarious favours of the great. We can see a certain academic self-consciousness in the way he presents his work: the first edition of his Roman tragedy *Sejanus* includes notes on the sources, and *Every Man Out of his Humour* includes a scientific discussion of the nature of 'humours', the elements whose imbalance turns men into eccentrics. Jonson took unusual pains to shape his career as a whole, including publishing his collected works in the Folio of 1616. The career itself was an original one. The Virgilian model, beginning with pastoral and going on to epic, that was followed by Spenser, Milton and Pope in their different ways, was not for Jonson. He turned to pastoral only at the end of his life, in the unfinished *The Sad Shepherd*, and epic always lay outside his range. He made what looks like an attempt to define that range in the Prologue to the Folio version of *Every Man in his Humour* (1598, revised by 1616) an early comedy rewritten and transferred from its original Italian setting to an English one. The Prologue introduces not only the new version of the play but in a sense the Folio itself. It mocks the theatre of romance, chronicle and spectacle, and offers instead a drama that is not just an alternative but an ideal. Following Sidney,[1] Jonson declares it makes no sense

> To make a child, now swaddled, to proceed
> Man, and then shoot up, in one beard, and weed,
> Past three score years: or, with three rusty swords,

And help of some few foot-and-half-foot words,
Fight over York and Lancaster's long jars,
And in the tiring-house bring wounds to scars.
He rather prays, you will be pleas'd to see
One such, to day, as other plays should be.

What is offered, specifically, is a drama that will use the theatre
realistically, reflect the life around it, and keep to the decorum of its
genre:

deeds, and language, such as men do use,
And persons, such as Comedy would choose
When she would show an image of the times,
And sport with human follies, not with crimes.

This has something of the quality of the Preface to *Lyrical Ballads*,
the deliberate announcement of a new literature for a new age. There
is even a rough similarity in the turning away from artificial language
towards plain words and the observation of common life. As an
account of what Jonson actually did it has severe limitations, as we will
see. But it proclaims accurately enough a deliberate art. So, more casually, does the Prologue to *Volpone* (1606): 'Nor made he his play for
jests stol'n from each table, /But makes jests to fit his fable'. This care
shows, right from the beginning. The first version of *Every Man in his
Humour*, set in Florence, is lighter and fresher than the usual Jonson
manner; when he rewrote it he not only added London detail but made
the language tougher and more concrete. But already he is adding to
the stock comic types – clever servant, jealous husband – a striking
precision in the creation of folly. The would-be gentleman Stephano
announces, 'I have bought me a hawk, and bells and all; I lack nothing
but a book to keep it by' (I. 1). The would-be poet Mattheo can 'write
you your half score or your dozen of sonnets at a sitting' (II. 3), in
direct contrast to Jonson's own careful art.

The anatomy of folly is the purpose that links the three 'comical
satires' *Every Man out of his Humour* (1599), *Cynthia's Revels* (1600) and
Poetaster (1601). But as the term itself is peculiar and original, so each
play is a fresh experiment in the creation of theatrical machinery. *Every
Man Out*, in its printed version, which according to the title page is
longer than the stage version (and we can well believe it), is the most
elaborate. It comes complete with essays on the characters and running
commentary by two onstage spectators: Mitis, who questions the
author's decisions, and Cordatus, who defends them. In the process
Cordatus comments on everything from practical playwriting to the

nature of comedy itself. The play is presented by the satirist Asper, whose opening statement strikes a note more appropriate for tragedy:

> To see the earth, crack't with the weight of sin,
> Hell gaping under us, and o'er our heads
> Black rav'nous ruin, with her sail-stretch'd wings,
> Ready to sink us down, and cover us . . .
>
> (Induction)

This apocalyptic fury seems oddly out of key with the satire on silly obsessions that follows; but it may be that Asper himself is subject to the author's scrutiny. He not only presents the play but impersonates its principal character, the envious railler Macilente, who has, like the other characters, a humour that needs to be cured. The performance, like Vindice's impersonation of Piato, may reveal something about Asper. There is something dark and crazy, Jonson seems to suggest, in satire itself. The scenes with Cordatus and Mitis are exercises in self-approval on Jonson's part, but the handling of Asper-Macilente conveys a deeper self-examination.

Cynthia's Revels turns specifically to the follies of the court; there is again a long run-up to the main action, beginning with a squabble among the actors, a prologue, and a mythological fantasy that grounds the play's satire on self-love in the story of Narcissus. Here, and at Cynthia's entrance later in the play, there are touches of the graceful lyricism of which Jonson was a master, but which he rarely used in the theatre. The opening and closing sequences also suggest a revival of the style of Lyly (this is, like Lyly's plays, a work for a children's company) and give a touch of conservative nostalgic fantasy to the exposure and cure of the foolish courtiers. In Poetaster Jonson reaches farther back for an image of good social order, to the age of Augustus. Ovid, Horace, Virgil, Maecenas and Augustus himself share the stage with buffoons drawn from the literary scene of contemporary London, including thinly-veiled caricatures of Marston and Dekker. Out in the streets the fops and poetasters hold sway; in the palace, behind closed doors, Augustus, surrounded by his poets, listens to Virgil read from the Aeneid. When the fools invade this closed world they are seized and forcibly, literally, purged. All these plays set up elaborate machinery by which folly may be judged and corrected, but in each case the initial impression of confidence is eroded if we look more closely. Every Man Out turns the satiric vision on satire itself, Cynthia's Revels makes the cure a matter of fantasy, and there is a wild card in the carefully stacked deck of Poetaster. When Ovid stages a blasphemous mock-banquet of the gods and Augustus banishes him from Rome, the play allows a real question as to whether the authorities have been too heavy-handed.

The good society has an obvious place for satire and epic; but Ovid's irresponsible romanticism, though not part of Jonson's own artistic programme, has its own claims in the free republic of literature, and Jonson allows those claims a sympathetic hearing which complicates the play's final judgement of art and society.

Asper promised to show 'the time's deformity /Anatomiz'd in every nerve and sinew' (Induction), and all three comical satires do so at what may seem like excessive length. But they are also eclectic in manner and unpredictable in their final effect. Jonson saw that stern authority was needed to correct this world but he also saw, as *Poetaster* in particular makes clear, that the machinery that surrounds authority can be a threat to free men. This idea is the spark that ignites *Sejanus* (1603). To Jonson's contemporaries, the play must have looked like an aberration: a popular comic writer had produced an over-dignified, over-learned tragedy on a classical theme and had of course failed. But a longer view suggests that *Sejanus* is not only a masterpiece in its own right but a major act of consolidation that made the rest of Jonson's dramatic career possible. In the comical satires we wonder why Jonson is asking us to take the trivial vices of society so seriously; in the second act of *Sejanus*, when Livia discusses her husband's murder and her beauty treatments in the same even tone, we know. We sympathize with the early satire on the corrupters of poetry and, behind it, of language; but we see how deep the issue goes when we see an historian on trial for treason because he wrote of a good past; and when words are redefined by the jackals of the state so that 'a prince's power makes all his actions virtue' (III), 'To be a spy for traitors, /Is honourable vigilance' (IV), and the final orgy of judicial cruelty is accompanied by cries of 'liberty' (V). Unlike *Poetaster* the play preserves Roman historical decorum; but its political analysis is so acute, so universal in its import, that we are not surprised to learn Jonson was hauled before the Privy Council on a charge of treason. The Rome of Tiberius is a society shaped by fear into a permanent reign of terror. The satiric commentator Arruntius asks,

>   May I think,
> And not be rack'd? What danger is't to dream?
> Talk in one's sleep or cough? Who knows the law?
> May I shake my head without a comment? say
> It rains, or it holds up, and not be thrown
> Upon the Gemonies?
>   (IV)

At the centre sits Tiberius, whose style of government is summarized in the command, 'Let all depart that chamber, and the next' (II). Sejanus himself, his upstart henchman, provokes Tiberius to further cruelties by playing on his fears. But Tiberius's fears include Sejanus himself, and he hires the equally vicious Macro to destroy him, 'That, while two poisons wrestle, we may live' (III). Human relations are reduced in his mind to chemical reactions, and the only aim of his elaborate statecraft is his own survival. It is not out of mere deference to history that Jonson has him spend the last two acts of the play on an island.

For Macro, as for Sejanus himself, the final determinant is power. But Macro prospers while Sejanus is destroyed, not just because he is more crafty but because he is better at combining his power drive with the final servility needed for survival in Tiberius's world. When he is taken into the Emperor's service he gives a chilling vision of just what this means:

> Were it to plot against the fame, the life
> Of one with whom I twinn'd; remove a wife
> From my warm side, as lov'd as is the air;
> Practise away each parent, draw mine heir
> In compass, though but one; work all my kin
> To swift perdition, leave no untrain'd engine
> For friendship, or for innocence; nay, make
> The gods all guilty: I would undertake
> This, being impos'd me, both with gain and ease.
> The way to rise is to obey and please.
> He that will thrive in state, he must neglect
> The trodden paths, that truth and right respect;
> And prove new, wilder ways; for virtue, there,
> Is not that narrow thing she is elsewhere.
>
> (III)

The warmth of the marriage bed is felt briefly, then dismissed; and for the rest of the speech normal human relations, even piety to the gods, become abstractions. In the new language of politics, they lose in translation.

Macro redefines virtue; and while there is virtue of the old style in this world it is beleaguered and passive, able only to protest and die. The historian Cordus gives us a glimpse of a past in which free debate was allowed and if anyone was attacked by a writer 'he words with words reveng'd' (III). The authorities are sufficiently cowed by his defence to spare his life, but they burn his books. Others are either killed, or spared on the insulting grounds that they are not dangerous:

'there's Arruntius too, he only talks' (II). He talks to some purpose, we may think, and says much that the audience wants to hear; but the barb sticks all the same. In part, Jonson is allowing real misgivings about the possibility of effective virtue in this world; but he also wants to put the focus on the self-destructiveness of evil. This is connected with the achievement of the play's structure. In the early comedies there is a quality of relaxed observation. In *Sejanus*, however, there is a constant pressure of intrigue, a tightly spiralling action that antici-pates *Volpone* and *The Alchemist*. At the centre of this is the title character. Sejanus is, by Renaissance or any other standards, an odd choice for a tragic hero: a secondary figure, a parasite who aspires to be at the centre of power but never makes it. He began his career as a passive homosexual prostitute, 'the noted pathic of the time' (I) and ends it in a more terrible passiveness, torn apart by the mob. He has no great last speech of the sort Chapman allowed Bussy and Byron, figures whose political positions are similar but whose aspirations to tragic dignity can be taken more seriously. In fact Tiberius, though miles away on Capri, dominates the last act with a brilliantly tortuous letter to the Senate, one whose lightest turns of phrase produce massive reactions from the terrified Senators.

Sejanus's final helplessness is the more striking in that he does seem for a while to be a centre of energy. The pace of the first scene quickens noticeably as soon as he appears. When he discusses a possible poisoner with Livia and her physician Eudemus, he shows the brisk-ness and precision of the true Jonsonian intriguer:

> LIVIA
>
> But he must be wrought
> To th'undertaking, with some labour'd art.
> SEJANUS
> Is he ambitious?
> LIVIA   No.
> SEJANUS
> Or covetous?
> LIVIA
> Neither.
> EUDEMUS
> Yet, gold is a good general charm.
> SEJANUS
> What is he then?
> LIVIA
> Faith, only wanton, light.
> SEJANUS
> How! Is he young? and fair?

EUDEMUS

A delicate youth.

SEJANUS
Send him to me, I'll work him.

(II)

In Act Five Sejanus swells with *hubris* and like other Jacobean tragic heroes begins to recreate the world on his own terms:

Great and high,
The world knows only two, that's Rome and I.
My roof receives me not; 'tis air I tread:
And, at each step, I feel my advanced head
Knock out a star in heav'n!

(v)

In his later defiance of Fortune, whose chapel he wrecks when the statue averts its face, he may resemble Tamburlaine. But he has none of Tamburlaine's capacity to translate his dreams into action. Tiberius and Fortune do for him in short order. There is, however, no satisfaction in his punishment, for the agents of his destruction are superior only in power. Tiberius has if anything degenerated on Capri, playing demented games of sex and death, 'acting his tragedies with a comic face' (IV). His bidding in Rome is done by Macro, who seems poised to become 'a greater prodigy in Rome than he /That now is fallen' (v), by the craven Senate, and by the mob

who never yet
Knew why to love, or hate, but only pleas'd
T'express their rage of power.

(v)

The victims include Sejanus's innocent children, who are introduced into the play only to be slaughtered. Any thought that there might be tragic justice in Sejanus's fall is finally overwhelmed by sheer disgust:

And because our laws
Admit no virgin immature to die,
The wittily and strangely cruel Macro
Deliver'd her to be deflower'd and spoil'd
By the rude lust of the licentious hangman,
Then, to be strangled with her harmless brother.

(v)

Finally the searchlight of the play's satire is turned into the heavens:

> Dost thou hope, Fortune, to redeem thy crimes,
> To make amends for thy ill-placed favours,
> With these strange punishments?
>   (v)

If Jonson glanced at Aristotle's *Poetics* before writing *Sejanus* he put it back on the shelf. Almost the last note is a deliberate blocking of one of the expected tragic emotions: 'he that lends you pity is not wise' (v). *King Lear* and *The Duchess of Malfi* show that satire can be an important element in traditional tragedy; but in *Sejanus* the satire is so relentless and pervasive that Jonson seems to be creating a new form. *Volpone* (1606), in some respects a companion play, shows a similar expedition to a frontier, raising the question of how severe a comedy can be and still remain comic. In his Epistle Dedicatory Jonson defends the harshness of the final judgements on the grounds of instructive justice, but the play is more daring than that. It shows a world as dehumanized in its own way as Tiberius's Rome: driven by greed, men will disinherit their children and prostitute their wives. Corvino, offering his wife to Volpone, regards her as a possession to be used, and says so to her face:

>   What, is my gold
> The worse for touching? clothes, for being look'd on?
> Why, this's no more.
>   (III. 7)

He also prostitutes language: 'a pious work, mere charity for physic, /An honest polity to assure mine own' (III. 7). Celia is warned, if she does not co-operate in this act of charity,

>   I will buy some slave,
> Whom I will kill, and bind thee to him, alive;
> And at my window hang you forth; devising
> Some monstrous crime, which I, in capital letters,
> Will eat into thy flesh, with aqua fortis,
> And burning corsives, on this stubborn breast.
>   (III. 7)

The cruelty of the final judicial punishments has been fairly prepared. Corvino's viciousness is, however, a worked-up rage. Volpone and his parasite Mosca are more truly appalling: they toss off quite coolly lines like Volpone's gloating over the day's purchase, 'Why, this is better than rob churches yet, /Or fat by eating, once a month, a man' (I. 5) and Mosca's dismissal of low-class parasites who must learn to 'echo my lord, and lick away a moth' (III .1). These lines, not Corvino's, catch the essential tone of the play: what it evokes is not horror or disgust but startled laughter.

As Tiberius on Capri acts his tragedies with a comic face, so *Volpone* has been described as 'a kind of comic imitation of a tragedy, with the point of Volpone's hubris carefully marked'.[2] In one sense Volpone is a traditional comic intriguer, running a confidence game in which he pretends to be dying in order to play, for his own profit, on the greed of those who expect to be his heirs. But the play's bold opening takes us deeper than that:

> Good morning to the day; and next my gold:
> Open the shrine, that I may see my saint.
> Hail the world's soul, and mine. More glad than is
> The teeming earth to see the long'd for sun
> Peep through the horns of the celestial Ram,
> Am I, to view thy splendour darkening his;
> That lying here, amongst my other hoards,
> Show'st like a flame by night; or like the day
> Struck out of chaos when all darkness fled
> Unto the centre. O thou son of Sol,
> But brighter than thy father, let me kiss,
> With adoration, thee, and every relic
> Of sacred treasure in this blessed room.
> Well did wise poets, by thy glorious name,
> Title that age, which they would have the best;
> Thou being the best of things: and far transcending
> All style of joy in children, parents, friends,
> Or any other waking dream on earth.
>
> (I. 1)

In the closed world of his bedroom Volpone creates his own blasphemous religion, with its own creation myth, its own age of innocence (Volpone goes on to declare that, like men of the Golden Age, he lives without working) and its own redefined morality. In the dismissal of normal human values we catch an echo of Macro. But like Chapman's heroes Volpone is a character in a play and cannot finally live by solipsism. As he delivers this speech Mosca is standing by, watching and finally interrupting, embodying the intrigue in which Volpone is involved and anticipating its outcome by the way he keeps pulling the dramatic focus away from his master.

What finally fascinates Volpone is not wealth but power; he enjoys not just making his dupes pay but making them squirm, 'letting the cherry knock against their lips, /And draw it by their mouths, and back again' (I. 1). This leads him, like Vindice, to run his own head into the noose. Virtue of a traditional kind is represented by the heavenly Celia and the good Bonario; but the moment when Bonario rescues Celia as Volpone is about to rape her is a moment of explosive comedy, and in the ensuing trial their truth and innocence are simply overpowered by the 'multitude and clamour' (IV. 6) of the court. The Avocatori, like the Senators of *Sejanus*, sway in every breeze but settle most confidently on the side of wrong. The punishments they deal out in the end are superficially appropriate but tainted at the source. There is no effective virtue or authority here; Volpone must, and does, destroy himself, taking one risk too many till he is driven to reveal himself rather than lose everything to Mosca. The final couplet, spoken from the bench, is 'Mischiefs feed /Like beasts, till they be fat, and then they bleed' (V. 12). The intent seems to be to imagine an animal fattened for slaughter; the actual effect is of an exploding leech.

Yet Volpone shows in the end a resilience that contrasts strikingly with the passiveness of Sejanus. He delivers himself into the hands of the Scrutineo with a sporting flourish: 'since we all can hope /Nought but a sentence, let's not now despair it' (V. 12); and when they have done their worst he breaks through the dramatic illusion itself and appeals directly to the audience:

> The seasoning of a play is the applause.
> Now, though the Fox be punish'd by the laws,
> He yet doth hope there is no suffering due
> For any fact which he hath done 'gainst you;
> If there be, censure him: here he doubtful stands.
> If not, fare jovially, and clap your hands.
>
> (Epilogue)

If Volpone is 'doubtful' so, perhaps, are we. Jonson has analysed Volpone's fundamentally inhuman quality with merciless clarity; but he has also given him remarkable energy and panache, and has refused to show an effective moral opposition to him within the play. We are now the final authorities; having questioned the Scrutineo's judgement we are left wondering if we can do any better. Jonson's disconcerting gaze is finally turned on us.

Epicoene, or The Silent Woman (1609) does not take such an obvious risk with the comic form as does *Volpone*; but it still questions the traditional structure and values of comedy in a fundamental way. The central character, Morose, has a farcical aversion to noise that represents not just a medical problem but a basic rejection of social life. He wants to retreat to the only company he finds tolerable: 'All discourses, but mine own, afflict me; they seem harsh, impertinent and irksome' (II. 1). We might expect to see this misanthropy rebuked by a depiction of social life as perfectly tolerable, even attractive, embodied in something like the final dance of *As You Like It*, from which Jaques retreats in wry but tolerant amusement. That would be in keeping with comedy's usual interest in working towards a harmonized society. What we get instead is an image of social life that seems to be a projection of Morose's own worst fantasies: a torrent of meaningless noise generated by fops, fools and shrewish women. Marriage itself, the end of Shakespearean comedy, is treated with sharp and searching irony. Morose intends to marry, simply as a way of disinheriting his nephew Dauphine; he demands, and thinks he has got, a silent bride. But Dauphine and his friends contrive a raucous bridal feast whose purpose is not to celebrate the marriage but to torment the bridegroom; the bride herself, the title character, turns out to be a shrill-tongued scold and in the final revelation a boy in disguise. 'Epicoene' is the clearest embodiment of the sexual ambiguity that is one of the play's recurring themes,[3] and of the spirit of paradox that pervades it. The happy ending of this comedy is not a marriage but a divorce. The moments of 'celebration' suggest that it is possible to consolidate society only for the purpose of aggression. The most intelligent character in the play, Truewit, makes it clear in the first scene that he sees through the emptiness of social life but can think of nothing better to do than to join in. To the question, 'Why, what should a man do?' he replies,

> Why, nothing, Or that which, when 'tis done, is as idle.
> Hearken after the next horse-race, or hunting-match, lay
> wagers, praise Puppy, or Peppercorn, Whitefoot, Franklin;
> swear upon the white mare's party; spend aloud, that my
> lords may hear you; visit my ladies at night, and be able
> to give them the character of every bowler or better o' the
> green. These be the things wherein your fashionable men
> exercise themselves, and I for company.
>
> (I. 1)

What keeps this world going is not love, marriage or employment but simply 'company', and the daily improvisation of essentially meaningless activity.

London itself, crowded, noisy and bustling, is a principal character in the play.[4] The Rome of *Sejanus* and the Venice of *Volpone* seem dutifully researched; London in *Epicoene* is evoked. Outside Morose's silent chamber are bells, cannons, street cries, rattling wheels on cobblestones. *The Alchemist* (1610) is even more self-consciously a London play: 'Our scene is London, ''cause we would make known, /No country's mirth is better than our own' (Prologue). Like *Volpone*, the play is shaped around a confidence trick, run by the alchemist Subtle, the mock-captain Face, and Doll Common, whose name identifies her sufficiently. They use the house which Face, in his other incarnation as Jeremy the butler, is supposed to be keeping for its absent master. To this house as to a magnet come a wide variety of characters, all driven by the common desire for gain without effort. The grandest of them is Sir Epicure Mammon, who wants the philosopher's stone to 'turn the age to gold' (I. 4) but whose dreams really involve transformation of a more destructive kind:

> Where I spy
> A wealthy citizen, or rich lawyer,
> Have a sublim'd pure wife, unto that fellow
> I'll send a thousand pound to be my cuckold.

FACE

> And I shall carry it?

MAMMON

> No. I'll ha' no bawds,
> But fathers and mothers. They will do it best,
> Best of all others. And my flatterers
> Shall be the pure and gravest of divines,
> That I can get for money. My mere fools,
> Eloquent burgesses, and then my poets,
> The same that writ so subtly of the fart,
> Whom I will entertain still for that subject.
>
> (II. 2)

The power of turning base metal into gold will allow him to turn humanity into dross.

We recognize the flattening of value as a theme carried over from *Sejanus* and *Volpone*; but Mammon's fantasies are too empty to be truly sinister, and the general tone of the play is correspondingly lighter. It shares with its predecessors a tightly spiralling action: as the intrigue gets more complex, Face and Subtle's attempts to keep it under control are increasingly desperate and ingenious. As in *Epicoene*, the resolution involves an ironic treatment of the principles of comedy itself, including some of Jonson's own earlier practice. Surly, who sees through all the tricks, is in a line of descent from the clear-sighted commentators who see through the fools of the comical satires. But as a card-sharp himself, he is in no position to sound superior; and

when he tries to join in the game by making a play for the rich widow
Dame Pliant he fails through lack of initiative and concludes in chagrin,
'Must I needs cheat myself, /With that same foolish vice of honesty?'
(v. 5). The final business of the ending is not to expose the truth and
restore lost property as is usual in comedy but to keep the game going.
The master of the house, Lovewit, returns unexpectedly. Face takes
the occasion to expel his partners but their escape suggests that somewhere else a new version of the game will go on; and back in the
original house Face, retranslated into Jeremy, consolidates his own
position by enlisting Lovewit. Lovewit not only keeps the goods the
dupes have brought to his home but, with Face's help, wins Dame
Pliant. The traditional comic resolution of marriage, here as in
Epicoene, is treated sardonically. Pliant is at least as mindless as her
name suggests. She is already second-hand goods, as Face reminds
Subtle when they prepare to interrupt their own competition for her
by letting another customer use her first:

> It is but one man more,
> Which on's chance to have her; and, beside,
> There is no maidenhead to be fear'd or lost.
>
> (iv. 3)

We are reminded of the casual way they share Doll Common: 'The
longest cut at night, /Shall draw thee for his Doll Particular' (i. 1).
Lovewit, as he himself points out, is breaking comic tradition by
getting the girl:

> if I have outstripped
> An old man's gravity or strict canon, think
> What a young wife and a good brain may do:
> Stretch age's truth, sometimes, and crack it too.
>
> (v. 5)

The old man is supposed to stand in the way of the lovers, and be
defeated in the romantic ending. But this ending is anything but
romantic; it is a moment of consolidation in an ongoing game of
cheating, in which the audience itself is enlisted by Face's last words:

> I put myself
> On you that are my country: and this pelf
> Which I have got, if you do quit me, rests
> To feast you often, and invite new guests.
>
> (v. 5)

As a host issuing a dinner invitation, he is once again usurping his master's function; and it would be easier for us to respond in a simply festive spirit if we had not seen what happened to Face's other guests.

Jonson's definitive treatment of the sort of festive occasion on which you have to keep hold of your wallet is *Bartholomew Fair* (1614). The Fair itself, a great local occasion, is not only created with a wealth of detail but shaped into a concentrated vision of man's lower nature. One of its principal locations is Ursula's pig-tent, a comic hellmouth that also serves as privy and brothel, where 'you may ha' your punk, and your pig in state, sir, both piping hot' (II. 5).[5] The line embodies both the reductiveness of the Fair and its concentrated energy. Another important location is Leatherhead's puppet-booth, where the old romantic story of Hero and Leander is reduced to a vulgar London setting and performed by small wooden actors whose dialogue consists largely of shouting mindless abuse at each other. In this the puppet-play resembles one of the Fair's key activities, the game of vapours, *'which is nonsense. Every man to oppose the last man that spoke, whether it concern'd him, or no'* (IV. 4). A vapour is the steam you get when you boil a humour. As social life seems to dissolve into noise, physical life seems to dissolve into elements. Ursula declares, 'I am all fire and fat, Nightingale. I shall e'en melt away to the first woman, a rib again, I am afraid. I do water the ground in knots as I go, like a great garden pot, you may follow me by the SS I make' (II. 2). The gamester Quarlous imagines, 'he that would venture for't . . . might sink into her, and be drown'd a week, ere any friend he had could find where he were' (II. 5).

If no one literally sinks into Ursula, several characters who might have seemed to embody higher forms of life sink into the Fair. Justice Adam Overdo, spying in disguise on the 'enormities' of the Fair, seems to be trying to imitate the careers of such disguised authority figures as the Duke in *Measure for Measure* and Altofront in *The Malcontent*. But when he calls himself a 'mirror of magistrates' (v. 6) he unconsciously echoes the title of a famous book about the falls of great men. He is imprisoned in the stocks and finally silenced when his wife is revealed dressed as a prostitute. The Puritan Zeal-of-the-Land Busy takes to the Fair more naturally; he is a creature of appetite, who is introduced 'fast by the teeth, i'the cold turkey-pie, i'the cupboard' (I. 6) and who is easily induced to go to the pig-tent, where he will 'eat exceedingly, and prophesy' (I. 6). Grace Wellborn has apparently no interest in the Fair: 'there's none goes thither of any quality or fashion' (I. 5) but once there she takes to it in her own way. In one of Jonson's most ironic treatments of the comic motif of courtship Grace, fought over by Quarlous and Winwife, makes herself the prize in a game of chance; we remember Face and Subtle drawing cuts for

Doll Common. Quarlous and Winwife seem prepared to settle the affair as between gentlemen, with drawn swords; Grace instead has each man write a name on her table-book, the issue to be settled by the first stranger to come along, who will be asked to mark one of the names. Significantly, the men take their names from tales of romance: Argalus from the *Arcadia*, Palemon from *The Two Noble Kinsmen* (the Shakespeare-Fletcher adaptation of *The Knight's Tale* in which the two heroes fight a tournament to settle their rivalry over the heroine). Jonson uses memories of romance for their obvious ironic value; and romance seems very remote indeed when Quarlous, having lost Grace, picks up the Puritan widow Dame Purecraft as a consolation prize: 'Why should not I marry this six thousand pound, now I think on't?' (v .2).

Jonson's ending is, however, celebratory in its own way. Overdo, having been advised by Quarlous, 'remember you are but Adam, flesh and blood! you have your frailty, forget your other name of Overdo, and invite us all to supper', issues what looks like a general invitation: 'I will have none fear to go along' (v. 6). The incorrigible innocent Bartholomew Cokes, who has in the course of the Fair lost 'myself, and my cloak and my hat, and my fine sword, and my sister, . . . and Mistress Grace (a gentlewoman I should ha' married) and a cutwork handkercher she ga' me, and two purses' (IV. 2), insists on bringing the puppets along too: 'we'll ha' the rest o' the play at home' (v. 6). Bartholomew, who insists that the Fair is *his* Fair because it bears his name, is given the last word Jonson usually reserves for the most successful or intelligent character in the play. In a final overturning of authority, the fool who has simply *enjoyed* the Fair despite his losses, and who is willing to prolong the party indefinitely, is allowed to have an odd wisdom of his own.

Jonson's drama is only part of a literary career that included court masques, non-dramatic poetry, criticism and table-talk. He set high standards for himself as a literary artist, and he required his audiences to rise to the often considerable demands he made on them. In his texts for the great masques he wrote for King James he tried to turn the genre from congratulatory spectacle to a means of educating the court by showing it a seriously-conceived vision of what it ought to be. When it became clear that the court was more interested in the stage spectacles devised by Inigo Jones, he was furious. Idealistic and censorious, Jonson could seem a forbidding character; but like Adam Overdo he had his frailty; and like Overdo he was finally as willing to throw a party as to deliver a lecture. *Bartholomew Fair* represents that side of his art most clearly.

It also represents in its most vivid and amusing form the mistrust of authority that makes Jonson in the long run a less conservative writer than Shakespeare or even Marston. Three figures of authority – Overdo, Busy, and Bartholomew's keeper Humphrey Waspe – end up side by side in the stocks, a satisfying picture of a world turned upside down. Initially, Jonson shaped comedy into an instrument of moral analysis and tragedy into satire. But in the process he showed his own rebellious spirit, resisting the popular and traditional forms that lay to hand; and, like the writers of Jacobean tragedy, he allows his rebels style and panache. Volpone is the key example: like Malevole and Vindice he is a role-player, exposing and correcting the vices of the world. But while they operate from a centre of injured virtue that is rendered insecure by their own fascination with the world they attack, Volpone's centre is his own unabashed, criminal desire for power, and in that he is secure. Clear-eyed about himself, he is masterly in exposing the world around him. The sheer variety of his roles, the completeness with which he not only fools but exposes his dupes, command our admiration. The cheaters of The Alchemist have a similar function: in the enclosure of Lovewit's house they create a series of parodies of the outside world, and the seemingly respectable figures who come from that world have their own desires revealed by their participation in the charade. Official morality lays a heavy hand on Volpone; but it is not clear that we are to approve of it, and the final touch of order in The Alchemist and Bartholomew Fair is much lighter. Jonson's rogues, including the villains of Sejanus, parody the normal world and corrupt its language. But they do so not out of any insecurity or uncertainty about themselves. They know what they want: power, money and pleasure. They are, like Jonson, outsiders; and Jonson at once judges them and gives them some of his own creative energy and critical acumen.[6]

Notes

1. See Sir Philip Sidney, An Apology for Poetry, edited by Forrest G. Robinson (Indianapolis, 1970), pp. 75–76.

2. Northrop Frye, The Anatomy of Criticism (Princeton, 1957), p. 165.

3. See Edward Partridge, The Broken Compass (London, 1958), pp. 161–77.

4. See L. G. Salingar, 'Farce and Fashion in The Silent Woman', Essays and Studies, 20 (1967), 29–46.

5. On the main symbolic locations of the Fair, see R. B. Parker, 'The Themes and Staging of Bartholomew Fair', University of Toronto Quarterly, 39 (1970), 293–309.

6. Jonson's later plays are discussed in Chapter 14.

Chapter 8

Middleton

Jonson shows a world that is, paradoxically, both dehumanized and vital. Whatever has happened to normal human relations, the central characters have an imaginative flair or at least an animal energy that give the plays scale and excitement. The early London comedies of Thomas Middleton (1580–1627) show a similar flattening of value, but the scale is smaller, the tone is cooler, and the characters' appetites meaner. They engage in intrigues for money, property and sex. They are role-players, like other principal characters of Jacobean drama. But while Shakespeare's tragic heroes are trying to construct significant identities in the face of chaos, Jonson's intriguers to express their own creative energy, and the heroes of *The Revenger's Tragedy* and of Marston's plays to meet a corrupt and duplicitous world on its own terms, role-playing in Middleton is more narrowly functional, a technical deception carried out as part of an intrigue for material gain. Jonson's London is a place where eccentrics jostle for attention, where social relations and their breakdown can be examined in depth; Middleton's London is a place where people make deals. The deals involve commodities or human beings treated as commodities. The scale is frequently small, as in *Your Five Gallants* (*c.* 1607), where the competitive trickery centres on such items as chains and cloaks – petty larceny at best. The principal aim of the characters in the *The Family of Love* (1602) is getting sex: but their desires are not so much grand passions as itches that need to be scratched. In *The Phoenix* (*c.* 1603), set ostensibly in Ferrara but suggesting a stylized London beneath the Italian names, we see the reduction of people to commodities when the Captain sells his wife and the justice Falso demands the sexual favours of his niece in order to save himself the trouble and expense of marriage. Occasionally, as in Jonson's comical satires, a stylized judgement will be passed on this world: the title character of *The Phoenix*, one of the disguised authority figures we meet so often in Jacobean drama, ends the play with a round of exposures and punishments. In *Your Five Gallants* the hero Fitzgrave exposes the rogues in a masque sequence that recalls a similar scene in *Cynthia's Revels*.

Game-like and consciously theatrical, these judgements do not seriously disturb the cool tone of the plays as a whole. Nor does the intrusion of the romantic 'golden' style of the lovers Gerardine and Maria into the low bawdry of *The Family Love*; the possibility that they represent a higher ideal of love is cancelled by the practical way Gerardine gets what he wants, tricking his way into Maria's room and getting her pregnant. Apparently out to judge his world, like Phoenix, Gerardine is really a part of it.

In other plays, including some of Middleton's best, the relation between cynical observation of the human animal and serious moral judgement is more problematic.[1] At times it seems that the more lively and engaging the comedy the more violent the recoil to moral disgust. *A Trick to Catch the Old One* (1605) presents one of the stock plots of the period, repeated with variations in Barry's *Ram Alley* and Massinger's *A New Way to Pay Old Debts*. A young prodigal manages by trickery to regain his lands from his usuring uncle, and while getting a good marriage for himself settles his former mistress by a trick marriage with another usurer. Youth triumphs over age, the country over the city, the old aristocratic life over the new commercialism. But it is all done in a surprisingly good-tempered manner, with no hard feelings at the end. In the subplot, on the other hand, we see the nasty life and miserable death of Dampit, who makes a shady living out of the law; the tone of his scenes is considerably darker. The usurers of the main plot are seen in action, to be enjoyed as players in a game. Dampit is relatively static, and is simply observed with distaste.

An equivalent and more puzzling split occurs in *A Mad World, my Masters* (1605). The main plot, like that of *A Trick to Catch the Old One*, is a youth-versus-age intrigue in which the tone is if anything more genial and the final distribution of prizes more even-handed. Through most of the play Follywit gulls his grandfather by a series of clever if criminal devices but is finally exposed and tricked into marrying the old man's courtesan. The grandfather himself, though not without a streak of meanness, exemplifies in his surface manner the geniality of his name, Sir Bounteous Progress. While the more simply effective hero of *Trick* is called Witgood, Follywit's double name expresses his double nature. The principal character of the subplot also has a double name. Penitent Brothel, that reflects this time a double vision in the plot as a whole. His successful attempt to sleep with Mistress Harebrain despite the efforts of her jealous husband is the occasion for bawdy, cynical comedy; then Penitent is suddenly transformed. He is driven into moral self-revulsion by reading a religious book, and by a succubus who appears in the form of Mistress Harebrain, driving him to wonder, 'What knows the lecher when he clips his whore /Whether

it be the devil his parts adore' (IV. 4). After its bawdy beginnings the
subplot comes to a sombre moral conclusion. But the tone of the
conclusion is a little uncertain, as we see in the speech that introduces
Penitent's reformation:

> Nay, I that knew the price of life and sin,
> What crown is kept for continence, what for lust,
> The end of man, the glory of that end
> As endless as the giver,
> To dote on weakness, slime, corruption, woman!
> What is she, took asunder from her clothes?
> Being ready, she consists of hundred pieces
> Much like your German clock, and near allied:
> Both are so nice they cannot go for pride,
> Beside a greater fault, but too well known,
> They'll strike to ten when they should stop at one.
>
> (IV. 1)

Here as elsewhere in Middleton repentance is triggered in part by a fear
of punishment; but the real difficulty is the way it is linked with stock
jokes about overdressed and lecherous women. If Middleton wants us
to take a new, serious view of these characters he is going an odd way
about it, raising the suspicion that he is either being ironic or simply
writing for effect.

The result of combining intrigue comedy with moral revulsion,
then, is instability. *Michaelmas Term* (1605) takes the route that will be
more characteristic of Middleton's major plays, keeping the tone
consistent and providing judgement through close analysis and
revealing juxtaposition. The principal character of the Induction,
Michaelmas Term himself, promises 'only . . . those familiar accidents
which happen'd in town, in the circumference of those six weeks
whereof Michaelmas Term is lord'. But he also suggests that this will
be more than just a slice of life:

> Lay by my conscience,
> Give me my gown, that weed is for the country;
> We must be civil now, and match our evil;
> Who first made civil black, he pleas'd the devil.

The play shows a systematic process by which characters from the
country, driven by greed and ambition, come to the city and are
destroyed by it. Middleton does not give a clear sense of what the
country is like, as Shakespeare did in *As You Like It* and Brome would
do in *A Jovial Crew*. Both these writers dramatize the country on stage

as a place of order and old-fashioned hospitality, where reciprocal social ties are maintained in a genial way. For Middleton in *Michaelmas Term* the country is simply the place his characters come from. It is defined not so much by what it is as by what the characters lose when they come to London: property, security, and moral coherence. In some cases their very identities are wiped out: Andrew Gruel becomes Andrew Lethe; his own mother quite literally does not know him, and he hires her as a servant. At the end of the play he can save himself from punishment only by acknowledging her and therefore, by implication, acknowledging himself. The effect is deepened by the parallel story of the Country Wench, who never does have a name; her father comes to the city to save her from the prostitution into which she has been lured by her desire to be a gentlewoman, and serves her in disguise without once recognizing her. In this case, though we expect the recognition scene that traditionally ends a comedy, we do not get it.[2]

The principal country gull is the appropriately named Easy. Like others who come to London he is concerned with being in the fashion, and is susceptible to such advice from city rogues as 'Then, for your observances, a man must not do so much as spit but within line and fashion. I tell you what I ha' done: sometimes I carry my water all London over, only to deliver it proudly at the Standard; and do I pass altogether unnoticed, think you?' (II. 1). When he enters into a ruinous bond with the usuring linen-draper Quomodo it is 'for fashion's sake' (II. 3). Quomodo himself, who operates an elaborate confidence game to cheat Easy of his land, seems to be the centre of the play's vision of London. But some curious ironies surround him. While the country gulls have dreams of London, Quomodo has dreams of the country:

> Oh, that sweet, neat, comely, proper, delicate parcel of
> land, like a fine gentlewoman i'th' waist, not so great as
> pretty, pretty; the trees in summer whistling, the silver
> waters by the banks harmoniously gliding. I should have
> been a scholar; an excellent place for a student, fit for my
> son that lately commenc'd at Cambridge, whom I now
> have plac'd at the Inns of Court. Thus we that seldom get
> lands honestly, must leave an heir to inherit our
> knavery.
> (II. 3)

His pastoral fantasy is a shopkeeper's dream of the good life. But more revealing in the long run is his desire to pass the land to his son. He knows that he is part of a life of process and change, and that he will have to get what he gets by knavery. But this self-awareness is ironically matched with a conservative streak; he wants to reinstitute in his own family the principle of inheritance he is violating in cheating Easy.

This accounts for Quomodo's apparently odd behaviour in the last movement of the play. Like Volpone he spoils his own victory by taking one risk too many: he pretends to die, to see how his son Sim will treat his inheritance. He knows the world well enough to fear what may happen, and to want to prevent it: 'I see before mine eyes that most of our heirs prove notorious rioters after our deaths, and that cozenage in the father wheels about to folly in the son' (IV. 1). He also wants to test the loyalty his wife and daughter will display after his death. Connected with his dream of the country is his dream of a happy family:

> A fine journey in the Whitsun holidays, i'faith, to ride
> down with a number of citizens and their wives, some
> upon pillions, some upon sidesaddles, I and little
> Thomasine i'th' middle, our son and heir, Sim Quomodo,
> in a peach-colour taffeta jacket, some horse-length or a
> long yard before us – there will be a fine show on's, I can
> tell you – where we citizens will laugh and lie down, get
> all our wives with child against a bank, and get up
> again.
>   (IV. 1)

This introduces the speech in which he plans his fake death to test his family and secure his inheritance; the two are clearly connected in his mind: 'I am jealous of this land as of my wife' (IV. 1). But the family he actually has is not the one he dreams of; it belongs to the fragmented world of self-seeking individuals in which he himself operates. The stage direction for his funeral specifies '*a counterfeit corse brought in . . .* Thomasine *and all the mourners equally counterfeit*' (IV. 4). Quomodo, however, is fooled by his wife's mourning; like any gull he sees what he wants to see. He then tries to contrive a comic recognition scene by writing his name on a document that, he realizes too late, has the effect of transferring all his land back to Easy. Once again a traditional comic device is ironically twisted. In fact Quomodo's wife cannot wait to claim Easy as her second husband, his daughter defies his wishes in her marriage, and Sim is cheated by Quomodo's own henchman Shortyard. In a scene parallel to the exposure of Andrew Lethe, Quomodo can stave off total ruin only by revealing his identity, and he can reveal his identity only by admitting his crimes.

Quomodo is master of the commercial world, which Middleton conceives as a world of cheating. He fails because he expects something more, wanting to restore the lost security that he and his kind have helped to destroy. In *A Chaste Maid in Cheapside* (1613) no one seems to expect even that much. This is Middleton's most comprehensive picture of human relations reduced to commodity transactions. Sir Walter Whorehound buys sex from Mistress Allwit by supporting the family, and Allwit buys security by going along with the arrangement. Touchwood senior, who cannot have sex without getting his partner pregnant, hires himself out as a fertility agent to the barren Sir Oliver and Lady Kix. And so on. The imagery is appropriately reductive. Sir Walter has brought his Welsh mistress to town to get her married off, or as he puts it, 'to turn thee into gold, wench' (I. 1). Touchwood junior puts it another way, declaring Sir Walter has 'brought up his ewe-mutton to find /A ram at London' (I. 1). Allwit, supporting himself by selling his wife, lives 'as other trades thrive, butchers by selling flesh, /Poulters by vending conies, or the like, coz' (IV. 1). A christening becomes an orgy of drunkenness and gluttony; a wench disposes of an unwanted baby by pretending it is a piece of meat and leaving it with two Promoters who are checking for violations of Lent. With all this behind us, when we come to the final scene and the play's young lovers, who have pretended to die, pop out of their coffins and are told, 'Here be your wedding sheets /You brought along with you' (V. 4) the association of shroud with wedding sheets does not suggest new life coming out of death so much as the climax of another vision of London, Blake's marriage hearse.

The lovers themselves, like other young lovers in Middleton, provide only a token romantic interest and a tone that is hardly romantic at all. Touchwood junior tells Moll,

> Turn not to me
> Till thou mayst lawfully; it but whets
> My stomach, which is too sharp-set already.
>
> (I. 1)

There is a chance for pathos when Moll is dragged away from her lover and physically abused by her cruel mother. But the pathos is cut across by farcical comedy as Moll's brother Tim offers to guard her with Henry V's sword borrowed from Westminster, and as she languishes near death competes with his tutor in a race to produce the first epitaph. There is a chance for moral judgement when Sir Walter, wounded in a duel, repents and denounces the Allwits. But his repentance, unlike that of Penitent Brothel, who converts his lover and her

husband, has no effect on anyone else, and since it is accompanied by
his financial ruin the Allwits simply get rid of him. This move is
accompanied by Allwit's bland rebuke, 'I thought you had been
familiar with my wife once' (v. 1). If there is a judgement here it is
the implicit judgement of Middleton himself, running through the
whole play: the characters, smug and self-confident as they appear, are
in fact the slaves of their own need for sex and material security, and
are not nearly so clever as they think they are. Allwit is the key
example: he boasts of the secure arrangement he enjoys with Sir
Walter, but any threat that Sir Walter could break the contract reduces
him to panic. In the end, the characters are content with survival. The
Yellowhammers, facing the apparent death of their daughter Moll,
worry briefly about what the neighbours will think but take comfort
from the fact that they still have a son to marry off: 'We'll not lose
all at once, somewhat we'll catch' (v. 2). The Allwits take stock and
decide to set up elsewhere; and their arrangement with Sir Walter looks
like being repeated by Touchwood senior and the Kixes: 'Get children,
and I'll keep them' (v. 4).

Middleton's city comedies, then, present a low view of humanity.
When he turns to tragedy in *Women Beware Women* (*c.* 1621) the effect
is not very different, and the result is a tragedy that has many affinities
with satiric comedy: the wide focus, quite unlike Shakespeare's concentration on a single hero; the heavy irony; the lack of any compensating
dignity. Even the title could be a comedy title: it identifies a principle,
not a character. The play's initial view of women seems to be, as in
A Chaste Maid in Cheapside, that they are commodities for men to trade
in. The Ward, about to marry Isabella, looks her over as though he
were buying a horse. One can understand her view of marriage: 'men
buy their slaves, but women buy their masters' (I. 2). At the start of
the play Leantio, a merchant's factor, has returned from a business trip
with a new wife, as one might return with an expensive souvenir; he
and his mother discuss Bianca in the third person, in her presence, as
though she were part of the furniture. He assumes that if he does not
lock her up he will lose her:

> 'tis great policy
> To keep choice treasures in obscurest places:
> Should we show thieves our wealth, 'twould make 'em
> bolder. (I. 1)

In turn, Middleton's depiction of the freedom women can enjoy is not
encouraging. The cynical widow Livia, the play's chief intriguer,
remarks that man

> tastes of many sundry dishes
> That we poor wenches never lay our lips to:
> As obedience forsooth, subjection, duty, and such
>   kickshaws,
> All of our making, but served in to them.
> And if we lick a finger then sometimes,
> We are not to blame; your best cooks use it.
>
> (I. 2)

The alternative to deprivation is furtive greed on a small scale. Livia's speech finds an echo when Leantio's mother, invited to a state banquet, takes two handkerchiefs 'to pocket up some sweetmeats' (III. 2).

For Isabella the alternative to marriage with the loutish Ward is an incestuous affair with her uncle Hippolito. Initially reluctant, she is tricked into compliance by Livia's claim that she is illegitimate and so it is not really incest. Her scruples vanish at once, and her appetite emerges in a speech that echoes Livia's view of women as cooks:

> I did but chide in jest; the best loves use it
> Sometimes, it sets an edge upon affection.
> When we invite our best friends to a feast
> 'Tis not all sweetmeats that we set before them,
> There's somewhat sharp and salt, both to whet appetite,
> And make 'em taste their wine well. So methinks
> After a friendly, sharp, and savoury chiding
> A kiss tastes wondrous well; and full o'th' grape.
>
> (II. 1)

Bianca is liberated from her marriage by an adulterous affair with the Duke of Florence, who is so impressed with her beauty he is even prepared to believe women have souls (III. 3). Bianca's fall, like Isabella's, is engineered by Livia. In a famous passage of *double entendre* Livia plays chess with Leantio's mother while the Duke seduces Bianca offstage. She has been led away on the pretext of viewing Livia's art collection; later she remarks sourly that she has seen 'the monument and all' (II. 2). Her sardonic acceptance of her fate, 'Come poison all at once' (II. 2), is as swift as Isabella's surrender. She quickly becomes impossible to live with, complains about the furnishings of Leantio's house, and finds no difficulty settling into her new role as the Duke's mistress. She blames her present behaviour on early repression:

> 'tis not good, in sadness,
> To keep a maid so strict in her young days;
> Restraint breeds wand'ring thoughts, as many fasting days
> A great desire to see flesh stirring again.
>
> (IV. 1)

But she is not so much liberated as lost. Leantio brought her, she thought at first, to a new life in Florence: 'I'll call this place the place of my birth now, /And rightly too: for here my love was born' (I. 1). At the end of the play, surveying the bloodbath in the court, she is simply bewildered: 'What make I here? These are all strangers to me' (V. 2). She tries for a *liebestod*, drinking from the 'cup of love' that has poisoned the Duke, and she draws a pat moral that reflects the play's title: 'Like our own sex we have no enemy, no enemy!' (V. 2). But what registers most strongly is the sense of lost identity; she is the tragic equivalent of Lethe and the Country Wench in *Michaelmas Term*.

Livia not only has more wit but, as a widow, more freedom. She uses her wit, however, to trap other women into sexual relationships. In the case of Isabella, she is acting from affection for her brother Hippolito; she refers to his 'ease' (II. 1) as though his incestuous desire were simply a physical pressure to be released. But while she takes pride in her 'craft t'undo a maidenhead' (II. 1), she becomes a helpless victim of her own desires when she first sets eyes on, of all people, Leantio. The small-minded businessman and the sophisticated society lady make an incongruous couple, and her temptation of him is fumbling: 'I'm cunning in all arts but my own love' (III. 3). Leantio himself has just been bought off by the Duke, and has started to complain the price is too low. Livia offers a chance of better maintenance, which he takes:

> LIVIA
> Do you but love enough, I'll give enough.
> LEANTIO
> Troth then, I'll love enough, and take enough.
> LIVIA
> Then we are both pleased enough.
> (III. 3)

The closest the play takes us to tragic recognition is the wry, sad awareness this ill-assorted couple shows of the smallness of their own satisfactions. This is paralleled in a later scene in which Leantio and Bianca maliciously congratulate each other on their new clothes.

As usual, Middleton's speciality is cynical observation. And there is little doubt that this time his scrutiny includes the characters' attempts to moralize about their lives. Leantio's self-congratulating speeches about the advantages of marriage amount to saying that it keeps one from adultery and provides plenty of opportunities for legal sex. Hippolito holds back from incest because of divine decree, and expects to be rewarded for his abstinence: his words, 'You see my honesty; /If you befriend me, so' (I. 2) are, I think, delivered with an eye cocked up to heaven. When Isabella offers herself he takes her.

Later he kills Leantio not so much because the tradesman is sleeping with Livia as because he is bragging about it. The most spectacular moral intervention comes from the Duke's brother, the Cardinal, who delivers a powerful tirade against adultery. He dwells on the responsibility of great men to set a good example, but his clinching argument is that sin leads to damnation: 'How dare you venture on eternal pain, /That cannot bear a minute's reprehension?' (IV. 1). His rhetoric is impressive, his intentions undoubtedly sincere; yet we notice, not for the first time, that Middleton's characters even at their most religious cannot get beyond Christianity as a superior form of fire insurance. The Duke repents and promises reform; but we learn in his ensuing soliloquy that his reform will consist of having Leantio killed so that he can marry Bianca and bed her legally, with the added advantage that a brief abstinence will make the pleasure 'seem new, fair, and fresh' (IV. 1). The Cardinal, to his credit, is not impressed. But he gives in when Bianca, having graduated from mistress to wife over the corpse of her husband, lectures him for lack of charity and for not appreciating her conversion. The Cardinal's moralizing, like Sir Walter Whorehound's, makes no headway in the world.

Final judgement is done by the characters on each other, as the masque to celebrate the Duke's wedding turns into an occasion for multiple murder. The death-in-a-masque device is one of the clichés of Jacobean drama, and writers were constantly looking for tricks to keep it fresh. Few go as far as Middleton in this play, and the result is wildly overelaborate. But the emblematic details are significant: Cupid's arrows, gold, cups for the bride and groom, incense for the marriage goddess – all are fatal. Given what love and greed have led to in this world, and given the kind of marriage that is being celebrated, we can see a connection between the masque and the play as a whole. It is also appropriate that Livia, arranger of illicit sexual affairs, should preside as Juno in her aspect as marriage goddess. There is a more general level of parody as well: the masque evokes a pastoral, mythical world utterly at odds with the coarse reality of the characters' lives; the story of a nymph unable to decide between two suitors recalls the story of Sidney's entertainment for Elizabeth, *The Lady of May* (*c.* 1578). If conventional morality is stymied, conventional romance is debunked. The ensemble quality of the scene also means that no character, not even Bianca, is put in the intense light we usually see fixed on a tragic hero. We are watching the fate of a group, a fate best summarized by Hippolito: 'Lust and forgetfulness have been amongst us, /And we are brought to nothing' (V. 2). The link with Andrew Lethe and other characters of *Michaelmas Term* is revealing. This is the tragic vision of a writer trained on comedy; we are brought in the end to see not the characters' greatness but their littleness.

It is a vision of great incisiveness and authority; but it is finally, deliberately, limited. The dispossessed heroes of other Jacobean plays want power, position, identity, something that guarantees their worth. Middleton's characters, starting from relatively secure positions, have smaller desires: a bit of money, a bit of land, a bit of sex. The intrigues they conduct in order to satisfy these desires show a low-level ingenuity quite different from the grand inventiveness of Jonson's heroes. At times – in the penitences of Penitent Brothel and Sir Walter Whorehound, or the sermons of the Cardinal – Middleton tries to oppose to this world of low intrigue a Christian denunciation of sin. But the rhetoric of hellfire and damnation remains disconnected from the world it attacks: the middle-class bedroom where quick, furtive sexual encounters take place never really seems like an anteroom of Hell. And the version of Christian morality espoused by Middleton's preaching characters is finally a morality of expediency: sin will lead to eternal torment, and the pleasure is just not worth the price. Far from exploding the material calculations of the commercial world, this 'morality' merely makes similar calculations on a grander scale. It is religion designed if not to keep men in awe, then to keep them in line. It is, in fact, the sort of religion we might expect in Middleton's own society, where the state enforced compulsory churchgoing for essentially political reasons. Of the radical morality of forgiveness and love proclaimed in the Gospels there is hardly a trace. Shakespeare dramatizes virtue in characters like Desdemona and Cordelia; Marston and Jonson, by conveying through imagery or ironically perverted language a sense of the positive values that are under attack. But morality in Middleton is a matter of rhetoric alone, overinflated and spiritually dead. The real criticism comes from within the material world itself, on its own terms. Success is chancy and the rewards are small. The characters are always congratulating themselves on their own cleverness but they are not quite so clever as they think: even Quomodo and Livia, among the most ingenious, stumble at last. In the more light-hearted plays, like *A Trick to Catch the Old One* and the main plot of *A Mad World, my Masters*, this does not matter, for the penalties for failure are small. Even in plays where the stakes seem higher to the characters, they never seem that high to us. We watch, mostly with sardonic detachment, as a sharply imagined but petty world goes about its business.[3]

Notes

1. This issue has been much debated in Middleton criticism, but the essential statement of the problem is still R. B. Parker, 'Middleton's Experiments with Comedy and Judgement', in *Jacobean Theatre*, edited by John Russell Brown and Bernard Harris, Stratford-upon-Avon Studies, 1 (London, 1960), pp. 179–99.

2. For an extended discussion of Middleton's treatment of traditional comic form, see George E. Rowe, Jr., *Thomas Middleton and the New Comedy Tradition* (Lincoln, 1979).

3. Middleton's later work, including his second major tragedy *The Changeling*, will be discussed in Chapter 12.

Chapter 9

Webster

The sharp satiric observation that is Middleton's special gift is found also in the plays of John Webster (*c.* 1580–*c.* 1634). But there is no pettiness here – or at least, not of Middleton's kind. The passions and desires of Webster's characters may in theory be reducible to the need for sexual satisfaction and material security; but in practice what is at stake is much larger: the dignity and integrity of human life, the need for freedom, and a heroic self-assertion in the face of chaos that matches that of Shakespeare's tragic heroes. Of Shakespeare's contemporaries only Chapman tries for anything like the heroic scale Webster attempts; but while Chapman's heroic visions are asserted in opposition to his own equally powerful sense of the pettiness of life, and thus remain somewhat disembodied, the heroic assertions of Webster's characters work *through* a world that they themselves perceive as broken and degraded, taking account of that world, taking account too of the fallibility of their own natures and the uncertainty of the spiritual universe. The result is heroic tragedy of an unusual kind, tragedy that has not so much faced and rejected the satiric vision – as we could say Shakespeare does in *Othello*, where Iago is finally swept aside – as absorbed it, preserved it and used it.

Webster is remembered principally for his two great tragedies, *The White Devil* (*c.* 1612) and *The Duchess of Malfi* (*c.* 1613); the rest of his career is relatively little known and little understood. We know that he had a citizen background; he was the son of a London coachmaker.[1] He wrote a number of works in collaboration, including two citizen comedies with Dekker, *Westward Ho* (*c.* 1604) and *Northward Ho* (*c.* 1605). He appears to have been an obliging collaborator, whose work is not obviously distinct from that of his colleague; but we see the stamp of his mind in the Italianate intrigue of the first play and the occasional flashes of sardonic observation in both works. His citizen background may account for some features of the two major tragedies: his fascination with the lurid horror that he imagines attends great princes; and his interest in the relatively disadvantaged. Each tragedy centres on a woman. Though one is a duchess and the other a courtesan they have in common problems of living in a world where the rules are set by men. The competing centre of attention in both plays is a sophisticated man with no natural position in society, who can survive only by finding work that degrades him – another version of the dispossessed hero. Webster shares the standard Jacobean qualities of fragmentation, uncertainty and tonal instability. He adds to this his own distinctive style: he writes in brilliant fragments, language that is deceptively simple, lines that strike fast and bite deep.

In *The White Devil* the speed of the writing is matched by the speed and complexity of the action. The play is full of surprises and reversals. Characters change suddenly before our eyes: 'Your reverend mother /Is grown a very old woman in two hours' (v. 4). The first scene opens with a single striking word, 'Banish'd?'; Duke Bracciano declares his love for Vittoria Corombona in three words, one of which is the name of Vittoria's brother, who will act as her pandar: 'Quite lost Flamineo' (I. 2). In both cases there is a striking sense of dislocation; and in the early scenes especially Webster deliberately makes it hard to get a fixed perspective on the action. When Vittoria and Bracciano meet, the dramatization of their growing, dangerous passion is surrounded by the commentary of eavesdroppers, pulling in opposite directions: the shock of Vittoria's mother Cornelia, the cynical appreciation of her brother (I. 2). The situation recalls the multiple eavesdropping scene in *Troilus and Cressida* (v. 2); but the clashes of tone, from moral horror to light bawdry, are sharper and the pace is much quicker.

The paradox of the title, initially a way of describing Vittoria's combination of beauty and corruption, anticipates a series of reversals that runs through the play. One of the most striking occurs when Vittoria enters the room in which Bracciano has just died, and sees him laid out in bed surrounded by confessors in the habit of Capuchins, complete with a crucifix and a candle. Her immediate reaction to this pious scene is 'O me! this place is hell!' (v. 3). In fact the 'confessors' are murderers in disguise, who have just killed the Duke. When the same killers, still disguised, come for Vittoria and Flamineo in the final scene, their leader Lodovico declares, 'We have brought you a masque' and Flamineo retorts sardonically, 'churchmen turn'd revellers!' (v. 6). At first the moral bearings of the play seem secure. Bracciano has had his wife and Vittoria's husband murdered to clear the way for their affair, and we see a clear connection between lust and murder. But when Vittoria is put on trial her guilt seems hardly to matter. She not only defends herself with wit and spirit –

> Sum up my faults, I pray, and you shall find
> That beauty and gay clothes, a merry heart,
> And a good stomach to a feast are all,
> All the poor crimes that you can charge me with.
>
> (III. 2)

– but scores some shrewd points against her accuser, Cardinal Monticelso: 'if you be my accuser /Pray cease to be my judge, come from
the bench' (III. 2). An adulteress deeply implicated in two murders
becomes a simple, pleasure-loving girl set upon by killjoy accusers
who will not even play fair. Bracciano, more deeply guilty than
Vittoria, shows his contempt for the whole proceeding by sitting on
the floor, on a rich gown which he ostentatiously leaves behind when
he stalks out half way through the trial. Before this he has appeared
only as a brutal man in the grip of lust; now, suddenly, we find
ourselves admiring his style. For the rest of the play the agents of
morality, Monticelso and Francisco de Medici, look increasingly
shady. Monticelso, we learn, has a book with the names of all the
notorious criminals in Rome, and we wonder why. Francisco insists
on involving himself in the final murder plot against Bracciano,
disguised as a moor, somewhat to the annoyance of the more
professional Lodovico who feels his employer has 'ridiculously engag'd
[himself] /Too far' (v. 5).

Early in his plot Francisco pretends love for Vittoria, remarking,
'My tragedy must have some idle mirth in't, /Else it will never pass'
(IV. 1). The play's tonal instability is seen here as a deliberate principle,
though the point is lightly expressed. The conscious preoccupation
with style is also characteristic of the play. Characters are put on
display, by others – 'mark this strange encounter' (III. 3) – and by
themselves:

> It may appear to some ridiculous
> Thus to talk knave and madman; and sometimes
> Come in with a dried sentence, stuff'd with sage.
> But this allows my varying of shapes –
> Knaves do grow great by being great men's apes.
>
> (IV. 2)

Here Flamineo, perhaps the play's most unstable character, is aware
of his instability and trying to control it by seeing it as a series of
performances. Lodovico is an artist in murder. He opens the play with
the threat, 'I'll make Italian cut-works in their guts /If ever I return'
(I. 1), and closes it with an artist's flourish: 'I limb'd this night-piece
and it was my best' (v. 6). Like Vindice he is content to die if he can
go with style.

That is one way in which characters in this fragmented world can
find integrity: construct a performance. Vittoria's way is not so much
to insist on her own role as to refuse to be type-cast by others. As she
opens her trial by refusing to be addressed either in Latin or in law-
jargon, so she refuses to have the conventional label 'whore' fastened
to her. She affects not to understand the word: 'Ha? whore – what's

that?' (III. 2). When Monticelso constructs a stock 'character' of a whore, she retorts simply 'This character escapes me' (III. 2)[2]. She will not be trapped in others' language, or in their stale imaginings. Flamineo presents a more complicated case, and his experience gradually emerges as the central experience of the play. He appears to have settled easily into the role of his sister's pandar, which he plays with cynical enthusiasm. But when his mother Cornelia objects, 'What? because we are poor, /Shall we be vicious?' his reply embodies both a frank awareness of the material problems of those cast adrift in an unstable society and an edgy defensiveness, a complaint that he is doing this only because he can find nothing better: 'Pray what means have you /To keep me from the galleys, or the gallows?' (I. 2). Having pandered for his sister he murders his brother Marcello, an act that drives his mother mad. His earlier defensiveness becomes a desperate attempt at callousness when he refers to Cornelia's mourning as 'superstitious howling' (v. 4). The sight of his mother, winding Marcello in his shroud and singing a dirge, finally breaks down Flamineo's pose of cynicism:

> I have a strange thing in me, to th' which
> I cannot give a name, without it be
> Compassion.
> (v. 4)

Like Vittoria at her trial he affects to find conventional moral language unfamiliar; but unlike her he accepts it, if only for a moment.
This is followed by a franker confession:

> I have liv'd
> Riotously ill, like some that live in court;
> And sometimes, when my face was full of smiles
> Have felt the maze of conscience in my breast.
> Oft gay and honour'd robes those tortures try –
> We think that cag'd birds sing, when indeed they
> cry.
> (v. 4)

This gives a fresh perspective on the conventionally cynical wit he displayed earlier in the play. At this point the ghost of Bracciano, the main cause of his corruption, appears to him, and while Flamineo's question, 'Pray, sir, resolve me, what religion's best /For a man to die in?' (v. 4) marks a return to his old cynical manner, it also signals a need to find some kind of certainty. He would still rather find it, however, in this world than the next, and when he goes to his sister's chamber to 'sum up all these horrors' his most obvious purpose is to 'be resolv'd what my rich sister means /T'assign me for my service' (v. 4).

The result, however, is not a final stability but one of the most complicated, difficult scenes in Jacobean drama. Flamineo fakes death in order to test Vittoria's loyalty, a test she spectacularly fails. He goes through a brilliant parody of a Jacobean death scene – 'There's a plumber, laying pipes in my guts, it scalds' (v. 6) – set up so that the audience itself will be fooled. Then he and Vittoria, along with Vittoria's attendant Zanche, have a real death scene, tied up and stabbed by Lodovico and his associates. All three meet their ends, at first, with remarkable courage and wit:

VITTORIA
                               'Twas a manly blow –
The next thou giv'st, murder some sucking infant,
And then thou wilt be famous.
FLAMINEO
                                 O what blade is't?
A Toledo, or an English fox?
I ever thought a cutler should distinguish
The cause of my death, rather than a doctor.
                                       (v. 6)

In death Flamineo and his sister are closer than at any other point in the play, but as Flamineo is admiring her courage she fades into despair and confusion: 'My soul, like to a ship in a black storm, /Is driven I know not whither'. She also offers something like conventional repentance: 'O my greatest sin lay in my blood. /Now my blood pays for't' (v. 6). The confusion, like the courage, is shared by Flamineo. But not the repentance:

                                I do not look
Who went before, nor who shall follow me;
No, at myself I will begin and end:
While we look up to heaven we confound
Knowledge with knowledge. O I am in a mist.
                                     (v. 6)

There is no better definition of what we might call the Jacobean world picture: man adrift in an incomprehensible universe, knowing only himself, and even then certain only of his death. It is not so much a picture, perhaps, as a confession of ignorance. There is no meaning, no value, no certain knowledge left. But to say that is to arrive at a point of rest, where all striving ceases. It is to accept death as the only reality. And the principal characteristic of this play has been its restlessness, its refusal to settle for any pat formula. And so Flamineo, having declared, 'O, I am in a mist', goes on talking. He greets his death, not with an acceptance of stasis but with a flash of defiance, ending, like the killer Lodovico, with a flourish: 'Let no harsh flattering bells resound my knell, /Strike thunder, and strike loud to my farewell' (v. 6). This contrasts with the deliberate limpness of Vittoria's last words: 'O happy they that never saw the court, /Nor ever knew great men but by report' (v. 6). The effect is not of a single, definitive reaction to death but of persistent shifting and variety. Flamineo and Vittoria are thinking, feeling, protesting and changing, right up to the end.

The White Devil has a hard-edged brilliance that finally limits its effect; but there are touches in it of a more gentle and humane vision: 'You shall see in the country in harvest time, pigeons, though they destroy never so much corn, the farmer dare not present the fowling-piece to them. Why? Because they belong to the lord of the manor; whilst your poor sparrows that belong to the Lord of Heaven, they go to the pot for't' (v. 1). This manner is extended in *The Duchess of Malfi*. The Duchess's secret marriage to her steward Antonio is at one level an assertion of simple, natural life:

> Why should only I,
> Of all the other princes of the world,
> Be cas'd up, like a holy relic? I have youth,
> And a little beauty.
>
> (III. 2)

She says of herself and Antonio,

> The birds that live i'th' field
> On the wild benefit of nature, live
> Happier than we; for they may choose their mates,
> And carol their sweet pleasures to the spring.
>
> (III. 5)

Later, in prison, she develops this image in a simple, familiar way: 'The robin redbreast, and the nightingale, /Never live long in cages' (IV. 2).

She is opposed by her brothers Ferdinand and the Cardinal, who turn from 'terrible good counsel' (I. 1) to murder. Ferdinand's oppression of his sister begins with a grotesque joke, 'I would . . . have a mathematical instrument made for her face, that she might not laugh out of compass' (I. 1), and ends in more deadly constriction as she is imprisoned, then strangled. So far, our sympathies would appear to be simple. But in the Duchess's determination to marry there is a complicating touch of arrogance:

> If all my royal kindred
> Lay in my way unto this marriage,
> I'd make them my low footsteps.
>
> (I. 1)

She takes obvious pride in the fact that her marriage is a contract before witnesses, legally valid but not sanctioned by the church: 'We now are man and wife, and 'tis the church /That must but echo this' (I. 1). When her waiting-woman Cariola objects to her trick of feigning a pilgrimage, the Duchess calls her 'a superstitious fool' (III. 2). But she is not consistent about this. She later accuses Ferdinand of violating 'a sacrament o'th' church /Shall make you howl in hell for't' (IV. 1), and tries to accept her trials with religious patience: 'naught made me e'er /Go right but heaven's scourge-stick' (III. 5). She is by turns natural, unorthodox, courageous, and in need of ordinary reassurance. Her appeal lies not in any one controlling virtue like courage or patience, but in the variety and vitality of her nature as a whole.

In the long ordeal that culminates in her death she is as deeply tried as any character in Jacobean drama. In her 'last presence-chamber' (IV. 2) she is presented first with antimasque of madmen, who spin grotesque variations on the themes of sex, death and religion, and then with a formal image of her mortality as the executioners enter with a coffin and the cords that will strangle her. Her exchange with Bosola, who is in charge of the ordeal, is both a parody of a masque in which a prince is complimented[3] and a tense debate about her very nature:

DUCHESS
  Who am I?
BOSOLA
  Thou art a box of worm-seed, at best, but a salvatory
  of green mummy! What's this flesh? A little crudded
  milk, fantastical puff-paste . . .
DUCHESS
  Am not I thy duchess?
BOSOLA
  Thou art some great woman, sure, for riot begins to sit
  on thy forehead, clad in gray hairs, twenty years sooner
  than on a merry milkmaid's. Thou sleepest worse than

> if a mouse should be forced to take up her lodging in a
> cat's ear: a little infant that breeds its teeth, should it lie
> with thee, would cry out, as if thou wert the more
> unquiet bedfellow.
>
> DUCHESS
> I am Duchess of Malfi still.
>
> BOSOLA
> That makes thy sleeps so broken . . . .
>
> (IV. 2)

Like Vittoria, the Duchess resists any attempt to reduce her to a
formula, of mortality or of greatness haunted by guilt. But she can
oppose to Bosola's generalized vision not a proper name (Webster
never gives her one) but a title. And the title conveys, by this point
in the play, an image of tormented greatness that bears out Bosola'a
point of view.

Apparently trying to reduce the Duchess to fear, Bosola is actually
testing her courage, and his admiration grows as she rises to the challenge. So does ours; but we also notice that while the Duchess displays
a wit and spirit akin to those of Flamineo and Vittoria, she betrays also
a desire to get the ordeal over before she cracks:

> BOSOLA
> Yet, methinks,
> The manner of your death should much afflict you,
> This cord should terrify you?
>
> DUCHESS
> Not a whit.
> What would it pleasure me to have my throat cut
> With diamonds? or to be smothered
> With cassia? or to be shot to death with pearls?
> I know death hath ten thousand several doors
> For men to take their exits; and 'tis found
> They go on such strange geometrical hinges,
> You may open them both ways – any way, for heaven-
> sake,
> So I were out of your whispering . . .
>
> (IV. 2)

Yet when her death comes she delays it a moment, to make a final
gesture of kneeling. This has a double effect: it signals her humility
before heaven, and it forces her executioners to change position in
order to accommodate her. It is the culmination of her effort to maintain control over her life. Even at this point the play is not finished

with her. Having apparently died with self-assertive courage, she revives briefly, calls for Antonio, and dies having received simple comfort from Bosola's news, only half-true, that her husband is alive and reconciled to her brothers. Dead by the end of Act Four, she survives through the last act in the echo from her tomb, in the visions seen by Antonio and Bosola, and in the torment of her brother Ferdinand, who tries to look at her after her death but cannot – 'Cover her face: mine eyes dazzle' (IV. 2) – and complains, in his later madness, 'I have cruel sore eyes' (V. 2).

The Cardinal is an enigmatic character: apparently uninvolved in the Duchess's death but later claiming responsibility for it, driven by no motive we can discern apart from a desire to express his power; apparently cold and resolute but collapsing hysterically when his life is threatened; and finally admitting as he dies that one relationship matters to him: 'Look to my brother' (V. 5). This makes sense as we look back through the play: we have seen him control and direct Ferdinand's hysteria as though he had no feelings of his own but had to live through his brother's. Ferdinand is a fuller and more tragic character, who is in some ways complementary to his sister; after her death we learn they are twins. As she experiences normal love in secret, he suppresses an incestuous desire that is never explicit but emerges in the compulsive sexuality of his language to her and his imaginings about her. As he imprisons the Duchess, he is himself imprisoned:

> thou hast ta'en that massy sheet of lead
> That hid thy husband's bones, and folded it
> About my heart.
>
> (III. 2)

In his final madness he tries to reveal his guilt by digging bodies out of churchyards:

>   two nights since
> One met the duke, 'bout midnight in a lane
> Behind Saint Mark's church, with the leg of a man
> Upon his shoulder; and he howl'd fearfully. . . .
>
> (V. 2)

In this phase of his madness he imagines he is a wolf. But his final delusion is that he is on a battlefield, leading a rally at a desperate moment, becoming the heroic prince he has always wished he could be. He says, after the tournament at the beginning of the play, 'When shall we leave this sportive action, and fall to action indeed?' (I. 1).

Entertaining Bosola's rudeness, he sees himself as a ruler accepting honest counsel (III. 1). Ferdinand is not a monster but the broken figure of a great Renaissance prince.

Antonio, his rival, speaks like a man who has read all the right conduct books, as in his praise of horsemanship (I. 1), but when we study him we sense there is something missing. He reacts hesitantly to the Duchess's proposal, and gives her at their final parting a kiss

> colder
> Than I have seen an holy anchorite
> Give to a dead man's skull.
>
>   (III. 5)

He dies after a weak attempt at reconciliation with her brothers, expressing a chagrin like Vittoria's: 'let my son fly the courts of princes' (v. 4). It is part of the irony of the Duchess's situation that the marriage on which she stakes so much is with a man who is not quite up to her weight. In the end the Duchess's strongest relationship is with Bosola. Like Flamineo he is trying to find maintenance in a world that will pay him only for crime, and reacting to this dilemma with conscious, ironic role-playing. He adopts the now stale pose of the court malcontent in the manner of Malevole; Antonio accuses him of 'out-of-fashion melancholy' (II. 1). He rails at the court, then allows himself to be hired by Ferdinand, protesting at his own corruption even as he allows it to happen. He tries to preserve some detachment from his role in the Duchess's ordeal by coming to her in disguise, turning his part into a performance. In the last act he adopts a new role as her avenger, a role which like his earlier performance as malcontent is already a little shopworn. His career as revenge hero ends ironically when he kills Antonio, 'the man I would have sav'd 'bove mine own life' (v. 4), by accident, 'such a mistake as I have often seen /In a play' (v. 5).

But in the plays of the period revenge killings are not usually accidental in quite this way. In *Antonio's Revenge* they are lurid and sensational, but purposeful in that the victim is punished for good reason. In *Titus Andronicus*, where Tamora is made to eat her sons, in *Hamlet*, where Claudius is killed with his own poison, and in *The Revenger's Tragedy*, where the Duke is made to kiss the poisoned lips of the woman he lusted after and killed, the manner of the killing is morally logical. Aesthetic design and nemesis come together. Even in the crazy last scene of *Women Beware Women* the individual deaths, using tricks like poisoned love-darts and showers of gold, are significant judgements on the victims. But Bosola simply kills the wrong man, by accident, in the dark – a dark equivalent to the mist that clouded Flamineo's eyes just before his death, an image of the fundamental uncertainty of life, the fear that it means nothing. As Bosola recounts his mistake he himself is dying, accidentally stabbed by the mad Ferdinand who is trying to kill his brother and has not even noticed Bosola. Just as Webster's characters see life drained of meaning, so Webster seems to be trying to drain meaning out of the action itself, leaving it as a series of random accidents.

But that would in itself be a pat, reductive statement about life, and Webster always resists such statements – even though he himself makes them with a power and authority unmatched in the period. It is the paradox of his vision of instability that instability itself cannot be proclaimed as a final truth: and so *The Duchess of Malfi*, while apparently depicting a world in chaos, resists that chaos by the conscious, deliberate shaping of its own art. It has a remarkable, pervasive symmetry of structure. Bosola's first confrontation in the play is with the Cardinal; then the two characters hardly meet until the last act, when Bosola confronts the Cardinal again and kills him. The military motif appears three times: once at the beginning, in the tournament; once at the mid-point, in an apparently irrelevant scene; and finally in Ferdinand's madness in the last act. Scene transitions reveal unexpected relationships: Bosola's tag, '*Though lust do mask in ne'er so strange disguise, /She's oft found witty, but is never wise*' (II. 3) is followed immediately by the entrance of the Cardinal and his mistress Julia, whom he later poisons. Lust is in a strange disguise indeed, and Julia's wit, which is considerable, cannot save her in the end. Having carried off the Duchess's body, in a touching expression of his final devotion to her, Bosola is then ordered to perform the same office for the dead Julia and remarks sourly, 'I think I shall /Shortly grow the common bier for churchyards' (v. 2). The line both calls attention to the parallel, and expresses Bosola's chagrin at the way the gesture is devalued by repetition. The Duchess, trying for patience in her imprisonment, declares, 'I am acquainted with sad misery, /As the tann'd galley-slave is with his oar' (IV. 2). One of the first things we learn about Bosola is that he was once a galley-slave for a murder performed at the Cardinal's bidding. His last words are 'mine is another voyage' (v. 5). Their meaning is enigmatic, but their echo of his earlier fate is clear. Whatever footing the characters try to find in the treacherous world they inhabit is insecure: the Duchess's marriage, Ferdinand's longing for heroic action, the role-playing of Bosola. But they are all part of a complex web of relationships, suffering together as well as alone, members one of another in a way that only the audience can see fully. By taking the risk of killing the Duchess in Act Four, Webster allows the last act to make this point, clearly and persuasively. Her story is finished only when the other lives she has touched are finished too.

The panoramic vision of the play is also a feature of Jacobean tragicomedy, of which Webster has left us one notable example in *The Devil's Law-Case* (*c.* 1617) We recognize in this play some of the issues of the tragedies, but with an appropriate reduction in scale. There may even be a certain feeling of moral security in the presence of the honest, good-natured lawyer Ariosto, though I think Webster is playing on our sense of paradox by linking those virtues with that profession. The merchant Romelio is a figure of some glamour but still a merchant. His oppression of his sister, whom he locks up because she will not marry the man he chooses, is an echo, but only a faint one, of Ferdinand's oppression of the Duchess. He becomes, like Bosola, a shape-shifter, disguising himself as a Jew to kill his sister's lover in what looks like a conscious imitation of Marlowe's Barabas. But, since this is a tragicomedy, Romelio's murderous intentions backfire; the stab he gives his victim cures him by allowing an old, dangerous wound to bleed freely. He also proves a life-giving figure in another ironic way: 'I have so much disorder'd the holy Order, /I have got this nun with child' (III. 3). There is jocular incongruity in Ariosto's final sentence on him, 'you shall marry that nun' (v. 5).

Before Romelio is to fight a dangerous duel, a Capuchin tries to bring him to piety:

CAPUCHIN
O, you have a dangerous voyage to take.
ROMELIO
No matter, I will be mine own pilot:
Do not you trouble your head with the business.

(v. 4)

He starts asking about the properties of different kinds of blades. Presented with a show of death-images recalling the *memento mori* passages in Webster's tragedies, Romelio pretends repentance only as a ruse to lock the Capuchin up: 'Wast thou not a-weary of his preaching?' (v. 4). He has his own version of the tragic characters' vitality in the face of death. But, since this is Webster, Romelio's resolution does not last; in the final scene he calls for the Capuchin to be unlocked, to come and pray for him, thereby helping precipitate the dénouement.

The swift action and sharp plot reversals operate benevolently, and Ariosto concludes:

Rareness and difficulty give estimation
To all things are i'th' world: you have met both
In these several passages: now it does remain,
That these so comical events be blasted
With no severity of sentence.

(v. 5)

It would be rash to attribute the dénouement either to heaven or to human will; rather it is the product of a complex tangle of accidents, misunderstandings and purposes misfired. The 'rareness and difficulty' that produce dark unsettling mystery in the tragedies here produce unexpected order. Granted this final difference, *The Devil's Law-Case* is akin to the great tragedies in its complexity and its celebration of human vitality.

Webster may have denied his characters heroic scale of a simple kind; whatever worldly greatness they have only sets off their corruption and ruin more dramatically. But they rise, circuitously, to heroic scale of another kind in the intensity with which they suffer and resist, the courage and honesty with which they face the mystery of their lives and deaths. It is here that the setting of the two great tragedies comes into play. For Marston and others, the 'Italian lascivious palace' is a hothouse of sex and violence whose corruption is intensified within a closed setting that seems to create infinite opportunities for bedding and killing. Webster's courts convey all of that and more. They are, like the English court Webster would have glimpsed through the perspective of his father's coach-maker's shop, places where opportunities for advancement are tantalizingly held out, where a talented man can make his way if he has the right combination of luck and corruptibility. In the ceremonies of tournament and masque they embody ideals of power, order and heroic value that the corrupt participants in these ceremonies are constantly betraying. And yet no writer of the period conveys so vividly as Webster does the sheer style and panache of the great. Bracciano and Vittoria defying the court at Vittoria's trial and the Duchess resisting her tormentors, may be images, respectively, of defiant guilt and tortured innocence; but they have this panache in common. One moment in particular may be taken as summing up Webster's combination of sardonic wit and heroic assertion. The Duchess declares that she could curse the stars; Bosola retorts, 'Look you, the stars shine still', to which the Duchess replies, 'O, but you must/Remember my curse hath a great way to go' (IV. 2). They agree on one thing: the remoteness of the stars. But the Duchess, by a witty paradox, not only increases that sense of remoteness and the feelings of absurdity and alienation that go with it, but insists on the power of her own voice to bridge the distance. And she goes further than Romeo, who merely defies the stars: she curses them, and accepts Bosola's interpretation that if her curse is effective they will stop shining. Human self-assertion can hardly go further than this. Whether or not her voice can reach the stars, we see in the rest of the play that it has reached Bosola. In Shakespeare, the answer to the absurdity that lies just on the edge of the tragic vision is love; in Webster, it is admiration.

Notes

1. On Webster's background and its implications for his work, see M. C. Bradbrook, *John Webster: Citizen and Dramatist* (New York, 1980).

2. The allusion is probably to the 'character' books so popular at the time, collections of stock character sketches – to one of which, *Sir Thomas Overbury his Wife . . . New News and Divers More Characters*, Webster may have contributed.

3. On the relation of this scene to the court masque see Inga-Stina Ekeblad [Ewbank], 'The Impure Art of John Webster', *Review of English Studies*, n.s. 9 (1958), 253–67.

Chapter 10

Popular Drama

Among the plays of Shakespeare's contemporaries, satiric comedies of London life and satiric tragedies set in the corrupt courts of Italy make up the bulk of the work that is widely studied today. It is a repertory drawn mostly from the private theatres and from the Chamberlain's-King's men (Shakespeare's company) in its more ambitious moments. But there was another face, both to that company's work and to the theatre scene generally. At the Globe, between performances of Shakespeare and Jonson, and at public theatres such as the Fortune and the Red Bull, one could see a range of plays designed less to startle and provoke, more to move and entertain. The distinction is crude, of course; who is to say that *Twelfth Night* and *The Alchemist* are not entertaining? But it may help to catch the difference between writers who pursued personal visions and took artistic risks and writers who produced a product to order and were willing to try anything they thought an audience might want. The best of them displayed both honest craftsmanship and real inventiveness, and managed to touch the nerves and imaginations of their audience in ways we can still appreciate. We can certainly admire the range over which they worked, which included domestic comedy and tragedy, chronicles, tales of fantasy and adventure, and, as we will see, one extraordinary experiment in the retelling of classical mythology for a popular audience. When they dealt with contemporary English life, the popular dramatists tended to romanticize it, though there are significant exceptions to this. When they worked in more exotic settings, they showed an interest not in Italian decadence but in possibilities for glamorous adventure, often involving travelling English heroes. Above all, theirs was an eclectic art, working for the effect of the moment, fundamentally good-natured in its view of humanity. But its best plays can be as critical and intelligent on their own terms as are the concentrated satiric works of the Jacobean writers we are more familiar with today.

Thomas Dekker (*c.* 1572–*c.* 1632) tried his hand at many forms of writing, including prose pamphlets commenting on the London scene.[1] He frequently worked in collaboration. With John Webster (a pairing of James Joyce and Arnold Bennett would be more surprising, but only a little) he produced two satiric comedies of London life for the private theatres, *Westward Ho* (1604) and *Northward Ho* (1605). His best known London play is *The Shoemakers' Holiday* (1599). The main drive of this work, based on Deloney's novel *The Gentle Craft* (1597–8), is celebration. Its leading character, Simon Eyre, is a shoemaker who fills the stage with noise and mirth, and never seems to do a stroke of work. Eyre rises to be Lord Mayor of London by a combination of shrewd business deals and luck. Both are only half glimpsed in Dekker's cleverly tactful dramatization. The play's main lovers, Lacy and Rose, plan to meet

> at Eyre's house
> Who now by death of certain aldermen,
> Is Mayor of London.
>   (IV. 3)

The fact that the most dramatic event in the life of the principal character is announced in a subordinate clause in a sentence about something else is a clue to the play's peculiar structure. The onstage plotting concerns two largely independent love stories. The first is the inter-class courtship of the aristocratic Lacy and the middle-class Rose, in which Lacy qualifies himself for marriage to a grocer's daughter by donning a shoemaker's apron and a maddening Dutch accent, thus proving himself a good fellow. The second, more serious and touching story concerns the shoemaker Rafe, pressed to the French wars, reported dead, and returning crippled just in time to rescue his faithful wife Jane from a second marriage. Eyre takes little part in either story but drifts freely through the play like a huge multicoloured balloon. Suppressing the process of his rise, Dekker concentrates instead on the celebratory energy which comes to a climax when the new Lord Mayor, in fulfilment of an old vow, feasts the apprentices:

> There's cheer for the heavens, venison pasties walk up and
> down piping hot, like sergeants, beef and brewis comes
> marching in dry fats, fritters and pancakes comes trolling
> in in wheelbarrows, hens and oranges hopping in porters'
> baskets, collops and eggs in scuttles, and tarts and custards
> comes quavering in in malt shovels.
>   (V. 2)

Eyre projects himself forward to the contemporary London audience as a figure of legend, to be commemorated in the feast that gives the play its title: 'Boys, that day you are free, let masters care, /And prentices shall pray for Simon Eyre' (v. 1). The lines seem designed to be fired at the audience, with a wink at the apprentices, who in being at the theatre that day are probably taking a holiday to which they are not entitled.

The play is less innocent than it may appear. Through the romance, and the Dick Whittington fantasy, we see touches of shrewd observation. In the Lacy–Rose plot Dekker allows us to see the class tension beneath the mutual politeness of the lovers' parents. Early in the play Lacy leaves for the wars, taking the young shoemaker Rafe with him and singling him out for special attention: 'Give me thy hand, /Thou shalt not want, as I am a gentleman' (I. 1). Even as he speaks we know he is planning to desert his command in order to win his love. At the end of the play the King wipes out his disgrace at a stroke:

> As for the honour which he lost in France,
> Thus I redeem it: Lacy, kneel thee down,
> Arise Sir Rowland Lacy.
>
> (v. 5)

Rafe regains his wife thanks to the quick action of his fellow shoe-makers; but nothing can give him two good legs again. Dekker does not insist on the point, but Lacy's promise, which he must know he cannot keep, brings the two men together for a moment and allows us to reflect on the relative fates of the common soldier and the gentleman. In Rafe's return crippled from the war, the play's usual vein of bawdy humour becomes a little nervous. Eyre's wife Margery, more flustered than usual, remarks, 'Trust me I am sorry Rafe to see thee impotent, Lord how the wars have made him sunburnt; the left leg is not well; 'twas a fair gift of God the infirmity took not hold a little higher, considering thou camest from France; but let that pass'. Her embarrassment deepens as she tries to account for the absence of Rafe's wife Jane:

> O Rafe, your wife, perdie we know not what's become of
> her; she was here a while, and because she was married
> grew more stately than became her; I checked her, and so
> forth; away she flung, never returned, nor said bih nor
> bah; and Rafe, you know, ka me, ka thee. And so as I tell
> ye – Roger, is not Firk come yet?
>
> (III. 2)

Often in Dekker catch-phrases and other tricks of speech are simply paraded; but he shows in this moment that he has an ear, and a sense of how people under pressure use clichés to cover discomfort.

Eyre is at once a romantic figure and a man in a real community: 'by the Lord of Ludgate, it's a mad life to be a Lord Mayor, it's a stirring life, a fine life, a velvet life, a careful life' (v. 1). When at the end of the play he confronts the King we see that his madcap manner is something he can turn on or off as the decorum of the situation requires:

EYRE
> I beseech your grace, pardon my rude behaviour, I am
> handicraftsman, yet my heart is without craft, I would
> be sorry at my soul, that my boldness should offend
> my King.

KING
> Nay, I pray thee, good Lord Mayor, be even as merry
> As if thou wert among thy shoemakers;
> It does me good to see thee in this humour.

EYRE
> Say'st thou so, my sweet Diocletian? Then hump,
> prince am I none, yet am I princely born, by the Lord
> of Ludgate my liege, I'll be as merry as a pie.

(v. 5)

After a few more lines of this sort of thing, the King turns to one of his nobles: 'Ha ha! Say, Cornwall, did'st thou ever see the like?' (v. 5). Throughout the last scene the easy relations of King and citizen show an ideally functioning society; but Dekker also allows the characters a certain self-consciousness in constructing this picture, and the King's delight in his mad Lord Mayor makes him sound for a moment like a visitor to a zoo.

The moments of disruption, however, are glimpses only. Dekker keeps the public action cheerful and the love stories gentle and lyrical in tone. Any class tension there might be in the Lacy–Rose story is finally smoothed over by the King, who disposes of it as easily as he disposes of Lacy's dishonour: 'Dost thou not know that love respects no blood?/Cares not for difference of birth, or state?' (v. 5). Hammon, who tries to marry Jane after Rafe's apparent death, could have been a villain: Dekker gives him his own loneliness, and his own pathos. We see the delicate balancing that is typical of Dekker at his best when Rafe leaves a last token for Jane as he departs for the wars:

> Now gentle wife, my loving lovely Jane,
> Rich men at parting give their wives rich gifts,
> Jewels and rings, to grace their lily hands;
> Thou know'st our trade makes rings for women's heels;

Here, take this pair of shoes cut out by Hodge,
Stitch't by my fellow Firk, seam'd by myself,
Made up and pink't, with letters for thy name,
Wear them, my dear Jane, for thy husband's sake,
And every morning when thou pull'st them on,
Remember me, and pray for my return;
Make much of them, for I have made them so
That I can know them from a thousand moe.

(I. 1)

We suspect at once that the shoes will be a recognition device later in
the plot, as of course they are. But Dekker also emphasizes that this
is a poor man's gift: it is for aristocratic lovers to use rings or jewels
as love-tokens. The gift reflects not only the affection of the couple
but the pride in craftsmanship, and the sense of community in the
shop, that we glimpse in other scenes involving the shoemakers. And
the speech as a whole is a moment of stillness at the end of a fast, noisy
scene.

The refrains of the two 'three-men's songs' that accompany the play
suggest the way it blends good nature with a certain underlying
sombreness:

O the month of May, the merry month of May,
So frolic, so gay, and so green, so green, so green;
O and then did I unto my true love say,
Sweet Peg, thou shalt be my summer's queen.

Cold's the wind, and wet's the rain,
    Saint Hugh be our good speed;
Ill is the weather that bringeth no gain,
    Nor helps good hearts in need.

The romance is more high-flown, and the austerity is sharper, in *Old
Fortunatus* (1599). Dekker is here, it seems, adapting an older two-part
play into a single work geared for court performance. The adventures
of the title character and his sons Ampedo and Andelocia centre on two
magic props: a purse of gold that never runs out, and a hat that at a
wish can transport its wearer anywhere in the world. But to this fairy-
tale material is added a framing allegorical action involving the figures
of Fortune, Virtue and Vice: the result is not a story of dreams come
true but a grim cautionary tale. Fortunatus's adventures are compressed
almost to the vanishing point; the emphasis instead is thrown on the
final emptiness of his pleasures in the face of death. He appears at first
to be 'one of Fortune's minions' (I. 1), as his name would indicate. He

is even allowed a kinship with Fortune's more famous minion, Tamburlaine; but as he declares, 'In these two hands do I gripe all the world' Fortune enters with '*three* Destinies *working*' and tells him, 'Thou art no son of Fortune, but her slave' (II. 2). He dies with the moral tag, 'behold in me /The rotten strength of proud mortality' (II. 2). His sons fare no better; even the more virtuous of the two, who sees the corruption the magic brings and tries to destroy it, is denounced by Virtue herself as too passive: 'He made no use of me, but like a miser /Locked up his wealth in rusty bars of sloth' (V. 2). The final debate of Vice and Virtue is settled when Fortune appeals directly to Queen Elizabeth, present in the audience; Vice flees from her presence and even Fortune submits to her. The quasi-religious adoration of the Queen that opens and closes the play recalls such earlier court shows as Peele's *The Arraignment of Paris* (*c.* 1581); but there is an extra level of suggestion when Virtue, punning on the name of one of the play's characters, the moralizing servant Shadow, appeals to the Queen on behalf of her fellow actors:

> All these that thus do kneel before your eyes
> Are shadows like myself; dread Nymph, it lies
> In you to make us substances.
>
> (v. 2)

Puck's reference to the actors as shadows was urbane and self-effacing. But after Dekker's depiction of the vanity of human wishes the emptiness of the theatrical illusion, to which only Elizabeth can give reality, seems also to reflect the emptiness of human life.

To moralize fantasy is an Elizabethan habit; in *Old Fortunatus* Dekker takes it so far that it kills the fun. He strikes a better balance in the two-part *The Honest Whore* (1604, *c.* 1605), the first part written in collaboration with Middleton. Here the scene is London, disguised as Milan, and the surface is apparently realistic. But the action proceeds in a series of exemplary set-pieces designed to show off the characters' virtues and vices in a striking way. The title character, Bellafront, is converted from prostitution to honesty by Hippolito in a long passage of rhetoric in the first play; in the second, Hippolito lapses into sin, tries to re-convert Bellafront with the same weapons, and fails. The scenes are consciously established as formal debates, and as mirror images of each other. In the subplot the patient linen-draper Candido is, like Hippolito and Bellafront, put on display. In the first play he shows that he can be patient under any provocation; in the second, that he can be angry when the occasion demands it. In the second part Dekker introduces Bellafront's father, Orlando Friscaboldo, a sentimental variation on the disguised intriguer of more hard-boiled Jacobean plays. Though he uses the methods of the rogue his kindness is unfailing and his tear-ducts are in good working order.

As in *The Shoemakers' Holiday*, the entertainment conveys some shrewd thinking about society. Candido's patience, for example, is both a serious moral virtue and a sign of his business sense. After a customer has tried to provoke him by demanding a pennyworth of expensive cloth cut from the middle of the bolt, he defends his acquiescence: 'A pen'worth serves him, and 'mongst trades 'tis found, /Deny a pen'worth, it may cross a pound' (Part One, i. 5). Candido is no fool: when another customer walks off with an expensive beaker he goes along with the theft as a joke, but retains a constable to get the beaker back. Having recovered his property he refuses to pursue the matter further: 'those have vexed spirits /That pursue lives' (Part One, i. 5). It is enough to secure his own interests; anything more would be useless aggression. The man who stole the beaker is properly impressed: 'Such a meek spirit can bless a commonweal' (Part One, i. 5). And indeed some serious thinking about social relations is going on through both plays. Part One ends with a visit to Bedlam, Part Two with a visit to Bridewell. We are used to deploring our ancestors' habit of finding amusement in madhouses; the Bedlam scene shows that our ancestors could deplore it too. One of the madmen is a citizen ruined by losses at sea. The visitors laugh at him at first, but he rounds on them: 'Do you laugh at God's creatures?' (v. 2). After he has exposed them to a painful, almost surrealist image of deprivation – 'you may look through my ribs, see how my guts come out, these are my red guts, my very guts, oh, oh!' the visitors cry, 'a very piteous sight' (v. 2). The pity in this scene is balanced by the Bridewell scene's tough appraisal of incurable vice. For all the talk of punishing and correcting whores, the Master has to admit that 'some going hence /Are, by being here, lost in more impudence' (v. 2), and this is just what we see. The play's main business is to give us striking images of sin renounced and patient, suffering virtue rewarded. But Dekker characteristically balances the fantasy with glimpses of incurable pain and untameable vice. Fairy godfathers like Orlando Friscaboldo can solve the problems of fictional characters. But the actual institutions of Dekker's London, Bedlam and Bridewell, can do nothing with society's misfits but lock them up. Dekker can write for effect, and can write sentimentally; but he can also use the fringe areas of his plays to suggest that the world is more intractable than conventional theatre allows. Even when he resorts to conventional theatrical methods there is a critical edge. Orlando Friscaboldo in his disguise, and Hippolito and Bellafront in their rhetorical displays of virtue, are put on show as creatures of a conscious theatrical artifice. The same is true of Simon Eyre in his flamboyant performance as the mad Lord Mayor of London, a performance that does not altogether conceal the shrewd businessman beneath. In other Jacobean plays such artifice conveys an insecurity about value and identity in a world of role-playing; in Dekker, it is rather a way of shaping the images of virtue for more effective display. But the consciousness of Dekker's artifice, shaded as it is by his shrewd knowledge of a grubbier and less satisfying world, implies an admission that the world is not always so neat as the popular theatre makes it seem.

The range of Thomas Heywood (*c.* 1574–1641) is if anything wider than that of Dekker, and the size of his output, mostly lost, is indicated by his boast that he had 'either an entire hand, or at least a main finger' in two hundred and twenty plays.[2] His best known work is the domestic tragedy *A Woman Killed with Kindness* (1603), an emotionally charged tale of adultery and remorse. The play opens with the wedding of Frankford and Anne. The couple are rich, cultivated and widely admired; Frankford keeps telling himself, and is told by others, that he has an ideal wife. The first threat to his complacency is indirect. The social pastime of the wedding feast leads to another social pastime, a morning of hunting and hawking, during which a brawl breaks out and two servants are killed. Frankford's friend Wendoll brings the news. Wendoll is himself an odd man out among the well-to-do gentry; Frankford calls him 'though of small means, yet a gentleman /Of a good house, though somewhat press'd by want' (scene 4), and his first function is to be the bearer of bad tidings. Frankford, nevertheless, adds him to his household, evidently seeing him as an ideal friend to match his ideal wife. Wendoll conceives a passion for Anne. He loathes himself for it and makes pathetic attempts to fight it off: 'I will not! Zounds, I will not! I may choose, /And I will choose' (scene 6). But these attempts only emphasize his final helplessness. Anne is equally helpless, falling almost at once: 'What shall I say? /My soul is wand'ring and hath lost her way' (scene 6). Confronting his wife with her guilt, Frankford is bewildered by the sheer unreasonableness of what has happened, and Anne can find no answers:

> Was it for want
> Thou play'dst the strumpet? Wast thou not supply'd
> With every pleasure, fashion, and new toy –
> Nay, even beyond my calling?
>
> ANNE
> I was.
>
> FRANKFORD
> Was it then disability in me,
> Or in thine eye seem'd he a properer man?

ANNE
> O no.

(scene 13)

The flat bewilderment of this moment is in a way more moving than Heywood's more overt attempts to play on our emotions; we touch here on the mystery of human frailty, and the promise of unadorned realism offered by the Prologue, 'a barren subject, a bare scene', is fulfilled.

Elsewhere Heywood's realism consists, more than Dekker's, of external details: 'Enter Frankford, *as it were brushing the crumbs from his clothes with a napkin, and newly risen from supper*' (scene 8); '*Enter* [Spiggot *the*] *Butler and* Jenkin *with a tablecloth, bread, trenchers, and salt*' (scene 11); '*Exeunt all* [*except* Wendoll *and* Jenkin], *the Carters whistling*' (scene 16). The last touch is particularly striking, following as it does a high-flown emotional scene in which the guilty lovers meet for the last time. For the carters, life goes on. Elsewhere Heywood uses domestic details for symbolic purposes. A card game becomes the occasion for relentless wordplay about the love-triangle; what works in the more artificial idiom of the chess scene in *Women Beware Women* looks a little contrived here. Having driven Anne from his house, Frankford searches the premises to make sure there is nothing left to remind him of her. This is a telling insight; but Heywood will not let it alone. Frankford finds her lute:

> O God, upon this instrument
> Her fingers have run quick division,
> Sweeter than that which now divides our hearts.

(scene 15)

He sends it to her, and she orders the servant Nicholas:

> Go break this lute upon my coach's wheel,
> As the last music that I e'er shall make –
> Not as my husband's gift, but my farewell
> To all earth's joy, and so your master tell.
> NICHOLAS
> If I can for crying.

(scene 16)

It was Nicholas, playing on an old loyalty – 'You knew me, sir, before you knew my mistress' (scene 8) – who first denounced the lovers. His tears thus doubly underline the pathos; but we may wonder if it needed to be underlined. The same deliberate playing on our emotions shows in Heywood's treatment of the couple's children, who are produced only when needed for maximum pathos after the adultery is discovered. Before this we had no reason to believe the couple had children or that they had been married more than a few days.

The most striking effect, of course, is Frankford's treatment of Anne, indicated by the title. His kindness consists in sending her to another house of his where all her material wants will be cared for; but she is never to see him or her children again. In response she starves herself to death, and Frankford breaks his own rule in time to appear at her deathbed for a touching reconciliation. Earlier, as he prepares to surprise the couple in bed, we see him consciously controlling himself, praying for patience; how hard patience comes is indicated when he nearly kills Wendoll and has to be restrained by a maid. Before passing his final sentence he retires into his study for a while. We see here a man controlling with some difficulty a natural impulse to revenge. But we have also to confront the dreadful paradox that the kindness is designed, quite consciously and deliberately, to kill. Frankford himself says so (scene 13). We are left wondering if we are seeing extraordinary charity or refined cruelty; if the impulse to revenge has been suppressed or concentrated with the intensity of a laser beam. Anne's brother, Sir Francis Acton, commenting on what Frankford has done, seems uncertain whether to condemn his mildness or praise his revenge (scene 17), and the confusion is revealing. But if we are disturbed in the right way by Frankford, we may also be a little disturbed, in the wrong way, by Heywood; Anne's fate seems consciously contrived to work out the implications of a familiar proverb; a certain glibness works against the attempt to move us in the final scenes. Wendoll is disposed of in a more convincing way. He flees the country, but looks forward to returning when the affair has blown over:

> And I divine, however now dejected,
> My worth and parts being by some great man prais'd,
> At my return I may in court be rais'd.
>
> (scene 16)

Again, the dramatization is glib; up to this point in the scene Wendoll has been torn with remorse, and his access of complacency seems to come from nowhere. But as an idea of what his future could be like, the resilience is interesting; and as a comment about the state of the world it balances the softer emotions of the play's last scene.

Later in his career Heywood returned to the theme of adultery and gave it a less striking but more subtle and accomplished treatment in the tragicomedy *The English Traveller* (c. 1625). The main plot begins with an even more comprehensive image of ideal social relations than the wedding in *A Woman Killed with Kindness*: a far-reaching web of friendship and mutual esteem, linking different households and crossing the generations. Decency and high-mindedness abound. Young Gerardine and Mistress Wincott, who is married to an elderly husband, are attracted to each other; but they go no further than an agreement to marry after her husband's death, which includes the provision that Gerardine will remain single till then. There are enough cross-purposes and misunderstandings to keep the plot going, but the characters' respect and affection for each other always prevent any serious damage. But in the midst of all this exemplary conduct Mistress Wincott is sleeping with Young Gerardine's friend Delavil. The revelation is not sudden and dramatic, as in *A Woman Killed*; it spreads like a slow dark stain, beginning with hints and dubious accusations, and is fully accomplished only near the end of the play. Mistress Wincott dies of remorse and Delavil, like Wendoll, flees, this time to an unknown future. But the friendship of Old Wincott and Young Gerardine seals over the disturbance:

> The lands that I have left,
> You lend me for the short space of my life;
> As soon as Heaven calls me, they call you lord.
> First feast, and after mourn; we'll, like some gallants
> That bury thrifty fathers, think't no sin
> To wear black without, but other thoughts within.
>
> (v. 2)

Heywood calls the play a tragicomedy and though the guilty wife, like Anne Frankford, dies, the label seems justified by the ease with which her death fades from our minds as the kindliness and security of the world at large are re-established.

In Old Wincott's speech the concentration on property and the reference to thrifty fathers, presumably with wastrel sons, suggest links with the comic subplot. Both stories play on an essential middle-class anxiety, the threatened house. Ideally a place of order and hospitality, it can also be a place of riot, and it can hide guilty secrets. Young Gerardine, left to himself at night in Wincott's house, explores it till he comes to Mistress Wincott's bedroom, where he hears two voices. In the subplot, based on Plautus's *Mostellaria*, Young Lionel, under the guidance of the debauched servant Reignald, takes over the house of his absent father and lives a life of riot. Our main interest is in the cleverness with which Reignald keeps the returned father at bay, among other tricks pretending the house is haunted. The gentleness of the main plot is balanced here by a raffish delight in the cunning of the trickster. Both stories end in repentance, though one is accompanied by death and the other by restoration. But the principal common factor is the haunted house, and the threat to middle-class security it embodies.

In both plays Heywood deals with forces that disturb the stability of society. Despite the escape of the guilty lover in each play, there is a final confidence in the threatened institutions. The wages of sin may be death or forgiveness, but the world around the sinner finally stands firm and is fundamentally good. Heywood has little of Dekker's sense that out in the streets there are unsolved problems. Elsewhere Heywood tends to be simply celebratory. The first part of *The Fair Maid of the West; or, A Girl Worth Gold* (*c.* 1600) puts the heroine Bess Bridges through her paces in a brisk tale of adventure that allows her to serve at a bar, wear men's clothes, fight, and lead a sea-voyage to exotic places, all the while displaying her patience, chastity, courage and generosity. The 1631 sequel is more given to Fletcherian contrivance and heroic debates on love and honour; the breezy high spirits of the original are more typical of Heywood. Bess is solidly English, a tanner's daughter who comes, in Shaw's phrase about Major Barbara, straight out of the heart of the whole people. The first play ends with Mullisheg, King of Fez, paying tribute to her and to her namesake Queen Elizabeth, the other Fair Maid of the West. That other Elizabeth is the subject of Heywood's two-part chronicle *If You Know not Me, You Know Nobody* (*c.* 1604, 1605). The first part concerns her troubles during the reign of her sister Mary; Elizabeth is a suffering Protestant martyr consoled by her faith and by the people's love. In a significant dumb-show, evidently representing a dream-vision, two friars try to kill her and two angels rescue her, leaving the Bible she was reading as she fell asleep open in her hand at a comforting text. The second play centres for much of its length on Thomas Gresham, whose wealth, enterprise and fiscal courage are celebrated in a series of colourful cartoon scenes. The focus shifts from the Queen to her subjects, whom we see going about their business and occasionally their pleasure. The two heroes come together when Elizabeth visits the Royal Exchange, Gresham's crowning achievement. Then we return to Elizabeth, as the play ends with the defeat of the Armada. Theatrically, all Heywood can do is have his characters stand around and describe what is happening out at sea; but the evocation of the famous events and the famous names seems to be enough. In *Henry V* Shakespeare gives a searching examination of the factors that produce a great national legend; Heywood is content to celebrate the legend.

The Queen Elizabeth plays show Heywood writing a national epic; they are serious in their way, but the main impression is of fast action and striking effects. The same is true of his most ambitious work, or at least his largest: the five-part cycle *The Golden Age*, *The Silver Age*, *The Brazen Age* and the two parts of *The Iron Age* (*c.* 1610–*c.* 1612). This is nothing less than a retelling of classical mythology from the opening quarrel of Titan and Saturn to the aftermath of the Fall of Troy. The sheer scale of the attempt is unmatched in the drama of the period; by Heywood's own account the performances drew on unusual theatrical resources and produced a real sense of occasion: 'these were the plays often, and not with the least applause, publicly acted by two companies, upon one stage at once, and have at sundry times thronged three several theatres with numerous and mighty auditories' ('Epistle to the Reader', *1 The Iron Age*). But Heywood is not Wagner. He is working for a popular, unlearned audience and is quite frank about it. In the *Epistle to the Reader* prefixed to the last play in the cycle he promises to print the whole work together in 'an handsome volume . . . with an explanation of all the difficulties, and an historical comment of every hard name, which may appear obscure or intricate to such as are not frequent in poetry'. In the puppet show of *Bartholomew Fair* Jonson insisted that the masses could take mythology only if it were vulgarized beyond recognition. Heywood does not quite do that; but he gives the stories in the form of a quick and varied narrative with lots of spectacular visual effects, suggesting that one precedent for what he was doing could be the miracle cycles that older playgoers would just remember: 'Hercules *fells* Pluto, *beats off the Devils with all their fireworks, rescues* Proserpine' (*The Silver Age*).

Occasionally a difficult moment is funked: Hercules, for example, battles the Nemean lion offstage while Juno and Iris comment. But Heywood and his theatrical collaborators shrink from very little. The death of Semele is the occasion for fire effects: '*Thunder, lightnings,* Jupiter *descends in his majesty, his thunderbolt burning. . . . As he toucheth the bed it fires, and all flies up.* Jupiter *from thence takes an abortive infant*' (*The Silver Age*). Elsewhere we have transformations: 'Gallus *sinks, and in his place riseth a cock and crows*' (*The Brazen Age*); elaborate settings: '*Two fiery bulls are discovered, the Fleece hanging over them, and the Dragon sleeping beneath them*; Medea *with strange fireworks hangs above in the air in the strange habit of a conjuress*' (*The Brazen Age*); and spectacular combats: 'Hector *takes up a great piece of a rock, and casts it at* Ajax, *who tears a young tree up the roots and assails* Hector' (*1 The Iron Age*, II). So much for the bare Elizabethan stage. For anyone interested in special effects these plays are a treasure-house.

Heywood's structure appears at first episodic, its overall shaping principle that of variety for its own sake: 'Loath are we, courteous auditors, to cloy /Your appetites with viands of one taste' (*The Brazen Age*). But as the plays progress we gradually become aware of Heywood's interest in the traditional idea that life deteriorated through the Ages. At first the sexual escapades of Jupiter are the occasion for comedy. The deception of Amphitrio gets its usual laughs, and Danae greets her fate with cheerful irony:

> If you but offer't, I shall cry outright.
> Oh God, how hoarse I am, and cannot! Fie,
> Danae thus naked, and a man so nigh!
>
> (*The Golden Age*, IV)

We are dealing with 'love and harmless lusts' (*The Brazen Age*). But the stories of Semele's fiery death and the rape of Proserpina introduce a more sombre note. When we come to Troy, Helen and Paris keep the tone light at first. Oenone's attempt to keep Paris from his fatal expedition to Greece is quickly brushed off:

OENONE
> Canst thou, o canst thou thy sweet life endanger,
> And leave thine own wife to seek out a stranger?

PARIS
> I can, farewell.
>
> (*1 The Iron Age*, I)

So is Menelaus's attempt to get Helen back:

MENELAUS
> Here honour dwells.

PARIS
> Here many a thousand kiss.

HELEN
> That way I should, because I know 'tis meeter.

MENELAUS
> Welcome.

HELEN
> But I'll this way, for Paris kisses sweeter.
>
> (*1 The Iron Age*, III)

But the tone darkens. Heywood is more explicit than Shakespeare about the unheroic nature of Hector's death; he makes it clear that Achilles leaves the killing entirely to his Myrmidons, and then stabs the dead body. The first Troy play ends with the madness and suicide of Ajax, a deepening sense of the futility of war, and a cynical epilogue by Thersites. In the second Troy play, the last of the series, the violence becomes extravagant. Paris, Hecuba, Polixenes and Andromache '*are all slain at once*' (*2 The Iron Age*, III). The carnage is just beginning, for Heywood's title page lists the deaths of sixteen characters followed by 'etc.'. In desperation to get it all done, he writes the following stage direction: '*A confused scruffle, in which* Orestes *kills* Pyrrhus, Pyrrhus, Orestes; Cethus *wounds* Pillades, Diomed, Menelaus, Ulysses, Thersites, *etc. All fall dead save* Ulysses' (v). After this we can admire the restraint of Webster and Middleton. More effective is the fate of Helen. As Troy burns she encounters the now leprous Cressida, and meditates on the frailty of beauty. In the last scene she is alone on stage, lamenting the ruin of her legend:

> [Is] this the beauty,
> That launch'd a thousand ships from Aulis gulf?
> Is such a poor repurchase now decay'd?
> See, fair ones, what a little time can do.
>
>   (v)

Then she strangles herself. This, we may reflect sadly, is what a middle-class moralist does with the legend of Troy. But after five plays of spectacle and adventure Heywood's decision to end it all with a single woman lamenting the mortality we all share has a certain poignant irony. The sole survivor is Ulysses, who announces in the epilogue his intention of returning to Penelope; but for Heywood the story is over. The vision of the new Troy that will rise in the form of London is placed early in the play, and goes for suprisingly little (II). Intent on ruin, Heywood for once passes up a chance for celebration.

We might summarize Heywood as quintessentially a man of the theatre. He uses its full resources with enthusiasm and frequently with daring; but he also uses them in an *ad hoc* way. His plays add up to a collection of striking effects: spectacle, pathos, adventure, rogue comedy. There is plenty to entertain, little to disturb – unless we are disturbed by the sight of a talented artist who has so little in the way of a central controlling vision. But that is to take Heywood on terms in which he himself seems not to have been interested. For Heywood the values that finally matter are theatrical ones. The theatre as he uses it is a splendidly versatile machine: it can deal in realism and in exotic spectacle, it can teach moral lessons and provide harmlessly amoral pleasures. The strongest impression his drama makes when taken as a whole is sheer delight in its own variety.

Dekker and Heywood are the best known of the popular dramatists. This is partly because of the quality of their best work, but partly also because a writer with a known name and a reasonably extensive canon stands a better chance of reprinting. Others were not so fortunate.

From the great range of popular drama we may select three anonymous plays, linked by the odd fate of having once been attributed to Shakespeare; no one now takes the attributions seriously, but the plays are conveniently anthologized in *The Shakespeare Apocrypha*.[3] All three were performed by Shakespeare's company, and they may stand as a representative sample of what his now forgotten contemporaries were up to. The Prologue to *The Merry Devil of Edmonton* (*c.* 1602) enjoins the audience to 'sit with a pleased eye, until you know /The comic end of this our tragic show'. The induction consciously reverses the ending of a famous tragedy, *Doctor Faustus*. We find the title character, Peter Fabell, waiting for a spirit to take him to Hell as the clock strikes. But when the spirit comes, Fabell tricks him into giving him seven more years, and by the end of the play nothing more is heard of the conjurer's approaching damnation. He uses the time to help a pair of young lovers cheat the girl's father: 'Let us alone, to bustle for the set, /For Age and Craft with Wit and Art have met' (I. 3). The combination of love and magic may recall Greene's *Friar Bacon and Friar Bungay*, (*c.* 1589) and the conflict of youth and age is one of the basic formulae of comedy. The girl's father has had her placed in a convent, from which her lover intends to steal her. The pre-Reformation setting allows some old-fashioned joking, particularly in Fabell's threat of the havoc his spirits will wreak among the nuns:

> I'll send me fellows of a handful high
> Into the cloisters where the nuns frequent,
> Shall make them skip like does about the Dale,
> And with the Lady Prioress of the house
> To play at leapfrog, naked in their smocks,
> Until the merry wenches at their mass
> Cry teehee weehee;
> And tickling these mad lasses in their flanks,
> They'll sprawl, and squeak, and prick their fellow nuns.
> Be lively, boys, before the wench we lose,
> I'll make the Abbess wear the Canon's hose.
>   (II. 2)

In the end Fabell hardly uses magic at all. As in *A Midsummer Night's Dream*, or Henry Porter's *Two Angry Women of Abingdon* (*c.* 1588), the characters go through a period of comic confusion in the dark, involving disguise, mistaken identity, deer-stealing, mock-ghosts, and false arrest. The love plot and the deer-stealing are linked by the priest and part-time poacher Sir John, using a peculiar logic of his own: 'Sir, to prove myself an honest man, being that I was last night in the forest stealing venison – now, sir, to have you stand my friend, if that matter should be call'd in question, I married your daughter to this worthy gentleman' (v. 2). Love and roguery make common cause, age and respectability, as usual, take a beating; the play follows, easily and undemandingly, some of the basic rules of comedy. We know that the result was popular enough to have annoyed Ben Jonson, for he refers sourly to it in the Prologue to *The Devil is an Ass*.

The London Prodigal (*c.* 1604) looks more ambitious. The wastrel Young Flowerdale is married to Luce, against her wishes, because her father mistakenly thinks Flowerdale a good financial investment. There is room for sombre reflection here on the abuse of marriage and on the rights of parents and children, particularly when Flowerdale's prodigality deepens from ordinary pleasure-seeking into something more desperate and ugly. Flowerdale Senior, apparently dead but actually spying on his son in disguise, offers some serious thoughts on the training of children, which he sees as the taming of animals (I. 1); he sees no real harm in the young man at first but is increasingly shocked as Flowerdale deteriorates. There seems no hope for him: 'On goes he that knows no end of his journey' (v. 1). But Luce, though she never wanted to marry him, becomes a Patient Griselda figure, and her loyalty finally shames him into repentance. Though it touches on serious questions, the ingredients of the story are in the end conventional: the disguised father, the faithful wife, the final forgiveness. So are the incidentals, including the dialect comedy that always threatens to break out in plays of this period. But the conventions in themselves have value: they imply something fundamentally secure, familiar, and reassuring in the play's vision. The scene in which Flowerdale begs from various representative characters shows a black-and-white, morally stable society in which people behave exactly as we would expect. The rakes and rogues who used to cater to his prodigality will have nothing to do with him; a grave citizen gives him money and a lecture, advising him not to count on begging; a citizen's wife gives him money but takes it back when he offers sexual services in exchange. Despite the occasional cruelty of individuals, Flowerdale's experience takes place in a society in which decent people behave decently and scoundrels do not. Apart from one surprise at the end, when in the general sharing of forgiveness and reconciliation Luce's sister announces she has renounced the idea of marriage, the play is designed to entertain us with a comfortably familiar story.

The same cannot be said of that grim little woodcut of a play, *A Yorkshire Tragedy* (*c.* 1606). This is a short play, part of a group called *Four Plays in One*, and its very brevity contributes to its power. It is in the tradition of murder plays based on real-life incidents, of which the most notable is *Arden of Faversham* (*c.* 1591). Here no saving conventions contain or neutralize the central character's drive to ruin. As if to emphasize their roles in society, the characters have no proper

names, only titles (Husband, Wife, Knight).[4] The Husband has a
solid, ancient position, which he is steadily destroying:

> Thy father's and forefathers' worthy honours,
> Which were our country monuments, our grace,
> Follies in thee begin now to deface.
>
> (scene 2)

The fact that the Husband is ruining his inheritance may be one reason
why he has no name. As in Marston, old, stable values are blighted.
And so is hope for the future. The Husband frustrates his own promise
– 'Much good has been expected in your life, /Cancel not all men's
hopes' (scene 2) – and that of his brother, who has been involved in
his debts. The Master of the brother's College complains, 'Oh, you
have killed the towardest hope of all our university. . . . Your brother,
a man who profited in his divine employments, might have made ten
thousand souls fit for heaven, now by your careless courses cast in
prison' (scene 4). The ruin is personal, social and spiritual; and it goes
on spreading.

The Wife, who tries to help him, recognizes not just compulsiveness
but bleak nihilism in his drive to self-destruction: 'Nothing will please
him, until all be nothing' (scene 3). She has arranged for him a place
at Court; but her smooth verse announcing the plan is assailed by his
jagged prose:

WIFE

> By this good means I shall preserve my lands,
> And free my husband out of usurers' hands;
> Now there is no need of sale, my uncle's kind;
> I hope, if aught, this will content his mind.
> Here comes my husband.
>
> (Enter Husband)

HUSBAND

> Now, are you come? Where's the money? Let's see the
> money! Is the rubbish sold, these wiseacres your lands?
> Why, when? The money! Where is it? Pour't down,
> down with it, down with it; I say pour't o'th' ground!
> Let's see it, let's see't.
>
> (scene 3)

The author dispenses with the picturesque, distorted imagery that
usually signals madness in the plays of this period and gives us instead
the frighteningly authentic sound of a mind turning in the grooves of
obsession.

The Husband kills two of his children, on stage. There is a certain contrived pathos in the death of the first: 'How shall I learn now my head's broke?' (scene 4), but no attempt at heightening in the second killing:

HUSBAND
    Strumpet, let go the boy, let go the beggar.
WIFE
    O my sweet husband!
HUSBAND
    Filth, harlot!
WIFE
    O, what will you do, dear husband?
HUSBAND
    Give me the bastard.
WIFE
    Your own sweet boy!
HUSBAND
    There are too many beggars.
                              (scene 5)

A servant who tries, and fails, to overpower him is astonished at the manic strength of a normally weak man (scene 7); he seems literally possessed. In the end he and his wife, whom he has wounded but not killed, are reconciled; but other attempts at comfort are blocked. The Husband prays to the dead children, but imagines, 'you are playing on the angels' laps, /And will not look on me' (scene 10); the Wife, told to take comfort in her remaining child, turns instead to futile plans for saving her husband, and the Master ends the play with a flat statement of ruin: 'Two brothers: one in bond lies overthrown, /This on a deadlier execution' (scene 10).

The domestic drama of the period deals naturally with threats to the security of the middle-class world, of which prodigality and adultery are the principal ones. It normally contains those threats by showing a fundamentally healthy society, and a fundamentally decent human nature, that allow kindness and forgiveness to have their way in the end; even tragedy is generally turned towards pity. But the threats are nonetheless real for being containable. The nameless Husband of *A Yorkshire Tragedy* shows the essential fear around which these plays are written: the threats to family, property and life itself that come not from ruffians in the streets – the law can always deal with those – but from an inexplicable darkness in the heart of the householder himself.

The Husband's madness, like the fall of Anne Frankford, is a mystery. In both cases there is a threat from within that destroys the comfortable home to which the domestic play aspires as its ideal, and destroys it for no discernible reason. Writers like Middleton and Jonson would have seen a reason: greed, lust and the desire for revenge naturally drive the characters of satiric drama. But for the popular playwright, it is natural to seek and defend comfort and security. The institutions of home and business, guaranteed by honest commercial enterprise and sexual continence, are what bind society together. The materialism that in Middleton narrows the human spirit is, for writers like Dekker and Heywood, simply a natural aspiration for the legitimate satisfactions the world can give. The drive to power and self-assertion is softened into a desire for possession, embodied in the security of home and shop. Good wives, like the reformed Bellafront and Mistress Flowerdale, remain loyal to their unworthy husbands because it is better to preserve the institution of marriage than to seek one's freedom by breaking it. Disloyal, adulterous wives lose not so much their immortal souls as their places in a world that could have given them security. And they themselves become, like the prostitutes who haunt the fringes of these plays, damaged goods. They command not admiration for their self-assertion or daring, but pity and regret for their folly. Webster's Vittoria would find no place here. The celebrations that open *A Woman Killed with Kindness* and close *The Shoemakers' Holiday* proclaim the satisfactions of security, good fellowship and mutual affection. Those who turn away from such satisfactions seem in the grip of an arbitrary, bewildering impulse to self-destruction. Given such comfort, who would want to throw it away? The popular dramatists have at least the honesty to ask the question; and the further honesty to admit they cannot answer it.

Notes

1. A convenient collection is *Thomas Dekker: Selected Prose Writings*, edited by E. D. Pendry, Stratford-upon-Avon Library, 4 (London, 1967).

2. 'To the Reader', *The English Traveller*, in *Thomas Heywood*, edited by A. Wilson Verity, Mermaid, (London, 1888) p. 154.

3. Edited by C. F. Tucker Brooke (Oxford, 1908).

4. The first scene involves three servants with proper names, who do not appear again. But the scene fits badly with the rest of the play, and is probably spurious.

Part Three:

Later Jacobean and Caroline Drama

Chapter 11
Fletcher and Company

The intense, satiric, questioning style we think of as 'Jacobean' was largely a product of the early years of the seventeenth century. Around 1610 a new manner becomes discernible: more relaxed and open, with, on the surface at least, a dignity and smoothness foreign to the temper of writers like Marston and Webster. Spiritually, the horizons of drama begin to shrink. The probing of the unseen world, the questioning of the gods, even of God, that runs from Marlowe through to Webster is replaced by a vision that is more purely social. It is not that the questions have been answered; they are no longer being asked. Class, breeding and behaviour are becoming more important than salvation and damnation. There is a conscious appeal to gentlemanly values: courage, honour, friendship. Characters are less inclined to shade into the angelic or the monstrous; instead, quirks of personality within a social context are observed. The change was gradual, and there was a good deal of overlapping. Such 'Jacobean' masterpieces as *Women Beware Women* and *The Duchess of Malfi* date well after 1610. And there is a kinship between the two styles. Beaumont and Fletcher, as we will see, combine a high heroic style with a low view of human nature; the same could be said of Webster, Marston or Chapman. The difference is that the contrast no longer seems shocking. It is observed, reported, accepted. The urgency has gone.

There is also a vein of the exotic and romantic that can be linked to the revival of romance drama, a key sign of which is the popularity around this time of the old romantic adventure-play *Mucedorus* (c.1590), a fine bit of Elizabethan popular nonsense that seems to have touched a vein of nostalgia in a more sophisticated audience. In early Jacobean drama we may not be able to tell one Italian court from another, but the sense of Italy is quite sharp, as is the sense of London in Middleton or Dekker. In Beaumont and Fletcher the setting may be called Rhodes, or Iberia, or Licia but it is really a place of the imagination, a precursor of the world of heroic drama where characters live in perspective sets and wear ostrich feathers in their helmets. Fletcher's comedy *The Woman's Prize* (c. 1605) is set in a London whose natives have names like Petronius and Moroso. Where Jonson, Middleton and

Dekker try to give a specific local flavour Fletcher tries to avoid it. He creates instead a world that belongs only on the stage. None of this means, however, that the plays can be dismissed as complacent entertainments for a bored aristocratic audience. They may not attack the nerves as the old ones did; but they still leave an alert audience with plenty to worry about.

John Fletcher (1597–1625) was a principal figure, perhaps the key one, in the change. We think of him as part of the team of Beaumont and Fletcher, and this was the most successful of his collaborations. But he also worked on his own, and after Beaumont's death he worked, though less effectively, with Massinger. Around 1613 he collaborated briefly with Shakespeare, certainly on *The Two Noble Kinsmen* (1613) and the lost *Cardenio* (*c.* 1612), possibly on *Henry VIII* (*c.* 1613).[1] *The Two Noble Kinsmen* shows the difference between the two writers most clearly, and is a convenient way of introducing some of the characteristics we may call 'Fletcherian'. The play is an adaptation of Chaucer's *Knight's Tale*, concerning the rivalry of Palamon and Arcite for the love of Emilia. The knights fight a tournament for her. Arcite, who has prayed to Mars, wins the tournament but is accidentally killed shortly afterwards; Palamon, who has prayed to Venus, loses the tournament but as the survivor wins the lady. Beneath the chivalry and romance there is a sense of the absurdity of life; this appears to be the principal common ground between Shakespeare and Fletcher, and may explain their interest in working together. But they express it very differently.

Shakespeare's vision is cosmic. Emilia, whose affections are divided, greets Arcite's initial victory with a lament for the sentence of death on Palamon: 'Is this winning? /O all you heavenly powers, where is your mercy?' (v. 3). Theseus, contemplating the final disposition of the two knights, similarly glances upwards: 'Never Fortune /Did play a subtler game' (v. 4). He concludes the play with a wry acceptance of life's absurdity, tinged with bitterness:

> O you heavenly charmers,
> What things you make of us! For what we lack
> We laugh; for what we have are sorry; still
> Are children in some kind. Let us be thankful
> For that which is, and with you leave dispute
> That are above our question. Let's go off,
> And bear us like the time.
> (v. 4)

When Fletcher's Arcite accuses Palamon, 'Fie, sir, /You play the child extremely' (ii. 1) there is a different tone, not thoughtful but sharp and exasperated. Here the absurdity belongs not to life in general but to particular people. Where Shakespeare's style is slow, controlled and difficult, Fletcher's is clear and direct, but more inclined to extremes. His characters are more given to idealistic gestures. Shakespeare's knights brood over the corruption of Thebes and plan to leave it (I. 2); Fletcher's Palamon, imprisoned by Theseus, cries, 'Where is Thebes now? Where is our noble country?' (II. 1). The disillusion of two young idealists has been replaced by a simple gentlemanly patriotism. At the same time the sex-drive of Fletcher's characters is much simpler. Shakespeare's Emilia speaks of the innocent, intense friendship she had with a girl who has since died, contrasting it with the experienced friendship of Theseus and Pirithous (I. 3). Fletcher's Emilia has a simpler view of human relations, saying of Narcissus, 'That was a fair boy, but a fool /To love himself, were there not maids enough?' (II. 1). Again we hear the note of comic exasperation. The leading character in Fletcher's subplot, the Gaoler's daughter who runs mad for love, sees her problem not as romance or sentiment but simple biology:

> Out upon't!
> What pushes are we wenches driven to
> When fifteen once has found us!
>
> (II. 3)

When Palamon and Arcite first see Emilia, Fletcher gives them not dignified rivalry but a childish squabble, behind which lies the same simple urge:

PALAMON
You love her, then?

ARCITE
　　　　　Who would not?

PALAMON
　　　　　　　　　　And desire her?

ARCITE
Before my liberty.

PALAMON
I saw her first.

ARCITE
　　　　That's nothing.

PALAMON
　　　　　　　　　But it shall be.

ARCITE
I saw her too.

PALAMON
　　　　Yes, but you must not love her.

ARCITE
    I will not, as you do, to worship her
    As she is heavenly and a blessed goddess.
    I love her as a woman, to enjoy her.
                                              (II. 1)

The whiplash speed, and the grand gesture followed by a sudden collapse, are among Fletcher's trademarks.

Henry VIII is a more controversial case. There would appear to be a Fletcherian manner at certain moments of the play, though whether this is to be accounted for by collaboration or influence is likely to remain unsettled. The matter of the play is weighty enough. The fall of Wolsey, Henry's break with Rome, his divorcing Katherine of Aragon to marry Anne Bullen, and a final prophecy of the golden age of Elizabeth, give us a panoramic view of English history at one of its crucial turning points. But along with the sheer breadth of vision goes a certain detachment, marked by a curious flippancy of manner. The Prologue declares that the play has designs on our emotions:

    I come no more to make you laugh. Things now
    That bear a weighty and a serious brow,
    Sad, high, and working, full of state and woe,
    Such noble scenes as draw the eye to flow,
    We now present.

The sense that we are being manipulated is confirmed by the Prologue's unexpectedly flippant conclusion: 'And if you can be merry then, I'll say /A man may weep upon his wedding-day'. The Epilogue is frankly jocular. In the main play, the King's divorce is high matter of state whose causes are variously attributed to his troubled conscience and his sexual infatuation with Anne Bullen: 'his conscience /Has crept too near another lady' (II. 2). There is plenty of spectacle, and there are grand scenes of farewell for Buckingham, Katherine and Wolsey, consciously balanced against the rise of Anne and the eventual triumph of Elizabeth. But the air of contrivance with which it is all done, and the clear-eyed vision of human pettiness in the private lives of the great, make this a more detached, even cynical play than the surface pomp and pageantry would suggest.[2]

Fletcher and Shakespeare made an unlikely team; the collaboration with Francis Beaumont (*c.* 1584–1616) appears to have been more sympathetic. Yet that too must have looked at first unlikely, judging by the earliest unaided work of the two men. Beaumont's *The Knight of the Burning Pestle* (*c.* 1607) and Fletcher's *The Faithful Shepherdess* (*c.* 1608) appear to have little in common apart from initial failure before an unprepared, uncomprehending audience. One is a rollicking burlesque, the other a grave pastoral exploring the themes of love and chastity. But each had something to contribute to the collaboration that lay ahead. *The Knight of the Burning Pestle* begins in the Blackfriars theatre, as a Citizen and his wife stop a performance of *The London Merchant*, which they imagine to be an anti-citizen piece, and demand instead that the company put on the sort of pro-citizen celebration Heywood was currently writing for the Red Bull:

CITIZEN
Why could you not be contented, as well as others,
with the legend of Whittington, or the life and death of
Sir Thomas Gresham, with the building of the Royal
Exchange? Or the story of Queen Eleanor, with the
rearing of London Bridge upon woolsacks? . . .

PROLOGUE
Why, what do you say to the life and death of fat
Drake, or the repairing of Fleet privies?
(Induction)

The interlopers are clearly out of place at this fashionable theatre and their taste is for a form of entertainment the company regards as dated and absurd. They want a part in the play for their apprentice Rafe as knight-errant. Rafe is an enthusiastic amateur actor whose repertoire includes such famous roles from the old heroic days of the theatre as Hotspur and Hieronimo, and who can always be counted on to scare the children. Rafe is given his chance, and the result is a burlesque of chivalry that shows old-fashioned courtesy adrift in a crass modern world.[3] Rafe complains: 'There are no such courteous and fair well-spoken knights in this age; they will call one the son of a whore, that Palmerin of England would have called fair sir; and one that Rosicler would have called right beauteous damsel, they will call damn'd bitch' (I). In one revealing scene, Rafe takes an inn for a castle manned by courteous knights, and assumes his host must be joking when he presents the bill. Cash also matters to the theatre company, who resist the Citizen's attempt to expand Rafe's part: 'In good faith, sir, we cannot, you'll utterly spoil our play and make it to be hissed, and it cost money' (III).

While the burlesque of *Pyramus and Thisbe* was securely contained within the structure of *A Midsummer Night's Dream*, the burlesque of *The Knight of the Burning Pestle* explodes the whole theatrical occasion. While Shakespeare's art draws everything together, Beaumont's is deliberately and startlingly centrifugal. At first Rafe is brought into scenes from the original play, *The London Merchant*; but his part finally

194 ENGLISH DRAMA: SHAKESPEARE TO THE RESTORATION

becomes quite independent, and deteriorates (or evolves) into a series of disconnected scenes designed to show him off in various roles: being wooed by a foreign princess, dressed as a May Lord, reviewing the militia, and finally playing a long death scene with an arrow through his head. The plot of *The London Merchant* would appear to trigger conventional sympathies: Luce is courted by the romantic lover Jasper and the foolish Humphrey, and of course prefers Jasper. But the Citizen's wife prefers Humphrey, and for Rafe Jasper is an enemy. The story's values and those of the onstage audience are at odds. Some story conventions are reversed: Old Merrythought, a prodigal father with a thrifty son, stays at home rioting while his sober family wanders helplessly through the streets. Others are presented with mocking self-consciousness, as when Luce insists, 'No man shall ever joy me as his wife, /But he that stole me hence' (I). Even the rhyming couplet, taken for granted in so much Elizabethan theatre, is burlesqued: 'Good Mistress Luce, however I in fault am /For your lame horse, you're welcome unto Waltham' (II). The sheer range of the play's mockery, making a clean sweep of everything from chivalric romance to citizen comedy, suggests a young writer who wants to announce his arrival on the scene by declaring the old conventions exhausted.

But the effect is not disturbing in the manner of Marston's *Antonio* plays. The prevailing spirit is good- tempered, and the final song unites the company in a celebration of mirth and harmony:

> Better music ne'er was known
> Than a quire of hearts in one. . . .
> Sing though before the hour of dying,
> He shall rise and then be crying.
> Hey ho, 'tis nought but mirth,
> That keeps the body from the earth.
>
> (v)

Death, burlesqued in the play itself, is allowed to be just serious enough to be worth laughing off. And the concord of hearts, mocked in the play's tongue-in-cheek love story, becomes unexpectedly real at the end of the play as the Citizen's wife addresses the audience:

> I thank you all, gentlemen, for your patience and
> countenance to Ralph, a poor fatherless child; and if I
> might see you at my house, it should go hard but I would
> have a pottle of wine and a pipe of tobacco for you, for
> truly I hope you do like the youth, but I would be glad to
> know the truth; I refer you to your own discretions,

whether you will applaud him or no, for I will wink and
whilst you shall do what you will – I thank you with all
my heart, God give you good night; come,
George.
       (Epilogue)

The citizens have disrupted the entertainment of a gentlemanly audience at a private theatre, and now they go back to the world they came
from. But they offer reconciliation and hospitality in their world in
return for the audience's sympathy for Rafe; it is a reconciliation of
stage with audience and of class with class. In the unexpected gentleness of the ending Beaumont may also be salving any hurt that may
have been caused by his caricature of the citizens. This is finally the
most amiable of English dramatic burlesques, and its initial failure is
a mark against the Blackfriars audience.

The failure of Fletcher's *The Faithful Shepherdess* is almost as
surprising, for this finely crafted and thoughtful play is also a tight and
lively theatre piece. Fletcher's epistle to the reader bitterly suggests that
the pastoral was not vulgar enough. Certainly these are very aristocratic and literary shepherds, but that should have given no trouble to
an educated audience. Perhaps, as the commendatory verses prefixed
to the first edition indicate, the audience was not really educated.
Fletcher uses this artificial mode for a serious exploration of sex, a
subject that was to concern him, not always so seriously, through
much of his career. The play's language is dominated by contrasting
images of hot lust and cold chastity. The title character, Clorin, begins
the play mourning her dead love, who is so much a living presence
for her that she apologizes for leaving his tomb to go on a brief errand
of mercy (IV. 5). Her virginity gives her a special power; the first sign
of this is the respect accorded to her by the Satyr, who acts as her
servant and messenger throughout the play, and whose rough nature
is tamed by her virtue:

                              Sure there is a power
In that great name of virgin, that binds fast
All rude uncivil bloods, all appetites
That break their confines.
                (I. 1)

We look forward for a moment to *Comus*. Clorin's opposite number
is the Sullen Shepherd. She heals injuries; he causes most of the damage
in the play. Her solitude is the ideal celibacy that allows charity to
spread more widely; his is simply antisocial and inhuman. His sex-
drive is indiscriminate: 'Now lust is up, alike all women be' (III. 1),

and he assumes that women's sexuality is as brutal as his: 'Women love only the opportunity /And not the man' (III. 1).

He is closest to being right in the case of Chloe, whose desire for sex is comically unbridled: 'It is impossible to ravish me, /I am so willing' (III. 1). Amarillis, though less indiscriminate, is equally aggressive, trying to win Perigot from his faithful lady Amoret even if it means enlisting the Sullen Shepherd. Male lust is represented by Alexis, whose willingness to meet Chloe on her own terms is contrasted with the shyness of Daphnis, who feels desire but, to Chloe's annoyance, can rein it in. Alexis, about to possess Chloe, is wounded by the Sullen Shepherd, and the moment is as overtly allegorical as similar moments in *The Faerie Queene*. He is yielding to, and injured by, the sort of lust the Sullen Shepherd represents. The most complex lovers are Perigot and Amoret, whose story is the central one. As he vows faithfulness to her, Perigot's language strays into compulsive images of heat, bestial violence and ultimate disorder:

> when I leave to be
> The true admirer of thy chastity,
> Let me deserve the hot polluted name
> Of a wild woodman, or affect some dame
> Whose often prostitution hath begot
> More foul diseases than ever yet the hot
> Sun bred through his burnings, whilst the Dog
> Pursues the raging Lion, throwing fog
> And deadly vapours from his angry breath,
> Filling the lower world with plague and death.
>
> (I. 2)

Innocent on the surface, the lovers are involved in a dark and violent action that suggests, given the play's allegorical machinery, something dangerous in their own sexuality. Amarillis, in the shape of Amoret, tempts Periogot to sex, and he tries in disgust to kill her; he misses the false Amoret but wounds the true one twice. The completeness of the illusion suggests that at some level he is acting out a conflict in his own sexual feelings for the real Amoret. Similarly, when Clorin tries to cure Amoret's second wound with a herb that works only on the chaste, it fails at first; the explanation turns out to be not that Amoret is literally corrupt, but that the lustful Chloe is hiding nearby and the herb is reacting to her presence. The suggestion may be, however, that there is something of Chloe hidden in Amoret.

The whole pastoral world is ordered and ceremonial. Dawn and sunset are signalled formally by the intoning of a priest of Pan, accompanied by an old shepherd ringing a bell. This is a nature religion, with its own daily offices. The rites of Pan both acknowledge and control man's lower passions, just as Clorin studies all herbs but eschews the dangerous ones. In the opening of I. 2, we see the priest formally purging the shepherds of whatever lustful desires a just-completed festival of Pan may have roused. Like love itself, the festival is right and necessary, but has a dark side that must be controlled. At the end of the play Clorin turns the shepherds over to the priest with the suggestion that though they have been cured of lust their continuing health must be constantly safeguarded:

> Now holy man, I offer up again
> These patients full of health, and free from pain;
> Keep them from after ills, be ever near
> Unto their actions.
>
> (v. 5)

Lust, temporarily amusing in the scenes with Chloe, is in the last analysis brutal and absurd; the ceremonies of the pastoral world, and the artifice of the play as a whole, are designed to contain and control it. In later plays by Beaumont and Fletcher, and by Fletcher alone, the absurd and reductive quality of passion will be even more apparent; the difference is that the aristocratic artifice that accompanies it will acquire an absurdity of its own.

In *Philaster; or, Love Lies Bleeding* (c. 1609) Beaumont and Fletcher combined in a successful tragicomedy that appears, unlike their earlier work, to have caught and perhaps helped to create the taste of the time. The action is fast, extravagant, and occasionally violent, but ultimately contained. The hero, in a sensational effect whose popularity is indicated by the play's subtitle, wounds both of the play's heroines, but not fatally. He himself calls for death in moments of stress, but when actually wounded declares, 'I must shift for life' (IV. 5). The inconsistency does not worry us, as it is part of the play's admitted and frequently self-conscious artifice. The characters' passions are at once extravagant and distanced. Arathusa can confess her love for Philaster only when he has turned his face away; the implied staging of their first love scene is of two opera singers facing the audience as they proclaim a shared passion. When Philaster learns that Arathusa has been unchaste, he rejects the slander at first:

> Set hills on hills betwixt me and the man
> That utters this, and I will scale them all,
> And from the utmost top fall on his neck,
> Like thunder from a cloud.

Then a few lines later he accepts it:

> The winds that are let loose
> From the four several corners of the earth
> And spread themselves all over sea and land
> Kiss not a chaste one. What friend bears a sword
> To run me through?
>
> (III. 1)

The audience does not yet know that the page Arathusa is accused with is a girl in disguise, and the slander is absurd. But we do not expect a tragic outcome, for there is enough absurdity in Philaster's passion, in which faith and jealousy are equally exaggerated and come out sounding much the same, to keep us from taking him seriously. Quieter, but just as artificial, is the lyrical melancholy of the accused page 'Bellario' (really Euphrasia) who loves Philaster and is quite content at the end of the play with a chance to see him regularly. The gesture and display, the quantifying of emotion, can take the seriousness even out of forgiveness:

> ARATHUSA
> I have a power to pardon sins as oft
> As any man has power to wrong me.
> CLEREMONT
> Noble and worthy.
>
> (V. 5)

As we remain cool to the characters' sufferings, we remain cool also to their final happiness.

The authors also keep us in touch with low reality. When Arathusa is lost in the wood, a courtier is irritated by the King's concern: 'Let him seek his daughter himself; she cannot stray about a little necessary natural business, but the whole court must be up in arms; when she has done, we shall have peace' (IV. 4). For Philaster's rival Pharamond, sex is also a necessary natural business. When Arathusa rejects his idea of anticipating the wedding night, he complains, 'The constitution of my body will never hold out till the wedding; I must seek elsewhere' (I. 2). When he tries the chaste court lady Gallathea, he gets nowhere: 'Gold? Now, as I live,' 'tis fair gold; you would have silver for it to play with the pages, you could not have taken me at a worse time' (II. 2). The witty put-down is as much a feature of the Beaumont and Fletcher style as is Philaster's hyperbole; indeed, the two are connected in a rhythm of strain and collapse that runs through their work.

One of the most complicated effects occurs during the hunting sequence when Philaster determines to avenge himself on Arathusa by killing her, and is interrupted:

PHILASTER
Are you at peace?

ARATHUSA
With heaven and earth.

PHILASTER
May they divide thy soul and body.
(Philaster *wounds her.*)

COUNTRY FELLOW
Hold, dastard, strike a woman! Th'art a craven. . . .

PHILASTER
Leave us, good friend.

ARATHUSA
What ill-bred man art thou, to intrude thyself
Upon our private sports and recreations?

COUNTRY FELLOW
God uds me, I understand you not; but I know the rogue has hurt you.
(IV. 5)

The Country Fellow has a point. He sees only the action, not the courtly values behind it, but his blunt comment helps us question the seriousness, not to say the humanity, of those values. At the same time he is socially out of his depth; this is a gentleman's (and lady's) game of passion and violence, and the victim herself is as annoyed with him as if she were interrupted while losing a tennis match. His reaction to the hunt, 'I can see nothing but people better hors't than myself, that outride me' (IV. 5), helps place him as an outsider. The distance between court and country has already been established in Philaster's pastoral reverie, in which he imagines a life of peace with a country girl who would rear 'at her big breasts /My large coarse issue' (IV. 3). This is what he claims to want, but his own words give him the lie, especially if we remember his description of Arathusa's breasts as 'two liquid ivory balls' (III. 1). The principal characters live in a courtly world and the country, as in many Restoration comedies, is like the dark side of the moon.

So is the city. Philaster, we are told, is loved by the people, and at the end of the play he is rescued not by his own efforts but by a rebellion of friendly citizens. This is not, however, a plea for a democratically supported monarchy. There is a sly suggestion that Philaster's popularity is a function of the people's stupidity (IV. 6) and while the mob is good-humoured and generally on the side of right it lacks the reality of the citizens in *The Knight of the Burning Pestle*, being characterized largely by mechanical jokes about trade.[4] Only in their exchange with Pharamond do we hear briefly something like the black comedy of a real mob:

> PHARAMOND
> You will not see me murdered, wicked villains?
> I CITIZEN
> Yes indeed will we, sir, we have not seen one for a
> great while.
> (v. 4)

That polite 'sir' makes the line perfect. This is, then, a courtly world in which other social classes appear only in caricatured form. And, like many courts in Beaumont and Fletcher, it is characterized by a missing centre. The King, who has deprived Philaster of his right, is a tepid and ineffectual villain whose struggles with his conscience are perfunctory and who dithers comically in the crisis of the rebellion: 'They will not hear me speak, but fling dirt at me, and call me tyrant. . . . O my wits, my wits!' (v. 3). In contrast to Marston's absurd but lurid villains, he is merely silly. He cannot even get a respectful hearing even from his courtiers:

> 'tis the King
> Will have it so! whose breath can still the winds,
> Uncloud the sun, charm down the swelling sea,
> And stop the floods of heaven; speak, can it not?
> DION
> No.
> (IV. 4)

Dion is equally scathing about Pharamond, 'who, but that people /Please to let him be a Prince, is born a slave' (III. 1). Putting the two moments together, we can see that beneath the satire on the stage tyrant is an impudence about the royal prerogative. Beaumont and Fletcher may have been entertaining an upper-class audience;[5] but the grand gestures and sensational actions are shot through with an irony that spares nobody. What makes it different from the irony of, say, Middleton, is a sense that the characters are more silly than corrupt, and that none of it finally matters very much.

A King and No King (*c.* 1611) uses the tragicomic form in a more complex and disturbing way. In bare outline the plot sounds like an unfair trick played on the audience. Arbaces, King of Iberia, has conceived an incestuous passion for his sister Panthaea; what looks like a tragic conclusion is averted by the last-minute revelation that Arbaces is not really the king and Panthaea is not his sister. However, the discovery should not surprise the audience as it surprises Arbaces. As in Jonson's *Epicoene*, where the heroine turns out to be a boy, we are fairly prepared by the title; and in the course of the play Beaumont and Fletcher hint far more broadly than Jonson does that there is a mystery to be revealed.[6] As in *Philaster*, though not to the same degree, various devices leave us detached. Through the last two acts, comic scenes with the bragging coward Bessus, and the more straightforward love interest of the subplot involving Arbaces' captives Tigranes and Spaconia, keep pulling the focus away from the principals as their passions get more dangerous. Ironically, every step Arbaces takes to his own apparent destruction works to the benefit of the minor lovers. When Arbaces sets himself on a tragic course – kill his friend Mardonius, rape Panthaea, commit suicide – the planned, deliberate quality keeps the temperature low:

> There is a method in man's wickedness,
> It goes up by degrees; I am not come
> So high as killing myself, there are
> A hundred thousand sins twixt me and it,
> Which I must do; I shall come too't at last.
>
>   (v. 4)

Compared with Othello or Macbeth, he does not really sound like a man heading for the brink. Mardonius calls his passion 'this raging folly' (IV. 2) and the long, tense, powerful scene in which he first recognizes his incestuous desires is punctured by Tigranes's aside, 'Pish, this is tedious' (III. 1).

But the play does more than tease its audience by presenting a fake-tragic action leading to a comic ending we should have expected all along. This time we are made to worry, as we are not in *Philaster*, about our own detachment; and about much else besides. Arbaces reveals his desires to the honest Mardonius, who denounces them; he then turns to the worthless Bessus, who accepts the role of go-between quite blandly – 'O, you would have a bout with her?' (III. 3) – and is prepared to go beyond the call of duty: 'when this is despatch'd, if you have a mind to your mother tell me, and you shall see I'll set it hard' (III. 3). The comedy this time is shocking. It presents Arbaces with such a brutal image of the implications of his desire that he temporarily recoils from it. And if we see in Bessus's cool reaction an image of our own detachment, we too may recoil. The issues of the play are finally serious; the identity game is not just a game. Early in the play Mardonius, in conversation with Arbaces, tries to get past two kinds of artificial identity: Arbaces's role as king, which restricts his personal relations, and his temperamental arrogance, which blocks his real virtue. Mardonius wants to bring out instead the essential man he would like for a friend:

MARDONIUS
> Would you but leave these hasty tempers, which I do
> not say take from you all your worth, but darken 'em,
> then you would shine indeed.

ARBACES
> Well.

MARDONIUS
> Yet I would have you keep some passions, lest men
> should take you for a god, your virtues are such.

ARBACES
> Why, now you flatter.

MARDONIUS
> I never understood the word. Were you no king, and
> free from these wild moods, should I choose a
> companion for wit and pleasure, it should be you; or
> for honesty, to interchange my bosom with, it would
> be you; or wisdom, to give me counsel, I would pick
> out you; or valour to defend my reputation, still I
> would find out you.

(I. 1)

'Were you no king' – this idea recurs throughout the scene, suggesting that the reasons for freeing Arbaces from his role go beyond the special problems of the incest plot. Yet as Mardonius describes his private virtues, he builds from the informal pleasures of companionship to more conventional virtues, and finally to the valour celebrated in Arbaces's first triumphant entrance as conqueror. Even as a private man he could show kingly virtue, perhaps more fully than he does as king; the paradox of the title can be turned more than one way.

When Arbaces first conceives love for his sister he refuses to accept her identity: 'She is no kin to me, nor shall she be' (III. 1). We see here the individual trying to redefine reality, with the arrogance of Coriolanus or of Chapman's tragic heroes. Though what he imagines is literally true, it is from his own viewpoint an impossible fantasy. The rules of society against which his imagination strains are likewise both effective and empty. He and Panthaea share a recognition that they are kept apart only by 'these mere sounds, /Brother and Sister' (IV. 4), yet on such 'mere sounds' depends the whole structure of convention that keeps man human:

>   he that undertakes my cure, must first
> O'er throw divinity, all moral laws,
> And leave mankind as unconfin'd as beasts.
>
> (III. 1)

In our final reception of the play the paradox may continue to disturb us past the technically happy ending: if names are so trivial, can so much pain and guilt really be undone by the simple device of changing them? As the play ends, Panthaea has not yet learned the truth about Arbaces, and he is teasing her with a riddle: 'that you will please to marry me, /If I can prove it lawful' (v. 4). If there is something technical and arbitrary about guilt, the same could be said of innocence. While Beaumont and Fletcher do not face the incest theme as squarely as Ford does in 'Tis Pity She's a Whore, the play may be not less about incest than it pretends, but more.

The principal themes are reflected through the subplots, giving the play a control at the level of ideas Philaster never aspires to. Bessus, like Arbaces, has an identity problem, a false reputation for courage. He wishes to shed it, as it gets him into trouble; like Parolles in All's Well That Ends Well he never fools himself. But he would also like to preserve it. He is teamed with two comic swordsmen, and among them they redefine reality by finding technical reasons for turning disgrace into honour: 'we are valiant to ourselves, and there's an end' (v. 3). Valour, like crime in the main plot, can be a state of mind. The subplot involving the captive prince Tigranes and his love for Spaconia includes a questioning of the social roles that define identity. When Spaconia's father thinks she has been unchaste he declares ironically, 'Forgive you, why I am no kin to you, am I?' (v. 2) and when Tigranes insists his intentions are honourable the old man becomes confused:

> TIGRANES
> Thou see'st thy Queen there.
> LIGONES
> Then have I made a fair hand, I call'd her whore; if I
> shall speak now as her father, I cannot choose but
> greatly rejoice that she shall be a queen; but if I should
> speak to you as a statesman she were more fit to be
> your whore.
>   (v. 2)

Tigranes's royalty, like that of Arbaces, complicates what should have been a simple happiness. From its title onwards the play toys with paradoxes involved in the necessary yet artificial roles in which people are cast by family and social relations. In a reversal of usual dramatic practice, the focus of the ending is not on the discovery that Panthaea is the true ruler of Iberia but on the discovery that Arbaces is not. The last words are 'I am prov'd no king' (v. 4). With delight and excitement, and still, we might note, issuing orders, Arbaces discards all the marks of respect that go with kingship; the play opens with a triumph, but the happy ending requires a triumph in reverse. In what may be a development from *The Knight of the Burning Pestle*, the last of the play's many paradoxes is a reversal of one of the built-in expectations of dramatic form.

The dignity that Philaster keeps losing and that Arbaces delightedly throws away might seem to be a necessary condition of tragedy. Here, we might suppose, the tricks used in tragicomedy to keep the stakes low and the temperature cool should have no place. But in *The Maid's Tragedy* (*c.* 1610) Beaumont and Fletcher keep violating this expectation. In one of the most brilliant scenes in the canon, Amintor learns on his wedding night that his bride Evadne is the King's mistress, that his job is to give her a respectable front, and that one of the conditions is he is not to bed her. The revelation occurs in stages, but the crucial turning point comes when Amintor wonders if she has vowed to preserve her maidenhead and Evadne replies, 'A maidenhead, Amintor, /At my years?' (II. 1). The joke is startling, brutal and revealing. In six words Evadne not only tells the truth about herself but reveals a wry, cynical acceptance of her condition, humiliates Amintor's innocent idealism, and comments on the way of the world. Bathos has seldom been used more powerfully. Amintor is lost and bewildered; he wants to behave as a hero should but his undignified situation gives him no chance:

> You powers above, if you did ever mean
> Man should be us'd thus, you have thought a way
> How he may bear himself, and save his honour;
> Instruct me in it, for to my dull eyes
> There is no mean, no moderate course to run,
> I must live scorn'd or be a murderer:
> Is there a third? Why is this night so calm?
>
> (II. 1)

That last line is one of the few hints of a spiritual dimension in Beaumont and Fletcher, and what it evokes is a silent universe, indifferent to the sufferings of man. The answer, for a while at least, seems to be a sad, cynical accommodation. Evadne unbends a little:

AMINTOR

What a strange thing am I?

EVADNE

A miserable one, one that myself
Am sorry for.

(II. 1)

The hero tries to adjust to his new life as a professional cuckold: 'Be careful of thy credit, and sin close, /'Tis all I ask' (II. 1). Later he notes with chagrin, as though it compounded the absurdity of his fate, that Evadne has slept peacefully, showing none of the conventional signs of guilt.

The title character, Aspatia, deserted by Amintor when he married Evadne, likewise suffers a descent to bathos. Her grief, even more than that of Bellario in *Philaster*, is consciously artificial. Proclaiming her solitude, she is generally surrounded by an admiring, weeping audience of maids. She is an artist in grief, and knows it: 'So with prayers I leave you, and must try /Some yet unpractis'd way to grieve and die' (II. 1). Though she says early in Act Two, 'This is the last time you shall look on me' (II. 1), she cannot grieve herself to death. She has to confront Amintor, disguised as her own brother, and provoke him into killing her. When he refuses she kicks him in exasperation. Finally he stabs her to death, and the scene circles back to pathos, but not before it has skirted the borders of farce. Bathos, less sharp but equally clear, affects Evadne's brother Melantius. He works himself up into killing the King in revenge for his family's dishonour; but he uses Evadne as his instrument, and makes sure that he himself escapes alive: 'To take revenge and lose myself withal /Were idle' (III. 2). In a series of cool comic scenes he gets the fort from Aspatia's weak and foolish father Calianax. Melantius talks at times like a tragic hero, but emerges in the end as a clever survivor.

The high talk, like that of the tragicomedies, is restrained in its effect by a tendency to quantify emotion. Amintor describes himself as 'nothing but a multitude /Of walking griefs' (III. 1). When Melantius denounces Evadne we are more aware of the cleverness with which he measures her guilt than of the moral indignation:

Thy body is too little for the story,
The lusts of which would fill another woman,
Though she had twins within her.

(IV. 1)

When Melantius finds Amintor dying his grief is presented as the reaction to mechanical stimulus:

> eyes, call up your tears,
> This is Amintor; heart, he was my friend,
> Melt, now it flows.
>
> (v. 3)

Calianax wishes he could do as well: 'My daughter dead here too, and you all have fine new tricks to grieve, but I ne'er knew any but direct crying' (v. 3). This is not the simple defence of sincerity we might have expected; it is touched with envy.

Values, like emotions, have something mechanical about them. For Melantius and Amintor the name 'friend' is a signal that triggers a response: 'to thyself murmur the name of friend, /And see what that will work' (III. 2). The name 'King' has the same effect on Amintor: 'Oh thou hast nam'd a word that wipes away /All thoughts revengeful' (II. 1). There is much fine talk of the sacredness of the royal office; but as in *A King and No King* its value hinges dangerously on mere words. The King himself is weak, corrupt and petty; again we see a courtly world collapsing around a missing centre. Even before we see him and realize the ludicrous disparity between man and office, even before the mockery beneath the opening wedding masque is revealed, a minor courtier casts a jaundiced eye on the masque and the whole courtly routine it exemplifies:

> they must commend their King, and speak in praise
> Of the assembly, bless the bride and bridegroom,
> In person of some god; they're tied to rules
> Of flattery.
>
> (I. 1)

The King cannot even lust grandly. His question to Amintor after the wedding night, 'What did you do?' (III. 1), suggests both nasty playfulness (the correct answer, he knows, is 'nothing') and schoolboy prurience. When in *The Revenger's Tragedy* the lecherous old Duke is made to kiss the poisoned skull of a lady he tried to debauch, the killing is an appropriate punishment for his lust. Beaumont and Fletcher go further: Evadne's killing of the King is presented as in itself a perverted sexual act. He wakes to find she has tied him to his bed: 'What pretty new device is this, Evadne?' As she stabs him repeatedly, the rhythm of the action echoes the rhythm of her words and the rhythm of the sexual act itself:

> Thou kept'st me brave at court, and whor'd me, King,
> Then married me to a young noble gentleman,
> And whor'd me still.
>
> (v. 1)

She penetrates his body as he had penetrated hers. The lustful tyrant who used others for his pleasure takes the passive role in this final coupling. It is not a grand ending.

At the end of the play Lysippus, the late King's brother, takes over the kingdom and offers a pat conclusion:

> on lustful kings
> Unlook't for sudden deaths from God are sent,
> But curst is he that is their instrument.
>
> (v. 3)

The choice of Evadne as regicide is a neat answer to the problem of killing a wicked king: find a wicked killer. As in *A King and No King* the play seems to be answering a riddle. But the overall effect is not so neat. When, her hands covered in the King's blood, Evadne encounters Amintor and demands, 'take me to thy bed' (v. 3) the shock is compounded by the fact that Amintor has just stabbed Aspatia to death. The play has shown grand gestures collapsing into bathos. When it probes beyond that, into the sexuality that provides so much of the play's bitter comedy, it finds not grand passion but excited cruelty. Beneath the surface drama of love and honour, loyalty and friendship, we catch a glimpse of something dark, nasty and alarming.

Fletcher returns to the sexual theme in two later, unaided tragedies, *Bonduca* (*c.* 1610) and *Valentinian* (*c.* 1611). Both carry on some of the experiments of *The Maid's Tragedy*, but without its concentrated power. The cast of *Bonduca* includes 'Petillius, a merry captain, but somewhat wanton' and 'Judas, a corporal, a merry hungry knave': odd characters, we might think, for a tragedy. To some extent the comic expectations these descriptions raise are borne out in the rest of the play. The Roman soldiers battling the Britons seem at times to be driven by two appetites, food and sex, which run together in their conversation and which betray them at various times into British ambushes. When Bonduca and her two daughters, trapped by the Roman army, commit suicide, the grandeur of their last gesture takes an odd twist as the Roman Petillius falls in love with the first daughter for her heroic death. Any dignity the idea may have is destroyed by the way he expresses it:

> What do I ail, i'th' name of heaven? I did but see her,
> And see her die; she stinks by this time strongly,
> Abominably stinks. She was a woman,
> A thing I never car'd for; but to die so,
> So confidently, bravely, strongly, O the devil,
> I have the bots, by –
>
> (v. 2)

The crazy tonal instability of this play makes one appreciate how much better the anticlimaxes were managed in the tragicomedies and *The Maid's Tragedy*. The hungry corporal Judas, a farcical buffoon for most of the play, kills an innocent child at the end and in return is beaten to death with a rock; his name at last means something, but the revelation of cruelty beneath the comedy seems forced and arbitrary.

Valentinian is better controlled. As in *The Maid's Tragedy*, the central problem is a lustful ruler, the emperor Valentinian, who rapes the chaste matron Lucina, leading her to commit suicide. There is at first a clear contrast between the dignified style of the noble Romans and the wry comedy of the corrupt courtiers. But when the emperor is murdered, Lucina's husband Maximus, who has been on the side of right, decides like Melantius to try to come out of the crisis with a whole skin, and even to exploit it: 'Why may not I be Caesar, yet no dying? /Why should I not catch at it?' If he succeeds, 'my wife was ravish'd well' (v. 3). He is killed at his own coronation by a poisoned laurel wreath; but that seems a more spectacular end than he deserves. Fletcher has already despatched him in his own more characteristic way, by revealing his ambition in coarse language and brutal comedy.

From the disillusioned wit that runs through his more serious work, we might expect Fletcher to write comedy with ease and confidence. He does; but his comedies are not his most interesting plays. They are if anything *too* easy, lacking the internal challenge that comes from the grappling of high and low styles in the major work. But his comedies include some lively entertainments, particularly concerned with the battle of the sexes. The theme can be traced through the history of comedy; Fletcher's treatment of it has an unsentimental frankness we do not always encounter in more famous examples. The most engaging of these comedies is *The Woman's Prize; or, The Tamer Tamed* (c. 1605) in which Petruchio, who has tamed his first wife, marries a second, Maria, who tames him. Petruchio's name embodies a witty allusion to *The Taming of the Shrew*; otherwise Fletcher's play is largely independent of Shakespeare's. It is emphasized that neither Petruchio nor Maria is a natural scold. Petruchio became one as the only way of surviving his termagant first wife, who 'turn'd his temper, /And forc'd him blow as high as she' (I. 1). Maria suppresses a naturally gentle disposition in order to tame Petruchio. She begins by denying her body to him, barricading herself in her room with her friends in a mock-heroic sequence that includes a drunken Army of Women who come to the aid of the besieged party. From then on Petruchio tries deception: pretending illness, pretending to travel, pretending to die. In each case she calls his bluff, mocking his extravagant gestures with extravagance of her own. He complains, 'could I find her /But constant any way, I had done my business' (IV. 2). Her art, like Fletcher's, is one of surprise. Fletcher emphasizes that the two really love each other, and this adds to the game-like quality of their conflict. The one occasion when this conflict seems serious is when he threatens to strike her; her sharp warning suggests that for once he has gone too far (IV. 2). In the end she submits to him as a conventionally obedient wife, but at her own volition, at a time chosen by herself, and after a full demonstration of her capacity for independence.

As role-player, and as wife, Maria is in control. The title character of *The Scornful Lady* (*c.* 1613; written with Beaumont) seems to take control even further, tormenting the Elder Loveless by her perverse behaviour. Though they have often kissed in private, she banishes him to travel for a year for the offence of kissing her in public. Through the rest of the play she and her lover try to out-bluff each other and she wins every round but the last. But while Maria's extravagant gestures are always clearly performances, the Lady is in the grip of a perversity she wishes she could control and cannot:

> a strange peevishness
> And anger, not to have the power to do
> Things unexpected, carries me away
> To mine own ruin.
>
> (v. 2)

Her attendant Abigail sums up the problem: 'this is still your way, to love being absent, and when he's with you, laugh at him and abuse him. There is another way if you could hit on't' (IV. 1). She has tried to play Loveless off against Welford, with some success. In the end the men make common cause and Loveless, like Abigail, appeals to standards of worldly common sense that make the courtship game look silly:

> For whose sake, [i.e., women]
> If we should leave our reason, and run on
> Upon our sense, like rams, the little world
> Of good men would laugh at us, and despise us.
>
> (v. 1)

Loveless finally goads the Lady into submission by introducing the disguised Welford as his fiancée, an ugly lady but tractable and a good housekeeper. Loveless marries and beds the Lady, whose sister takes the rejected fiancée to bed with her by way of consolation, with the expected results when Welford reveals his true sex. Welford has said of the sisters, 'I care not which I have' (v. 1). The same unsentimental attitude lies behind the masculine preening the two men indulge in the next morning. Petruchio and Maria seem to be headed for a life of witty companionship, for which Maria's games have prepared them. In *The Scornful Lady* the courtship game is revealed as silly and perverse, and neither party really wants to play; but there seems little more to marriage than a good night's free sex. Loveless's conclusion is blunt: 'Would every dogged wench had such a day' (v. 4). We may wonder in the end about the full significance of his name.

The Woman's Prize allows women the initiative in both plots; in the subplot, Livia, caught in a conventional rival-wooer story, manages her own affairs quite nicely without much help from her lover Rowland, whom she describes as 'the prettiest puling piece of passion' (I. 2). In the subplot of *The Scornful Lady* the prodigal Younger Loveless not only marries a rich widow but establishes the household on his own terms, with a place for his drunken companions. Here, in both plots, the men finally take the initiative. Two of Fletcher's later comedies, *The Humorous Lieutenant* (1619) and *The Wild-Goose Chase* (1621), seem to tilt the balance back to the women, but the appearance is deceptive. The title character of *The Humorous Lieutenant* is an eccentric soldier who fights like a hero when sick and in pain and is quite useless when healthy; though the odd quirk reflects a psychological truth about the way some people react to affliction, Fletcher seems most interested in the oddness. But the play centres on Celia, whose wit and stubborn will allow her to breeze through the trials her persecutors set for her. As one of the parties to a plot on her chastity complains, 'She is perilous crafty; /I fear too honest for us all too' (III. 2). But when she is restored to her lover she decides arbitrarily to prolong their difficulties herself. The witty old soldier Leontius has to bring her to heel using reverse psychology. Like Arbaces, she is given a new identity at the end of the play; she is really Enanthe, daughter to a neighbouring king. But at a psychological level she has already been revealed as not quite the woman we took her for; she is more vulnerable to her own whims, and to the manipulation of others, than she first appeared.

The Wild-Goose Chase concerns the attempt of Oriana to capture the young rake Mirabell, who says of his conquests, recorded in a book, 'I enjoy'd 'em at my will, and left 'em' (II. 1). Their first interview is unpromising; he is offensively cynical and she is reduced to one-line pleas that get nowhere. Later she pretends to be engaged, a device borrowed from *The Scornful Lady*, and then to go mad. The first device appeals to his male self-esteem, the second to his compassion. He is shown to have both qualities, and they balance each other. Neither trick works; but on the second occasion he dismisses her with a challenge: 'From this hour I disclaim thee /Unless thou hast a trick above this; then I'll love thee' (IV. 3). But just as there are hints that Mirabell may not be quite the brutal rake he claims, so Oriana is not altogether the strong, witty lady the plot advertises. Much of the contriving is done by two male allies, her brother and a tutor. And the last, successful trick is unsettling. She impersonates a rich, glamorous lady, who so impresses Mirabell that he proposes to her. On the surface he falls in love with a deception, and his acceptance of the rich lady is really an insult to Oriana, who is not like this at all. Or is she? When he accepts her as herself, he praises her wit, and adds, 'and yet, perhaps, I knew you' (V. 6). We are left wondering if he has really seen through the deception all along; if he is trying to redeem his own credit, Falstaff-fashion; or if he has seen in the glamorous lady an inner truth about Oriana revealed in the disguise. When he specifies, 'these fine clothes you shall wear still' (V. 6), he may be trying to keep an inner truth about her alive, or prolonging a deception. This time Fletcher teases the audience right to the end.

The control and authority of Maria, confirmed when she surrenders them, make her exceptional among Fletcher's characters. They are more commonly helpless: manipulated by others, subject to quirks and passions of their own, unable to do more than struggle. Arbaces and Philaster both have princely glamour; but one is saved from disaster by a plot trick contrived by a minor character, the other by a rather silly mob. Even the tragic figures are subject to lapses in dignity. Fletcher and his associates brought into the theatre qualities of glamour and easy-going wit that would feed the drama for generations to come. Over the next two centuries their progeny are far more numerous than those of Shakespeare or Jonson. But while there are touches of pity, admiration and even kindliness in their work they did not in the end replace the scepticism of earlier Jacobean drama with a more positive vision. They simply expressed it with a new, studied casualness.

Honour, friendship, loyalty, wit – these are the values of this genteel, self-contained world. They are expressed as gestures, but the characters take them just seriously enough to free them from the questioning they would have undergone in earlier Jacobean drama. In moments of crisis they are concerned, like Amintor on his wedding night, to find the right gesture for the occasion. One thinks of gesture, not style, because each occasion is a new challenge. The heroes of Chapman and the more impressive heroes of Webster find a style, and sustain it so that it is ingrained in them. The heroes of Beaumont and Fletcher by comparison live for the moment; they are always collapsing and having to start again. And they have no alternative world to which they can turn for guidance. The traditional integrity of fixed social roles and moral values, lost but still recoverable or imaginable, that Shakespeare locates in the countryside of *As You Like It* or Marston in the citadel of *The Malcontent*, find no expression here. In the courtly plays, the country and the city are simply caricatured, leaving the court as the only world there is. When Fletcher's comedies move out of that court into the lives of the gentry, they depict a collection of free-wheeling individuals with no community around them. There is nothing like the fully realized London of Jonson, Middleton or Dekker, with its streets, shops and familiar place names. We are dimly aware of houses, and of open spaces around them, but little more. The reduction of value to gesture in the tragedies and tragicomedies, and of sexual relations to an improvised game of one-upmanship in the comedies, is connected with this lack of community. The characters cannot settle into the fixed human relationships Shakespeare provides in his images of order; they have to make up their lives as they go along. The same is true even in the courtly settings. These settings are a little more fully realized than the others, but while the benevolent rulers Shakespeare sometimes provides and the corrupt rulers more often depicted by his Jacobean contemporaries, give a strong, clear centre to the courts they govern, the rulers of Beaumont and Fletcher are weak and trivial even in their crimes. It becomes the private responsibility of the courtiers to decide how gentlemen ought to behave. Even Arbaces, the strongest and most striking ruler-figure in the canon, turns out not to be a king at all. His kingship is a mistake, preventing him from leading the free life to which he is entitled as a private man.

Improvising their behaviour around a missing centre, the characters are still not altogether free. They are frequently gripped by a sex-drive Fletcher imagines as a sharp, simple hunger, as comic as the literal hunger that occasionally afflicts the buffoons in his subplots.[7] They are also gripped, especially in the comedies, by a sheer perversity that seems at best an unexamined reporting of human oddity and at worst a lazy way to keep the plot going. In both cases Fletcher shows, with clinical coolness, how people react to stimuli. This reductive view of humanity is linked to the anticlimaxes that are so striking a feature of the Beaumont and Fletcher style. Improvising, indulging in gestures, responding to stimuli, the characters have no protection against a final banality. If the charge of complacency so often levelled at the Beaumont and Fletcher canon has any merit, it may lie in the fact that the playwrights, particularly Fletcher, seem so unperturbed by what they are reporting.

Notes

1. The title page of the 1634 edition of *The Two Noble Kinsmen* identifies Fletcher and Shakespeare as the authors; the case for divided authorship of *Henry VIII* rests on internal evidence alone. For a survey of the authorship question, inclined to play down the role of Fletcher, see R. A. Foakes, Introduction to the Arden edition of *Henry VIII* (London, 1957, revised 1964), pp. xvii–xxvii. The case for a substantial role for Fletcher has been argued by Marco Mincoff, '*Henry VIII* and Fletcher', *Shakespeare Quarterly*, 12 (1960), 239–60. On *Cardenio* see Kenneth Muir, *Shakespeare as Collaborator* (London, 1960), pp. 148–60.

2. For a view of the play as essentially Fletcherean and the worse for it, see Robert Ornstein, *A Kingdom for a Stage* (Cambridge, Mass., 1972), pp. 203–20.

3. W. B.'s Epistle to Robert Keysar, accompanying the 1613 edition, notes with pride that the play antedates the appearance of *Don Quixote* by a year.

4. This goes much further in *A King and No King*, in which the citizens who greet Arbaces's return from the war are so stupid as to appear hardly human.

5. This view of them, still a common one, is conveyed in Lawrence B. Wallis, *Fletcher, Beaumont, and Company: Entertainers to the Jacobean Gentry* (New York, 1947).

6. Fletcher is often criticized for his surprise endings. He has been defended on this point, with particular reference to this play, by Clifford Leech, *The John Fletcher Plays* (London, 1962), pp. 16–21.

7. There are examples in *Bonduca* and in *Love's Cure; or, The Martial Maid* (*c.* 1625).

Chapter 12
Middleton, Rowley and Company

Running parallel with the work of Fletcher and his associates is a range of plays, generally written in collaboration, in which the concentration of earlier Jacobean drama is replaced by a more relaxed social vision and a greater variety of tone. While the multiple actions of plays like *Women Beware Women* and *The White Devil* contribute to a single vision of the world, the multiple actions of the new plays do not. The stories may be connected by plot devices, family or business relationships among the characters, or loose similarities of theme, but there is no longer the sense that a single coherent investigation is being conducted. Many of the plays are tragicomedies, putting the characters seriously at risk but bringing them to final happiness. Even the plays that are formally tragedies, bringing the central characters to death, stop well short of the wholesale slaughters of earlier Jacobean tragedy, and contain comic material whose independent value makes the overall effect of the plays something other than tragic.[1] This multiple vision is generally concerned with social themes. Sex, money, property and honour are all investigated, but more with an open curiosity about how the characters will behave under pressure than with the satiric assumption that they will behave badly. In some cases values that would earlier have been mocked are allowed to have unexpected gravity and seriousness. The satiric intensity of earlier Jacobean drama could not be sustained for long, and in these later plays we see a recoil from it.

A Fair Quarrel (1617), written in collaboration by Thomas Middleton and William Rowley (*c.* 1585–1626), is a case in point. The central story concerns the duelling code. The principal antagonists are the Colonel and Captain Ager, whose rivalry is sparked initially by quarrels among their friends as to the two men's relative worth. The grand gestures and fast plot turns that follow recall Beaumont and Fletcher; but this time the characters' values are grounded in a solidly realized community. At first the quarrels look like the effect of youth and hot blood; as the merchant Russell comments, 'Here's noble youths! Belike some wench has cross'd 'em, /And now they know not what to do with their blood' (I. 1). The connection between valour and sexuality is also suggested when one of Ager's friends calls his relative moderation 'a virtue as rare as chastity in youth' (I. 1). But the touchiness that leads to the play's quarrels is also a function of membership in a community of gentlemen, 'the fellowship of honour' (II. 1). The principal quarrel is touched off when the Colonel calls Ager 'the son of a whore'. His mother, Lady Ager, rather than have him fight, pretends the charge is true. Ager sees her alleged misconduct as an offence not against chastity as such but against a community of men, particularly his father and himself:

> He I call'd father
> Deserv'd you at your best, when youth and merit
> Could boast at highest in you; y'ad no grace
> Or virtue that he match'd not, no delight
> That you invented but he sent it crown'd
> To you full wishing soul.

LADY AGER

> That heaps my guiltiness.

CAPTAIN AGER

> Oh, were you so unhappy to be false
> Both to yourself and me, but to me chiefly?
> What a day's hope is lost, and with it
> The joys of a just cause!

(II. 1)

That the women are counters in a game of honour played by the men is confirmed when the Colonel decides to mark his reconciliation with Ager by giving his sister in marriage. When she hesitates, he is indignant:

> Is it so burdensome for thee to love
> Where I forgive? Oh, wretched is the man
> That builds the last hope of his saving comforts
> Upon a woman's charity!

(IV. 2)

Under this pressure, she submits. While casualness about naming characters is frequent in the plays of this period, it may not be an accident that the playwrights give her no proper name, identifying her only as 'the Colonel's sister'. There is an undercurrent of misogyny throughout the play; even the chastity of Lady Ager, as she herself suggests, is admirable because it is exceptional (III. 3). Ager himself will not fight for it without confirming that the slander is false since, much as he loves his mother, 'my judgement tells me she's but a woman, /Whose frailty let in death to all mankind' (II. 1). The last embrace of the play, we notice, is between two men.

The modern reader might expect to see these self-centred male values exploded; but Middleton and Rowley are writing for their time, not ours. Some internal criticism is allowed: Ager delivers a lecture against duelling that the Colonel admits 'mov'd a little with me' (III. 1), and the Colonel tries to prevent a new flare-up between them by warning Ager, 'rage will force me do what will grieve honour' (III. 1). But peacemaking by outsiders is discredited. In the opening scene the merchant Russell acts as peacemaker, but his motives are cynical. He is plotting to deprive the men of their swords so that when his daughter's lover Fitzallen is arrested for debt the others cannot rescue him. When Lady Ager slanders herself to keep her son from fighting, her ruse fails; the Colonel accuses Ager of cowardice, and they fight anyway. She sees this as

> a judgement plain; truth's angry with me,
> In that I would abuse her sacred whiteness
> For any worldly temporal respect.
>
> (III. 3)

To have something to fight for is to have something to believe in; from the title onwards, the play registers strongly the *need* for a good quarrel. Ager's friends, when he refuses to fight the Colonel over the slander to his mother, accuse him of having missed a great opportunity: 'Why would you cozen yourself so and beguile /So brave a cause, manhood's best masterpiece?' (II. 1). They insist that more is at stake for Ager than his mother's reputation:

> If you fail virtue here, she needs you not
> All your time after, let her take this wrong,
> And never presume then to serve her more.
>
> (III. 1)

When the Colonel responds by calling Ager a coward, he is delighted and relieved: 'Oh, heaven has pitied my excessive patience, /And sent me a cause' (III. 1).

The importance of a cause is implicitly confirmed by the comic subplot involving the foolish Cornishman Chough, who goes to the Roaring School to learn a comic version of the quarrelsomeness of the

more serious characters. One of the factors that makes roaring comic
is that it is a game played for its own sake. Nothing is at stake, no
blood is shed, and its only purpose is to serve as an excuse for a drink:
'there must be wine ready to make all friends, for that's the end of
roaring; 'tis valiant but harmless' (IV. 1). There are some points of
contact. One of the Colonel's friends is an instructor at the Roaring
School, and in the comic jargon that forms a major part of roaring
there may be a general parody both of the serious characters' touchiness about words, and of their fencer's jargon: 'An absolute punto,
hey?' ''Twas a passado, sir' (III. 1). But on the whole the comedy of
the roaring scenes is amiable rather than satiric, and their principal
function seems to be to enhance by contrast the seriousness of the main
characters.

As the foolish suitor to Russell's daughter Jane, Chough has a plot
function like that of the Heir in *Women Beware Women*. But while the
Heir was a subhuman lout, Chough, though foolish, is attractively
good-natured. The love-plot itself is connected much more loosely to
the rest of the play. Jane and Fitzgrave have a contractual marriage,
but not a church one. Jane's pregnancy is treated first as a guilty secret
and finally as a device to bring the lovers together: when he hears of
it Russell abandons his attempt to get a good (i.e., rich) marriage for
her and palms her off on Fitzgrave, seeing himself as a man cleverly
getting rid of damaged goods: 'We old men have pretty conceits sometimes' (V. 1). Before revealing he is the father Fitzgrave drives a hard
bargain and gets Jane's dowry increased. Though Jane shows wit and
spirit defending her chastity against the physician who is treating her,
and who assumes that having fallen once she will fall again, the final
disposition of this plot is clever and cynical. While the play's other
gentlemen dispute points of honour Fitzgrave gets a good rich
marriage, exemplifying no value more serious than a quick eye for the
main chance. This plot, like the comic roaring scenes, contributes to
the play's variety of tone, but in this case we are not invited to judge
the behaviour of one set of characters by that of another.

Middleton and Rowley's most important collaboration is *The Changeling* (1622). The principal story of this play, mostly the work of
Middleton, revives the satiric concentration of earlier Jacobean drama.
Beatrice-Joanna hires the ugly servant de Flores, for whom she feels
a compulsive loathing, to murder her fiancé Alonso, freeing her to
marry her lover Alsemero. She thinks this will get both the victim and
the murderer out of her life, as de Flores will be forced to flee. But
de Flores has other ideas. His price for the killing is not her money
but her body. The scene in which he demands his fee is one of the
greatest in Jacobean drama. It simply has not occurred to Beatrice-
Joanna that she has made anything more than a business arrangement.

Step by step de Flores insists on her moral involvement and its logical consequences. It is hard work:

> I'm in a labyrinth,
> What will content him? I would fain be rid of him.
> (to de Flores) I'll double the sum, sir.
>
> (III. 4)

When she grasps the fact of his demand she still fails to see its moral logic:

> Why, 'tis impossible thou canst be so wicked,
> Or shelter such a cunning cruelty,
> To make his death the murderer of my honour!
> Thy language is so bold and vicious,
> I cannot see which way I can forgive it
> With any modesty.
>
> DE FLORES
>   Push, you forget yourself!
> A woman dipp'd in blood, and talk of modesty?
>
> (III. 4)

Whatever irony may have touched the notion of honour in *A Fair Quarrel*, there was nothing like this.

De Flores forces her to realize not just that she is in his power but that her very identity is determined by what she has done. Not only is her honour empty; so is the social position on which it depends:

> Push, fly not to your birth, but settle you
> In what the act has made you, y'are no more now,
> You must forget your parentage to me:
> Y'are the deed's creature.
>
> (III. 4)

She comes to accept de Flores; her tribute, 'The east is not more beauteous than his service' (v. 1) includes a bawdy pun on 'service' and a parody of the traditional romantic notion of lover as servant, yet its acceptance of de Flores is quite sincere. This is not so much a radical change in her as the revelation of a truth that was latent from the beginning, a fascination that emerged first as compulsive hatred: 'my loathing /Was prophet to the rest, but ne'er believ'd' (v. 3). His fascination with her has been clear all along. De Flores, like Bosola and Flamineo, is a dispossessed gentleman forced into service. Sardonically aware of his own humiliation, he recognizes his infatuation as a sickness but is unable to stop himself:

> Why, am not I an ass to devise ways
> Thus to be rail'd at? I must see her still!
> I shall have a mad qualm within this hour again,
> I know't.
>
> (II. 1)

There is nothing grand in the passion that brings them together. Their sexual fantasies suggest not intercourse but mutual masturbation: de Flores handles her gloves and thinks of thrusting 'my fingers /Into her sockets here' (I. 1); she confesses to her husband, 'I have kiss'd poison for't, strok't a serpent' (v. 3). Conversely, while there is much fuss about chastity in the play it seems to be largely a technical thing. De Flores insists that half his price is an intact maidenhead (III. 4); Alsemero tests his wife's virginity with a liquid that will make a virgin yawn, sneeze and then laugh. The sheer absurdity of the device reflects the absurdity of a sexual code that sees virtue as a physical condition. It is also a bargaining point. Virginity in *Measure for Measure* and *Pericles*, to take only two examples, had an almost religious value; its preservation was a matter of spiritual life and death. Here it is a counter in a series of transactions, and Beatrice-Joanna's dilemma is that of a merchant who has struck the same bargain with two different customers and cannot satisfy them both. When she tries to use grander language than this, the play's irony closes in on her.

The tragedy, however, is not only concentrated on Beatrice-Joanna and de Flores but confined to them. There are suggestions that the setting, a citadel full of secret passages and threatened by fire in the last act, is a reflection of the nature of Beatrice-Joanna in particular. But for all the distress the final revelations cause, she and de Flores are isolated from the other characters. We might have expected otherwise. The comic subplot, in which Isabella, wife of a madhouse keeper, preserves her virtue in the face of a jealous husband, a lecherous servant, and two foolish lovers who have disguised themselves as patients in order to court her, has occasional points of similarity with the plot of the main action, and one striking thematic connection, when de Flores's words, 'I coupled with your mate /At barley-brake; now we are left in hell' (v. 3) recall a game played by the madmen, with offstage shouts of 'Catch there, catch the last couple in hell!' (III. 3). The real madhouse patients, as opposed to the comic counterfeits who figure in the action, are glimpsed only occasionally; but this makes their presence if anything more compelling, suggesting a half-seen irrational power. Their master's plan to use them as part of the entertainment for Beatrice-Joanna's wedding confirms their connection with the obsessions that drive the principal characters. But for the most part the comedy of the madhouse scenes, like that of the Roaring School in *A Fair Quarrel*, is surprisingly innocuous. The only madmen we see at any length are the counterfeits, and Isabella's cool, inventive wit means she has little difficulty keeping the troublesome men at bay. Moreover, the ending of the play takes an unexpectedly genial turn, beginning with a connection between the two plots. The idea of the 'changeling', initially a reference to one of the counterfeit madmen, is applied to all the characters, beginning with the principals:

> Here's beauty chang'd
> To ugly whoredom; here, servant obedience
> To a master sin, imperious murder.
>
> (v. 3)

But as the idea of change spreads, it becomes largely positive: 'Your change is come too, from an ignorant wrath /To knowing friendship'; 'I see all apparent, wife, and will change now /Into a better husband'. The principle, applied across the cast, is increasingly neat and reductive, and dissipates the power of the central action. The tone of the last few minutes is reassuring:

> justice hath so right
> The guilty hit, that innocence is quit
> By proclamation, and may joy again.
>
> (v. 3)

Alsemero's last speech, comforting Beatrice-Joanna's father, shades into an epilogue that appeals not for the audience's applause but for its 'smiles': 'If these appear, all griefs are reconcil'd'. The considerable reputation of this play, which holds the modern stage as well as any non-Shakespearean play of the period, is based largely on the satiric rigour of its central scenes; but the comic subplot makes its own independent statement, and it allows a final relaxation that makes the play quite different from its predecessors.

The dangers inherent in the wide focus and mixed tone of *A Fair Quarrel* and *The Changeling* can be appreciated by a glance (it is worth no more) at *Anything for a Quiet Life* (*c.* 1621). Middleton may have been the sole author, though Webster is sometimes proposed as collaborator; whatever the truth about the authorship, there does not seem to be a single controlling intelligence at work. The first scene is a considerable technical feat, laying out a wide network of social, financial and sexual relationships over a great variety of characters. But this time there are so many plots at work that none of them achieves more than limited and conventional treatment. Two gallants cheat a mercer and a barber; a lawyer's wife defends her chastity against a lord by pretending she loves his page, who is really the disguised wife of one of the gallants (the reason for the disguise is never clear); the mercer, meanwhile, tries to cope with his shrewish wife by applying the motto of the play's title; and in the plot that emerges as the central one Lady Cressingham destroys her husband's household by her profligacy, making him sell his land, disinherit his son and put his younger children out to board. The issue, the destruction of an old estate, seems serious. But it is resolved by a flagrantly unconvincing surprise twist in which the wicked stepmother turns out to have been just pretending and we are asked to forget that any of it happened. A similar arbitrariness dogs the main plot of Webster and Rowley's *A Cure for a Cuckold* (*c.* 1624), in which Clare commands her lover Lessingham, 'Kill for my sake the friend that loves thee dearest' (I. 1). The command is in fact a riddle whose significance keeps shifting through a series of plot twists: unexpected revelations of feeling, love-friendship debates, points of gentlemanly honour (recalling *A Fair Quarrel*), and outbreaks of jealousy and intrigue. By the time the plot, appropriately described as 'this labyrinth, this toil' (v. 1), has run its course the audience may be past caring what the characters do next. The playwrights seem to be reaching for eccentric novelty. But that same interest may also be credited with two of the play's more engaging characters, the 'honest thief' Rockfield, a dispossessed younger son who, though very much in need of money, is too gentlemanly to succeed in his trade; and the old mariner Compass, who gives the play its title. Returning after a long sea voyage to find his wife pregnant, Compass not only forgives her but claims the child for his own and wipes the stain of his wife's guilt and his own cuckoldry by staging a mock-death: 'I will go hang myself two hours, and so long shalt thou drown thyself' (IV. 1). After a playful courtship in which they pretend to be meeting each other for the first time, he marries her again. As one of the other characters remarks, 'This is a new trick' (v. 1). So, in a way, was Clare's. But Compass's trick reflects a human reality: the wish that we could indeed forget and forgive the past, and make broken relations new. And while Middleton's trick with Lady Cressingham was just a playwright's gimmick, Compass's contrivance is made the natural extension of a salty but compassionate comic personality.

The music for his second wedding precipitates the resolution of the main plot, just as the gentle end of the subplot of *The Changeling* seems to seep upwards into the main body of the play. In the tonal mix of both plays the low-life comedy has an overall healing effect. But in

The Witch of Edmonton (1621) the low-life characters contribute what we might have expected, and get only occasionally, in *The Changeling*: an undercurrent of the dark and irrational that affects the higher world. The title page identifies the authors as Rowley, Dekker and John Ford (1586–*c*. 1640) adding tantalizingly, 'etc'. While there are some jumps in style beyond what the material needs, the collaborators have worked together intelligently. This time the surprise twists are in the opening scene; they reflect not the playwrights' interest in teasing the audience but the confused and equivocal situation the characters have made for themselves. Frank Thorney has been having an affair with Sir Arthur Clarington's maid Winnifred. She is pregnant; he has married her, but wants to keep aloof until he has secured his inheritance. We suspect he is playing a double game; but then we learn that Sir Arthur, who has rebuked Frank but offered to provide for the couple, has also been enjoying Winnifred and plans to use the marriage as a cover for his continued pleasure. He in turn is surprised when Winnifred refuses to co-operate, insisting on taking her marriage seriously. Frank, trying to win round his father without revealing the truth, is instead pressured into a bigamous second marriage with Susan Carter; his father is in financial straits and this is the only way to save the estate. Sex, marriage and property are all bound up, and Frank comments bitterly on the way he has been used: 'When I was sold, I sold myself again; /Some knaves have done't in lands, and I in body' (III. 2). Frank's susceptibility to conflicting pressures is the centre of a whole tangle of broken promises and dishonest deals.

The story of the witch, Mother Sawyer, is at first glance a bold contrast with all this equivocation in high life. Cursed and persecuted, accused of witchcraft, she responds like Shylock by executing the villainy she has been taught and becomes a witch indeed. Her familiar, a black dog, makes what looks like a straightforward deal with her: revenge on her enemies, in exchange for her soul. But he too equivocates: though he will not allow her any evasion, he reveals after she has made the compact that his power is limited (II. 1). He also offers her love in place of the hate she gets from the villagers, and the grotesque physical affection that develops between them – 'Let's tickle' (IV. 1) – produces some of the darkest comedy in the play. The hatred that surrounds Mother Sawyer suggests a dark underside in the country itself. Her chief persecutor, Old Banks, is 'loving to the world, /And charitable to the poor' (II. 1), but cannot keep himself from abusing an old woman. She calls him 'this black cur /That barks and bites' (II. 1) and a moment later the dog first appears; her persecutor and her familiar are mysteriously connected. The authors do not sentimentalize Mother Sawyer; she causes real misery. But we can also see that she has been *made* a witch, and the evil that drives her has a social as well as a supernatural dimension. Publicly accused, she counter-attacks by seeing her evil as an image of the way the whole world behaves:

> A witch? Who is not?
> Hold not that universal name in scorn then.
> What are your painted things in princes' courts,
> Upon whose eyelids Lust sits blowing fires
> To burn men's souls in sensual hot desires,
> Upon whose naked paps a lecher's thought
> Acts sin in fouler shapes than can be wrought?

JUSTICE
> But these work not as you do.

SAWYER
>   No, but far worse:
> These by enchantments can whole lordships change
> To trunks of rich attire, turn ploughs and teams
> To Flanders mares and coaches, and huge trains
> Of servitors, to a French butterfly.
> Have you not city-witches who can turn
> Their husbands' wares, whole standing shops of wares,
> To sumptuous tables, gardens of stol'n sin,
> In one year wasting what scarce twenty win?
> Are not these witches?

>   (IV. 1)

As in *Michaelmas Term* and *The Revenger's Tragedy*, established property is sold for transient luxury; land becomes money. The old woman is here the vehicle for far-reaching satire in the old Jacobean manner; and just as we may be thinking the effect is a bit glib, she includes seducers in her list of witches and Sir Arthur, his conscience stung, leaves the stage.

Mother Sawyer and her dog reflect an irrational level in the whole community. The villagers complain, 'Our cattle fall, our wives fall, our daughters fall, and maidservants fall; and we ourselves shall not be able to stand, if this beast be suffered to graze amongst us' (IV. 1). The bawdy jokes show that the powers and the fears the witch releases are largely sexual. Frank's mental disturbance in his scenes with Susan seems at first independent. But as they try to comfort each other their exchange of vows, 'I am all yours', 'and I all thine' (II. 2) recalls the dog's first words to Mother Sawyer: 'Ho! Have I found thee cursing? now thou art mine own' (II. 1). In a later scene the dog rubs against Frank, the idea of killing Susan comes into his head, and he stabs her to death.

For the clown Cuddy Banks, on the other hand, the witch is simply his favourite character in the Morris Dance (III. 1) and though he falls in with the dog their relations are surprisingly innocent. He expects the dog to get him Susan's sister Katherine, but he gets a ducking instead, and this time the bawdy puns – 'thinking to land at Katherine's dock, I was almost at Gravesend' (III. 1) – simply keep the tone light. The spirit who impersonates Katherine says of Cuddy, 'We can meet his folly, /But from his virtues must be runaways' (III. 1). He himself sums up the innocence of his relations with the dog:

CLOWN
    I entertain'd you ever as a dog, not as a devil.
DOG
    True; and so I us'd thee doggedly, not devilishly. I have
    deluded thee for sport to laugh at.
                                                (v. 1).

They finally lose patience with each other and separate, the dog declaring, 'I am for greatness now, corrupted greatness' (v. 1). The dog's interventions in the festive rural life Cuddy represents are eerie: when he joins the Morris Dance, invisible to all but Cuddy, the fiddler suddenly finds he cannot play, the dog plays instead, and as he finishes the Constable comes to arrest two innocent men for Susan's murder. But the good nature of Cuddy himself, which links him to Chough and Compass, makes him one character the powers of darkness cannot touch.

As in *The Changeling*, evil fails to take a complete and final hold on the world. This may be one reason why, though Susan, Frank and Mother Sawyer die, the play's title page advertises a tragicomedy. Though the witch goes off with curt warnings against trusting the devil, and with an unsettling complaint that the curses of the onlookers are distracting her from repentance, Frank is allowed a full repentance and a long, affectionate farewell to the survivors. He has earlier toyed with the idea of wishing man were not immortal, so that he would not have to answer for his sins, but has rejected it:

                              This were a fine reign,
        To do ill, and not hear of it again.
    Yet then were man more wretched than a beast;
    For, sister, our dead pay is sure our best.
                                                (IV. 2)

There is some irony in the ending. Sir Arthur is identified as the real culprit, yet he gets off with a fine. But there are suggestions that he too is on the way to repentance. In the end Old Carter, Susan's father, welcomes Winnifred into his house and commends her to his surviving daughter: 'Come to me, Winnifred, shalt be welcome; make much of her, Kate, I charge you; I do not think but she's a good wench, and hath had wrong as well as we. So let's every man home to Edmonton with heavy hearts, yet as merry as we can, though not as we would' (v. 3). The soft tone recalls the ending of *The Changeling*; but that was too smooth and contrived to be fully persuasive. This offer of restoration is more convincing for being a bit clumsy. Like the play as a whole it shows that the mixed, open vision of late Jacobean tragicomedy, though it always runs the danger of glibness and sentimentality, could carry integrity and conviction in its depiction of the ordinary decency that saves the world from total corruption. The eclecticism of these later plays includes an assertion of positive social values: the gentlemanly honour of Ager and the Colonel, the charity of Compass. The focus, even in the latter case, is social rather than spiritual. As in Beaumont and Fletcher there is no questioning of the heavens, and even Mother Sawyer's role as a witch is more a social than a spiritual phenomenon. What separates these plays from the work of Beaumont and Fletcher is that the values they depict are grounded in communities we can actually see. They are created by a combination of Jacobean satire on materialism and deception, and the interest in security and comfort we saw in popular drama. In *The Changeling* the genial and satiric visions are kept apart until the end, and expressed in sharply alternating scenes. In *The Witch of Edmonton* they blend in a rounded vision of a rural community, capable at once of kindness and meanness, hospitality and cynicism. This ability to depict not just a collection of characters getting through a plot but a whole world going about its business will be carried over into Caroline drama.

Notes

1. On the importance of tragicomedy at this period, and its value as a form, see Jacqueline Pearson, *Tragedy and Tragicomedy in the Plays of John Webster* (Totawa, N. J., 1980), pp. 7–49.

Chapter 13
Ford

In plays like *The Witch of Edmonton* the individuality of the collaborators is to some degree submerged in the group enterprise. One of the collaborators, Dekker, was a leading exponent of the old, robust popular school. Another, John Ford (1586–*c*. 1640), was just beginning a career that was to make him the most original and imaginative playwright of the Caroline period, a specialist in refined and courtly drama. The individuality of Ford is not yet apparent in this early play, and he seems to work easily with Dekker and the others. But his later, independent work shows the stamp of a very distinctive mind. Paradoxically, one of his peculiarities is the way he uses conscious allusion to earlier drama. His tragedy *Love's Sacrifice* (published 1633) is full of echoes of *Othello* and of the tragedies of Webster. *Perkin Warbeck* (published 1634), in its opposition of the pragmatic politician (Henry VII) and the doomed, romantic figure who has a much fuller sense of the mystique of kingship (Perkin himself), recalls *Richard II*, and there are verbal echoes of this and other Shakespearean history plays. *'Tis Pity She's a Whore* (published 1633) presents two young lovers, aided by a bawdy nurse, in opposition to their society; we think of *Romeo and Juliet*. These echoes are not the signs of a tired, imitative art. The allusiveness, for one thing, is consciously advertised; sometimes it is the first thing the audience is given. The opening of *Love's Sacrifice*, 'Depart the court?', is meant to recall the famous 'Banisht?' that opens *The White Devil*; in its tone and phrasing the first speech of *Perkin Warbeck* ('Still to be haunted, still to be pursued . . .') recalls, with equal deliberateness, the opening of *Henry IV Part One* ('So shaken as we are, so wan with care . . .'). Ford's awareness of the literary past advertises a reach and grandeur like that of earlier drama, something that had been lost in the more relaxed manner of the later Jacobeans. But he is not just turning the clock back; the old material is there to be re-shaped in a new way. In *Perkin Warbeck* the mystique of royalty is represented not by a king but by a pretender, and the young lovers of *'Tis Pity She's a Whore* are brother and sister.

One consequence of this conscious originality is a certain difficulty in finding an attitude to the characters' behaviour, a difficulty which bothers not just the audience but the characters themselves. We see this in *'Tis Pity*. Giovanni and Annabella are entering unknown territory. The fact that Giovanni's principal adviser, and the main opponent of his love, is a friar, not only recalls *Romeo and Juliet* but emphasizes that the lovers are breaking not just a sexual taboo but a religious one. Giovanni, we are told, is a brilliant student, a young man with an inquiring mind; for him incest and religious freethinking go together. When he and Annabella confess their love, their exchange of vows is ceremonial; they kneel together, and the liturgical repetition of their language suggests a need not just to abandon the old religion but to construct a new one based on their love:

ANNABELLA
        On my knees,   *She kneels.*
Brother, even by our mother's dust, I charge you,
Do not betray me to your mirth or hate:
Love me or kill me, brother.
GIOVANNI
        On my knees,   *He kneels.*
Sister, even by my mother's dust I charge you,
Do not betray me to your mirth or hate:
Love me, or kill me, sister.

(I. 2)

They seem tentative and fearful, and they deal with those fears by codifying them. In swearing by their common mother they are evoking the very relationship that makes their love sinful. The loyalty they demand of each other is part of a shared recognition that they are both outlaws. Giovanni tells the Friar, 'Your age o'errules you: had you youth like mine, /You'd make her love your Heaven, and her divine' (II. 5). Out of context this would sound conventional; but Giovanni in the most literal sense has made of his love a new religion.

His commitment to it, however, is steadier than Annabella's. She becomes pregnant, and is hastily married to Soranzo; this makes her position more complicated than Giovanni's. For a while the Friar terrifies her into repentance with a lecture on the torments of Hell (II. 6), yet when Soranzo discovers her pregnancy she defies him with brazen, impudent wit: 'Let it suffice, that you shall have the glory /To father what so brave a father got' (IV. 3). As he beats her, she laughs and sings. Yet not long afterwards she repents again, this time on her own initiative, and her last thoughts are governed by conventional piety. Giovanni has his own instability, but his is more a matter of style. Speaking of their love, he veers between lyricism and innuendo:

Hear her but speak, and you will swear the spheres
Make music to the citizens in Heaven;
But father, what else is for pleasure framed
Lest I offend your ears shall go unnamed.

(II. 5)

The descent to schoolboy naughtiness reminds us that the consummation of their affair was accompanied by the coarse bawdry of the old nurse Putana: 'and I say still, if a young wench feel the fit upon her, let her take anybody, father or brother, all is one' (II. 1). Giovanni's love for Annabella never wavers, but his attitude to her marriage does. He himself suggests it as a practical measure, as soon as they have made love, and his tone is surprisingly brusque: 'You must be married, mistress. . . . /Someone must have you' (II. 1). But when the Friar proposes the idea he rejects it: 'Marriage? Why, that's to damn her; that's to prove /Her greedy of variety of lust' (II. 5). With painfully cynical jealousy he attributes Annabella's repentance to the notion that Soranzo has been more interesting in bed:

What, changed so soon? Hath your new sprightly lord
Found out a trick in night-games more than we
Could know in our simplicity?

(v. 5)

It is a sign of Giovanni's fundamental challenge to convention that he makes his sexual relations with Annabella sound innocent and her relations with her husband perverted.

The instability of Giovanni's language and his difficulty in finding a steady attitude to Annabella's marriage reveal that his defiance of convention is cynical as well as romantic, and that his confidence in Annabella is not nearly so great as his confidence in himself. Towards the end of the play they move apart; as she reverts to piety, he becomes a Marlovian rebel imposing his imagination on the universe:

why, I hold fate
Clasped in my fist, and could command the course
Of time's eternal motion, hadst thou been
One thought more steady than an˙ebbing sea.

(v. 5)

From the beginning he has seen himself marked out for a special destiny: ''tis not, I know, /My lust, but 'tis my fate that leads me on' (I. 2). Invited to Soranzo's birthday feast, he knows he is going into danger and replies, 'tell him I dare come' (v. 3). Like Romeo's 'Is it e'en so? Then I defy you' stars!' this shows him at once accepting his fate and making that acceptance an act of his own defiant will. His final gesture is to kill Annabella and appear at the feast with her heart impaled on his dagger.[1] It is an assertion of his power not just over her but over his whole world: 'The glory of my deed /Darkened the mid-day sun, made noon as night' (v. 6). In his last interview with Annabella he begins by denying a traditional Heaven or Hell, but tells her, 'Go thou, white in thy soul, to fill a throne /Of innocence and sanctity in Heaven' (v. 5). The incongruity disappears if we see this not as the Friar's heaven but one of Giovanni's own imagining, in which incestuous love has made Annabella a saint. The characteristic Jacobean doubt about the next world, like Julia's 'I go, /I know not whither' (*The Duchess of Malfi*, v. 2), is replaced by something more prescriptive: 'Where'er I go, let me enjoy this grace, /Freely to view my Annabella's face' (v. 6).

In the drama of the period incest is a vehicle for the expression of illicit desire, a challenge to the fundamental conventions of society. In *Women Beware Women* it is mean and furtive, like the other passions of that play; in *The Duchess of Malfi* it is a dark secret, never quite admitted, that destroys Ferdinand from within, while giving him a kind of tormented grandeur. In *A King and No King* Beaumont and Fletcher bring incest into the open, using it to probe the artibrariness of human relations but not really committing themselves to a defence of it as a legitimate exercise of freedom. At the literal level of the plot they finally shrink from the thing itself. Ford does not. And he makes it the vehicle for a daring assertion of human will: Giovanni, like Bussy d'Ambois, aspires heroically to be a law unto himself. Moreover, the play's sympathy for the lovers is increased by its sardonic depiction of the conventional society that defines them as criminals. Annabella's marriage is cobbled up with cynical haste; her husband is mainly concerned with the outrage to his own male ego, and has himself been guilty of sexual misconduct of a more ordinary kind; and the chief authority figure is a Cardinal whose principal actions are to pardon murder and to seize the estate of the lovers' family for the Church. The Friar, the most serious and well-meaning spokesman for convention, is curiously negative. His religion is one of fear and prohibition; his first words are 'Dispute no more' (I. 1). As the action approaches its final crisis he flees the city. Even the writing of the play supports the lovers, though this may be unintentional: against the background of the drab, tired revenge story that forms the balance of the action, they stand out in high relief. It is the lovers themselves who generate misgivings about their affair: the instability of Giovanni's language, the final piety of Annabella. As he uses her for his last grand gesture, she resists: 'Brother, unkind, unkind' (v. 5). He hardly seems to notice her resistance. Ford shows the excitement of Giovanni's attempt to construct an original morality, but he also shows the human cost.

The hero of *Perkin Warbeck* is in his own way as original as Giovanni. To revive the English history play after it had been dead for over a generation (the Prologue admits as much) is itself a challenge to fashion; to make its hero a minor pretender deepens the challenge; and to allow him a degree of passion and conviction that finally tips the scales in his favour is to challenge more than just theatrical assumptions. Perkin's insistence that he is the last of the Plantagenets, the younger of the princes allegedly murdered by Richard III, never wavers. When sentenced to the Tower at the end of the play he calls it 'Our childhood's dreadful nursery' (v. 2), keeping his claim intact in the final collapse of his fortunes. He makes his death, a minor episode in actual history. sound like the end of an era:

> the glorious race
> Of fourteen kings, Plantaganets, determines
> In this last issue male.
>
> (v. 3)

The play leaves the literal truth of his claim unexamined; the conviction Perkin carries is a matter of style. As the Scottish King James IV puts it, 'He must be more than subject who can utter /The language of a king, and such is thine' (II. 1). Such a claim, we might think, is easily overthrown; but Ford allows it real authority. He sets Perkin against Henry VII, who is clearly the effective King of England, but whose public image as a wise and gentle ruler conceals a hard-nosed, cynical politician, skilled in the art of buying loyalty:

> the two hundred marks
> Your majesty convey'd a' gently pursed
> With a right modest gravity.
>
> (III. 3)

Henry is surrounded by admiring followers, whose comments shade from ''Tis a King /Composed of gentleness' (II. 2) to 'cards well shuffled /And dealt with cunning bring some gamester thrift' (IV. 4). In their one meeting Henry takes the obvious line on Perkin: 'The player's on the stage still, 'tis his part; /A' does but act' (v. 2). But Perkin has a surprisingly effective rejoinder: Henry is King only because he happened to win the battle of Bosworth:

> The tale is soon applied:
> Fate, which crowned these attempts when least assured,
> Might have befriended others like resolved.
>
> (v. 2)

In terms of legitimacy there is little to choose between them. As one of Perkin's followers puts it, 'For my own part, I believe it is true, if I be not deceiv'd, that kings must be kings and subjects subjects. But which is which – you shall pardon me for that' (v. 2).

As in *'Tis Pity*, Perkin's appeal is qualified not by the opposition but by his own party and his own behaviour. He has a set of ludicrously stupid followers, whom he persists in calling 'Peers of England' (v. 3) right to the end. He flees from a crucial military encounter before the battle even takes place. His wife Katharine says all that can be said with confidence on his behalf when she states, 'You have a noble language, sir; your right /In me is without question' (III. 2). What she leaves unsaid is equally significant. But her continued loyalty to Perkin as her husband is a clue to the way Ford ultimately uses his dynastic claim, and to the positive value that lies behind it. Our sympathy for Perkin's view of himself as Richard IV is the vehicle not for a Pirandello-like questioning of the nature of reality but for an assertion of the integrity of the individual will in sticking to its commitments. It is at this level that Perkin really is a king – in his love: 'We reign in our affections, blessed woman!' (v. 2); and in his brave defiance of death: 'so illustrious mention /Shall blaze our names, and style us Kings o'er Death' (v. 3). As Giovanni's rebellion is not just sexual, Perkin's is not just political. Each man makes a large claim for the individual's right to see the world on his own terms. The difference is that Perkin is more consistently dignified and sympathetic than Giovanni, and this difference is largely a matter of style: at this level Perkin never falters as Giovanni does.

The importance of style in achieving self-definition and establishing value is one of the keys to *The Broken Heart*. This play is perhaps Ford's fullest and most original achievement. Here the allusions to earlier drama have virtually disappeared, as though Ford no longer feels the need to test his own vision against those of other writers. Instead of a single rebel standing out against his community we are shown a group tragedy that involves the community itself. The setting is a court; but this court is far removed from the decadent palaces of Jacobean drama. It is an artificial but decorous and dignified world; the high style of the principal figures is defined, as often in Ford, against the comic vulgarity of the minor courtiers. A line from *Perkin Warbeck*, 'Princes are but men /Distinguished by the fineness of their frailty' (IV. 5) captures the special quality of this world. Two other plays give useful sidelights. In *The Lover's Melancholy* (1628) and *The Fancies Chaste and Noble* (published 1638) Ford allows some traditional misgivings about the court while moving to a final assertion of its value determined by the comic structure of the plays. In The *Fancies Chaste and Noble* Octavio, Marquis of Sienna, runs a private establishment given to artistic pleasures and peopled by the collection of ladies who give the play its title. Dark suspicions about the nature of the establishment are dispelled in the last act: it really is a salon, not a bordello, and Octavio is revealed as a figure of stern but benevolent authority. *The Lover's Melancholy* allows some conventional but effective satire on the empty display of court life, but the play's main sufferers from mental disturbance, the Prince Palador and the old lord Meleader, are cured in courtly terms: the first by a masque that reveals the source of his melancholy, the second by the restoration not just of his lost daughter but of the badges of his former office. In the first scene the traditional tale of a music contest between a human and a nightingale, in which the nightingale loses, asserts the primacy of art; and this prepares us for a benevolent use of artificial devices at the end of the play. *The Broken Heart* (published 1633) is equally positive in its assertion of courtly value, but this time the medium is tragedy.

The philosopher Tecnicus gives us what looks like a way of reading the play when he lectures his pupil Orgilus on the nature of honour:

> Honour consists not in a bare opinion
> By doing any act that feeds content,
> Brave in appearance, 'cause we think it brave.
> Such honour comes by accident, not nature,
> Proceeding from the vices of our passion,
> Which makes our reason drunk. But real honour
> Is the reward of virtue, and acquired
> By justice or by valour, which for basis
> Hath justice to uphold it.
>
> (III. 1)

In its contrast between private values and absolute, objective ones this looks back to the debate on value between Troilus and Hector in *Troilus and Cressida*. It also reads like a rebuke to Giovanni and Perkin Warbeck. But while Tecnicus helps to define the play's interests, his judgement is not the final one. The principal characters hold, intensely, to private codes of behaviour; but in the long run the play endorses these codes and the community sanctions them.

Ithocles, having returned in triumph from the wars, falls in love with the princess Calantha. He recognizes in this love a dangerous ambition and thinks wistfully of being able to control it by keeping his soul in order; but he knows the attempt will fail:

> Morality applied
> To timely practice keeps the soul in tune,
> At whose sweet motions all our actions dance.

But this is form of books and school-tradition.
It physics not the sickness of a mind
Broken with griefs. Strong fevers are not eased
With counsel, but with best receipts and means;
Means, speedy means and certain; that's the cure.

(II. 2)

In fact Calantha favours his love and even the foreign prince Nearchus,
who might have married her, decides to further it in private. But
Ithocles's fate is complicated by a rash action in his past: he forced his
sister Penthea away from her betrothed lover Orgilus and trapped her
in a loveless marriage with the jealous old lord Bassanes. Penthea
rejects Orgilus's renewed advances, even to the extent of speaking
frankly to him only when he has crossed to the other side of the stage
and resumed the disguise in which he first approached her:

PENTHEA

                    My true love
    Abhors to think that Orgilus deserved
    No better favours than a second bed.
ORGILUS
    I must not take this reason.
PENTHEA
                        To confirm it,
    Should I outlive my bondage, let me meet
    Another worse than this and less desired
    If of all the men alive thou shouldst but touch
    My lip or hand again!

(II. 3)

The fierceness of her rejection reflects a conviction that her marriage
has corrupted her own nature:

                    she that's wife to Orgilus and lives
    In known adultery with Bassanes
    Is at the best a whore.

(III. 2)

She has in effect re-defined herself. But the internal tension destroys
her: her mind breaks down, and she starves herself to death, seeing the
act as punishment on her own polluted blood (IV. 2).

Orgilus, who has been driven through most of the play by bitter
resentment of Ithocles, avenges Penthea's death by trapping Ithocles
in a trick chair and stabbing him. But what begins as a scene of revenge

becomes a scene of mutual admiration between gentlemen. Ithocles
defies his killer bravely, and Orgilus is impressed:

> By Apollo,
> Thou talk'st a goodly language. For requital,
> I will report thee to thy mistress richly.
>
> (IV. 4)

Ithocles is equally gallant in return: 'Nimble in vengence, I forgive
thee. Follow /Safety, with best success. O may it prosper!' (IV. 4).
Even the trick chair has a double effect: it is an unfair contrivance
suggesting a mechanical code of honour; but it also allows Ithocles a
dignified position in which to die. Orgilus too dies with dignity. He
chooses to bleed to death; his execution is presented as a decorous court
ceremony, and the poetry of his end conveys the slow fading of a
human life. Though he is being punished as a criminal, the tone is very
different from the horror and revulsion that surrounded Giovanni. He
dies, like Penthea, in quiet, and Bassanes celebrates his courage:

> This pastime
> Appears majestical. Some high-tuned poem
> Hereafter shall deliver to posterity
> The writer's glory and his subject's triumph.
>
> (v. 2)

In one of the play's most striking passages Calantha, in the middle
of a dance, is told of the deaths of her father, her lover and Penthea.
She goes on dancing. But in the last scene she reveals the truth:

> O my lords,
> I but deceived your eyes with antic gesture,
> When one news straight came huddling on another,
> Of death, and death, and death. Still I danced forward;
> But it struck home, and here, and in an instant.
> Be such mere women, who with shrieks and outcries
> Can vow a present end to all their sorrows,
> Yet live to vow new pleasures, and outlive them?
> They are the silent griefs which cut the heart-strings.
> Let me die smiling.
>
> (v. 3)

Like the lovers of 'Tis Pity, but much more elaborately, she devises
a ceremony that both codifies her values and destroys her. Unlike them
she is surrounded as she dies by wonder and admiration.

The suppressed feeling that destroys from within is a motif that ties the play together. Penthea, having rejected Orgilus, expresses the love and pity she has been concealing:

> I fear I was too rough. Alas, poor gentleman,
> 'A looked not like the ruins of his youth,
> But like the ruins of those ruins. Honour,
> How much we fight with weakness to preserve thee!
>
> (II. 3)

Concealing his love from Calantha, Ithocles is stricken by illness; Penthea tells the Princess that before he will confess his love to her, 'First, his heart /Shall fall in cinders, scorched by your disdain' (III. 5). Calantha, apparently rejecting Penthea's plea on behalf of her brother, declares, 'Lady, /Your check lies in my silence' (III. 5). Beneath that silence, and intensified by it, her love goes to work. Orgilus catches this aspect of the play's atmosphere following the song that marks Penthea's death:

> A horrid stillness
> Succeeds this deathful air. Let's know the reason.
> Tread softly. There is mystery in mourning.
>
> (IV. 3)

These suppressed feelings issue in ceremonial deaths that produce public wonder. To the tragic emotions of pity and terror Ford adds admiration. Bassanes is an interesting test case. In the early scenes he is a stock jealous husband, and his language is gross: 'I'll tear thy throat out, /Son of a cat, ill-looking hound's-head' (II. 1). Then this jealousy comes to a head and breaks; he not only repents but attempts to join the dignified sufferers who form the play's centre. He assists in the execution of Orgilus, suggesting not only a reconciliation between the characters but a community of gentlemen to which they both belong: 'I'll be as nimble . . . stretch out /Thine arm with vigour and unshook virtue' (V. 2). But while he would like to die like the others his style betrays him: 'Ere I speak a word /I will look on and burst' (IV. 2). In the end he is sentenced to live, and be Sparta's marshal. The verdict distresses him; but it also helps to define the deaths of the others as an achievement reflecting the fineness of their natures. Life is for those who are coarse enough to survive. The true aristocrats form a community governed by suppressed, intense feeling and a commitment to codes of behaviour that may look artificial and peculiar from outside, but acquire conviction as the play draws us into its special world.

Later Jacobean plays like *The Changeling* and *The Witch of Edmonton* seemed content in the end to take charity and tolerance as their positive values. Ford restores the heroic scale. His heroes, like those of Shakespeare, Chapman and Webster, assert their wills and values with a defiant, amoral grandeur. Like the earlier heroes they work through style and role-playing. But while Giovanni and Perkin are isolated against a shrunken conventional world and Giovanni in particular cannot sustain his own role consistently, the figures of *The Broken Heart* make up a community of their own. The fineness and frailty of which Perkin speaks give Ford's vision a softer texture than that of the earlier playwrights. His heroes, even Giovanni, are more delicate than robust. But the soft texture, simply because it is made so palpable in Ford's language, means that when he comes in *The Broken Heart* to create a whole community of heroes who finally support each other, that community, closed and special though it is, is solidly realized as the courts of Beaumont and Fletcher are not. It is a self-sufficient world; one feature of the Jacobean manner that does not return in Ford is the probing of the heavens. Even Giovanni's impiety consists not so much of defying God as of redefining divinity in earthly and sensual terms. The ceremonies of *The Broken Heart* – music, candles, white robes, an altar covered in white – may suggest the High Anglicanism Archbishop Laud was introducing into the English church. But they are the ceremonies of a secular church whose commandments direct not moral conduct but feeling and style.

Notes

1. While Ford has been accused of sensationalism at this point, Ronald Huebert has shown that the ripping open of Annabella's breast is a logical culmination of the play's imagery. See *John Ford: Baroque English Dramatist* (Montreal, 1977), pp. 144–50.

Chapter 14

Caroline Drama

Apart from the achievement of John Ford, the drama of the reign of Charles I has frequently been regarded as a charming backwater. As England approached the great crisis of the Civil War, the story goes, dramatists amused their audiences with escapist entertainment. This view is not altogether fair. Some dramatists at least were concerned, directly or implicitly, with issues of the day,[1] and the censorship discussed in the Introduction had to be as active as ever. But Caroline drama's claim to serious attention does not rest just on occasional topicality. It is true that the satiric rigour of early Jacobean drama had long faded; the new manner is more relaxed. In tragedy, the great solitary heroes are gone, and with them the dark questioning of man's place in the universe. Only Ford aims at the heroic scale. But there is still a keen scrutiny of men and women in society, and the conclusions are not always complacent. The frank artifice associated with Fletcher and his colleagues persists, and with it goes a tendency to hold artifice itself up for examination.

The word 'Cavalier', so often associated with these plays, suggests a doomed romantic charm. But their range of manner is much wider than that. We can sample that range by placing together two plays of the mid-1630s, *The Wits* (1634) by Sir William Davenant (1606–68) and *Aglaura* (1637) by Sir John Suckling (1609–42). *The Wits* concerns the attempt of the Elder Pallatine and the humorous old knight Sir Morglay Thwack to live in town on their wits alone, abandoning their estates and looking to the ladies for maintenance. The Elder Pallatine is outsmarted by his younger brother, who has him arrested in an abandoned brothel, inhabited only by 'a melancholy race of old /Norman spiders that came in with the Conqueror' (II. 3), and then trapped in a trunk. The victim claims to appreciate his brother's wit, but his offer of reconciliation is couched in aggressive language: 'I've a great mind to kiss thee . . . and eat up thy lips so far, /Till thou'st nothing left to cover thy teeth' (v. 3). The play's fun is rough and brutal, and through its depiction of London we glimpse the city that will be Hogarth's. The imagery is of the order of, 'Your dog, tied to a bottle, shall not outrun me' (v. 2). When Young Pallatine's lady asks for a share of his winnings he replies,

> What need it, Luce? A virgin may live cheap;
> They're maintain'd with as small charge as a wren
> With maggots in a cheesemonger's shop.
>
> (III. 2)

The value of settled country life, taken seriously elsewhere in the period, means little to these characters. As Young Pallatine and his assistant Pert steal the Elder Pallatine's jewels, they remark that these are his flocks and herds: 'A little room contains them all /At last' (II. 3). As in Middleton's city comedies, inheritance has become a commodity, but this time the idea is simply accepted as the way of the world. In *A New Way to Pay Old Debts*, as we will see, Massinger sees the military life as a gentleman's redemption; here, Pert returns from the wars remarking, 'we have been to kill we know not whom /Nor why' (I. 1).

Tough and cynical, this play anticipates the more hard-boiled Restoration comedies. Like them, and unlike the comedies of Fletcher, it gives us a palpable London. Suckling's courtly drama is at first glance more high-minded, a point in the line of heroic tragedy, geared to admiration, that runs from Marston's *Sophonisba* through Beaumont and Fletcher to the heroic plays of the Restoration. While Davenant catches the sexuality of his characters in lines like

> there is a small parcel
> Of man that rebels more than all the rest
> Of his body.
>
> (I. 1)

Suckling's characters debate the role of physical pleasure in love as a philosophical problem; more, one suspects, because Platonic love was a fashionable topic than because it is a necessary question of the play. For the sensualists in the debate, Love is an epicure whose kitchen contains

> Hearts newly slain
> Serv'd up entire, stuck with little arrows
> In stead of cloves . . . .
> Sometimes a cheek plumpt up
> With broth, with cream and claret mingled
> For sauce, and round about the dish
> Pomegranate kernels, strew'd with leaves of lilies.
>
> (I. 5)

Even the heroine Aglaura, urging her husband not to consummate their marriage at a time of danger, speaks as a connoisseur: 'Gather not roses in a wet and frowning hour; /They'll lose their sweetness then, trust me they will sir' (III. 2). The first version of the play ends with complicated multiple killings that inspire both reflections on the mystery of life, 'Why, 'tis to be benighted to eternity, /To sit i' the dark, and do I know not what' (v. 1), and a certain flippancy: 'What have we here? a churchyard?' (v. 3). Both the bewilderment and the joke can be seen as echoes of Webster. But the joke also signals a lack of final commitment, confirmed in the second version when the blood-bath is replaced by a happy ending, introduced by an apologetic new Prologue: ''Tis strange, perchance, you'll think, that she that died /At Christmas, should at Easter be a bride', and accompanied by a new philosophy:

> This violence of Fortune cannot last ever:
> Who knows but all these clouds are shadows
> To set off your fairer days?
>   (v. 1)

Fortune, like love, plans like an artist, for effect. Marston's switch of genres in the Antonio plays was deliberately shocking; this seems more simply an exercise in style. Davenant parades his cynicism, making it a way of life for his characters, part of the play's rough manner. Suck-ling's cynicism runs deeper: beneath the elegant surface there is a final indifference. It is relevant to note here that of the two Suckling is more obviously re-working material from earlier drama.

By 1625 most of the major figures of the earlier period were gone. Ben Jonson survived. His survival was not always a happy affair: sick, neglected by the court, at odds with the theatre public, his longevity must have looked like a misfortune. But he was not content to decom-pose slowly like a great beached whale. The new age brought a new manner to his writing.[2] Though it belongs to the later years of the previous reign *The Devil is an Ass* (1616) anticipates his later manner, and indeed a good deal of Caroline drama, in important respects. Its satire is by Jonson's earlier standards mild and diffuse; business, fashion and social climbing are the main targets. Jonson is more creatively engaged in playing with the dramatic medium itself. He revives with apparent mockery those old dramatic stand-bys the Devil and the Vice; they make by their complaints about the state of the world a point the play itself does not make very clearly: that in the way of wickedness modern fashionable London is leaving Hell far behind. More pervas-ively, they make us conscious of the play as play. In a similar vein the principal fool, Fitzdottrel, spends the early scenes fussing with anxiety to see a new play called *The Devil is an Ass*.

Jonson's interest in the manner and behaviour proper to a gentleman, a key theme in his non-dramatic poetry, surfaces here in the attempt of Wittipol, aided by his friend Manly, to win Fitzdottrel's wife. Fitzdottrel lends her to him for fifteen minutes' conversation, under restricted conditions, in return for a rich cloak. Wittipol takes the occasion to begin his courtship. Fitzdottrel's bargain recalls Corvino's use of Celia in *Volpone*; but the courtship taking place under special, artificially created conditions looks forward to the Court of Love scenes in *The New Inn*. More tricks follow, but in the end the Lady makes it clear to Wittipol that she wants not a lover but the aid and counsel of an honest friend. Wittipol, urged by Manly, agrees: 'Virtue shall never ask my succours twice' (IV. 6). The last trick sees the men getting Fitzdottrel's estate to use it for his wife's interest. Manly's appeal to Wittipol's virtue as a gentleman gives the play unexpected gravity, though the trickery of the plot complicates the effect: as he makes his most dignified pronouncements Wittipol is wearing a dress. Fitzdottrel himself is not just a fool but the bankrupt heir of what had been a sound family:

> What will the ghost of my wise grandfather,
> My learned father, and my worshipful mother,
> Think of me now?
>
> (IV. 7)

The play contains more invention than Jonson can co-ordinate; the playing with theatrical illusion, the satire, and the gentlemanly virtue, do not quite work together. In *The Staple of News* (1626), however, artifice and satire are fused. The central action, in which the prodigal Pennyboy Junior courts the Lady Pecunia only to lose her and be taught the careful use of riches, borrows its obvious allegorical shape from the morality. Pecunia herself is the centre of a deliberately trivial secondary creation. She is an artificial sun who 'makes it Spring /Where'er she favours' (IV. 2); her worshippers are 'a kind of dancing engines all' (IV. 2). At times she seems to be literally what she represents, as when she complains of the usurer Pennyboy Senior, 'Once he would ha' smothered me in a chest /And strangled me in leather' (IV. 3). The prodigal describes his passion for her in appropriately trivial language: 'such motions as the sunbeams make /Against a wall, or playing on a water' (II. 5). When the prodigal's father, who has been spying on him in disguise, reveals himself and denounces both his son and the worthless cheaters he is spending his money on, he sets up against the parody world that surrounds Pecunia the picture of a true, good society in which everything is in place:

A worthy courtier is the ornament
Of a king's palace, his great master's honour.
This is a moth, a rascal, a court rat,
That gnaws the commonwealth with broking suits
And eating grievances.

(IV. 4)

And so on, through the roles of Soldier, Herald, Doctor and Poet. The artificiality of the prodigal's world is in itself the point: it is a parody of the world as it ought to be. But that ideal world remains offstage, and the bearings of the play as a whole are less fixed than may at first appear. The moralizing father himself falls foul of the cheating lawyer Picklock, and has to be rescued by his penitent son; he plays the traditional role of moral agent less securely than we might have expected. The Gossips who act as onstage, commenting audience are for the most part simply the butts of Jonson's ridicule, teaching the audience the right way to judge by showing them the wrong way. But Mirth plays for both sides: in the Second Intermean she defends and interprets the author as sympathetically and seriously as Cordatus in *Every Man Out of his Humour*; in the Fourth she turns against him with the others. In different ways characters we might have taken as our guides let us down; despite its clear moralizing structure the play is less confident than it looks.

The richest, most difficult and controversial of Jonson's last plays is *The New Inn* (1629).[3] Instead of setting up sound values against an artificial parody-world as he does in *The Staple of News* Jonson expresses those values *through* artifice. Lovel, 'a complete gentleman, a soldier, and a scholar' ('The Persons of the Play'), stands for the gentlemanly world. He claims that to make a boy a page is

the noblest way

Of breeding up our youth, in letters, arms,
Fair mien, discourses, civil exercise
And all the blazon of a gentleman.

(I. 3)

He expresses pious admiration for the late Lord Beaufort, who trained him in the dual life of arms and studies. The Host of the New Inn, though he likes Lovel, questions his idealistic view of the world:

Ay, that was when the nursery's self was noble,
And only virtue made it, not the mercate,
That titles were not vented at the drum
Or common outcry.

(I. 3)

He looks back to a time when 'Every house became /An Academy of honour' (I. 3); for him that time is gone. But Jonson, old though he is, does more than lament a good dead past. Lovel has fled to the Inn through despair at his frustrated courtship of the unpredictable Lady Frampul, only to find her a fellow guest. They are brought together in two elaborate set-piece scenes in which a Court of Love is created, presided over by the Lady's maid Prue. In each scene Lovel is to discourse on a set subject for an hour, and then be given a kiss by the Lady. The subjects are Love and Valour. Lovel defines them in a high-minded, academic way: Love is a matter of the soul, not the body; Valour should never be confused with anger or exercised for a trivial cause. All this is rendered ironic by Lovel's failure to control his own passions: when the game is over he flies into a rage because it could not last longer. There is further irony in the artifice by which the Court is established: Prue is dressed up in a borrowed gown, the parties swear on 'Love's Missal . . . *Ovid de arte amandi*' (III. 2), and so on. And yet through the artifice Lovel gets his way. He may not live up to his own ideals but he defends them so eloquently that the Lady falls in love with him. If the Court is a contrived secondary world it is also, unlike the court of Pecunia, a place where serious ideals can flourish.

It is set against a vulgar below-stairs life of noise, cheating and social pretence, which the Host, who sees himself as a laughing philosopher, tolerates and even encourages. The game of dressing-up, played seriously in the main plot where Prue's fine dress is a clue to her inner worth, takes an ugly turn in the story of the tailor Stuffe, whose habit it is, when he has made a fine gown, to dress his wife in it and carry her off for a dirty weekend in which they act out the fantasy of a great lady slumming with her servant. Fly, the Inn's resident parasite, parodies the military theme by creating a mock-militia below stairs. Another kind of threat is embodied in the bankrupt citizen Bat Burst:

> He had no father, I warrant him, that durst own him;
> Some foundling in a stall, or the church porch,
> Brought up i' the Hospital, and so bound prentice,
> Then master of a shop, then one o'th' Inquest,
> Then breaks out bankrupt, or starts alderman:
> The original of both is a church porch.
>
> (IV. 2)

He has not only no secure position but no real identity and, most important for this play, no father. In the background of *The New Inn*, emerging in the controversial last scene, is the tangled plot of a broken family reunited. The Host is really Lord Frampul, the drunken Irish nurse is his wife, Lady Frampul his daughter, and the boy Frank his other daughter. The family broke up over the wife's failure to produce a son: to ensure, in other words, the most conventional route of inheritance. Though he does not make much of this theme, Jonson, whose own father died before he was born, is concerned not just with lovers but with parents and children. In a revealing detail, Lady Frampul admits that Lovel is old enough to be her father (III. 2); it is evidently not just a lover she wants. The resolution is conveyed in a tricky combination of graceful lyricism and overelaborate plotting that makes the final effect uncertain. But we may suggest that as Jonson both mocks the artifice of the Court of Love and allows it to make a serious point, he may be doing the same with the artifice of his own play.

The happiness of the play's end is made wistful by the Epilogue's sharp reminder of the sick, neglected author 'set round with pain'. The play itself was a humiliating failure at its first performance. Jonson threatened to abandon the stage altogether, but the mood did not last. The subtitle of *The Magnetic Lady; or, The Humours Reconciled* (1632) suggests a conscious attempt to tie his career together. The play itself, however, is a sad, weak performance. It was fresh ground that proved more fertile, as this most urban of playwrights turned to scenes from country life: comically, in the rustic wooing of *A Tale of a Tub* (1633),[4] and more gracefully in the light-hearted pastoral *The Sad Shepherd*, left unfinished at Jonson's death. But *The New Inn*, with its thoughtful examination of codes of conduct both amorous and gentlemanly, and its balanced treatment of artifice, at once sympathetic and sceptical, stands as his most important contribution to Caroline drama.

It is particularly characteristic of its period in two respects: in its concern for the behaviour of a gentleman, a concern it shares with *The Devil is an Ass*; and in its balanced, exploratory treatment of artifice. The retreat to the country in Jonson's last plays may also convey a desire to return to an old, ordered society, the life Shakespeare touches on occasionally and Middleton shows his country gulls throwing away when they come to London. There is certainly nostalgia as well as mockery in his recollections of earlier drama. And the concern for the recovery of old values is conveyed in the spectacles Fitzdottrel and Pennyboy junior present as they squander their inheritances in a crass new society, just as Lord Frampul has abandoned his family to travel with gypsies and puppet-masters. But at least Frampul has moved through a world of rural shows and pastimes, settled at a country inn, and recovered his family there. Restoration is to be found, Jonson suggests, through the exercise of art – even the low popular art he used to despise – and through the pastimes of the country. Richard Brome, the most notable playwright among Jonson's protégés, the so-called 'tribe of Ben', will re-examine this theme in *A Jovial Crew*.

The idea of the squandered inheritance returns in *A New Way to Pay Old Debts* (*c.* 1621), by Philip Massinger (1583–1640). The comedy carries a pun in its title, for it shows a new way to play old material. The plot, in which an ex-prodigal recovers his estate by pretending a rich marriage, is borrowed from Middleton's *A Trick to Catch the Old One*, but there is none of Jonson's occasional nostalgia in the reminiscence. Massinger makes the story very much his own, giving it a new gravity of manner and a sharp class-consciousness. Welborne, the prodigal, has ruined an estate which, like that of *A Yorkshire Tragedy*, symbolized the good order of country life; his father 'bare the whole sway of the shire; kept a great house; /Reliev'd the poor, and so forth' (I. 1). He has also ruined the tradesmen who depended on him; we are reminded that when a man in this position falls he takes others with him. Though Welborne plans to restore himself by trickery, pretending a marriage to the rich Lady Allworth so that the usurer who ruined him, Sir Giles Overreach, will advance him money again, Massinger emphasizes not the fun of the game but the class solidarity Welborne appeals to. When Lady Allworth at first demurs he reminds her 'The blood that runs in this arm is as noble /As that which fills your veins' and appeals to his friendship with her late husband: "Twas I that gave him fashion; mine the sword /That did on all occasions second his' (I. 3). At the centre of this high-toned world is 'the gallant-minded, popular Lord Lovell' (II. 1), whose reputation depends on 'that fair name, I in the wars have purchas'd' (III. 1). Though nominally concerned with money and land, *A New Way to Pay Old Debts* keeps invoking the sword. Lady Allworth passes on her late husband's advice to her stepson:

> If e'er my son
> Follow the war, tell him it is a school
> Where all the principles tending to honour
> Are taught, if truly followed.
>
> (I. 2)

In the end Welborne is not content with paying his debts; he must recover his reputation as a gentleman by taking military service under Lord Lovell.

Against this community Overreach opposes himself virtually as a natural force. For him class conflict is a biological necessity,

> there having ever been
> More than a feud, a strange antipathy
> Between us, and true gentry.
>
> (II. 1)

Class difference is expressed comically when Overreach's lawyer Marrall dines with Lady Allworth and the servants mock his table manners. It becomes more serious when Lovell insists that to marry Overreach's daughter Margaret would be to 'adulterate my blood' (IV. 1). Margaret expresses the same view, in more practical imagery suited to her class: 'tissues match'd with scarlet suit but ill' (III. 2). Overreach, on the other hand, is obsessed with the idea of having his daughter styled 'honourable'. It is part of a campaign whose purpose he declares: 'I must have all men sellers, /And I the only purchaser' (II. 1). In this case he wants to buy a title. He has already created a reign of terror in the countryside:

> He frights men out of their estates,
> And breaks through all law-nets, made to curb ill men,
> As they were cobwebs.
>   (II. 2)

When Lovell asks him if he is not moved by the curses of the families he has ruined, he replies,

>   Yes, as rocks are
> When foamy billows split themselves against
> Their flinty ribs; or as the moon is mov'd
> When wolves with hunger pin'd howl at her
>   brightness.
>   (IV. 1)

We may find his language too extravagant to take seriously, but Lovell is shocked by it: for him, a few minutes' conversation with Overreach is worse than anything he has had to endure in war. Yet Overreach is a vulgar tradesman after all. He calls Margaret 'the blest child of my industry and wealth' (III. 2) as though he got her in the way of business. When he uses his sword, it is to threaten as a bully; the threats include an attempt to kill Margaret. Defeated, he runs mad, imagining himself in a battle. So did Ferdinard in *The Duchess of Malfi*, but Overreach cannot match Ferdinand's crazy heroism:

>   my sword
> Glu'd to my scabbard, with wrong'd orphans' tears,
> Will not be drawn.
>   (V. 1)

He has tried to be a law unto himself, like some heroes of early Jacobean tragedy: 'Why, is not the whole world /Included in my self?' (V. 1). But in the end he is judged not just as a failed hero but as a *parvenu*.

The manner of his defeat is, however, unsettling. Welborne uses Overreach's creature Marrall against him, playing on Marrall's discontent with his bullying master, and leading him on with rich promises. But when Marrall has served his purpose Welborne loftily rejects him, an ending even Marrall seems to accept: 'This is the haven /False servants still arrive at' (v .1). We take the point; but we cannot help noticing how much Welborne has depended on the disloyalty he now punishes. Marrall's defeat of Overreach involves a trick with disappearing ink. This may symbolize a basic human wish that all awkward legal documents could self-destruct so neatly; but it gives the ending a fantastic, artificial quality. Welborne's restoration is also touched by irony. The innkeeper Tapwell, who has wronged him, fears the worst:

> When he was rogue Welborne, no man would believe him
> And then his information could not hurt us.
> But now he is right worshipful again,
> Who dares but doubt his testimony?
>
> (IV. 2)

The play as a whole shows, with evident satisfaction, an aristocratic world closing ranks against a vulgar intruder. But Massinger allows a certain scepticism about the means, and about the prejudices built into the class system the play generally supports.

It is also clear that the problem is not just an attack from outside by Overreach. The problem began at the centre when Welborne squandered his own estate. In *The City Madam* (*c.* 1632) the problem also begins at the centre, with Sir John Frugal's failure to control his social-climbing wife and their equally foolish daughters who, because there is no son in the family, swell 'with hopes beyond their birth and scale' (I. 1). This disruption at the centre may explain the title of the play, which is otherwise puzzling since Lady Frugal does not appear to be the central character. There is a more fundamental disruption in the past, and again the principles of inheritance are involved: Sir John's father favoured his younger brother Luke; denied his birthright, Sir John built up wealth by his own efforts, acquiring the double status of citizen and gentleman, while Luke squandered the inheritance. Luke, now apparently repentant, lives in the house as resident poor relation, subjected to persistent insults by the women and treated with caution by his brother. As a test on Luke's apparent good nature, Sir John pretends to retire to a monastery, leaving him in charge of the family. At the same time the girls' suitors, who have been put off by their extravagant demands (if they marry, the women will own the estates and the husbands will live on pensions) pretend to embark on a three-year voyage. At first Luke seems to encourage the fantasies of the women, but he soon springs his trap and reveals the cruelty of his nature, dressing them in coarse habits with the ironic comment, ''Till now you ne'er look'd lovely' (IV. 4). By the end of the play he plans to send them to America as human sacrifices for the Indians: 'they are burdensome to me, /And eat too much' (V. 1).

Like Overreach, Luke is a fantasy-menace, the money-grubbing citizen turned monster. But he is more complicated, both in his own nature and in Massinger's use of him. He is acting in part out of ambition: he celebrates his new wealth in a manner that recalls Volpone, noting with delight that his financial power extends through all England and lamenting, like Alexander the Great, that 'there is /No more to be exhausted in one kingdom' (IV. 2). But he is also reacting to real injuries: Massinger makes the women's initial treatment of him vicious enough to make his counter-attack understandable. He is also driven by self-contempt, knowing his degradation was of his own making: 'I am not worth their pity' (III. 2). The extravagant courses he urges on the foolish apprentices Tradewell and Goldwire are the courses that ruined him, and there is an edge of irony when he praises 'the raptures of being hurried in a coach /To Brentford, Staines or Barnet' (II. 1). Though his motives are twisted the crimes and follies he punishes by his cruelty are real: in that way he acts as a scourge, both for Sir John and for the playwright. He tells Lady Frugal,

> I laugh, and glory that I have
> The power in you to scourge a general vice,
> And rise up a new satirist. . . .
> (v. 4)

She accepts correction:

> I am sick, and meet with
> A rough physician. O my pride and scorn!
> How justly am I punish'd!
> (IV. 4)

The plot works in a moralizing way, exposing and correcting vice. But it embodies an uncomfortable irony for which there is a modern parallel in Brecht's *The Good Person of Setzuan*. Gentle and good-natured, Sir John cannot control his own household. It takes his brother, his mirror-opposite, to apply the rough medicine needed for the job. The irony extends from the morality to the medium itself. As Marrall's disappearing ink brings a note of contrivance to the resolution of *A New Way to Pay Old Debts*, so Sir John's plot is consciously artificial. Sir John introduces it with the promise 'It may produce /A

scene of no vulgar mirth' (II. 3) and concludes, after the final resolution, 'You have seen, my lord, the pageant' (v. 3). The last scene does
indeed have the quality of pageant. Luke, celebrating his triumph by
dining symbolically alone, is presented with a show based on
Orpheus's rescue of Eurydice, ending with pleas from his own victims
which demonstrate that he, unlike Pluto, cannot be moved to tears.
Luke himself becomes at this point a figure in the pageant, which is
designed to show off his true nature. The suitors return through the
medium of trick-pictures coming to life. The ending, like that of *A
New Way*, is theatrically satisfying but the artifice on which that
satisfaction depends is even more overt.

Both comedies show Massinger seemingly concerned with social
issues like class and money, breeding and behaviour, but implicitly
admitting that his solutions depend on stagy contrivance. The whole
question of theatre as a moral instrument is given searching examination in his tragedy *The Roman Actor* (1626). Massinger creates a
corrupt and fearful Rome, closely modelled on that of Jonson's *Sejanus*,
in which

> To be virtuous
> Is to be guilty. They are only safe
> That know to soothe the Prince's appetite,
> And serve his lusts.
>
> (I. 1)

The difference is that Domitian, unlike Jonson's Tiberius, does not
bother to be subtle; he is extravagantly open in his lust and violence.
In this Rome, language is dangerous: '*The* Guard *lead off* Lamia, *stop-
ping his mouth*' (II. 1). One thinks of the silencing of the historian in
Sejanus. The actor Paris and his colleagues are arrested for disrespect
to people of rank: Paris replies, in an extended set speech, that the stage
is the school of morality and that if the wicked see themselves in the
figures on stage the actors cannot help it. As *A New Way to Pay Old
Debts* survived into the nineteenth century because Overreach was a
great part for a star actor, so *The Roman Actor*, with the alternative title
The Drama's Vindication, survived on the strength of this speech.[5] But
that is to stop where Massinger barely started. Whatever role as moral
teacher Paris may have is compromised by his dependence on the
Emperor: as one of his fellow players tells him, 'While you hold your
grace and power with Caesar, /We from your bounty find a large
supply' (I. 1). Anyone interested in topical significance is invited to
ponder the fact that this play was performed by the King's Men.

The difficulty does not stop there. One of Caesar's creatures asks
Paris to put on a play called *The Cure of Avarice* to reform his miserly
father. Paris promises,

Your father looking on a covetous man
Presented on the stage as in a mirror
May see his own deformity, and loath it.

(II. 1)

This traditional claim for the moral power of drama is put to a practical
test before our eyes. The play fails; the miser remains stubbornly
himself. The only effect of the performance is that the Emperor's
mistress Domitia becomes sexually infatuated with Paris, who had
played the part of the doctor who cures the miser. Instead of curing
disease the play spreads it. While expressing her contempt for the
theatre by forcing her rival Domitilla to act a part as humiliation,
Domitia also becomes caught up in the illusion: she has Paris play a
despairing lover, and takes his performance for reality. In conversation
with him later, she insists that his performances of virtuous characters
must somehow reflect his own inner virtue:

As vessels still partake the odour
Of the sweet precious liquors they contain'd,
Thou must be really in some degree
The thing thou dost present.

He replies that if this were true he would also partake in the nature
of the vicious characters he portrays. But he concludes:

O gracious madam,
How glorious soever, or deform'd,
I do appear in the scene, my part being ended
And all my borrowed ornaments put off,
I am no more nor less than what I was
Before I enter'd.

(IV. 2)

As an actor his job is to be versatile, and the parts he plays have no
reference to his true nature.
But what is that true nature? As though his professional adaptability
has gone too deep into his private life (meaning that Domitia has a case
after all, though she does not fully understand it) Paris as a character
is curiously elusive. He speaks in ringing tones of the moral function
of art; with the Emperor and his mistress he is as obsequious as any
court toady. When Domitia tries to seduce him he resists because his
loyalty to his master will look better to posterity, yet when she starts
to kiss him he surrenders 'since it is your will' (IV. 2). The drama's
laws the drama's patrons give, and Paris cannot shake off his
professional habits. When the Emperor discovers them together Paris

asks for death so eloquently that his master is tempted to spare him rather than lose such a fine speaker. Instead, he has Paris and his actors perform a scene from *The False Servant*, imitating exactly the sequence of courtship and discovery we have just witnessed, and ending with the intervention of the wronged master, played by Caesar himself:

CAESAR
    O villain! Thankless villain! I should talk now,
    But I have forgot my part. But I can do,
    Thus, thus, and thus.   *Kills* Paris.
PARIS
               Oh, I am slain in earnest.
                                (IV. 2)

Death in a play is by now an old trick, going back to *The Spanish Tragedy*, but Caesar's failure to remember his lines is an interesting variation: the play becomes reality only by breaking down as a play. In its normal condition the theatre is, as Paris has described it, pure illusion.

Paris's last words are characteristically opaque. They are a bare statement of fact: we may read into them shock, discovery, or expectation fulfilled, as we like; the character's own mind remains unrevealed. It is Caesar who claims our attention, justifying the killing as his way of honouring 'Rome's bravest actor' (IV. 2), stressing his own role as connoisseur and patron of the arts. If the relationship between art and performer remains a mystery, the relationship between art and authority is held up as a paradox: Caesar loves Paris's skill but cannot tolerate his disloyalty, and honours him by giving him a death scene such as no other actor has ever had. *The False Servant* also reveals Massinger's own artifice. As soon as Caesar gets the idea, Paris's colleagues appear, instantly ready. The artifice of *The Roman Actor* itself, like that of *The Cure of Avarice*, is morally directed, witnessing against the Emperor. His obsession with doing things openly –

                              Nero and Caligula
Commanded only mischiefs, but our Caesar
Delights to see 'em.
           (III. 1)

– becomes his undoing. Two of his victims, by their exemplary courage under torture, display the limits of his power, leaving him briefly humbled: 'By my shaking /I am the guilty man, and not the judge' (III. 2). At the end their ghosts return to haunt him, as they threatened to do; he dreams they have stolen the statue of his patroness

Minerva, and wakes to find the statue really gone. The equation of dream and play is a traditional one,[6] found in *A Midsummer Night's Dream* and Brome's *The Antipodes*, and Caesar's discovery of reality in apparent illusion may be seen as nemesis for the way he kills Paris. He is finally murdered at the hour predicted by an astrologer; like a character in a play, which he is, he has a predetermined end.

The play both exemplifies and questions the moral power of art. It is turned against Caesar, and turned against itself, and we are left to wonder if *The Roman Actor* can succeed where *The Cure of Avarice* failed. There is a simpler scepticism in *Believe as You List* (1631), which begins at a point where many plays of the period end. Antiochus, the lost ruler of Carthage, appears as a beggar just as his former subjects are looking to the gods to provide deliverance from the Roman yoke 'when least expected' (I. 2). They recognize him instantly. There is never a problem about his identity, as there is about Perkin Warbeck's claim to be Richard the Fourth.[7] The problem is that his potential friends and allies are intimidated by the Romans, and he is betrayed and imprisoned. He endures his sufferings with dignity, and with what he himself calls 'passive fortitude' (V. 2) but the effect is to show Ulysses defeated by Penelope's suitors. The play originally told the story of the modern Spanish pretender Don Sebastian and was revised back into classical times after being rejected by the censor; it has been seen as a veiled comment on the misfortunes of Frederick of Bohemia, who was betrayed by the pro-Spanish policy of the English court, though the parallels are far from exact.[8] But besides this topical interest there is a formal interest. Massinger starts with a traditional ending and produces from it a drama of frustration. Though it is too monotonous to be as effective theatrically as the other three plays under discussion, *Believe as You List* exemplifies in a peculiarly clear way one of the features of Massinger's art; it presents a sharply dramatic solution to a serious problem, and then erodes our confidence in that solution.

Massinger deals with such traditional themes as material greed and corrupt authority. To that extent he is the heir of Middleton, Marston and Jonson. The positive values he sets up are gentlemanly honour (expressed in social conduct and military enterprise) and the stable life of the country or city household. But the fundamental value is the moral power of art itself, and Massinger, by questioning that power even as he asserts it, puts all his other positive values in doubt. The power of art to rebuke society and show images of the good life is part of Massinger's own inheritance as a playwright, and he seems always on the point of doing what his heroes do – losing his inheritance, even giving it away. His plays, for the most part, end with images of order restored; but the power of *Believe as You List* lies in its simple depiction of irretrievable loss.

The view of Caroline drama as escapist entertainment is closer to the truth, though still not adequate, when applied to the plays of James Shirley (1596–1666). His comedy *Hyde Park* (1632) has a late-Jacobean multiplicity of effect: there are three plots, each with a different set of ground rules. In the simplest, Bonavent, missing for seven years and presumed dead, returns just in time to rescue his wife from an unsatisfactory second marriage; Shirley, unlike Massinger, uses the old trick quite straightforwardly. If that story is essentially romantic, the story of Julietta is unexpectedly moral. Her lover Trier tests her chastity by setting Lord Bonvile to seduce her. Bonvile approaches her with cynical wit, claiming a natural sympathy with ladies:

> there's no handsome woman
> Complains that she has lost her maidenhead
> But I wish mine had been lost with it.
>
> (II. 3)

Like Manly persuading Wittipol, she urges him to think of his position:

> 'Twere better not to have been born to honours
> Than forfeit them so poorly; he is truly
> Noble, and best justifies his blood,
> When he can number the descents of virtue.
>
> (V. 1)

After some initial reluctance he is persuaded. Julietta, insulted by Trier's test of her, throws him over in favour of an honourable marriage with the reformed lord. Virtue Rewarded. The most interesting of the three stories, drawing on comedy's traditional fascination with warring couples, concerns the witty lovers Carol and Fairfield, who fight their way to an understanding through a series of mutual challenges. Fairfield's opening gambit is to demand that Carol not love him, his principle being 'What woman are forbidden /They're mad to execute' (III. 2). He binds her to accept his demand before revealing what it is, allowing her first to state whatever exceptions she likes. Having gone through the obvious ones – she will not love him, lie with him, or give him her estate – she comes down to finer details:

> I will not be confin'd to make me ready
> At ten, and pray till dinner: I will play
> At gleek as often as I please, and see
> Plays when I have a mind to't.
>
> (II. 4)

We are seeing one of the ancestors of the Proviso scene in *The Way of the World*, in which Mirabell and Millamant bargain their way to marriage. Fairfield's ploy fails, as he presses his advantage too quickly. Carol, though she tries to make a frank declaration, finds she cannot: 'By all the faith and love of mankind, /Believe me now – It will not out' (III. 2). After a few more rounds, however, the lovers declare themselves 'Each other's now by conquest' (v. 1).

Each plot entertains the audience in its own way; there are no organic connections between them. If there is common ground it lies in the depiction of a fashionable world going about its pleasures, drinking, dancing and placing wagers. Hyde Park itself is used for races, between horses – a horse race occurs just offstage, and the losing jockey comes in covered with mud – and between footmen. Carol asks, with genuine interest, 'Do they run naked?' (III. 1). In this play Shirley is content to record the pastimes of the town; *The Lady of Pleasure* (1635) is more critical. Aretina opens the play with a sigh of relief at having returned to London and escaped the country, where the only pleasures are

> to hear a fellow
> Make himself merry, and his horse, with whistling
> 'Sellinger's Round'.
> (I. 1)

Her Steward insists on the other side of country life, its ideals of order and responsibility:

> You liv'd there
> Secure and innocent, belov'd of all,
> Prais'd for your hospitality, and pray'd for.
> (I. 1)

Aretina is made to see the waste and vanity of the city. Her husband frightens her by pretending to squander his estate in gambling; her nephew gets drunk and makes a pass at her, declaring, 'You have a soft hand, madam; are you so /All over?' (v. 1); and her lover, whom she has tricked into bed, thinks he has been sleeping with a devil. As her husband Bornwell puts it in his last speech, 'Our pleasures cool' (v. 1). Shirley's satire is less indignant than Jonson's or Marston's, but he shows clearly enough the emptiness of a world in which ''Tis sin enough to have your clothes suspected' (III. 2).

Like the women of *The City Madam*, Aretina is cured in part by trickery. Even when he turned to tragedy Shirley retained an interest in games of mutual challenge and deception. In *The Traitor* (1631) the

lustful but weak and vacillating Duke of Florence presides over a softened version of the 'Italian lascivious palace' of Jacobean drama.
Sciarrha, pretending to seduce his sister Amidea for the Duke,
describes ironically the pleasures of the court:

> dance, kiss
> The amorous lords, and change court breath, sing loose
> Belief of other heaven, tell wanton dreams . . . .
>
> (ii. 1)

He is really testing her, in a situation reminiscent of Vindice's attempt
on his sister in *The Revenger's Tragedy*; but the tone is noticeably
lighter. Sciarrha is less bothered by the Duke's lust than by the offence
to his family. Are there no brothels, he asks, 'that we are come /To
supply his blood out of our families?' (ii. 1). He forms an unlikely and
unstable alliance with the traitor of the title, the Duke's kinsman and
favourite Lorenzo. Lorenzo, who practises killing the Duke by stabbing his picture, is simply ambitious for himself; he scorns Sciarrha's
'dust and heraldry' (iv. 2). While the two join forces against the Duke,
each is also concerned to get the advantage over the other, and Shirley
seems more interested in the tricks they play than in the opposed values
they represent or the moral significance of their alliance.

Amidea, who would rather reform the Duke than kill him, succeeds
for a while as does Julietta in *Hyde Park*, by asking him to take a
serious view of his high position. She reinforces the argument by
threatening to kill herself. But her victory is temporary, as Lorenzo
turns the Duke back to his old ways; and there is in her devotion to
chastity not only Sciarrha's sense of family but a certain decorative
quality. She aspires to have her name 'stand in the ivory register of
virgins /When I am dead' (ii. 1). In the end Sciarrha kills her; and the
Duke, coming to her bed, finds a corpse. Shirley does not play this
for the grotesque necrophilia of *The Second Maiden's Tragedy*; Amidea
is rather 'an excellent pattern, /As she now stands for her own
alabaster' (v. 1), an elegant image of dead virtue. But the dominant
tone of the last scene is caught in the moment when the Duke's
opponents, after professing mutual friendship, finally turn on each
other:

LORENZO
  (*Aside*) How hastily he climbs the precipice
  From whence one fillip topples him to ruin. –
  We two shall live like brothers.
SCIARRHA
                                   Stay. We two?

> Now I consider better I have no mind
> To live at all, and you sha' not.
>
> (v. 3)

Brisk and surprising, going to the brink of comedy, Shirley's tragedy is summed up by a minor character: 'I never heard /Such killing stories' (v. 3).

That line suggests Shirley knows exactly what he is doing; he is not trying to create a more dignified type of play and failing. The Prologue to *The Cardinal* (1641) is engagingly frank: 'A poet's art is to lead on your thought /Through subtle paths and workings of a plot'. The Epilogue opens with a pratfall:

> (*Within*) Where's Master Pollard! Where's Master Pollard, for the epilogue?
>
> *He is thrust upon the stage, and falls.*

In between, Shirley tells a complicated tale centred, once again, on a weak ruler: in this case, a vacillating King swayed by the Cardinal of the title, as the Duke of *The Traitor* was swayed by Lorenzo. Here, however, the implications of the King's weakness are more serious. Half way through the play the intended husband of the Duchess Rosaura is killed during their wedding masque (Shirley is never bashful about using the old tricks) and the Duchess demands justice:

> if here
> Such innocence must bleed, and you look on,
> Poor men, that call you gods on earth, will doubt
> To obey your laws.
>
> (III. 2)

The vehemence of her plea conveys a fear, entirely justified, that the King will not do his duty; the lesson for any kings who happen to be in the audience is clear enough. The killer Columbo argues on the other side, calling the murder

> An act your honours and your office, sir,
> Is bound to build a law upon, for others
> To imitate.
>
> (III. 2)

His honour, as he conceives it, has been wronged; he intended to marry the Duchess himself. In the manner of Chapman's Bussy, he expects the King to confirm what he, as a gentleman, has decided is law for him. The King at first rules against Columbo; then under pressure from the Cardinal, who is Columbo's uncle, he changes his mind. At this point another courtier remarks bitterly, 'I'll be now /Of no religion' (IV. 1).

Columbo is a gallant but rough-natured soldier; after being greeted by him a court lady remarks, 'He has been taught to kiss' (I. 2). One of his officers who counsels a war of attrition is dismissed for cowardice. But at least he shows a certain flair. In his final duel he somehow gets two swords, and throws one away, declaring, 'I scorn a base advantage' (IV. 3). He is killed almost at once. His chief antagonist the Duchess is more cautious. Like the Duchess of Malfi she insists, dangerously, on marrying to her own liking; but though she has some of the earlier Duchess's fascination with risk she goes to work more carefully, first tricking Columbo into surrendering his claim on her and then getting the King's approval over the Cardinal's protests. She pretends madness as a defensive tactic and recovers her wits with almost comic speed as soon as she thinks the danger is over. The manner of her death is appropriate: the Cardinal poisons her with what she thinks is an antidote. The King's reaction, 'Thou'rt not so horrid?' (V. 3), suggests how far Shirley is playing for effect; but the effect has its point: the Duchess is destroyed for trying to play it safe. The Cardinal's statement of purpose is revealing: 'I am sure /You sha' not now laugh at me' (V. 3). But the last laugh is on him. Thinking he is mortally wounded, he has taken the poison himself and confessed all. He is then told, much to his chagrin, that his wounds were harmless. The Prologue teases us with the suggestion that the play is going to be a comedy, and in the self-mocking trickery of its action it very nearly is. The Cardinal himself, who is far from being the leading character in the first four acts, is, we suspect, honoured with the play's title because he plays its cleverest trick. The attempts to pass him off as lurid Jacobean villain are less persuasive than the comic exasperation of a minor character who calls him an 'o'ergrown lobster' (V. 2). The excitement of the last scenes, caught in the line, 'What will become of her, and me, and all /The world in one small hour?' (V. 3), is the excitement of following a complicated plot. In both tragedies Shirley takes a serious enough interest in the responsibilities of rulers and the difficulties of living by a code of honour; and *The Cardinal* in particular has some shrewd insights into human weakness. But his heart seems to be in spinning tales of adventure.

Richard Brome (*c*. 1590–*c*. 1652) was a prolific writer who worked in a variety of forms, but his two best plays are comedies, and both show the interest in artifice, at once playful and serious, that is characteristic of the period. Peregrine, the hero of *The Antipodes* (1636), has addled his brains with travel books. He is so ruled by his obsession that after three years he has not consummated his marriage and his wife Martha has run mad with frustration. The cure involves making him believe he has travelled to the Antipodes; after taking a sleeping-draft he wakes to find himself in 'anti-London', whose citizens are created for him by a company of players. Dream and play are implicitly connected by this device. As there is something odd and eccentric about the problem, recalling Fletcher's interest in abnormalities, so the solution involves going into a private fantasy world. The players are run by Letoy, a 'fantastic lord' who prides himself on being 'without precedent for my humour' (I. 2), and on being self-sufficient: 'Stage-plays and masques are nightly my pastimes /And all within myself' (I. 2). His servants are his company and he writes all his own plays. Self-enclosed though it is, his art succeeds where *The Cure of Avarice*, in *The Roman Actor*, failed. Drawn right into the illusion, Peregrine, thinking he is King of the Antipodes and Martha is a princess destined to be his bride, takes her offstage and consummates the marriage at last. At this point both are cured. The play is for Peregrine an erotic dream leading to an orgasm; or as one character puts it, 'They have been in th'Antipodes to some purpose' (v. 2). But while consummation produces the final cure, it takes illusion to make it possible.

In creating the fantasy world of the Antipodes Brome constantly varies his tactics, and part of the fun is that we are never sure what is coming next.[9] Sometimes it is predictable nonsense: deer chasing hounds, sheep worrying foxes. Sometimes the inversions convey wish-fulfilment: a Gentleman begs two sergeants to arrest him and they refuse. But the satire can be more barbed, suggesting through irony that contemporary England is itself upside-down:

> DIANA
> Who be their usurers?
> LETOY
> Soldiers and courtiers chiefly,
> And some that pass for grave and pious churchmen.
> DIANA
> How finely contrary th'are still to ours!
>
> (III. 1)

The irony can work another way, as when we are told that only in the Antipodes does the King have true subjects. Some of the paradoxes, like those of Butler's *Erewhon*, tease us into thinking about institutions we take for granted:

> the law punisheth
> The robb'd, and not the thief, for surer warning
> And the more safe prevention.
>
> (IV. 1)

The obvious jokes in which traditional sex-roles are reversed, with a woman fencing for a prize and a man being ducked as a scold, lead Peregrine to think about what is 'proper to each sex' and his Doctor expresses relief that at least he knows there is a difference (IV. 1). The fantasy at this point is clearly leading toward the cure. And we are told early in the play that the Antipodean world is an image of Europe: 'They under Spain appear like Spaniards, /Under France Frenchmen, under England English' (I. 3). Brome is serving notice that this invented world will make us think about the world we live in.

The fantasy of *A Jovial Crew* (1641) is slightly less overt but more pervasive. Oldrents, whose very name evokes a settled world free of the ravages of inflation, embodies the country virtues of generosity and hospitality, winning 'all the praises of the rich, /And prayers of the poor' (I. 1). But Brome is also prepared to admit that Oldrents is too good to be true, for the hospitality of his house is shown in a long comic set piece full of running gags, including servants with identical beards, that takes us to the border of farce, and over. Against Oldrents's settled life we see the free life of the beggars who give the play its title. If he keeps to the old rents, they are free of material demands altogether:

> We have no debt or rent to pay,
> No bargains or accounts to make:
> No land or lease to let or take.
>
> (I. 1)

Yet the beggars are also admitted to be, like Oldrents, fantastic. In their first two scenes they are presented in theatrical tableaux: '*He opens the scene; the* Beggars *are discovered in their postures*' (I. 1); '*Randall opens the scene. The Beggars are discovered at their feast. After they have scrambled a while at their victuals, this song*' (II. 2). Their world, like Letoy's Antipodes, is a play-within-the-play presented to the other characters as onstage audience: 'See in their rags, then, dancing for your sports, /Our clapperdudgeons and their walking morts' (II. 2).

Like the Antipodes, the beggars' invented world is a reflection of the real one, covering a range of society: 'Hedge-ladybirds, hedge-cavaliers, hedge-soldier, hedge-lawyer, hedge-fiddlers, hedge-poet, hedge-players, and a hedge-priest among 'em' (V. 1). It is also possible for the other characters, as for Peregrine, to move into this world, with curative effect. Oldrents's steward Springlove gets the itch to join the beggars every year; and Oldrents's daughters, tired of their father's melancholy, run away with their lovers for the same purpose. They could not do better, for Oldrents's melancholy is caused by the prophecy that his children will be beggars, and by acting the prophecy out in a harmless way they effect his cure. Springlove tells the men that the discomfort of their first night as beggars is merely 'your birth-night into a new world' (III. 1), making the positive value of this secondary creation sound for a moment quite serious. In the last act the beggars become literally players, offering Oldrents a choice of entertainments, all with titles that reflect the action of the play proper: *The Two Lost Daughters*, *The Vagrant Steward*, *The Old Squire and the Fortune-Teller*, *The Beggar's Prophecy*. Oldrents rejects all of these as being too close to home, and selects *The Merry Beggars*, whose title is the subtitle of Brome's own play. The inner play reflects the main one, and adds new information: Springlove is Oldrents's son, and the grandson of Wrought-on, who was cheated out of his estate by Oldrents's grandfather. Through the illusion the surrounding reality is illuminated in two directions: a lost child is discovered and an old guilt is revealed.

Springlove is careful to exonerate Oldrents himself from blame, but his revelation tells us that the wealth which allows Oldrents to be so generous is not fairy gold from a magic crock: it comes from the dirty traffic of a more brutal world than the play has shown. Similarly, the beggars' life, as the lovers find after their first uncomfortable, sleepless night, is not all fun and freedom: 'We look'd upon them in their jollity, and cast no further' (III. 1). The reality includes begging itself, at which the men are ludicrously incompetent: unable to adjust to the beggars' scale of living, they ask for far too much. For the women, it includes the threat of sexual assault, with the suggestion that if they were as poor as they look they would have no recourse. The play is for the most part a pleasant fantasy in which one good way of life illuminates and restores another; but around the fantasy there are dark edges. Some of the jokes have an extra sting. When the gentlemen-beggars make their extravagant demands a passer-by remarks, 'The court goes a-begging, I think' (III. 1). Had the financially hard-pressed King been in the audience his smile at this point might have been a little grim. As the stormclouds of civil war gathered, the life of the beggars may have looked attractive for more than its material simplicity: 'No alter-ation in a commonwealth, /Or innovation, shakes a thought of theirs' (IV. 2). The beggar-musicians have joined the Jovial Crew because they were 'within the reach of the lash of the law for singing libelous songs at London. . . . They can sing anything most tunably sir, but Psalms' (I. 1). London, we remember, was a stronghold of the Puritans.

A Jovial Crew was in fact performed just before the theatres closed for a generation. Brome's Epistle to Thomas Stanley tells us 'it had the luck to tumble last of all in the epidemical ruin of the scene and now limps hither with a wooden leg to beg an alms at your hands'. If its picture of the good life is a self-admitted illusion, the reasons go deeper than Brome's interest in playing with theatrical artifice. It is in fact tempting to see Caroline drama as living knowingly on the edge of crisis, to relate Shirley's vacillating rulers to the shifty Charles, to imagine Luke Frugal with close-cropped hair. Certainly the romantic strain in this drama can be traced to a real frustration. The military adventures of the reign were mostly embarrassing failures, with the 1625 raid on Cadiz setting the tone; all those evocations of war as the school of honour are setting up an ideal against a depressing reality. We may object that dramatists are no more prescient than anyone else, and that no one at the time could have been expected to fortell the extraordinary events that lay over the horizon. But there are some eerie moments. Shirley's Duchess Rosaura warns the Cardinal to see himself and reform 'before the short-haired men /Do crowd and call for justice' (II. 3). Brome's Poet-Beggar imagines an allegorical Utopia: 'I would have the country, the city, and the court, be at great variance for superiority. Then would I have Divinity and Law stretch their wide throats to appease and reconcile them; then would I have the soldier cudgel them all together and overtop them all' (IV. 2). Both plays belong to 1641, when the crisis was well under way but its full shape was not yet clear. Much of Caroline drama presents an enclosed and courtly artifice, not unlike the play-world of the court itself, with its lavish masques and splendid paintings. But the shrewdest of these playwrights knew, or sensed, that artificial worlds are made to be broken.

If that is attributing too much prescience to them, we can at least see in Caroline drama a prophetic reflection of a society in danger of losing confidence in itself. The lost inheritance is a central theme; it runs through Jonson, Massinger and Brome. As Jonson in *The New Inn* is concerned with the recovery of parents, so Massinger and Brome are concerned with the recovery or securing of estates. But all these playwrights know that their images of the good life are created by theatrical artifice, and with varying degrees of explicitness they say so. And the central authority figures – the moralizing father of *The Staple of News*, Sir John Frugal in *The City Madam*, the King in *The Cardinal* – are all in some way flawed. Like those of Beaumont and Fletcher, these plays combine a consciously artificial surface and a missing centre. But we cannot accept them so complacently, for this time there is a fuller analysis of a society we recognize as real. Caroline drama anatomizes country, town and court. It does not probe the mind or spirit as the greatest Jacobean plays did; but it mirrors England. At times it shows the gentry and aristocracy a flattering image of themselves: witty, honourable and courageous. But its recurring theme of a lost inheritance was a warning that should not have gone unheeded.

Notes

1. See Martin Butler, *Theatre and Crisis 1632–1642* (Cambridge, 1984).

2. On the change in Jonson's manner in his later years, see Anne Barton, *Ben Jonson, Dramatist* (Cambridge, 1984), pp. 219–351.

3. The controversy over whether Jonson has written an experimental play or just a bad one can be sampled in Harriet Hawkins, 'The Idea of a Theatre in Jonson's *The New Inn*', *Renaissance Drama*, 9 (1966), 205–26 and Richard Levin, 'The New *New Inn* and the Proliferation of Good Bad Drama', *Essays in Criticism*, 22 (1972), 41–47.

4. Traditionally this play has been regarded as a late revision of an early work. The case for seeing it as entirely a product of Jonson's last years is made by Barton, *Ben Jonson, Dramatist* pp. 321–37.

5. See *The Plays and Poems of Philip Massinger*, edited by Philip Edwards and Colin Gibson, 5 vols. (Oxford, 1976), III, 11–12.

6. See Jackson I. Cope, *The Theatre and the Dream: From Metaphor to Form in Renaissance Drama* (Baltimore, 1973).

7. This play and *Perkin Warbeck* are compared by Philip Edwards, 'The Royal Pretenders in Massinger and Ford', *Essays and Studies*, 27 (1974), 18–36.

8. See Edwards and Gibson, III, 297–8.

9. Ian Donaldson, *The World Upside-Down* (Oxford, 1970), pp. 78–98, relates the play to the satiric tradition of inverted worlds.

Epilogue

The 1642 Order of Parliament closing the theatres may have looked
at the time like a temporary measure. It gave as its reason the idea that
such a frivolous pastime as drama was inappropriate in a time of
national turmoil. Such measures had been taken before. The 1647
ordinance against playing, however, was a much more principled statement of the fundamental Puritan opposition to drama. Playing was not
just wrong for the present time; it was wrong altogether.[1] Given the
state of the theatre from about 1620 onwards, it may also appear that
a sick beast was being knocked on the head. Only the King's Men,
Shakespeare's old company, survived through the entire period. Other
companies struggled and died. Yet the theatre itself proved hard to kill.
Though in the Commonwealth period not much significant new work
was done, it is not altogether a blank page in the history of English
drama. Plays that could not be performed could at least be printed, and
were. Many of these, including such significant works as *Women
Beware Women* and *The Changeling*, might otherwise have been lost.
A number of theatres were pulled down. But playing continued in
private houses, and short entertainments called 'drolls' were put on in
the Red Bull, which was frequently raided by the authorities. From
1656 onwards William Davenant, author of *The Wits*, staged spectacles
with music, including *The Siege of Rhodes* (1656; traditionally the first
English opera), *The Cruelty of the Spaniards in Peru* (1658), and *The
History of Sir Francis Drake* (c. 1658). The use of music to make the
entertainments in question something other than 'plays' is curiously
prophetic of the way early nineteenth-century London theatres evaded
the licensing regulations by staging shows with music – hence the term
'melodrama'.

When the theatres reopened at the Restoration, Davenant and
Thomas Killigrew were given the monopoly; both had been playwrights before the closing of the theatres. One sometimes hears the
complaint that the Interregnum produced a break in the tradition of
English theatre, so that there is no continuity in England with the
theatre of Shakespeare as there is in France with the theatre of Molière.

This is not altogether true; or if there was a break it is better located in the nineteenth century with the replacement of a repertory system with long runs, stock sets and stock characters with productions designed around individual plays, and a rowdy audience in the same light as the actors with a well-behaved audience sitting in the dark. The interruption in the seventeenth century was less radical in its effect than the revolution in the nineteenth. Two small details may be cited; they suggest the traditional conservatism of the theatre. There is a story that Betterton learned the playing of Shakespeare's Henry VIII from Davenant, who learned it from John Lowin, the original Bosola in *The Duchess of Malfi* and possibly the original Iago. Lowin, the story goes, learned it from Shakespeare.[2] Easier to authenticate is the history of a piece of business in *A Midsummer Night's Dream*. In Edward Sharpham's comedy *The Fleer*, published in 1607, occurs the line, 'Faith, like Thisbe in the play, a has almost kill'd himself with the scabbard' (Sig. E$_1$ v). In 1942 Margaret Webster was able to describe this business as 'still in common use'.[3] It took more than an Act of Parliament to kill a traditional gag. When regular playing resumed at the Restoration the theatres that staged the first works of the new era were part of a line of continuity that went back to Shakespeare and earlier, a line that turned and twisted but was never really broken. Its playwrights were the heirs of Shakespeare and Jonson, of Beaumont and Fletcher, of Brome and Shirley.

What they did with their inheritance is matter for another volume. But it may be as well to look back over the journey we have come in this one. Shakespeare tamed and ordered the rough, eclectic art of Elizabethan drama as he found it. But his own experimental insight, working on the social order imagined by comedy and history, led him to study the psychological truth behind the patterns of convention. Man naturally makes pictures of order, but they do not always take full account of his own complex, intractable nature. This leads Shakespeare in his tragedies to examine the way men and women betray their own ideals, in themselves and in those they love; in the process, however, he reveals how much people matter to each other, and this becomes the key to his final romances. His Jacobean contemporaries are more comprehensively sceptical. In their plays the ordered society Shakespeare occasionally imagines is replaced by a brutally competitive world governed by greed and sexual desire, a world in which heroism constantly threatens to collapse into triviality. The dispossessed hero, dealing in disguise with a world he despises yet wants to succeed in, unsure even of his own nature, is a recurring figure on whom the general uncertainty of Jacobean drama centres. But there are flares in the darkness: notably the energy of Jonson's heroes and the tormented heroism of Webster's. Something that looks like a higher style returns in Beaumont and Fletcher, but behind the heroic facade is an almost clinical view of man as a creature of low impulse; to that extent their plays carry on from earlier Jacobean drama. A more securely positive vision comes out of the popular drama, with its relaxed appreciation of society in its more genial phases: charity, comfort, neighbourliness. This enters the more diffuse and varied drama of the later Jacobean and Caroline theatre, just as something of Websterian heroism is recovered in Ford. But the social vision of these later plays, concerned as it is with honour, chastity and correct behaviour generally, involves a narrowing of the spiritual range of earlier, more sceptical drama. And this more amiable manner does not mean a full recovery of confidence. In Massinger and Shirley, as in Beaumont and Fletcher, private virtue has to do what it can in a world where the centres of authority are weak. Knowing what we know, it is tempting to read back into these plays the coming crisis of the Civil War. We should not do this too glibly; certainly the playwrights were no more conscious than their contemporaries of what was coming. But the lingering uncertainty of their art meant that in this period, as in others, literature was an index to the health of the society that fostered it.

Notes

1. See Philip Edwards, 'Society and the Theatre', *The Revels History of Drama in English*, IV (London, 1981), 61–3.
2. See E. K. Chambers, *The Elizabethan Stage*, II (Oxford, 1923), 329.
3. *Shakespeare Without Tears* (New York, 1942, revised Cleveland 1955), p. 157.

Chronology

*Note: Dates of plays are mostly approximate and refer to composition, not publication.
Dates of other works refer to publication.*

DATE	PLAYS	OTHER WORKS	HISTORICAL/CULTURAL EVENTS
1590	Greene *James IV* Peele *Old Wives' Tale* Shakespeare *Comedy of Errors* *1 Henry VI*	Sidney *Arcadia* I–III Spenser *Faerie Queene* I–III	
1591	Anon *Arden of Faversham* Shakespeare *2 Henry VI*	Sidney *Astrophil and Stella* Spenser *Complaints*	
1592	Marlowe *Doctor Faustus* *Edward II* Nashe *Summer's Last Will and* *Testament* Shakespeare *3 Henry VI* *Titus Andronicus*	Daniel *Delia* Greene *Groatsworth of Wit* Nashe *Pierce Penniless*	Plague: theatres close for 2 years Greene d.
1593	Shakespeare *Richard III* *Two Gentlemen of* *Verona*	Hooker *Ecclesiastical Polity* I–IV Shakespeare *Venus and Adonis* Sidney *Arcadia* I–V	Marlowe d.

DATE	PLAYS	OTHER WORKS	HISTORICAL/CULTURAL EVENTS
1594	Shakespeare *Love's Labour's Lost* *Taming of the Shrew*	Davies *Orchestra* Nashe *Unfortunate Traveller* Shakespeare *Rape of Lucrece*	Period of bad harvests begins Admiral's Men and Chamberlain's Men consolidated
1595	Shakespeare *Midsummer Night's Dream* *Richard II* *Romeo and Juliet*	Sidney *Defence of Poesy* Spenser *Amoretti* *Epithalamion*	Raleigh's voyage to Guiana Drake and Hawkins d.
1596	Chapman *Blind Beggar of Alexandria* Shakespeare *King John* *Merchant of Venice*	Spenser *Faerie Queene* I–VI *Epithalamion* *Four Hymns*	Shirley b.
1597	Chapman *Humorous Day's Mirth* Shakespeare *1 Henry IV*	Bacon *Essays* Hooker *Ecclesiastical Polity* v	English campaign in Low Countries
1598	Jonson *Every Man in His Humour* Shakespeare *2 Henry IV*	Marlowe *Hero and Leander* Stow *Survey of London*	Poor Law established

DATE	PLAYS	OTHER WORKS	HISTORICAL/CULTURAL EVENTS
1599	Dekker *Old Fortunatus* *Shoemakers' Holiday* Heywood *Four Prentices of London* Jonson *Every Man out of his Humour* Shakespeare *Henry V* *Julius Caesar* *Much Ado About Nothing*	James VI *Basilikon Doron* Marston *Scourge of Villainy*	Essex campaigns in Ireland Globe Theatre built Bishops order burning of satires Spenser d.
1600	Heywood *1 Fair Maid of the West* Jonson *Cynthia's Revels* Marston *Antonio and Mellida* *Antonio's Revenge* Shakespeare *As You Like It* *Merry Wives of Windsor* *Twelfth Night*	Fairfax, translation of Tasso's *Jerusalem Delivered* Kempe *Nine Days' Wonder* Marlowe *All Ovid's Elegies*	East India Company chartered Fortune Theatre built
1601	Dekker *Satiromastix* Jonson *Poetaster* Shakespeare *Hamlet*	Daniel *Works* Rosseter and Campion *Book of Airs*	Essex rebels and is executed
1602	Chapman *Gentleman Usher* *Sir Giles Goosecap* Middleton *Family of Love* Shakespeare *Troilus and Cressida*	Campion *Art of English Poesy*	Bodleian Library founded

DATE	PLAYS	OTHER WORKS	HISTORICAL/CULTURAL EVENTS
1603	Heywood *Woman Killed with Kindness* Jonson *Sejanus* Marston *Malcontent* Middleton *Phoenix* Shakespeare *All's Well That Ends Well* *Othello*	Daniel *Defense of Rhyme* Dekker *Wonderful Year* Drayton *Barons' Wars* Florio translation of Montaigne's *Essays*	Elizabeth I d. Accession of James I Theatre companies under royal patronage
1604	Chapman *All Fools* *Bussy d'Ambois* *Monsieur d'Olive* Dekker & Middleton *1 Honest Whore* Dekker & Webster *Westward Ho* Heywood *1 If You Know Not Me, You Know Nobody* Marston *Fawn* Shakespeare *Measure for Measure*	James I *Counterblast to Tobacco* Middleton *Black Book*	Peace with Spain Hampton Court Conference

DATE	PLAYS	OTHER WORKS	HISTORICAL/CULTURAL EVENTS
1605	Chapman *Widow's Tears* Chapman, Jonson & Marston *Eastward Ho* Dekker *2 Honest Whore* Dekker & Webster *Northward Ho* Fletcher *Woman's Prize* Heywood *2 If You Know Not Me, You Know Nobody* Marston *Dutch Courtesan* Middleton *Mad World, My Masters Michaelmas Term Trick to Catch the Old One* Shakespeare *King Lear*	Bacon *Advancement of Learning* Camden *Remains* Drayton *Poems*	Gunpowder Plot
1606	Anon *Revenger's Tragedy Yorkshire Tragedy* Jonson *Volpone* Marston *Sophonisba* Shakespeare *Macbeth*	Dekker *Seven Deadly Sins of London*	

DATE	PLAYS	OTHER WORKS	HISTORICAL/CULTURAL EVENTS
1607	Beaumont *Knight of the Burning Pestle* Chapman *Conspiracy & Tragedy of Byron* Middleton *Your Five Gallants* Shakespeare *Antony and Cleopatra*		Settlement of Virginia
1608	Fletcher *Faithful Shepherdess* Shakespeare *Timon of Athens*	Dekker *Bellman of London*	King's Men lease Blackfriars Theatre Milton b.
1609	Beaumont & Fletcher *Philaster* Chapman *May Day* Heywood & Rowley *Fortune by Land and Sea* Jonson *Epicoene* Shakespeare *Coriolanus* *Pericles*	Shakespeare *Sonnets* Spenser *Mutabilitie*	

DATE	PLAYS	OTHER WORKS	HISTORICAL/CULTURAL EVENTS
1610	Beaumont & Fletcher *King and No King* *Maid's Tragedy* Chapman *Revenge of Bussy* *d'Ambois* Dekker & Middleton *Roaring Girl* Heywood *Golden Age* Jonson *Alchemist* Shakespeare *Cymbeline*	Donne *Pseudo-Martyr*	Galileo's discoveries with telescope reported
1611	Anon *Second Maiden's Tragedy* Fletcher *Monsieur Thomas* *Valentinian* Heywood *Silver Age* *Brazen Age* Jonson *Catiline* Shakespeare *Winter's Tale* *Tempest* Tourneur *Atheist's Tragedy*	King James Bible Chapman *Iliad* Donne *Anatomy of the World* *Ignatius his Conclave*	
1612	Heywood *1 & 2 Iron Age* Middleton *No Wit, No Help Like* *a Woman's* Shakespeare *Henry VIII* Webster *White Devil*	Bacon *Essays* (enlarged) Donne *Second Anniversary* Heywood *Apology for Actors*	Prince Henry d.

DATE	PLAYS	OTHER WORKS	HISTORICAL/CULTURAL EVENTS
1613	Beaumont & Fletcher *Scornful Lady* Fletcher & Shakespeare *Two Noble Kinsmen* Middleton *Chaste Maid in Cheapside* Webster *Duchess of Malfi*	Campion *Two Books of Airs*	Princess Elizabeth marries Elector Palatine Globe Theatre burned
1614	Fletcher *Wit Without Money* Jonson *Bartholomew Fair*	Raleigh *History of the World*	Second Globe built
1615	Middleton *More Dissemblers Besides Women* *Witch*	Chapman *Odyssey*	
1616	Fletcher *Mad Lover* Jonson *Devil is an Ass* Middleton *Hengist, King of Kent*	Chapman *Whole Works of Homer* James I *Works*	Jonson First Folio Harvey lectures on circulation of the blood Beaumont d. Shakespeare d.
1617	Fletcher *Chances* Fletcher & Massinger *Knight of Malta* *Queen of Corinth* Middleton & Rowley *Fair Quarrel* Webster *Devil's Law-Case*		

DATE	PLAYS	OTHER WORKS	HISTORICAL/CULTURAL EVENTS
1618	Fletcher *Loyal Subject* Massinger, Middleton & Rowley *Old Law*	Stow *Summary of English Chronicles*	30 Years War begins Raleigh executed Jonson walks to Scotland
1619	Fletcher *Humorous Lieutenant* Massinger & Field *Fatal Dowry*	Kepler *De Cometis*	
1620	Fletcher & Massinger *Custom of the Country* *False One* May *Heir*	Bacon *Novum Organum* Dekker *Dekker his Dream*	Pilgrims settle at Plymouth, Massachusetts
1621	Chapman *Chabot, Admiral of France* Dekker, Ford & Rowley *Witch of Edmonton* Fletcher *Wild Goose Chase* Massinger *Maid of Honour* *New Way to Pay Old Debts* Middleton *Anything for a Quiet Life* *Women Beware Women*	Burton *Anatomy of Melancholy* Hall *Works*	Bacon impeached

DATE	PLAYS	OTHER WORKS	HISTORICAL/CULTURAL EVENTS
1622	Massinger *Duke of Milan* Middleton & Rowley *Changeling* Rowley *Match at Midnight* Webster *Appius and Virginia*		
1623	Massinger *Bondman* Middleton & Rowley *Spanish Gypsy*	Daniel *Whole Works* Wither *Hymns and Songs of the Church*	Prince Charles and Buckingham travel to Spain Shakespeare First Folio
1624	Fletcher *Rule a Wife and Have a Wife* *Wife for a Month* Massinger *Parliament of Love* Middleton *Game at Chess* Rowley & Webster *Cure for a Cuckold*	Donne *Devotions*	War with Spain
1625	Heywood *English Traveller* Massinger *Unnatural Combat* Shirley *Love Tricks*	Dekker *A Rod for Runaways*	James I d. Accession of Charles I Charles I marries Henrietta Maria of France Fletcher d.
1626	Jonson *Staple of News* Massinger *Roman Actor* Shirley *Wedding*	Roper *Life of Sir Thomas More*	Bacon d.

DATE	PLAYS	OTHER WORKS	HISTORICAL/CULTURAL EVENTS
1627	Davenant *Cruel Brother* Massinger *Great Duke of Florence*		Middleton d.
1628	Davenant *Albovine* Ford *Lover's Melancholy* Shirley *Witty Fair One*	Coke *Institutes*, I Earle *Microcosmography*	Petition of Right Buckingham assassinated
1629	Brome *City Wit* *Northern Lass* Jonson *New Inn* Ford *Broken Heart*	Andrewes *96 Sermons*	Parliament dissolved
1630	Heywood *2 Fair Maid of the West*	Taylor *Works*	Massachusetts Bay Colony settled
1631	Massinger *Believe as You List* Shirley *Changes* *Humorous Courtier* *Love's Cruelty* *Traitor*	Heywood *England's Elizabeth*	Donne d. Dryden b.

DATE	PLAYS	OTHER WORKS	HISTORICAL/CULTURAL EVENTS
1632	Brome *Queen's Exchange* Ford *Love's Sacrifice* *'Tis Pity She's a Whore* Jonson *Magnetic Lady* Massinger *City Madam* Shirley *Arcadia* *Ball* *Hyde Park*	Donne *Death's Duel*	? Dekker d. Locke b.
1633	Heywood *Maidenhead Well Lost* Ford *Perkin Warbeck* Jonson *Tale of a Tub* Nabbes *Covent Garden*	Donne *Poems* Herbert *Temple* Prynne *Histriomastix*	Laud Archbishop of Canterbury
1634	Brome & Heywood *Late Lancashire Witches* Davenant *Love and Honour* *Wits* Milton *Comus* Rutter *Shepherds' Holiday*		Ship-money levied Chapman d. Marston d. ? Webster d.
1635	Brome *Sparagus Garden* Ford *Fancies Chaste and Noble* Marmion *Antiquary* Shirley *Lady of Pleasure*	Browne *Religio Medici* Quarles *Emblems*	

DATE	PLAYS	OTHER WORKS	HISTORICAL/CULTURAL EVENTS
1636	Brome *Antipodes* *Queen and Concubine* May *Old Couple*		Book of Canons imposed on Scotland
1637	Brome *English Moor* Suckling *Aglaura*		Hampden tried for refusal to pay Ship-money Scots reject Laud's new liturgy Jonson d.
1638	Brome *Damoiselle* Davenant *Unfortunate Lovers* Suckling *Goblins*	Milton *Lycidas* Peacham *Truth of our Times*	Scottish Covenant
1639	Brome *Mad Couple Well Matched* Shirley *Politician*		First Bishop's War against Scotland
1640	Brome *Court Beggar* Shirley *Imposture*	Donne *80 Sermons*	Short Parliament Long Parliament begins Scots invade northern England ? Ford d. Massinger d.
1641	Brome *Jovial Crew* Killigrew *Parson's Wedding* Shirley *Cardinal*	Jonson *Timber*	Strafford executed Grand Remonstrance Heywood d.

DATE	PLAYS	OTHER WORKS	HISTORICAL/CULTURAL EVENTS
1642		Denham *Cooper's Hill* Milton *Reason of Church Government*	First Civil War begins Battle of Edgehill Theatres closed Newton b.
1643		Milton *Doctrine & Discipline of Divorce*	Westminster Assembly
1644		Milton *Of Education* *Areopagitica*	Battle of Marston Moor Globe Theatre pulled down
1645		Howell *Epistolae Ho-Elianae*	Battle of Naseby Prayer Book abolished Laud executed
1646		Suckling *Fragmenta Aurea*	End of First Civil War
1647		Andrews *Private Devotions*	Scots deliver Charles I to Parliament Playing resumes briefly and is forbidden Beaumont and Fletcher Folio
1648		Herrick *Hesperides* Hooker *Ecclesiastical Polity*, VI, VII	30 Years War ends Second Civil War Pride's Purge Further orders against playing
1649		Donne *50 Sermons* Milton *Tenure of Kings & Magistrates*	Charles I executed Monarchy and House of Lords abolished Cromwell campaigns in Ireland

DATE	PLAYS	OTHER WORKS	HISTORICAL/CULTURAL EVENTS
1650		Taylor *Holy Living* Vaughan *Silex Scintillans*	
1651		Hobbes *Leviathan* Taylor *Holy Dying*	
1652			War against Dutch begins ? Brome d.
1653		Walton *Compleat Angler*	Rump Parliament dissolved Cromwell becomes Lord Protector
1654		Milton *Defenso Secunda*	War against Dutch ends
1655			Rule of the Major- Generals Jamaica captured
1656	Davenant *Siege of Rhodes*		
1657			
1658	Davenant *Cruelty of the Spaniards* *in Peru*	Browne *Urn Burial*	Cromwell d.
1659			Protectorate abolished Rump Parliament restored

DATE	PLAYS	OTHER WORKS	HISTORICAL/CULTURAL EVENTS
1660			Restoration of Charles II Act of Indemnity and Oblivion Theatres re-open

General Bibliographies

Note: Each section is arranged alphabetically. Place of publication is London unless otherwise noted.

(i) Historical and cultural background

Akrigg, G. V. P.   *Jacobean Pageant* (Cambridge, Mass., 1962). (The court of James I.)

Black, J. B.   *The Reign of Elizabeth* (Oxford, 1956).

Buxton, J.   *Elizabethan Taste* (1963). (Especially on the Elizabethan fondness for elaborate art.)

Byrne, M. St. C.   *Elizabethan Life in Town and Country*, 8th ed. (1970). (Draws closely on contemporary sources.)

Craig, H.   *The Enchanted Glass* (New York, 1936). (Elizabethan psychology.)

Davies, G.   *The Early Stuarts* (Oxford, 1937).

Judges, A. V., ed.   *The Elizabethan Underworld* (1930).

Lee, S. L. and C. T. Onions, eds.   *Shakespeare's England*, 2 vols. (Oxford, 1916). (Richly detailed survey of social life.)

Mathew, D.   *The Social Structure of Caroline England* (Oxford, 1945).

Neale, J. E.   *Queen Elizabeth I* (1934).

Rowse, A. L.   *The England of Elizabeth: The Structure of Society* (1950). (Lively if somewhat romanticized.)

Stone, L.   *The Crisis of the Aristocracy 1558–1641* (Oxford, 1965). (Economic problems and the class structure.)
The Family, Sex and Marriage in England 1500–1800 (New York, 1977). (Full of important evidence, though its bleak view of Elizabethan family life is controversial.)

Tillyard, E. M. W.   *The Elizabethan World Picture* (1943). (Influential on the Elizabethan belief in order and degree. Its picture of a conservative culture has been challenged but cannot be ignored.)

Trevelyan, G. M.   *English Social History*, vol. 2 (New York, 1942). (Covers the period from the Elizabethan age to the Restoration.)

Wilson, J. D., ed.   *Life in Shakespeare's England* (Cambridge, 1911). (Collects contemporary writing that reflects daily life.)

Wright, L. B.   *Middle-Class Culture in Elizabethan England* (Chapel Hill, 1953). (Unreliable as social history, but valuable as a survey of popular literature.)

Wrightson, K.   *English Society 1580–1680* (1982).

Zeeveld, W. G.   *The Foundations of Tudor Policy* (Cambridge, Mass., 1948). (Political ideas and policies.)

(ii) Theatres, actors and audiences

Armstrong, W. A.   *The Elizabethan Private Theatres: Facts and Problems* (1958).

Beckerman, B.   *Shakespeare at the Globe 1599–1609* (New York, 1962). (On performance conditions.)

Bentley, G. E.   *The Jacobean and Caroline Stage*, 7 vols. (Oxford, 1941–68). (Standard reference work.)
The Profession of Dramatist in Shakespeare's Time 1590–1642 (Princeton, 1971). (Clear and useful survey.)
The Profession of Player in Shakespeare's Time 1590–1642 (Princeton, 1984). (Clear and useful survey.)

Bentley, G. E., ed.   *The Seventeenth Century Stage* (Chicago, 1968). (Valuable essays on a variety of topics in theatre history.)

Bradbrook, M. C.   *The Rise of the Common Player* (1962). (The development of the acting profession.)

Chambers, E. K.   *The Elizabethan Stage*, 4 vols. (Oxford, 1923). (Standard reference work.)

Cook, A. J.   *The Privileged Playgoers of Shakespeare's London 1576–1642* (Princeton, 1981). (Valuable study of the audience and the social background.)

Foakes, R. A. and R. T. Rickert, eds.   *Henslowe's Diary* (1961). (Perhaps the single most important source of evidence for Elizabethan theatre practice.)

Greg, W. W.   *Dramatic Documents from the Elizabethan Playhouses*, 2 vols. (Oxford, 1931). (Useful collection of primary evidence.)

Gurr, A.   *The Shakespearean Stage 1574–1642* (Cambridge, 1970).

Harbage, A.   *Annals of English Drama 975–1700*, revised by S. Schoenbaum (Philadelphia, 1964). (Useful chronological list of plays, including theatrical information.)

Hillebrand, H. N.   *The Child Actors* (Urbana, 1926).

Nungezer, E.   *A Dictionary of Actors* (1929). (Useful collection of information on Elizabethan actors.)

Orrell, J.   *The Quest for Shakespeare's Globe* (Cambridge, 1983). (The likely dimensions of the Globe Theatre.)

Shapiro, M.   *Children of the Revels* (New York, 1977). (Wide-ranging study of children's companies and their plays.)

Smith, I.   *Shakespeare's Blackfriars Playhouse* (New York, 1964).

Wickham, G.   *Early English Stages 1300–1660*, 3 vols. (1959–81). (Especially on the mediaeval heritage of the Elizabethan theatre.)

(iii) General criticism

Barroll, J. L., A. Leggatt, R. Hosley and A. Kernan.   *The Revels History of Drama in English, III* (1975). (1576–1613; includes material on the theatres.)

Bradbrook, M. C.   *Themes and Conventions of Elizabethan Tragedy* (Cambridge, 1935). (Pioneering study; includes the Jacobean period.) *The Growth and Structure of Elizabethan Comedy* (1955). (Wide-ranging survey.)

Brooke, N.   *Horrid Laughter in Jacobean Tragedy* (Totatwa, N. J., 1979). (Deals with black comedy but also ranges more widely.)

Brown, J. R. and B. Harris, eds.   *Jacobean Theatre*, Stratford-upon-Avon Studies I (1960). (Essays on a variety of playwrights.)

Butler, M.   *Theatre and Crisis 1632–42* (Cambridge, 1984). (The political dimension of Caroline drama.)

Dollimore, J.   *Radical Tragedy* (Brighton, 1984). (Presents Jacobean drama as radically sceptical and subversive.)

Doran, M.   *Endeavors of Art: A Study of Form in Elizabethan Drama* (Madison, 1954). (Important study of dramatic conventions.)

Edwards, P., G. E. Bentley, K. McLuskie, and L. Potter.   *The Revels History of Drama in English, IV* (1981). (1613–1660; includes material on the theatres.)

Ellis-Fermor, U.   *The Jacobean Drama* (1936).

Gibbons, B.   *Jacobean City Comedy*, 2nd ed. (1980). (Jonson, Marston and Middleton against their social background.)

Harbage, A.   *Cavalier Drama* (New York, 1936). *Shakespeare and the Rival Traditions* (New York, 1952).

	(Prejudiced and should be read with caution, but an important study of the differences between public and private theatres.)
Kirsch, A. C.	*Jacobean Dramatic Perspectives* (Charlottesville, 1972).
Knights, L. C.	*Drama and Society in the Age of Jonson* (1937). (Seminal work on Jacobean drama and its social background.)
Leggatt, A.	*Citizen Comedy in the Age of Shakespeare* (Toronto, 1973). (Social themes in comedies dealing with the middle class.)
Levin, R.	*The Multiple Plot in English Renaissance Drama* (Chicago, 1971). *New Readings vs. Old Plays* (Chicago, 1979). (Entertaining attack on some recent trends in criticism of Renaissance drama.)
Ornstein, R.	*The Moral Vision of Jacobean Tragedy* (Madison, 1960).
Ribner, I.	*The English History Play in the Age of Shakespeare*, revised ed. (1965).
Waith, E.	*The Herculean Hero* (New York, 1962). (On the heroes of Marlowe, Chapman, Shakespeare and Dryden.)
Weimann, R.	*Shakespeare and the Popular Tradition in the Theatre*, ed. R. Schwartz (Baltimore, 1978).

Individual Authors

Notes on biography, major works and criticism

Each entry is divided into three sections:
(a) *Outline of author's life and principal works*. Unless otherwise specified, dates of
   plays refer to composition, not publication. We can assume that in most cases
   production followed shortly after composition; publication was often delayed
   for many years.
(b) *Biographies*. Place of publication is London unless otherwise stated. This
   section appears in only a few entries. Information on most of these authors is
   sketchy, and book-length biographies are not always available. The more
   general critical books and the better editions (see below) generally contain
   biographical information.
(c) *Selected critical works*, listed chronologically. Place of publication is London
   unless otherwise stated.

   Modern editions are not cited. Shakespeare's plays are of course widely available
in separate editions. At the time of writing the Arden Shakespeare series
(Methuen) is the most thorough and complete. The Oxford Shakespeare, still in
progress, is comparable. Also recommended are the revised New Cambridge
Shakespeare (in progress), the New Penguin Shakespeare (nearly complete) and
the Signet Classic Shakespeare (complete). The major plays of Shakespeare's
contemporaries are available in a number of series, of which the most thorough
(comparable to the Arden Shakespeare) is the Revels Plays, published originally
by Methuen and currently by Manchester University Press. Plays are also
available in the New Mermaid series (Ernest Benn), the Regents Renaissance
Drama series (University of Nebraska Press), and the Cambridge University
Press series of *Selected Plays* of the major dramatists.

BEAUMONT, Francis (*c.* 1584–1616), born at Gracedieu, Leicestershire, attended
   Bradgates Hall (later Pembroke College), Oxford and the Inner Temple.
   After the initial failure of his dramatic burlesque *The Knight of the Burning
   Pestle* (*c.* 1607), began a successful collaboration with John Fletcher,
   including *Philaster* (*c.* 1609), *The Coxcomb* (*c.* 1609), *The Captain* (*c.* 1610),
   The Maid's Tragedy (*c.* 1610), *A King and No King* (*c.* 1611) and *The
   Scornful Lady* (*c.* 1613). Stopped writing for the stage *c.* 1613, when he
   married the heiress Ursula Isley and retired to the country.

   See: FLETCHER, John.

BROME, Richard (c. 1590–c. 1652). A servant and protégé of Ben Jonson; his plays occasionally recall Jonson's in detail, though not usually in spirit. They include: *The City Wit* (c. 1629), *The Northern Lass* (1629), *The Queen's Exchange* (c. 1632), *The Late Lancashire Witches* (with Thomas Heywood; 1634), *The Sparagus Garden* (1635), *The Queen and Concubine* (c. 1636), *The Antipodes* (1636), *The English Moor* (1637), *The Damoiselle* (c. 1638), *A Mad Couple Well Matched* (c. 1639), *The Court Beggar* (1640), *A Jovial Crew* (1641).

> Kaufman, R. J. *Richard Brome: Caroline Playwright* (1961). (Critical biography.)

CHAPMAN, George (c. 1560–1634), born in Hitchin, Hertfordshire; may have been associated with the 'School of Night', a group of freethinkers connected with Sir Walter Raleigh. Early non-dramatic verse includes: *The Shadow of the Night* (1594) and *Ovid's Banquet of Sense* (1595). Wrote early plays (many now lost) for the Admiral's Men, including: *The Blind Beggar of Alexandria* (1596) and *An Humorous Day's Mirth* (1597), a forerunner of Ben Jonson's comedy of humours. After the turn of the century, wrote plays for the children's companies, including *The Gentleman Usher* (c. 1602), *Sir Giles Goosecap* (c. 1602), *All Fools* (c. 1604), *Monsieur d'Olive* (c. 1604), *Bussy d'Ambois* (c. 1604), *The Widow's Tears* (c. 1605), *Caesar and Pompey* (c. 1605), *The Conspiracy and Tragedy of Charles, Duke of Byron* (c. 1607), *May Day* (c. 1609), and *The Revenge of Bussy d'Ambois* (c. 1610). His later tragedy *Chabot, Admiral of France* (c. 1621), survives in a version by James Shirley, and a revised version of *Bussy d'Ambois*, apparently prepared by Chapman himself (though this has been disputed) was published in 1641. Completed Marlowe's unfinished *Hero and Leander* (1598). His translation of Homer's *Iliad* (1611) and *Odyssey* (1615) is the subject of a well-known sonnet by Keats. Was in the service of Prince Henry as 'sewer in ordinary'. Collaborated with Ben Jonson and John Marston on *Eastward Ho* (1605) and was imprisoned with Jonson because of anti-Scottish jokes in the play. Later quarrelled with Jonson, siding with his adversary Inigo Jones. Died in London.

> See: Jacquot, J. *George Chapman: Sa Vie, sa Poésie, son Théâtre, sa Pensée* (Paris, 1951). (Includes discussions of Chapman's life and philosophy.)
>
> Rees, E. *The Tragedies of George Chapman: Renaissance Ethics in Action* (Cambridge, Mass., 1954).
>
> MacLure, M. *George Chapman: A Critical Study* (Toronto, 1966). (Important general study; includes biography.)
>
> Grant, T. M. *The Comedies of George Chapman: A Study in Development* (Salzburg, 1972).
>
> Ide, R. S. *Possessed with Greatness: The Heroic Tragedies of Shakespeare and Chapman* (Chapel Hill, 1980).

DAVENANT, Sir William (1606–68), son of a tavern-keeper, born and educated at Oxford. Important transitional figure whose career spans the interval between the closing of the theatres and the Restoration. Early plays include: *The Cruel Brother* (1627), *The Tragedy of Albovine* (c. 1628), *Love and Honour* (1634), *The Wits* (1634) and *The Unfortunate Lovers* (1638). Helped keep theatre alive during the Commonwealth; his *Siege of Rhodes* (1656) is considered the first English opera. Davenant and Thomas Killigrew were given the monopoly on theatre in London at the Restoration.

Harbage, A. *Sir William Davenant: Poet Venturer 1606–1668*
(Philadelphia, 1935). (Critical biography.)

DEKKER, Thomas (*c.* 1572–*c.* 1632), born and died in London. Possibly of
Dutch extraction. A prolific author and collaborator whose extant work
includes: *Old Fortunatus* (1599), *The Shoemakers' Holiday* (1599), *Patient
Grissell* (with Henry Chettle and William Haughton; 1600), *Satiromastix* (an
attack on Ben Jonson; 1601), *1 & 2 The Honest Whore* (with Thomas
Middleton; 1604; *c.* 1605), *Westward Ho* (with John Webster; 1604),
Northward Ho (with Webster; 1605), *The Whore of Babylon* (*c.* 1606), *The
Roaring Girl* (with Middleton; *c.* 1610), *If It Be Not Good, the Devil is in It*
(*c.* 1611), *The Virgin Martyr* (with Philip Massinger; *c.* 1620), *The Witch of
Edmonton* (with John Ford and William Rowley; 1621). Self-consciously a
London writer, he also wrote civic pageants and prose pamphlets; many of
the latter deal with London life in a satiric or moralizing way: including
The Wonderful Year (1603), *The Seven Deadly Sins of London* (1606), *News
from Hell* (1606), *Lantern and Candlelight* (1608), *The Bellman of London*
(1608), *The Gull's Hornbook* (including satire on fashionable theatregoers;
1609), *The Four Birds of Noah's Ark* (1609), and *Work for Armourers* (1609).
Writes of the plague, and of prison life, having spent some time in prison
for debt.

See: Jones-Davies, M. T. *Un Peintre de la Vie Londonienne: Thomas
Dekker*, 2 vols. (Paris, 1958). (Extensive study of Dekker against
his background.)
Price, G. R. *Thomas Dekker* (New York, 1969).
Hoy, C. *Introductions, Notes and Commentaries to Texts in the Dramatic
Works of Thomas Dekker*, 4 vols. (Cambridge, 1980). (Rich and
informative.)
Champion, L. S. *Thomas Dekker and the Tradition of English Drama*
(New York, 1985).

FLETCHER, John (1579–1625), born at Rye, Sussex, probably attended Bene't
(later Corpus Christi) College, Cambridge. His father, President of that
College, became Bishop of London in 1595 but died debt-ridden the
following year. Wrote *The Woman's Prize* (*c.* 1605) and *The Faithful
Shepherdess* (*c.* 1608) independently. Collaborated with Francis Beaumont
on *Philaster* (*c.* 1609), *The Coxcomb* (*c.* 1609), *The Captain* (*c.* 1610), *The
Maid's Tragedy* (*c.* 1610), *A King and No King* (*c.* 1611), and *The Scornful
Lady* (*c.* 1613); with William Shakespeare on *Cardenio* (*c.* 1612; lost), *The
Two Noble Kinsmen* (1613) and possibly *Henry VIII* (*c.* 1613); and with
Philip Massinger (q.v.) on *Sir John Van Olden Barnavelt* (1613), *The Custom
of the Country* (*c.* 1620), and several other plays. Later independent plays
include *Bonduca* (*c.* 1610), *Monsieur Thomas* (*c.* 1611), *Valentinian* (*c.* 1611),
Wit Without Money (*c.* 1614), *The Mad Lover* (*c.* 1616), *The Chances*
(*c.* 1617), *The Loyal Subject* (1618), *The Humorous Lieutenant* (1619), *The
Wild Goose Chase* (1621), *Rule a Wife and Have a Wife* (1624), *A Wife for a
Month* (1624). Principal dramatist for the King's Men after the death of
Shakespeare.

See: Waith, E. M. *The Pattern of Tragicomedy in Beaumont and Fletcher*
(New Haven, 1952).
Leech, C. *The John Fletcher Plays* (1962). (Unusually sympathetic.)
Danby, J. F. *Elizabethan and Jacobean Poets* (1964). (First published as
Poets on Fortune's Hill, 1952; includes two essays on Beaumont and
Fletcher.)

FORD, John (1586–c. 1640), born at Islington, Devonshire, and attended the Middle Temple, from which he was expelled in 1605 for not paying his buttery bill. Early non-dramatic writings include the poems *Fame's Memorial* (1606) and *Christ's Bloody Sweat* (1613), and the prose pamphlets *Honour Triumphant* (1606), *The Golden Mean* (1613), *A Line of Life* (1620). Collaborated with Thomas Dekker and William Rowley on *The Witch of Edmonton* (1621). Independent plays, which for the most part are unusually difficult to date, include *The Lover's Melancholy* (1628, published 1629), *The Broken Heart, Love's Sacrifice, 'Tis Pity She's a Whore* (all published 1633), *Perkin Warbeck* (published 1634), *The Fancies Chaste and Noble* (published 1638) and *The Lady's Trial* (licensed 1638, published 1639).

See: Sensebaugh, G. F. *The Tragic Muse of John Ford* (Stanford, 1944). (Sees Ford as radical and sceptical.)

Oliver, H. J. *The Problem of John Ford* (Cambridge, 1955).

Leech, C. *John Ford and the Drama of his Time* (1957).

Stavig, M. *John Ford and the Traditional Moral Order* (Madison, 1968). (Sees Ford as a traditionalist.)

Huebert, R. *John Ford: Baroque English Dramatist* (Montreal, 1977). (Relates Ford's style to developments in the visual arts.)

Farr, D. M. *John Ford and the Caroline Theatre* (1979). (Especially on the staging of Ford in small theatres.)

HEYWOOD, Thomas (c. 1574–1641), born in Lincolnshire, probably the son of a clergyman, may have attended Emmanuel College, Cambridge. Actor as well as playwright, was under contract to Philip Henslowe (c. 1596) and later shareholder of Worcester's (later Queen's) Men. Prolific author and collaborator, much of whose output is lost. Surviving plays include *The Four Prentices of London* (c. 1599), *1 & 2 The Fair Maid of the West* (c. 1600, c. 1630), *The Royal King and the Loyal Subject* (c. 1602), *A Woman Killed with Kindness* (1603), *The Wise Woman of Hogsden* (c. 1604), *1 & 2 If You Know Not Me, You Know Nobody* (c. 1604, 1605), *The Rape of Lucrece* (c. 1607), *Fortune by Land and Sea* (with William Rowley; c. 1609), *The Four Ages* (c. 1610–c. 1612), *The English Traveller* (c. 1625), *A Maidenhead Well Lost* (c. 1633), *The Late Lancashire Witches* (with Richard Brome; 1634). Non-dramatic work includes an Ovidian narrative poem, *Oenone and Paris* (1594 and a defence of the theatre, *An Apology for Actors* (1612). Died in London.

Clark, A. M. *Thomas Heywood: Playwright and Miscellanist* (Oxford, 1931).

See: Cromwell, O. *Thomas Heywood: A Study in the Elizabethan Drama of Everyday Life* (New Haven, 1928).

Grivelet, M. *Thomas Heywood et le Drame Domestique Élizabéthain* (Paris, 1957).

JONSON, Ben (1572–1637), born in London, the posthumous son of a minister and stepson of a bricklayer. Educated at Westminster School, under the antiquarian William Camden, whose influence he acknowledged warmly in later life. Apprenticed as a bricklayer, and saw military service in the Low Countries in early 1590s. Became an actor and playwright; early work mostly lost, except for the comedy *The Case is Altered* (1598). May have written the 'additions' to *The Spanish Tragedy*. His dramatic canon, as defined by the plays whose publication he himself arranged, includes *Every*

Man in his Humour (1598; revised by 1616), *Every Man out of his Humour* (1599), *Cynthia's Revels* (1600), *Poetaster* (1601), *Sejanus* (1603), *Volpone* (1606), *Epicoene* (1609), *The Alchemist* (1610), *Catiline* (1611), *Bartholomew Fair* (1614), *The Devil is an Ass* (1616), *The Staple of News* (1626), *The New Inn* (1629), *The Magnetic Lady* (1632), *The Tale of a Tub* (1633; regarded by some as a revision of an early play), and the pastoral *The Sad Shepherd*, left unfinished at his death. One of the most important poets of his time; non-dramatic poetry published in three collections: *Epigrams, The Forest* (both published in his Folio *Works*, 1616) and *Underwoods* (published in the posthumous *Works*, 1640). Wrote the texts for numerous masques for the court of King James I, but quarrelled with the designer Inigo Jones and fell out of court favour after the accession of Charles I. In and out of trouble for much of his life, imprisoned for his part in the lost play *The Isle of Dogs* (1597) and for anti-Scottish jokes in *Eastward Ho* (with George Chapman and John Marston; 1605). Killed the actor Gabriel Spencer in a duel (1598); branded and released after pleading benefit of clergy. A Roman Catholic between 1598 and *c.* 1610, he was employed by the government in its investigation of the Gunpowder Plot. Took a walking tour to Scotland (1618–19), where he stayed with William Drummond of Hawthornden, who recorded his conversation. Literary opinions also recorded in the form of critical jottings in the posthumous *Timber* (1640). Opinionated and gregarious, he was the centre of a literary circle and an influence on younger writers. Suffered a paralytic stroke in 1628; buried in Westminster Abbey in an upright position, presumably to save money.

Chute, M. *Ben Jonson of Westminster* (New York, 1953). (Lively and informative.)

Miles, R. *Ben Jonson* (1986). (Detailed and evocative biography.)

See: Partridge, E. B. *The Broken Compass* (1958). (Language and theme in the major plays.)

Barish, J. A. *Ben Jonson and the Language of Prose Comedy* (Cambridge, Mass., 1967).

Blissett, W. F., J. Patrick and R. W. van Fossen, eds. *A Celebration of Ben Jonson* (Toronto, 1973).

Beaureline, L. A. *Jonson and Elizabethan Comedy: Essays in Dramatic Rhetoric* (San Marino, 1978).

Duncan, D. *Ben Jonson and the Lucianic Tradition* (Cambridge, 1979). (Jonson's use of irony and paradox.)

Leggatt, A. *Ben Jonson: His Vision and his Art* (1981). (Connects Jonson's plays, poems and masques.)

Barton, A. *Ben Jonson, Dramatist* (Cambridge, 1984). (Important on Jonson's romantic and Elizabethan qualities, and on changes in his later manner.)

Maus, K. E. *Ben Jonson and the Roman Frame of Mind* (Princeton, 1984). (How the classics shaped Jonson's imagination.)

MARSTON, John (1576–1634), probably born at Coventry, educated at Brasenose College, Oxford and the Middle Temple. Early work includes satiric poetry, *The Metamorphosis of Pygmalion's Image and Certain Satires* (1598), and *The Scourge of Villainy* (1598, expanded 1599); these were included among the books burned by order of Archbishop Whitgift and Bishop Bancroft (1599). Turned to the stage, with *Jack Drum's Entertainment* (*c.* 1600), *Antonio and Mellida* (*c.* 1600), *Antonio's Revenge* (*c.* 1600), *What You Will* (*c.* 1601), *The Malcontent* (*c.* 1603), *The Fawn* (*c.* 1604), *The Dutch Courtesan* (*c.* 1605) and *Sophonisba* (*c.* 1606). Most of his work was for children's companies, though a revised version of *The Malcontent* was performed by the King's Men. Tragedy *The Insatiate Countess* (*c.* 1608) left unfinished; collaborated with George Chapman and Ben Jonson on *Eastward Ho* (1605); may have revised the anonymous *Histriomastix* (*c.* 1599); some scholars believe this play to be entirely his. Shareholder in the Blackfriars Theatre, 1604–8, and wrote all his plays for it in that period. Ordained priest 1609; held the living at Christ Church, Hampshire 1616–31. Died in London.

See: Caputi, A. *John Marston, Satirist* (Ithaca, N.Y., 1961).
        Finkelpearl, P. J. *John Marston of the Middle Temple: An Elizabethan Dramatist in his Social Setting* (Cambridge, Mass., 1969). (Marston's Inns of Court background and its significance for his drama.)
        Scott, M. *John Marston's Plays: Theme, Structure and Performance* (1978).
        Geckle, G. L. *John Marston's Drama: Theme, Images, Sources* (Rutherford, Madison and Teaneck, 1980).

MASSINGER, Philip (1583–1640), born at Salisbury, attended St Alban Hall, Oxford. Wrote initially in collaboration, especially with John Fletcher, whom he succeeded as principal dramatist of the King's Men. Their collaborations include *The Knight of Malta* (*c.* 1617), *The Queen of Corinth* (*c.* 1617), *Sir John van Olden Barnavelt* (*c.* 1619), *The Custom of the Country* (*c.* 1620), *The False One* (*c.* 1620), *The Double Marriage* (*c.* 1621), *The Spanish Curate* (*c.* 1622), *The Little French Lawyer* (*c.* 1623). Other collaborations include *The Old Law* (with Thomas Middleton and William Rowley; *c.* 1618) and *The Fatal Dowry* (with Nathan Field; 1619). Independent works include *The Maid of Honour* (*c.* 1621), *A New Way to Pay Old Debts* (*c.* 1621), *The Duke of Milan* (*c.* 1622), *The Bondman* (1623), *The Parliament of Love* (1624), *The Unnatural Combat* (*c.* 1625), *The Roman Actor* (1626), *The Great Duke of Florence* (*c.* 1627), *Believe as You List* (1631), *The City Madam* (*c.* 1632). Died in London.

See: Dunn, T. A. *Philip Massinger* (Edinburgh, 1957).
        Howard, D., ed. *Philip Massinger: A Critical Reassessment* (Cambridge, 1985). (Essays challenging old critical assumptions.)

MIDDLETON, Thomas (1580–1627), born and died in London, attended Queen's College, Oxford. Early life embroiled in lawsuits about the family estate. Early non-dramatic work includes the poems *The Wisdom of Solomon Paraphrased* (1597), *Micro-Cynicon: Six Snarling Satires* (1599) and *The Ghost of Lucrece* (1600); also the prose pamphlets *The Ant and the Nightingale* (1604) and *The Black Book* (1604). Extant plays include *The Family of Love* (*c.* 1602), *The Phoenix* (*c.* 1603), *1 The Honest Whore* (with Thomas Dekker; 1604), *Michaelmas Term* (1605), *A Mad World, My Masters* (1605), *A Trick to Catch the Old One* (1605), *Your Five Gallants* (*c.* 1607), *The Roaring Girl* (with Dekker; *c.* 1608), *No Wit, No Help Like a Woman's* (1612), *A Chaste Maid in Cheapside* (1613), *The Witch* (*c.* 1615), *More Dissemblers Besides Women* (*c.* 1615), *Hengist, King of Kent* (*c.* 1616), *A Fair Quarrel* (with William Rowley; 1617), *The Old Law* (with Rowley and Philip Massinger; *c.* 1618), *Anything for a Quiet Life* (possibly with John Webster; *c.* 1621), *Women Beware Women* (*c.* 1621), *The Changeling* (with Rowley; 1622), *The Spanish Gypsy* (with Rowley; 1623), and *A Game at*

Chess (1624). The latter, an allegory of relations between England and Spain, caused a scandal by its caricature of the Spanish Ambassador. Also wrote civic pageants and served as City Chronologer from 1620 to his death. Plays sometimes attributed to him include *Blurt, Master Constable* (1602), *The Puritan* (*c.* 1604), *The Revenger's Tragedy* (*c.* 1606) and *The Second Maiden's Tragedy* (*c.* 1611).

See: Schoenbaum, S. *Middleton's Tragedies* (New York, 1955). (Includes essays on *The Revenger's Tragedy* and *The Second Maiden's Tragedy*.)
Barker, R. H. *Thomas Middleton* (New York, 1958).
Holmes, D. M. *The Art of Thomas Middleton: A Critical Study* (Oxford, 1970).
Lake, D. J. *The Canon of Thomas Middleton's Plays* (Cambridge, 1975). (Thorough study of authorship problems.)
Rowe, G. E. Jr. *Thomas Middleton and the New Comedy Tradition* (Lincoln, 1979).
Heinemann, M. *Puritanism and Theatre: Thomas Middleton and Opposition Drama under the Early Stuarts* (Cambridge, 1980). (Places Middleton against his social and political background, challenging the assumption that his plays are pro-aristocratic and anti-citizen.)
Friedenreich, K., ed. *'Accompaninge the Players': Essays Celebrating Thomas Middleton 1580–1980* (New York, 1983).

ROWLEY, William (*c.* 1585–1626), actor as well as playwright, his roles included the Fat Bishop in Thomas Middleton's *A Game at Chess*. Though much of his work was done in collaboration, his independent plays include *A Shoemaker a Gentleman* (*c.* 1608), *A New Wonder, a Woman Never Vexed* (*c.* 1610), *All's Lost by Lust* (*c.* 1619) and *A Match at Midnight* (1622). Most important collaborations were with Middleton, with whom he wrote *A Fair Quarrel* (1617), *The Old Law* (also with Philip Massinger; *c.* 1618), *The Changeling* (1622) and *The Spanish Gypsy* (1623). Collaborated with Thomas Heywood on *Fortune by Land and Sea* (*c.* 1608), with Thomas Dekker and John Ford on *The Witch of Edmonton* (1621) and with John Webster on *A Cure for a Cuckold* (*c.* 1624).

See: MIDDLETON, Thomas.

SHAKESPEARE, William (1564–1616), born at Stratford-upon-Avon, son of the glover John Shakespeare, who held various civic offices but fell on hard times in the late 1570s. Presumably attended the local grammar school. Married Anne Hathaway, eight years his senior, in 1582, six months before the birth of their first child. In London, working as a playwright, by 1592. Became actor and shareholder in the Lord Chamberlain's company (1594). Published narrative poems, *Venus and Adonis* (1593) and *The Rape of Lucrece* (1594). Sonnets circulated privately, published without his authorization (1609). Purchased property in and around Stratford; obtained a coat of arms for his father (1596). Established himself as the leading English playwright. Plays include *1, 2 & 3 Henry VI* (*c.* 1590–2), *The Comedy of Errors* (*c.* 1590), *Titus Andronicus* (*c.* 1592), *Richard III* (*c.* 1593), *The Two Gentlemen of Verona* (*c.* 1593), *The Taming of the Shrew* (*c.* 1594), *Love's Labour's Lost* (*c.* 1594), *Romeo and Juliet* (*c.* 1595), *Richard II* (1595), *A Midsummer Night's Dream* (*c.* 1595), *King John* (*c.* 1596), *The Merchant of Venice* (*c.* 1596), *1 & 2 Henry IV* (1597, *c.* 1598), *Henry V* (*c.* 1599), *Much Ado About Nothing* (*c.* 1599), *Julius Caesar* (1599), *The Merry Wives of Windsor* (*c.* 1600), *As You Like It* (*c.* 1600), *Twelfth Night* (*c.* 1600),

Hamlet (*c.* 1601), *Troilus and Cressida* (*c.* 1602), *All's Well That Ends Well* (*c.* 1603), *Othello* (*c.* 1603), *Measure for Measure* (1604), *King Lear* (*c.* 1605), *Macbeth* (*c.* 1606), *Antony and Cleopatra* (*c.* 1607). *Timon of Athens* (*c.* 1608), *Coriolanus* (*c.* 1609), *Pericles* (*c.* 1609), *Cymbeline* (*c.* 1610), *The Winter's Tale* (*c.* 1611), *The Tempest* (1611), *Henry VIII* (*c.* 1612), *The Two Noble Kinsmen* (with John Fletcher; 1613). Bought a London house 1613, but seems to have retired for the most part to Stratford, where he died.

> Chambers, E. K. *William Shakespeare: A Study of Facts and Problems.* 2 vols. (Oxford, 1930).
> Alexander, P. *Shakespeare's Life and Art*, new edition (New York, 1961).
> Eccles, M. *Shakespeare in Warwickshire* (Madison, 1961).
> Schoenbaum, S. *William Shakespeare: A Documentary Life* (Oxford, 1975).

See: Bradley, A. C. *Shakespearean Tragedy* (1904). (Essays on *Hamlet, Othello, King Lear* and *Macbeth*. Despite an approach to character that now looks outmoded, this remains a major work.)
O'Dell, G. C. D. *Shakespeare from Betterton to Irving*, 2 vols. (New York, 1920). (Standard work of stage history.)
Knight, G. W. *The Wheel of Fire* (1930). (Idiosyncratic and often brilliant essays on the tragedies.)
Tillyard, E. M.W. *Shakespeare's History Plays* (1944). (Influential study of the plays as taking an official, conservative line.)
Granville-Barker, H. *Prefaces to Shakespeare*, 2 vols. (Princeton, 1946, 1947). (Criticism by a theatre professional who influenced modern Shakespeare production.)
Knight, G. W. *The Crown of Life* (1947). (On the final plays.)
Goddard, H. C. *The Meaning of Shakespeare* (Chicago, 1951). (Eccentric, provocative.)
Mahood, M. M. *Shakespeare's Wordplay* (1957). (One of the best studies of Shakespeare's language.)
Bullough, G. *Narrative and Dramatic Sources of Shakespeare*, 8 vols. (1957–75). (Standard collection of sources and analogues.)
Barber, C. L. *Shakespeare's Festive Comedy* ((Princeton, 1959). (Relates the comedies to social ritual.)
Charney, M. *Shakespeare's Roman Plays: The Function of Imagery in the Drama* (Cambridge, Mass., 1961).
Reese, M. M. *The Cease of Majesty* (1961). (On the history plays.)
Rossiter, A. P. *Angel with Horns* (1961). (Lively essays on a variety of plays.)
Righter [Barton], A. *Shakespeare and the Idea of the Play* (1962).
Trewin, J. C. *Shakespeare on the English Stage 1900–1964* (1964).
Frye, N. *A Natural Perspective: The Development of Shakespearean Comedy and Romance* (New York, 1965). (On structure and convention.)
Edwards, P. *Shakespeare and the Confines of Art* (1968). (On Shakespeare's attitude to his medium.)
Traversi, D. *An Approach to Shakespeare*, 2 vols., revised edition (1968). (Sensitive essays on language and value.)
Vickers, B. *The Artistry of Shakespeare's Prose* (1968).
Goldman, M. *Shakespeare and the Energies of Drama* (Princeton, 1972). (Especially on the theatrical impact of the plays.)

Ornstein, R. *A Kingdom for a Stage* (Cambridge, Mass., 1972). (Challenges the conservative reading of the histories.)
Young, D. *The Heart's Forest: A Study of Shakespeare's Pastoral Plays* (New Haven, 1972).
Leggatt, A. *Shakespeare's Comedy of Love* (1974). (Essays on individual plays from *The Comedy of Errors* to *Twelfth Night*.)
Cantor, P. A. *Shakespeare's Rome: Republic and Empire* (Ithaca, N.Y., 1976). (Sees the Roman plays reflecting different stages in the development of Roman society.)
Bevington, D. *Shakespeare*, Goldentree Bibliographies (Arlington Heights, 1978). (A particularly useful bibliography, thorough and intelligently selective.)

SHIRLEY, James (1596–1666), born in London, educated at Merchant Tailor's school and Saint Catherine's College, Cambridge. Was at various times a clergyman and (after his conversion to Roman Catholicism) a schoolmaster, and (1636–40) a theatre manager in Dublin. According to one story, Archbishop Laud objected to his ordination because he had an unsightly mole on his face. Plays include *Love Tricks* (1625), *The Wedding* (c. 1626), *The Witty Fair One* (1628), *The Traitor* (1631), *Love's Cruelty* (1631), *The Humorous Courtier* (c. 1631), *The Changes* (c. 1631), *Hyde Park* (1632), *The Ball* (1632), *The Arcadia* (c. 1632), *The Lady of Pleasure* (1635), *The Politician* (c. 1639), *The Imposture* (1640), *The Cardinal* (1641). Masques include *The Triumph of Peace* (1634) and *Cupid and Death* (1653). Succeeded Philip Massinger as principal dramatist of the King's Men. Died, evidently of shock, in the aftermath of the Great Fire of London.

Nason, A. H. *James Shirley, Dramatist: A Biographical and Critical Study* (New York, 1915).

SUCKLING, Sir John (1609–42), chiefly noted for his lyric poetry, also wrote plays, including *Aglaura* (1637) and *The Goblins* (1638). Financed the lavish production of *Aglaura* from his own pocket. Invented cribbage. A Royalist leader, he fled to Paris after the failure of a plot to free Strafford. Allegedly committed suicide.

Squire, C. L. *Sir John Suckling* (Boston, 1978). (Biographical and critical introduction.)

TOURNEUR, Cyril (c. 1580–1626), place and date of birth obscure, seems to have spent much of his life abroad on military and diplomatic service. Non-dramatic work includes a verse satire, *The Transformed Metamorphosis* (1600), a prose 'character' of Robert Earl of Salisbury published just after Salisbury's death (1612) and a funeral poem on Sir Francis Vere (1609). The satiric prose pamphlet *Laugh and Lie Down* (1605) is sometimes attributed to him. *The Atheist's Tragedy* (c. 1611) is the one surviving play confidently attributed to him; his tragicomedy *The Nobleman* (c. 1612) has been lost. *The Revenger's Tragedy* (c. 1606) was not attributed to him until 1656; though the play is usually printed under his name the attribution is controversial, with many scholars favouring Thomas Middleton. Died in Ireland while returning from the Cadiz expedition.

See: Murray, P. B. *A Study of Cyril Tourneur* (Philadelphia, 1964).

WEBSTER, John (c. 1580–c. 1634), educated at the Merchant Tailor's school and
the Middle Temple. His reputation rests on the two great tragedies *The
White Devil* (c. 1612) and *The Duchess of Malfi* (c. 1613) and the
tragicomedy *The Devil's Law-Case* (c. 1617). *Appius and Virginia* (1622)
may have been written in collaboration with Thomas Heywood. Wrote a
new induction for *The Malcontent* (1604) when it was performed by the
King's Men. Collaborated with Thomas Dekker on *Westward Ho* (c. 1604)
and *Northward Ho* (c. 1605), and with William Rowley on *A Cure for a
Cuckold* (c. 1624).

Bradbrook, M. C. *John Webster: Citizen and Dramatist* (New York,
1980). (Webster's London background.)

See: Bogard, T. *The Tragic Satire of John Webster* (Berkeley and Los
Angeles, 1955).

Dent, R. W. *John Webster's Borrowing* (Berkeley, 1960). (Evidence
for Webster's working methods.)

Leech, C. *Webster: The Duchess of Malfi* (1963).

Morris, B., ed. *John Webster*, Mermaid Critical Commentaries
(1970). (Including essays on Webster in performance.)

Berry, R. *The Art of John Webster* (Oxford, 1972). (Themes and
techniques in the major plays.)

Pearson, J. *Tragedy and Tragicomedy in the Plays of John Webster*
(Totawa, N. J., 1980).

Bliss, L. *The World's Perspective: John Webster and the Jacobean Drama*
(New Brunswick, N. J., 1983).

Index